DRAMA CONTEMPORARY
India

PAJ BOOKS

Bonnie Marranca & Gautam Dasgupta

Series Editors

PLAYS BY

Girish Karnad

Kavalam Narayana Panikkar

Usha Ganguli

Tripurari Sharma

Mahesh Dattani

Datta Bhagat

EDITED BY ERIN B. MEE

DramaContemporary
India

A PAJ BOOK   *The Johns Hopkins University Press Baltimore and London*

The Johns Hopkins University Press
2715 North Charles Street
Baltimore, Maryland 21218-4363
www.press.jhu.edu

Library of Congress Cataloging-in-
Publication Data will be found at the end
of this book.
A catalog record for this book is available
from the British Library.

ISBN 0-8018-6621-9
ISBN 0-8018-6622-7 (pbk.)

To my mother and father, who, through their own example,

have taught me to recognize good writers and good writing

Contents

ACKNOWLEDGMENTS xi

INTRODUCTION 1
A NOTE ON TRANSLATION 21

THE FIRE AND THE RAIN
by Girish Karnad, translated by the author 23

ARAMBA CHEKKAN
by Kavalam Narayana Panikkar,
translated by the author and Erin B. Mee 83

RUDALI
by Usha Ganguli, translated by Anjum Katyal 111

THE WOODEN CART
by Tripurari Sharma, translated by Mohit Satyanand 169

TARA
by Mahesh Dattani 229

ROUTES AND ESCAPE ROUTES
by Datta Bhagat, translated by Maya Pandit 283

GLOSSARY 345
NOTES ON CONTRIBUTORS 359

Acknowledgments

FIRST AND FOREMOST, I want to thank the playwrights and translators whose work appears here: they have been extremely helpful and generous as this volume has progressed.

I am grateful to the National School of Drama, New Delhi, for photos of performances of *The Wooden Cart* and *The Fire and the Rain,* to Vivek Mansukhani for photos of *Tara,* to Anjum Katyal, Naveen Kishore, and Usha Ganguli for photos of *Rudali,* and to Sudhir Mungi for photos of *Routes and Escape Routes.*

My thanks to Anjum Katyal for all her help and advice, to Eleanor Zelliot for her help with portions of the introduction and the glossary, to the entire Sopanam company (especially K. Sivakumar, P. V. Malini, P. Gopinath, C. Sreekumar, G. Ayyappan, B. Krishnakumar, K. T. Abraham, Sunitha, Sujatha, and Vasudevan Namboothiri) for everything, and to Sadasivan, Mohit Satyanand, and Arun Mehta for endless help of all kinds whenever I have asked for it. Special thanks to Judith Jerome for her insightful comments on the introduction.

Special and heartfelt thanks to Jennifer Greenfield who has been so supportive of my interest in Indian plays over the years, to Rob Coburn for the same, and to Richard Schechner for his constant encouragement.

Finally, thanks go to my husband, Shanker Satyanath, who makes everything worth it.

DramaContemporary
India

Introduction

INDIA as it is currently configured is the largest and most populous democracy in the world. It is also one of the most culturally diverse countries in the world. Each of India's twenty-six states has its own political and social history, its own performing art traditions, and its own language—there are fifteen nationally recognized languages in India, and 844 recognized dialects. It is useful to think of states in India the way we think of countries in Europe: as a group of related entities with distinct cultures.

The term "theater" in India encompasses a wide range of performance events, including ritual performance such as *ramlila* and *theyyam*, classical dance-dramas such as *kathakali* and *kuttiyattam*, folk performance such as *chhau* and *therukkuttu*, "living newspaper" productions, theater for educational purposes, and large-scale commercial plays and musicals. Theater is performed in fields, market places, and temples, in private living rooms, in front of government offices, and on proscenium stages. It is performed as part of religious festivals, for secular entertainment, and for tourist consumption. Modern drama is a subset of "theater" but is nonetheless connected to, and influenced by, many of these other performance forms.

Four men are credited with creating a modern dramatic literature in India: Vijay Tendulkar in Marathi, Badal Sircar in Bengali, Mohan Rakesh in Hindi, and Girish Karnad in Kannada. Their plays have become landmarks of modern Indian drama, and at first glance it would seem an obvious choice to publish a collection consisting primarily of their work. However, with the exception of Karnad, their most famous plays are thirty years old and are easily available in print.[1] For this volume, I wanted newer plays written in a variety of styles, and I wanted to expose readers to some of the extremely talented playwrights they might not already know.

This volume focuses specifically on contemporary plays from India (not including the diaspora) written in the last four to fifteen years. Each of the six plays in this volume is written from a different perspective and in a different style, and each deals with an issue of current importance. In addition to the fact that each play is excellent and important in its own right, these plays as a group demonstrate (although they do not, and could not possibly *represent*) the enormous range of playwriting in India today.

Five of the plays in this volume belong to aesthetic movements which are also, or which are closely related to, social movements: *The Fire and the Rain* by Girish Karnad and *Aramba Chekkan* by Kavalam Narayana Panikkar both belong to what is known as the theater of roots movement; *Rudali* by Usha Ganguli belongs to the women's theater movement; *The Wooden Cart* by Tripurari Sharma, though not itself a street theater piece, developed out of street theater performances; and *Routes and Escape Routes* by Datta Bhagat belongs to a category of writing known as Dalit Sahitya, or literature of the oppressed. *Tara,* by Mahesh Dattani, was written in English, but it challenges the norms of English-language playwriting in India.

The theater of roots movement began after India's independence in 1947 when a group of playwrights and directors wanted to create a theater that did not follow British colonial models for modern theater prevalent at the time. They turned to their roots in indigenous (or traditional) classical, ritual, and folk performance to see what could be used in the creation of a *modern Indian* theater. Thus, the theater of roots movement can best be understood as a way of decolonizing the theater, as a politically driven search for an indigenous aesthetic and dramaturgy. I include two plays from this movement because it is the most influential theatrical movement of the last fifty years. Girish Karnad and Kavalam Narayana Panikkar are two of the leading playwrights of the roots movement.[2]

Usha Ganguli believes that the stage is a place from which women can voice their indignation. Many women in India resist the term *feminist* because they feel it refers primarily to the concerns of middle-class white women in the United States and not to the issues they face on a daily basis. Consequently, much of what I would call feminist theater is referred to as women's theater, of which there are many types. There are street theater performances dealing with female infanticide and dowry deaths, solo performances telling the story of the *Mahabharata* from Draupadi's point of view (Draupadi is the main female character in the *Mahabharata, The Great War of the Bharatas,* one of India's most famous epic poems), workshops with sex workers in Kalighat, and plays about adolescent women.[3] Ganguli chose to produce, write, direct, and act in *Rudali* specifically because it focuses on the life of a woman.

The political street theater movement in Delhi gained momentum in the early 1970s with the work of Safdar Hashmi and Badal Sircar (whose company, though based in Calcutta, performed often in Delhi). Sircar began performing in the streets to reach audiences who either would not or could not come to a theater hall to see a performance.[4] Hashmi dedicated himself to creating political theater "that would effectively express the emotions and concerns of India's working class."[5] Tripurari Sharma was deeply influenced by the work of Sircar and Hashmi and took her own plays to the streets. Not all her work is street theater, but all her work reflects the concerns and agendas of the movement. Sharma is dedicated to giving voice to those who are not often heard and to political issues which are not being discussed. In conversation, as well as in her methods of work and in her productions, Sharma is not interested in providing answers or solutions to problems. She is more interested in opening up dialogue, presenting multiple points of view, and providing a forum for exchange. Many parts of *The Wooden Cart*— which focuses on the social stigmas surrounding leprosy—were originally presented as street theater pieces, but the version published here is not actually a street theater piece. It developed out of interviews with patients and workshops with paramedical doctors and was presented at the National School of Drama.

Mahesh Dattani writes in English for an urban audience. English is dismissed by some in India as the foreign language of colonization, but it is one of India's officially recognized languages. It is often used by people from different states (who speak different languages) to communicate with one another, it is used by the upper classes, and it is studied by those aspiring to be middle class—those for whom a knowledge of English would open up a myriad of job possibilities. It is spoken, however, by a very small percentage (some say as small as five percent) of the population, most of whom live in cities. In the theater, English has been used much more frequently as a language of translation than as a language of original composition; plays written in other Indian languages achieve national recognition through translation into English, but plays originally written in English have, until recently, stayed on the fringes of the theater scene. This is, in part, because English-language theater has been heavily influenced by British drawing-room comedy and is therefore associated with light entertainment for the urban elite, a perception Dattani has done much to change. Dattani's plays are not mindless fluff: he takes as his subject the complicated dynamics of the modern urban family. Dattani's characters struggle for some kind of freedom and happiness under the oppressive weight of tradition, cultural constructions of gender, and repressed desire. Their dramas are played out on multilevel sets where interior and exterior become one and geographical locations are collapsed; in short, his settings are as fragmented as the families who inhabit them.

Datta Bhagat is a Dalit writer. *Dalit* means "ground down" or "depressed" in Marathi and is the term used by politicized ex-Untouchables to describe themselves with respect to the oppression they have endured. Dalit Sahitya is a socioliterary movement begun by Buddhists in Maharashtra (former Untouchables who converted to Buddhism to rid themselves of discrimination based on caste) demanding, through literature, social change and economic justice. Arjun Dangle, a Dalit poet, describes Dalit Sahitya as that "which acquaints people with the caste system and untouchability in India, [with] its appalling nature, and [with] its system of exploitation."[6] Bhagat's play *Routes and Escape Routes* is significant because it is the first modern Dalit play to reach a large and diverse audience.

GIRISH KARNAD AND *The Fire and the Rain*

Karnad was born in 1938 in Matheran, near Bombay (now Mumbai). He was educated at the Karnatak University in Dharwad and at Oxford, where he was a Rhodes Scholar. He wrote his first play, *Yayati*, during an emotional crisis brought on by his decision to attend Oxford, a crisis in which he felt he would have to choose between a future in England and a future in India. Karnad chose to use the story of Yayati, which comes from the *Mahabharata*, because the myth reflected his particular anxieties in that moment. However, while the theme of the play came from an Indian source, Karnad was forced to use a Western dramatic structure because there was none in his own modern tradition to which he could relate.[7] In an attempt to find an indigenous structural model for his work, Karnad turned to traditional performance.

Hayavadana, Karnad's third play, is one of the first modern Indian plays using traditional performance to receive national attention, and it established Karnad as one of India's most important modern playwrights. In *Hayavadana* Karnad makes use of "tradition" both in terms of form and in terms of content, by blending indigenous folk elements with a specifically Indian story in a multilayered structure that is typical of many Indian folk and classical performance forms. He mobilizes and juxtaposes several different genres, each with its own inherent logic, its own textures, and its own perspective, so that the central story is reflected in various forms and commented on in many ways. In his most recent play, *The Fire and the Rain,* Karnad continues to use and refer to traditional performance in order to make strong political and social statements about contemporary life.

The Fire and the Rain opens with an elaborate *yajña* (a fire sacrifice intended to preserve the world from physical and moral chaos). However, not long after the image of this Brahminic ritual is presented, Karnad begins to turn it upside down: this is not a reverent play espousing Brahmin ideals. On a political level, *The Fire and the Rain* exposes the hypocrisy and brutality of Brahmin priests and the failure of religion. On a personal level, it reveals the ways in which jealousy can destroy a family (and by implication an entire community and possibly the cosmos itself). By the end of the play one Brahmin (Yavakri) has been granted power by the gods—a power he uses solely to get revenge on his own uncle. Another Brahmin (the chief priest of the *yajña*) kills his father and pins the blame on his brother Arvasu. Arvasu, who breaks caste by falling in love with the daughter of a hunter and joining a troupe of actors, is the hero of *The Fire and the Rain.* His acting company performs a play (technically a ritual performance) at the *yajña* which breaks the cycle of vengeance and revenge and brings release from anger. As anger melts away, the rains come, ending a crippling drought.

Indra, who is god of the firmament, a personification of the atmosphere, and the lord of the rains, appears in the play in several forms. At one level he is a mythological figure. At another level, he appears as a character played by an actor in the play-that-is-a-ritual-performance within the ritual (*yajña*), that is in turn performed within the play (*The Fire and the Rain*). Finally, Indra appears in the ritual as a *murthi,* as an actual *manifestation* of the deity being propitiated at the *yajña*. In other words, Indra is *actually present*—as opposed to being *represented*. To "see" Indra in the context of a ritual is to receive *darshan*. *Darshan* refers to the "visual perception of the sacred," and, more specifically, to the contact between devotee and deity which takes place through the eye.[8] *Darshan* occurs when human sight mixes with divine insight to dispel illusion. *Darshan* helps us to see clearly, to understand: seeing, being seen, and coming to see are conflated; sight becomes insight, and the spectator is transformed into a seer. Significantly, *darshan* is an indigenous visual practice stemming from traditional performance: Karnad has reminded spectators of, and asked them to practice, an indigenous way of seeing. By placing a ritual in the context of a play, Karnad has asked them to apply this indigenous way of seeing to a contemporary play and has forced spectators to practice "complex seeing," or seeing that simultaneously acknowledges several different realities.

The Fire and the Rain was commissioned by the Guthrie Theater in Minneapolis after a successful production of one of Karnad's earlier plays. It was first performed in a Hindi-language translation at the National School of Drama in Delhi, in 1996.

KAVALAM NARAYANA PANIKKAR AND *Aramba Chekkan*

While Karnad makes his living in film, as a writer and actor, and is not attached to a specific theater company, Kavalam Narayana Panikkar is the artistic director of the Sopanam Theater in Thiruvananthapuram, Kerala. As such, he writes almost exclusively for his own company and directs most of his own plays, which makes it difficult to separate his texts from the way he envisions them in performance.

Panikkar was born in 1928 in the village of Kavalam in Kerala. He grew up hearing folk songs, attending ritual performances, and seeing classical dance-drama, all of which have had an enormous impact on his work. Panikkar began his career as a poet, and his first play, *Sakshi*, grew out of public performances of his poems and songs. Panikkar continues to write poetry, and the influence of poetry on *Aramba Chekkan* is obvious. In fact, for Panikkar, theater is *drishya kavya*, or visual poetry—poetry for the eyes as well as for the ears.

Panikkar's search for a form of modern theater that is "Indian" led to an exploration of Sanskrit drama. Panikkar is well known not only as a Malayalam playwright (Malayalam is the language spoken in Kerala) but as a director of Sanskrit plays, particularly the plays of Bhasa, which were written some time in the first few centuries A.D. The dramaturgical structure of Bhasa's plays, as well as their aesthetics, have influenced Panikkar enormously.

Bhasa's plays were discovered in 1912 in Thiruvananthapuram. When they were discovered, scholars realized that these were the texts being performed in the dance-drama form called *kuttiyattam*. The plots of most of Bhasa's plays come from the *Mahabharata* and the *Ramayana,* so the *kuttiyattam* spectator already knows the story before the performance begins. Consequently the emphasis of the performance is not on *what* the story is (the plot) but on *how* it is told (what the performers make of it). A performance of a Bhasa play in *kuttiyattam* can take anywhere from five to thirty-eight nights to perform. On the first night of performance, one of the main characters will enter and present his or her personal history, some important events leading up to the play, and possibly the story of the play from that character's point of view. Most of this will be improvised by the performer, who follows guidelines set out in acting manuals passed on from teacher to student. A performer may spend up to three hours illuminating three lines of text by making political and social analogies, exploring emotional associations, and telling related or background stories. One by one the other characters appear and do the same thing. On the last night of performance "the play"—or what those of us brought up on mainstream text-driven plot-oriented theater would consider "the play," in other words, what was written by the playwright—is performed. "The play" is only one-fifth or one-thirty-eighth of the experience. The spectators' experience is not horizontal: they do not follow the plot in a linear fashion across time; they have a series of vertical experiences in which each moment is explored fully before the story moves on. Panikkar has adapted the dramaturgical structure of *kuttiyattam* in his own plays and productions. For example, his production of Bhasa's *Urubhangam* (*The Shattered Thigh*), which is twelve pages in the Penguin edition, is ninety minutes long. His production is not simply an interpretation of the script, but an elaboration on it. When he directs his own plays, he elaborates on them; and he expects other people, when they direct his plays, to elaborate as well—he even says of certain moments "here is a place where the director can elaborate."

In this situation body language, or the ability to communicate nonverbally, becomes vitally important. One of Panikkar's colleagues (another member of the roots movement) says that in this kind of theater "the actor's role is not to interpret the character psychologically but to create a celebration of emotions [or emotional elaboration] . . . via the body."[9] This is a reference to *rasa*. According to the *Natyasastra*, the Sanskrit treatise on drama, the goal of Sanskrit is to create *rasa*. *Rasa* literally means "juice" or "flavor," but it refers to the emotional essence of a production, to that which can be tasted in performance. *Rasa* exists neither in the performer nor in the spectator but in the interaction between the two, because *rasa* is experienced when various inner states or emotions, present in the spectator as latent impressions from one's past experiences, are awakened by the performer. Panikkar refers to the actor-in-character as a "*katha patram*" (literally "story vessel"). For Panikkar the actor is a vessel containing and communicating (or pouring out) the emotional essence of the story so it can be felt by the spectator.

In the summer of 1996, Panikkar invited me to direct a play with his company and suggested I find a story for him to adapt. I have always loved the story of Orpheus and Eurydice, and I felt Panikkar would too, so I gave him an outline of the myth. Panikkar usually focuses on Kerala mythology as the inspiration for his plays, and in that respect *Aramba Chekkan* is not typical of his work. It is, however, representative of the way Panikkar creates modern plays from mythology, or, as he puts it, "myths [for a] modern sensibility."[10] I chose to include *Aramba Chekkan* in this anthology because I think it will be interesting for an audience familiar with the myth of Orpheus and Eurydice to see how Panikkar has transformed it and made it his.

While Panikkar was writing *Aramba Chekkan,* he was directing a production of Kalidasa's *Vikramorvasiyam* (a Sanskrit play) and was haunted by the relationship between the two leading characters: by the way Puruva takes Urvashi (who, in Panikkar's interpretation, represents nature) for granted. For Panikkar *Aramba Chekkan* also became a story about the way people take nature for granted. In *Aramba Chekkan* nature has two distinct manifestations: its wild, destructive side represented by the cruel animals who ultimately tear Aramban to pieces and its loving, fertile side represented by

Chekki, who gets her name from an orange forest flower that grows in Kerala. Chekki is "the flower of the forest."[11] In this version Aramban is a singer, but he doesn't start out as a singer: his ability to sing is a gift from nature (from Chekki). *Aramba Chekkan* is about the knowledge man gains when his relationship with nature blossoms. The second half of the play, which takes place in the underworld, focuses on how man treats nature. Yama, the god of death, is supposed to judge the souls that come to him. He is supposed to judge man's behavior toward nature. But he is confused—he cannot decide who is to blame for the destruction of nature. Clearly, the characters in *Aramba Chekkan*, like the characters in Panikkar's other plays, are not individuals with personal psyches, they are personifications of themes, ideas, and drives.

USHA GANGULI AND *Rudali*

Usha Ganguli began her career as a Bharatanatyam dancer, but she took to acting in 1970, appearing in Rustom Bharucha's production of Kroetz's *Request Concert* and with the Sangeet Kala Mandir in Calcutta. In 1976 she formed her own theater company, Rangakarmee. Rangakarmee is an unusual phenomenon in the Bengali group theater scene in Calcutta. It functions as other Bengali group theaters do: it is composed of theater enthusiasts who have other jobs to support themselves during the day (Rangakarmee usually rehearses in the evening) and who are best described as amateurs with professional standards of performance and production. They subscribe to an alternative, experimental, noncommercial ethic, defining themselves in opposition to the "professional" commercial scene. They are an accepted part of the group theater scene. However, Rangakarmee performs in Hindi, because that is Ganguli's first language. The fact that Ganguli has managed to establish her company as a Hindi-speaking theater for a largely Bengali-speaking audience is, as Anjum Katyal, who translated *Rudali* into English, says, a remarkable achievement.[12]

Rangakarmee, says Ganguli, was formed to create "meaningful theatre for the masses." She describes her work as "theatre with a cause" and her audience as "the average citizen" of Calcutta, the "person who is bogged down by his daily life and helplessness." Rangakarmee attempts, with its productions, to provide "a space in some corner of his over-exploited mind, to question."[13]

Theater, in Ganguli's opinion, should "show what truth is, how it is."[14] She is interested in "realistic" theater that portrays the real lives of ordinary individuals rather than mythological figures or archetypes. Rangakarmee's first production was an adaptation of Ibsen's *A Doll House*, and after several productions on other subjects, Ganguli wanted to focus again on women, specifically Indian women. Ganguli turned to the novel *Rudali* by Mahasweta Devi, one of India's most important writers, and adapted it for the stage.

Although the final script is Ganguli's, *Rudali* was developed in workshops with several other Bengali play- and screenwriters and the occasional input of Mahasweta Devi herself. Ganguli took the several Bengali versions that emerged and compiled them into one script, which she then translated into Hindi.

Mahasweta Devi's novel centers around Sanichari, a poor, exploited, low-caste village woman struggling to survive in a rich-eat-poor world. The novel is a critique of the nexus between the socioeconomic and religious systems in place in Sanichari's village. One by one Sanichari's relatives die, and she is unable to cry. She is so worried about the cost of the rituals surrounding death that she does not have the time or energy to mourn: she cannot *afford* to mourn. In Sanichari's village, when a member of a wealthy family dies and there are not enough women in the family to mourn, mourners are hired—the more *rudalis* (hired mourners), the greater the family's prestige. Grief and mourning are commodified. Sanichari goes into business as a *rudali,* and the novel ends with a triumphantly subversive act: she arrives at a funeral with so many *rudalis* in tow that the heirs know nothing will be left of their inheritance. Sanichari has not only given employment to every woman she can find, she has bankrupted a rich family.

Ganguli's play shifts the emphasis slightly from class to gender; Sanichari represents not an oppressed class, but an oppressed woman. Ganguli says her play is about "all" of us and that Sanichari represents "women in general." "I believe that the Indian woman, whether it's Sanichari or someone from the middle or upper class, is highly exploited in our society. Somehow in *Rudali* I see Sanichari protesting against society [as a] whole." Anjum Katyal notes that in Mahasweta Devi's novel the upper classes exploit the lower classes, whereas in Ganguli's play men exploit women.[15] Nonetheless, Ganguli's play retains Mahasweta Devi's economic critique. Ganguli sees the biggest difference between the novel and the play in the ending: she feels that Mahasweta Devi's ending is too optimistic, and therefore untruthful. "Truth has to be bitter and uncompromising," she says. "So was my end."[16] At the end of Ganguli's play, Sanichari is alone on stage: she clearly misses her only real friend, Bikhni, who is now dead. In spite of her sorrow, she resolutely decides to go on.

Rudali opened on 29 December 1992 and played for months to packed houses.

TRIPURARI SHARMA AND *The Wooden Cart*

Tripurari Sharma was born in 1956, received a degree in English literature from Delhi University in 1976, and graduated from the National School of Drama in 1979. Sharma's work takes several forms: she and her company, Alarippu, perform plays in the streets, she develops plays and productions collectively in community workshops, and she directs classical plays in mainstream theater spaces. Sharma has dealt with a broad range of subjects: communalism, the effect of the dollar on the Indian economy, and governmental corruption.

Sharma first developed a script collectively when she was asked by a group of factory workers to create, with them, a production about working conditions. Because no extant script was appropriate, the group created the play by using acting exercises to extend and develop stories told by the factory workers. After this experience, Sharma was asked by Manushi, a women's group, to do a workshop with college girls. They created a piece about how it feels to be a woman, how it feels to be "not exactly discriminated against, [but] treated differently, [about] the constant search for identity, for friendship," and for understanding.[17] In the course of creating the piece, many of the women expressed their anger, sorrow, and bitterness. In some situations, Sharma says, "you don't have to do anything—you don't have to probe, you don't have to make [the actors] become aware of their anger, you just have to create the space" for them to speak.[18]

The Wooden Cart began when UNICEF asked Sharma to run some workshops as part of a communication package designed to educate people about leprosy and to deal with prejudices blocking the diagnosis and treatment of the disease. After one performance of a workshop she conducted with para-medical doctors in a leprosy-prone area, a villager stepped into the playing space to say "I'm cured of leprosy, and I'm saying this so that [others] who might be hiding [their disease] will see that there is no reason to hide." In this moment Sharma realized that "theatre is a forum. It's not so important for the play to say everything, the fact that you bring something out in the open in itself sends out vibrations which are in some way liberating, and get people talking. Earlier I felt it was necessary to put everything about the issues into the play, to make everything clear, but the fact that you create this forum is itself an event, and it leads to many other kinds of events."[19]

As her research continued, Sharma began to focus more and more on the social stigmas attached to leprosy. For example, she hadn't known that the illness is not in the fingers, that the illness is somewhere else but manifests itself in the fingers because they have lost their sensitivity. "This is emblematic of the way we deal with things," she says. "We always try to deal with the symptoms of something when the cause is somewhere else. Like the slums: we deal with the slums, but the slums are here because there's a problem in the village, and people migrate to the city. We aren't going to solve the slum problem by attacking the slums. In that way leprosy became a metaphor for me, it became a metaphor for other things." What inspired Sharma most while working on the play were the stories of courage and creativity she encountered. "These were people who have suffered so much rejection, and have survived with so much depth, so much understanding of life. Many of them lost everything, and they have begun again, and they have made some sense of their lives in their own way. They were rejected by their families, they were forced to leave their homes, and they found ways of making new families, and some of the families they formed were very unconventional. These are the people who are stigmatized, who are put off in a category. These are the people society has thrown away, but they are doing marvelous things." When UNICEF suggested that she turn her material into a play, Sharma wrote *The Wooden Cart*, which is really a play about social stigma. As she says, "leprosy is incidental to the story really; the woman in the play who is thrown out of her house could have been thrown out for many other reasons. It's about what she makes of her life."[20]

When I asked Sharma whether she thought she could change anyone's mind through performance, she said: "It's very difficult to measure how people change by seeing plays. I believe there is a basic goodness in people, and I feel that if a play points out something positive, it appeals to that positiveness in them. . . . If they didn't get support from outside, then the negative which exists would get strengthened, which is why I feel it is important, even if I am unable to measure, or to feel that I'm doing a very important social service by changing people's minds, [to keep working,] because somewhere it will strengthen something positive, which will have an effect. . . . I don't think . . . that in forty-five minutes you can change a forty-five-year experience, but I feel that it adds to something somewhere—it gives people something to think about and keep in mind."[21] Sharma's strength as an artist lies in presenting "other" points of view in a way that they cannot be ignored: she provides a place in which people can listen to each other and exchange views.

MAHESH DATTANI AND *Tara*

Mahesh Dattani was born in 1958 in Bangalore. When he was ten his parents, who moved to Bangalore from the northwestern state of Gujarat, took him to see a Gujarati play. Attending Gujarati plays was one way for Dattani's parents to stay in touch with their community, and attending this play was a big family event. Dattani was struck by the dazzling costumes, by the gaudy sets, and by the surreal world of the theater, but he never dreamed of being part of it.

In the early 1980s, while in college, Dattani joined the Bangalore Little Theatre: he took workshops, directed plays, and acted. In 1984 he founded his own company, Playpen, and began to look for Indian plays in English, which proved more difficult than he had anticipated. "Like many urban people in India, you're in this situation where the language you speak at home is not the language of your environment, especially if you move from your hometown. And you use English to communicate, so you find that you're more and more comfortable expressing yourself in English. I found I could only do theatre in English [. . . but] I wanted to do more Indian plays [and that] became a kind of challenge, because there weren't many good translations—or, there may have been good translations, but they didn't do anything for me."[22] Eventually Dattani solved this problem by writing his own plays, starting with *Where There's a Will*.

Dattani is concerned with the "invisible issues" in Indian society. Sexuality and homosexuality are taboo subjects, but Dattani pulls them out from under the rug and places them on stage for public discussion. His most recent play, *On a Muggy Night in Mumbai,* centers around a gay man, Kamlesh. Kamlesh, who has been dumped by his lover Ed, finds out that Ed has proposed to his sister Kiran. Ed wants his marriage with Kiran to function as a smokescreen so he can secretly continue his relationship with Kamlesh. Ed resorts to this strategy because he can't face coming out in Indian society. Dattani's treatment of this triangle is the only treatment of issues affecting the gay community—and the only sympathetic treatment of homosexual characters—that I have found in any modern Indian play. *On a Muggy Night . . .* caused a stir in Mumbai, where it was both lauded and reviled, largely because of its subject matter. "You can talk about feminism," Dattani says, "because in a way that is accepted. But you can't talk about gay issues because that's not India, it doesn't happen here." Because Dattani does talk about gay issues, some people dismiss his writing, saying it is "not Indian." When I asked Dattani how he would respond, he said: "I am Indian: this is my time and this is my place, . . . I'm reflecting that in my work, and that makes it Indian."[23]

Other people claim Dattani's work is "not Indian" because he writes in English for the proscenium stage, to which Dattani replies: "Does [Indian theatre] mean traditional theatre forms? Yes, they're wonderful, they're very sophisticated, they're impressive, but are they really India? . . . Are they really reflecting life as it is now? . . . What we need to do now is look at those forms and say we're approaching the twenty-first century, this is who we are and this is our legacy, so where do we take that. That's not happening, and that's a matter of serious concern."[24]

Tara centers on the emotional separation that grows between twins who had been conjoined, following their discovery that their physical separation was manipulated by their mother and grandfather to favor the boy (Chandan) over the girl (Tara). Tara, a feisty girl who isn't given the opportunities her brother has (although she may be smarter), eventually wastes away and dies. Chandan escapes to London, changes his name to Dan, and attempts to repress the guilt he feels over his sister's death by living without a personal history. Woven into the play are issues of class and community, and the clash between traditional and modern lifestyles and values.

Dattani sees *Tara* as a play about the gendered self, about coming to terms with the feminine side of oneself in a world that always favors what is "male," but many people in India see it as a play about the girl child. One of my students at New York University wrote her final paper on *Tara* for a course I taught on Indian performance. She agreed with Dattani that Tara and Chandan are two sides of the same self rather than two separate entities, and she stated that Dan, in trying to write the story of his own childhood, must write Tara's story if he is to rediscover the neglected half of himself and become whole. Another student pointed out that Dattani focuses on the family as a microcosm of society in order to dramatize the ways we are socialized to accept certain gendered roles and to give preference to what is "male."

All of Dattani's plays are first workshopped with his company, Playpen, where he puts the finishing touches on his dialogue in rehearsal, with the input of the actors. After its Bangalore premiere with Playpen in 1990, *Tara* went on to be produced in Mumbai and in Delhi, where it received rave reviews.

DATTA BHAGAT AND *Routes and Escape Routes*

The Dalit movement began as a political movement among the Mahars, a caste of Untouchables in Maharashtra. The Mahars traditionally worked in their villages as watchmen and messengers, and as the people responsible for removing dead cattle and other animals.[25] They could not eat with members of a higher caste or drink water from the same well; they were prevented from entering temples at all and from entering certain other buildings through the front door; and they were denied access to education. However, the Mahars were also the singers, dancers, comedians, and drummers of *tamasha,* a form of popular theater which has had a significant influence on modern Marathi drama. As such, they have their own oral tradition of stories and songs.

In the 1920s, Dr. B. R. Ambedkar emerged as the "father" of the Dalit movement. A lawyer, writer, reformer, and politician, Ambedkar worked to educate and politicize Mahars in Maharashtra and to fight for their rights. He founded newspapers to unify Untouchables, and educational organizations that to this day run colleges in several major cities. As a delegate to the Round Table Conferences of 1930–32, he championed reserved seats for Untouchables in the legislature.[26]

In 1956, Ambedkar led millions of Untouchables in a mass conversion from Hinduism to Buddhism. This conversion was a rejection of everything associated with caste Hinduism—Hindu mythology and notions of rebirth, pollution, and untouchability—in favor of a religion that did not legitimize caste hierarchy. Historian Eleanor Zelliot points out that "while the newspapers may be seen as a symbol of the whole paraphernalia of modernity, the educational institutions as the means for opportunity, the political stress as a basic urge to participate in government and to maintain unity, the conversion to Buddhism provided psychological freedom."[27]

Thus, Untouchables became Dalits: "Dalit," says Dangle, "is not a caste but a realization."[28] In the 1960s, Dalits began writing about their experiences: Dalit poetry, novels, and autobiographies began to appear, and in the 1970s this outpouring of work was recognized as Dalit Sahitya (literature of the oppressed). Many people think of Dalit Sahitya as the most important literary movement of the last fifty years in India.

In the theater, politically active Dalits stopped participating in tamasha (which took its plots from Hindu mythology) after the Buddhist conversion. They reconstructed tamasha so that it focused on the life of Ambedkar and on the Buddhist conversions, and they called it Ambedkari Jalasa. They performed Jalasa to spread the teachings of Ambedkar and to create greater political awareness among both Untouchables (those who had not yet converted to Buddhism or become politically active) and Dalits.

Datta Bhagat traces the beginning of Dalit theater to the beginning of Ambedkari Jalasa; he traces the beginning of modern Dalit theater to the rise of Dalit Sahitya. Bhagat feels that the Dalit movement, Dalit literature, and Dalit theater are interdependent, and that the growth of the Dalit movement depends on the theater, which provides a public forum to debate problems raised by the movement.

Bhagat is interested in social reconstruction and social change. Most of his plays deal with the sociocultural conflict between Dalits and Hindus, and their respective outlooks. In his play *Ashmak* (*The Piece of Stone*), Bhagat presents the conflict between two ideologically opposed attitudes: a ruler seeks power by offering his subjects material wealth in exchange for their ability to reason; he is opposed by Chakshu, a man who believes that reason is what separates man from animal. In *Jahaz Futley Aahe* (*The Broken Ship*), an old man divides to conquer: five young people of different castes are so busy fighting over petty issues that they are never able to unite and take on the bigger problems in their community.

Routes and Escape Routes dramatizes the conflict between three characters typifying different positions within the Dalit movement. Kaka, Satish, and Arjun each represent a different generation of the movement: Kaka is an unquestioning follower of Ambedkar; Satish is an educated activist who teaches in college; and Arjun is a radical student activist. *Routes and Escape Routes* asks: what is the future of the Dalit movement, what kind of movement is it becoming? The "action" in the play takes place offstage. Onstage, Bhagat focuses on the intellectual transformation of the characters. He focuses on the importance of listening to another person, of being able to hear and acknowledge another person's point. The events of the play are located in the exchanges of view. Consequently, in production Bhagat does not want the *mise-en-scène* to overwhelm the dialogue: he has cautioned directors to focus on the way each character's perspective affects and influences the other characters, and not to focus as much on the physical world of the play.

Routes and Escape Routes was first produced in December 1987 at the Tilak Smarak Mandir in Pune.

How should directors approach these plays? Dattani's advice to anyone directing his play is to "relate the play to their audience first, not to try and find the 'authentic Indianness' in the play, . . . because that's when you get very clichéd and boring, and you're not translating to an audience."[29] Karnad echoes Dattani when he says "a play works only at the moment of performance and therefore at a given historical cultural moment. The director (as well as the actors) would be well advised to explore the inwardness of the characters as human beings rather than as Indians." The most dangerous temptation, he says, is to create an exotic Indian ambiance, because that results in kitsch.[30]

What will these plays mean to an American reader or audience member? Datta Bhagat points out that his plays deal with the universal phenomenon of the "downtrodden" from within the specific framework of Indian society.[31] Sharma's play is about the universal phenomenon of rejection: it is about how people are rejected and how, despite that rejection, they accept themselves and make something of their lives. Although some of the specifics in these plays may initially be unfamiliar, I believe they have the power to speak to audiences in the United States. I hope readers will find these plays as moving, as interesting, as full of anger, hope, fear, love, despair, and triumph, as I do. I hope people will be as challenged by them aesthetically, intellectually, and politically, as I have been. I think these plays open up other ways of seeing and experiencing the world, and they force us to look at things we might otherwise overlook. I hope that each play, and this collection as a whole, will take people on a journey. As Mahesh Dattani points out, however, the journey need not be to India: it can be a journey into one's self from a stance outside one's own cultural viewpoint.[32]

NOTES

1. Oxford University Press has published a volume titled *Three Modern Indian Plays* containing the work of Karnad, Sircar, and Tendulkar, as well as a collection of Karnad's plays titled *Three Plays* and a collection of Tendulkar's plays called *Five Plays*. Rupa has published Rakesh's play *Adhe Adhure*. Plays by other well-established Indian playwrights are available through Seagull Books, 26 Circus Avenue, Calcutta 700 017, India.

2. For more information on the theater of roots, see Suresh Awasthi, " 'Theatre of Roots': Encounter with Tradition," *TDR* 33, 4:48–69.

3. For more information on some of these workshops and productions, see *Seagull Theatre Quarterly* 9.

4. Badal Sircar, "Our Street Theatre," *Sangeet Natak* 69 (1983): 22.

5. Eugène van Erven, *The Playful Revolution* (Bloomington: Indiana University Press, 1992), 141.

6. Arjun Dangle, *Poisoned Bread* (Bombay: Orient Longman, 1992), 264.

7. Girish Karnad, "Author's Introduction," *Three Plays* (Delhi: Oxford University Press, 1994), 3–4.

8. Diana L. Eck, *Darshan* (Chambersburg, Pa.: Anima Books, 1985), 3, 7.

9. H. Kanhailal, quoted in "Theatre in Manipur Today," *Seagull Theatre Quarterly*, 14/15 (1997): 51, 78.

10. Erin B. Mee, "Folk Philosophy in K. N. Panikkar's Poetic Theatre of Transformation," *Seagull Theatre Quarterly* 7 (1995): 58.

11. Erin B. Mee, "Kavalam Narayana Panikkar: Meaning into Action," *Performing Arts Journal* 55 (1997): 7.

12. Anjum Katyal, letter to the author, 6 January 2000. It is interesting to note, however, that Rangakarmee's most recent piece, *Mukti* (*Freedom*), is written in Bengali.

13. Usha Ganguli, letter to the author, 22 April 1998.

14. Ibid.

15. Anjum Katyal, "Metamorphosis of Rudali," *Rudali* (Calcutta: Seagull Foundation for the Arts, 1997), 28–29, 36–44.

16. Usha Ganguli, letter.

17. Tripurari Sharma, interview with the author, 30 August 1996.

18. Erin B. Mee, "Tripurari Sharma: Out in the Open," *Performing Arts Journal* 55 (1997): 14.

19. Ibid., 15.

20. Tripurari Sharma, interview with the author, 8 July 1999.

21. Mee, "Tripurari Sharma," 18.

22. Mahesh Dattani, interview with the author, 27 August 1996.

23. Erin B. Mee, "Mahesh Dattani: Invisible Issues," *Performing Arts Journal* 55 (1997): 25, 24.

24. Ibid., 24–25.

25. See Eleanor Zelliot, "Dalit Sahitya: The Historical Background," in *An Anthology of Dalit Literature* (Delhi: Gyan Publishing House, 1992), 2.

26. Ambedkar advocated policies not unlike affirmative action in the United States. See *Ambedkar* in the glossary.

27. Quoted in Vinay Dharwadker, "Dalit Poetry in Marathi," in *World Literature Today* 68, no. 2 (1994): 320.

28. Dangle, *Poisoned Bread,* 264.

29. Mee, "Mahesh Dattani," 22.

30. Girish Karnad, letter to the author, 26 May 1998.

31. Datta Bhagat, letter to the author, 15 June 1998.

32. Mee, "Mahesh Dattani," 22.

A Note on Translation

INDIAN ENGLISH, like British English, is very different from American English—especially when spoken. Indian English has absorbed idiomatic phrases, words, and grammatical constructions from other Indian languages. The Indian translators whose work appears in this volume have retained these phrases and grammatical constructions because they have become part of the English language as it is spoken in India. It is important to remember that these translations reflect the way characters do or would speak English in India, rather than the way they would speak English if they were American and living in the United States. I have included a glossary of unfamiliar words and expressions at the end of the volume.

The Fire and the Rain

by Girish Karnad

TRANSLATED FROM KANNADA BY THE AUTHOR

CHARACTERS

(in order of appearance)

THE KING

PARAVASU, the chief priest of the fire sacrifice

THE PRIESTS

THE BRAHMA RAKSHASA, a demon soul

A COURTIER

THE ACTOR-MANAGER

ARVASU, Paravasu's younger brother

THE ACTOR-MANAGER'S BROTHER

NITTILAI, a hunter girl

ANDHAKA, a blind man, Yavakri's servant

VISHAKHA, Paravasu's wife

YAVAKRI, Paravasu's cousin

RAIBHYA, Paravasu's father

NITTILAI'S BROTHER

NITTILAI'S HUSBAND

VOICE OF INDRA, the king of gods

CROWDS, BRAHMINS, SOLDIERS, GUARDS, VILLAGERS, AUDIENCE, SOULS

The National School of Drama Repertory Company in *The Fire and the Rain*
Photographs courtesy of the National School of Drama, Delhi

Prologue

It has not rained adequately for nearly ten years. Drought grips the land. A seven-year-long fire sacrifice (yajña) is being held to propitiate Indra, the god of rains.

Fire burns at the center of steplike brick altars. There are several such altars, at all of which priests are offering oblations to the fire, while singing the prescribed hymns in unison.

The PRIESTS are all dressed in long, flowing, seamless pieces of cloth and wear sacred threads. The KING, who is the host, is similarly dressed but has his head covered.

PARAVASU is the conducting priest (adhvaryu). He is referred to as the chief priest, since he is the most important of them all. It is his responsibility to see that there are no errors, either of omission or of commission, in the performance of the sacrifice. He is about twenty-eight.

It is an impressive panorama.

The BRAHMA RAKSHASA, a Brahmin soul trapped in the limbo between death and rebirth, is moving around outside the sacrificial precincts, though no human eye can see him.

The afternoon session is over. The PRIESTS begin to disperse.

A COURTIER enters with the ACTOR-MANAGER. The latter is made to stand at a distance from the fire sacrifice, since as an actor he is considered low-born. The COURTIER rushes into the protected enclosure of the fire sacrifice and talks to the KING. The PRIESTS surround them. There is heated discussion.

KING: (*Explodes.*) No, impossible! It's not possible.

PRIEST 1:   But where is the troupe?

COURTIER: At the city gates. Waiting.

PRIEST 2:   Let them come, Your Majesty. Please—

KING: I am not stopping them. They can come, by all means. But I won't have that boy—

PRIEST 3:   It's three years since we saw a play.

PRIEST 4:   And there was a time when we had four plays a month!

PRIEST 3:   These endless philosophical discussions, metaphysical speculations, debates. Every day! Surely, a sacrifice doesn't have to be so dreary.

PRIEST 2:   We need a play to freshen our minds.

PRIEST 1:   Fortunately this troupe is here—

PRIEST 4:   Do let them perform, Your Majesty.

KING: But why do they insist on him? He is not even an actor by birth—

COURTIER: The Manager says all his actors have fled to other lands. He needs an actor. And this one, he says, is good—

KING: But the Chief Priest won't agree.

PRIEST 1:   Why don't we ask him? (*Calls out.*) Sir—

PARAVASU: (*Entering.*) Did someone call me?

KING: (*To* COURTIER.) You tell him.

COURTIER: Well, sir . . . it's like this. There's a troupe of actors at the city gates. They are keen to stage a play in honor of the fire sacrifice.

PARAVASU: I thought the famine had decimated all the troupes.

COURTIER: That's precisely it. This one has come specially for us—against all odds. (*Points to the* ACTOR-MANAGER.) That's the Manager of the troupe. He has come with a specific plea. He'll make his submission from a distance. (PARAVASU *nods. The* COURTIER *shouts to the* ACTOR-MANAGER.) You may shout out whatever you have to say, but please face away from the sacrificial enclosure so you don't pollute it.

ACTOR-MANAGER: (*Stands facing away from the sacrificial enclosure and declaims theatrically.*) Sirs, as is well known to you, Brahma, the Lord of All Creation extracted the requisite elements from the four Vedas and combined them into a fifth Veda and thus gave birth to the art of drama. He handed it over to his son, Lord Indra, the God of the Skies. Lord Indra, in turn, passed on the art to Bharata, a human being, for the gods cannot indulge in pretence. So if Indra is to be pleased and bring to an end this long drought which ravages our land, a fire sacrifice is not enough. A play has to be performed along with it. If we offer him entertainment in addition to the oblations, the god may grant us the rains we're praying for.

(*Long pause.*)

PARAVASU: Surely you don't need me to decide on this?

COURTIER: (*Hesitating.*) The problem is . . . there aren't enough actors to stage a play. They want to bring a new actor with them. (*Pause.*) Your brother.

PARAVASU: (*Quietly.*) Arvasu!

COURTIER: (*Hurriedly.*) I told the Actor-Manager, "Anyone but him! He's forbidden to step in here!" But the Manager says there's no play without him. Not enough of a cast!

KING: They are twisting our arms. They know the priests are desperate for some entertainment.

(*A long pause.* PARAVASU *is silent. The* PRIESTS *anxiously wait for his reaction.*)

COURTIER: The Manager says that he has a special message from your brother for you. He will repeat it if permitted to do so. Your brother has taught him what to say. The exact words.

(PARAVASU *nods.*)

KING: (*Anxious.*) Is that all right with you? I mean . . . everyone will hear.

PARAVASU: And why shouldn't they?

COURTIER: (*Shouts to the* ACTOR-MANAGER.) If you have anything to add, you may do so.

ACTOR-MANAGER: A message from a brother: Dear elder brother, you once said to me: "The sons of Bharata were the first actors in the history of theater. They were Brahmins, but lost their caste because of their profession. A curse plunged them into disrepute and disgrace. If one values one's high birth, one should not touch this profession." And I accepted this. But today I am a criminal. I have killed my father, a noble Brahmin. I already stand tarnished. I may now become an actor. This follows from your own words. So please do not bar the way now.

(*A long pause. Everyone looks eagerly at* PARAVASU.)

KING: The fire sacrifice is nearing completion. We have conducted it without a blemish for nearly seven years. And you have guided us. Let's just complete it. Let it rain. Once it rains, we can have as many plays as we like. As a sacrifice approaches completion, demons gather in the shadows. The danger of disruption increases. You said so yourself. To permit a condemned criminal in the vicinity of our sacrificial fires, to risk . . . at this stage—

PARAVASU: Perhaps the sacrifice needs danger.

KING: But you drove him away yourself. You called him a demon.

PARAVASU: Perhaps you can't keep demons away from the sacrifice. It's a bond we can't break. Let's have the play. We shall all watch.

(*The* COURTIER *bows, runs to the* ACTOR-MANAGER, *who nods enthusiastically. They depart. The* PRIESTS *disperse discussing the play.*

The troupe comes on stage: It consists of only three men, the ACTOR-MANAGER, *his* BROTHER, *who is limping, and* ARVASU, *Paravasu's brother, aged about eighteen. They all carry bundles of costumes.* ARVASU *is also carrying a mask. A couple of women provide music, with a few wind instruments and a drum.*

The KING, PARAVASU *and the other* PRIESTS *sit in front. Behind them gathers the general populace.*

The ACTOR-MANAGER *starts singing the benedictory verse. The stage darkens, leaving* ARVASU *in a pool of light.*)

ARVASU: He's agreed, Nittilai! He'll be there to watch the play! But where are you? Why aren't you here? Nittilai! Nittilai! I am going to act on stage! I hope you are watching. Please, please, watch. The play is about to begin. Yes, after all these years, it's going to happen. But you know, and Brother knows, and I know that this isn't the real thing. This is a fiction, borrowed from the myths. The real play began somewhere else. A month ago. A month? . . . Was it really that recent? It seems ages and ages of darkness ago. You and I were going to get married. Begin a new life. And I had to meet the elders of your tribe.

(NITTILAI, *a girl of fourteen, comes and stands next to* ARVASU. *Though they are obviously fond of each other, they do not touch, except when specified.*)

Act One

NITTILAI: Oh! Don't go on about it! I told you! There's nothing to worry about. The elders will gather under the big banyan tree and ask a few questions. You answer them—

ARVASU: I couldn't sleep a wink last night. Woke up in a cold sweat every time I thought of your elders—

NITTILAI: You are a fusspot. You've known them for years. And after all, every young man about to get married goes through it. Just declare—

ARVASU: Yes, I know. I know. Just stand there and say: "I want to take her as my wife. I am potent. I can satisfy all her needs . . ."

NITTILAI: (*Shyly.*) Yes, more or less, that!

ARVASU: And in public!

NITTILAI: Of course. What's the point of saying it to yourself? (*Laughs.*) Don't worry. It's nothing . . .

ARVASU: Nothing, yes. For the young men of your tribe! But I am a Brahmin. To say all that in plain, loud words to a smirking, nudging, surging multitude. No hymns to drown out one's voice. No smoke to hide behind. It's dreadful. I hope there won't be too many people there—

NITTILAI: The whole village will be there.

(ARVASU *groans.*)

And some from the neighboring villages.

ARVASU: Are the elders brutal?

NITTILAI: Of course not. But the young men could be—

ARVASU: What young men?

NITTILAI: Your friends. My brothers. Others attending the council. They have a field day usually.

ARVASU: I am not coming!

NITTILAI: Let no evil spirit hear you. Don't be silly, Arvasu. Father has told the young men not to get carried away. He likes you. In any case, there are very few men left because of the famine. The women will be there of course. In hordes. It's not often that they get a Brahmin groom—

ARVASU: To chew on, you mean? Your women can be more lewd than your men.

NITTILAI: It's their prerogative. Come on now, you keep bragging about how, given a chance, you could stun thousands with your wit and eloquence.

ARVASU: I was talking as an actor. But this is real. Me as myself.

NITTILAI: Yes. (*Pause.*) And have you faced your own people? Told them yet? (*No reply.*)

You haven't, have you? Do you feel ashamed?

ARVASU: Ashamed? Let me show you. Here! (*Grabs her hands and pulls her near.*)

NITTILAI: (*Scandalized.*) Let go of me! Let me go! What'll everyone say?

ARVASU: Why? Don't I have my rights . . . ?

NITTILAI: Not until we're married. Until then the girl is not supposed to touch her husband-to-be. That's our custom . . .

ARVASU: Mother of mine! I'm about to jettison my caste, my people, my whole past for you. Can't you forget a minor custom for my sake?

NITTILAI: It's a nice custom. Sensible. Worth observing.

ARVASU: All these days I couldn't touch you because Brahmins don't touch other castes. Now you can't touch me because among hunters, girls don't touch their betrothed. Are you sure someone won't think of something else once we're married?

(*She stops him and points. They are at some distance from the hermitage of Yavakri's father. A blind man, called* ANDHAKA, *who is a* shudra *by caste, is sitting by the gate.* ARVASU *nods, signals to her to watch. Then proceeds toward the hermitage, moving zig-zag, trying to camouflage his walk.*)

ANDHAKA: Who's that? Arvasu?

(NITTILAI *doubles up with laughter.* ARVASU *jumps up and down in mock frustration, but is actually quite annoyed with himself.*)

ARVASU: Curse your years! *Curse your ears!*

NITTILAI: (*To* ANDHAKA.) He was trying to walk so you wouldn't guess who it was.

ANDHAKA: They all try that. But I can always tell. Just as you can recognize a man by his face—I can recognize him by the sound of his steps.

ARVASU: I'll fool you yet, old man!

ANDHAKA: I wish you luck. But in the meantime you two have cheered my heart, children. Made my ears happy . . .

NITTILAI: You mean you already know?

ARVASU: We thought we'd surprise you.

NITTILAI: You never move out of here. Yet you hear of everything . . .

ANDHAKA: You two are brave. It's one thing to frolic together as children. But you're not children any longer. You're old enough to know that the world can be cruel and ruthless.

NITTILAI: Even now he hasn't told his family.

ANDHAKA: Fair enough! "You must always extract the honey without ruffling the bees."

ARVASU: I keep telling her, no one cares! The one advantage of this famine—

NITTILAI: Don't say that! That's not nice.

ARVASU: I know. Nevertheless. The famine has sent my relatives fleeing to the city. The last thing they want is to send a daughter back to this cursed land. So they couldn't care less whom I marry.

ANDHAKA: (*Not unkindly.*) Besides, you're not known to be bright. You are not in demand. That's an advantage.

(ARVASU *makes a wry face.* NITTILAI *giggles silently.*)

ARVASU: Actually, I did have some moments of panic. But then the other day as I sat thinking—(*For* ANDHAKA's *benefit.*) "trying hard" to think, if you like—it suddenly occurred to me how stupid I was being. I'll never be learned like father or uncle. I shan't ever conduct the royal sacrifice like Paravasu or perform penance like cousin Yavakri. All I want is to dance and sing and act. And be with Nittilai. It doesn't matter a flake of cow dung to my father whether I'm alive or dead. My sister-in-law lives wrapped up in a world of her own. That leaves only my brother—

ANDHAKA: A hard man, who will not be crossed.

ARVASU: Hard? Never to me. To me he's been a mother, father, brother, nurse, teacher—everything rolled into one. He who taught me to win at marbles and play tunes on reeds. I owe everything to him.

ANDHAKA: And what if he forbids you now?

ARVASU: I'll tell him: "I can't give up Nittilai. She is my life. I can't live without her. I would rather be an outcaste!"

ANDHAKA: Beautiful! Beautiful! Such moving words.

(NITTILAI *laughs happily.*)

But Paravasu is not one to be easily moved, I warn you.

ARVASU: You'll see. The only reason I haven't told him yet is that the sacrifice is about to end. And he *is* the Chief Priest. It's important that he is not disturbed . . .

(NITTILAI *nods in agreement.*)

ANDHAKA: But surely he'll hear about your meeting with her tribal elders this afternoon?

ARVASU: How was I to know her father would call this Council so suddenly? He never asked me.

NITTILAI: So Father's to blame? Do you know why Father called the elders in such haste? He always says: "These high-caste men are glad enough to bed our women but not to wed them."

ARVASU: All right! Now I'll wed you so you can—

NITTILAI: (*Screams.*) Shut up!

(*They all laugh.*)

ANDHAKA: Your cousin Yavakri will be so happy.

ARVASU: Is he in?

ANDHAKA: No. In fact he said he was heading in the direction of your hermitage.

ARVASU: We are on our way there too. He's sent word asking me to meet him there.

NITTILAI: It would have been so convenient if you could have finished talking to him here. We could have gone directly to our village . . .

ANDHAKA: Yavakri gets no peace here. It's this endless stream of visitors. Morning to night. Ceaseless. Learned men, ascetics, pundits, all dying to find out how he talked to the god, what Lord Indra said, the details of his austerities, what hymns he chanted . . .

ARVASU: (*lo* NITTILAI.) You see? It's no small matter. Don't joke about it.

ANDHAKA: She joked about it? What did she say?

(NITTILAI *glares at* ARVASU *as though to say, "There! You've done it!"* ANDHAKA *is getting more and more agitated.*)

Speak up, child. You joked about what?

NITTILAI: I only said I didn't know why Yavakri had to spend ten years in the jungle—

ANDHAKA: He was seeking God so he could ask for Universal Knowledge?! And gods don't yield to men so easily. He had to mortify himself, practice austerities, fast, meditate, pray.

NITTILAI: I know, but—

ANDHAKA: Ten years of rigorous penance. And still Lord Indra would not oblige. Finally, Yavakri stood in the middle of a circle of fire and started offering his limbs to the fire—first his fingers, then his eyes, then his entrails, his tongue, and at last, his heart—that's when the god appeared to him, restored his limbs, and granted him the boon.

NITTILAI: (*Simply, with no offense meant.*) Did he tell you all this, Grandfather?

ARVASU: Don't be silly. A man of his stature wouldn't talk about himself.

NITTILAI: Then how does everyone know what happened in a remote corner of the jungle—miles away from the nearest prying eye?

ANDHAKA: Every Brahmin on the face of this earth wants to gain spiritual powers. But few succeed. In my lifetime I have known only two who did. Your uncle and your father, Arvasu. But they got their knowledge from human gurus. By diligent study. Yavakri has gone beyond even them. He received his knowledge from the gods, direct! Your uncle was sure he would fail. How he tried to dissuade the boy from taking on this ordeal. But I said to him, "Master, let him go to the jungle. You don't know your son. I do. I brought him up on this lap of mine. He will succeed in anything he tries, you mark my words!" If my Master had listened to me, he would be alive today. But he died of a broken heart. (*Pause.*) I waited. Right here. For ten years. I took care of this hermitage for the day when my Yavakri would return home. And now he has come back. In triumph. The whole world is at his feet.

NITTILAI: But what I want to know is, why are the Brahmins so secretive about everything?

ARVASU: Oh God! She's got into one of her argumentative moods! (*Walks off a little distance. Stands concentrating.*)

NITTILAI: (*Continuing.*) You know, their fire sacrifices are conducted in covered enclosures. They mortify themselves in the dark of the jungle. Even their gods appear so secretly. Why? What are they afraid of? Look at my people. Everything is done in public view there. The priest announces that he'll invoke the deity at such and such a time on such and such a day. And then there, right in front of the whole tribe, he gets possessed. And the spirit answers your questions. You can feel it come and go. You *know* it's there. Not mere hearsay . . .

ANDHAKA: Take care, child. The gods that their priests seek are far mightier than yours. Don't talk of the two in the same breath.

NITTILAI: My point is, since Lord Indra appeared to Yavakri and Indra is their God of Rains, why didn't Yavakri ask for a couple of good showers? You should see the region around our village. Parched. Every morning, women with babes on their hips, shrunken children, shriveled old men and women gather in front of my father's house—for the gruel he distributes. No young people. They have all disappeared! And Father says all the land needs is a couple of heavy downpours. That'll revive the earth. Not too much to ask of a god, is it?

ANDHAKA: (*Half-agreeing.*) But they say that such powers shouldn't be used to solve day-to-day problems. They are meant to lead one to . . . to . . . inner knowledge.

NITTILAI: What's that?

ANDHAKA: I don't know. That's what Yavakri's father used to say.

NITTILAI: Then what's the use of all these powers?

ANDHAKA: Ask Yavakri, when you meet him. He won't mind. In fact, he'll like it. He's a gentle soul.

NITTILAI: Actually, I want to ask Yavakri *two* questions. Can he make it rain? And then, can he tell when he is going to die? Just two. What is the point of any knowledge, if you can't save dying children and if you can't predict your moment of death.

ARVASU: (*From far.*) Now, guess what animal this is!

NITTILAI: He can't think of anything else! (*But closes her eyes and listens.*) All right.

(ARVASU *charges, pretending to be a wild animal.*)

ANDHAKA: (*Listens.*) A wild horse . . . No! A boar? I know. A bison!

NITTILAI: Yes. A bison. That was good.

ARVASU: (*Ecstatic.*) Triumph! They say one shouldn't imitate! One should embody the essence. Only the essence! It means I have captured the essence of a bison!

NITTILAI: You don't need to try. You were born with it.

ARVASU: That's why the hunters love me!

(*They all laugh.*)

NITTILAI: Let's go.

ANDHAKA: Wait, child. I know you're restless to reach your village. But Yavakri wants you to meet him when the sun's overhead, doesn't he?

ARVASU: "Exactly." I don't know why. But his message said "exactly." Neither earlier. Nor later. Exactly when the sun's overhead.

ANDHAKA: So you've time. Stay and chat. Listening to you makes me feel happy.

ARVASU: The question is how do you capture the essence of the gods in your footsteps, since a god's feet never touch the earth?

(*The stage darkens.*

Lights come up in another part of the stage, representing the hermitage of Raibhya, father of Arvasu. VISHAKHA, *aged about twenty-six, is pouring water into a metal urn. She has scooped out water from holes dug in the wet sand and collected it in the pot. She must have been an attractive person once but now looks angry and haggard. She looks around furtively. There's no one around. She picks up the pot, puts it on her waist and starts for home.* YAVAKRI *is standing right in the middle of her path. She stops but avoids looking at him. A long pause.*)

VISHAKHA: (*Without looking at him.*) Please . . .

YAVAKRI: At last, a word! After waiting for four days. I practically had to wrench it out of you by blocking your path. (*As he moves aside and sits down on a rock,* VISHAKHA *takes a few steps towards her house.*) Stay, Vishakha, please. There's no one in your house. Your father-in-law has gone out. Your brother-in-law is never home. What's the hurry?

VISHAKHA: My father-in-law will be back tomorrow. Speak to him then.

YAVAKRI: It's not the need to speak to him that brings me here.

VISHAKHA: I can't stay here chatting with a stranger.

YAVAKRI: A stranger! (*Laughs.*) That's good.

VISHAKHA: I am a married woman.

YAVAKRI: I know you are. The first piece of news to greet me on my return was that you had married Paravasu. And I was shattered. But it was silly of me not to have expected it. Ten years is a long time. Ten years of silence is longer still. Can't we just talk? (*Pause.*) Ten years ago I swore to you that I would not look at another woman. I kept my word.

VISHAKHA: That's over and done with now.

YAVAKRI: Don't think I regret it. No, not for a moment. But doesn't that give me some right to say: "Please put the pot down for a few minutes and talk to me?"

(VISHAKHA *makes a move to go.*)

Vishakha, after ten years in solitude, I am hungry for words.

(*Startled,* VISHAKHA *looks up at him for the first time.*)

VISHAKHA: They say that pleased with your rigorous penance, Lord Indra has granted you Universal Knowledge. I don't feel equal to the task of—

YAVAKRI: Universal Knowledge! What a phrase! It makes me laugh now. But do you know it was in order to win some such grandiose prize that I went into the jungle? You put it so simply in that one sentence. So beautifully. You go into the jungle. You perform austerities in the name of some god. You stand in a circle of fire. The pressure of your austerities forces the god to grant you your wish. And you get "Universal Knowledge." Victory! (*Pause.*) It wasn't at all like that, you know.

VISHAKHA: (*Gently.*) Why?

YAVAKRI: For a start, life in the jungle is sheer hell. Flies, giant ants, beetles, pests, leeches attacking at the suspicion of moisture, vipers lurking in bowls of dust. The relentless heat. Not demons but mosquitoes to torture you—

VISHAKHA: Perhaps that's how the gods test one.

YAVAKRI: One would expect the appearance of a god to be a shattering experience. Concrete. Indubitable. Almost physical. But though I think Indra came to me several times, I was never certain. The first time he appeared he said, "No, Yavakri, you can't master knowledge through austerities. It must come with experience. Knowledge is time. It is space. You must move through these dimensions." I said, "No, I must have it. Grant me all knowledge." He laughed and said, "You are being silly." That's it! Common dialogue. Not very profound. And when the god disappeared, nothing was left behind to prove he had ever been there. I looked around. The same old black scorpion. The same horned chameleon. The shower of bird shit around me. So was it all a hallucination caused by something I'd eaten that morning? Or was it fever working on my brain? So I go on. Another year. Or perhaps two. Then the god comes again. "Why are you being so stubborn?" he chides. "You can't cross a full stream on a bridge of sand." I insist that my demands are met. Another trite exchange of words . . .

VISHAKHA: But you did win in the end?

YAVAKRI: Yes, one day I decided I had won. So I have come back. I have no clear recollection how I arrived at that conclusion. (*Laughs.*) Some knowledge, but probably little wisdom. I know now what *can't* be achieved. That itself is wisdom, isn't it? But I mustn't complain. I think I have some mystical powers I hadn't before. Mastered a few secret arts. Got a few *mantras* at my fingertips. You'll see for yourself soon.

VISHAKHA: Me? No, thank you.

YAVAKRI: The strangest thing, however, is that I've discovered a corner within me, left untouched by those ten years! Undisturbed by all that self-lashing! So if you feel insulted by what I am going to tell you, go away. I won't see you again. In that case, let these be the last words I speak to you. (*Pause.*)

The day I decided my penance was over I fell down in a dead faint. I don't know how long I was in that state. It was terrible exhaustion, the pain of sheer relief. And when I opened my eyes, do you know the first thing that I thought of? Ten years ago I had come to your house to bid you goodbye. And you led me quickly to the jack-fruit grove behind your house. You opened the knot of your blouse, pressed my face to your breasts, then turned and fled. I stood there stunned. The trees were loaded with fruit. Many were ripe and had split open and the rich golden segments poured out. The sweet sick smell of the jack-fruit, the maddening hum of a fly. The smell of your body. Ten years later I opened my eyes and I knew I was hungry for that moment.

VISHAKHA: I can't believe it! The whole world may be singing your praises. But you haven't grown up! These ten years have not made any difference to your teenage fantasies. That's all gone, Yavakri. Indra may be immortal. But my breasts hang loose now. (*Laughs.*)

YAVAKRI: Why are you laughing?

VISHAKHA: I have been trembling at the sight of you these last three days. Now, I only feel sorry.

YAVAKRI: Good. I told you you could go home if you were angry. But you are not angry. My tale only makes you feel sorry for me. So you can stay?

VISHAKHA: The moment I heard you say you were hungry for words, I knew it was too late to go. I couldn't walk out on you after that. I had lost the initiative, missed the moment of decision. Because I know that hunger well, Yavakri. That's why I should have gone back without saying a word to you.

YAVAKRI: Don't go, Vishakha!

VISHAKHA: Have I gone? I am still here. You are a fool, Yavakri. And you talk like one.

(YAVAKRI *goes to her. There's a pause.* VISHAKHA *looks at him steadily, smiling. He embraces her. She pushes him away, puts the pot down on the ground.*)

YAVAKRI: You want to hit me? Go ahead . . .

VISHAKHA: It's not you I am worried about. It's the water. I have dug it out like precious gold. You are hungry for words. And so am I. So let's talk. Sit down.

YAVAKRI: You and Indra. That's right. The presiding deities of my life. It's because of you two that I have avoided women altogether until now. Conserved my seed like you conserve your water. Now as I sit in front of you, I want to betray Indra—he left me ignorant . . .

VISHAKHA: They say Indra has a thousand eyes. (*Laughs.*) He could have opened at least one for you.

(YAVAKRI *tries to kiss her.*)

YAVAKRI: Shush now.

VISHAKHA: What do you mean "Shush?" What you have done is to rekindle my need to talk. I thought it was dead and gone. Gently! Don't rush. Oh, Yavakri! The pleasure of calling someone a fool. Of the desire welling up inside one to protect him. I live in this hermitage, parched and wordless, like a she-devil. And words are like water—precious. I was afraid to bathe. Now I want to drown. Listen to me. You went away. I was married off—

YAVAKRI: Your father must have felt relieved that I went away. Paravasu was a better match. I was only his miserable cousin.

VISHAKHA: Yes, Father was happy. I was married off to Paravasu. I didn't want to, but that didn't matter. The night of the wedding, my husband said to me: "I know you didn't want to marry me. But don't worry. I'll make you happy for a year." And he did. Exactly for one year. He plunged me into a kind of bliss I didn't know existed. It was heaven—here and now—at the tip of all my senses. Then on the first day of the second year of our marriage, he said: "Enough of that. We now start on our search." And then—it wasn't that I was not happy. But the question of happiness receded into the background. He used my body, and his own body, like an experimenter, an explorer. As instruments in a search. Search for what? I never knew. But I knew he knew. Nothing was too shameful, too degrading, even too painful. Shame died in me. And I yielded. I let my body be turned inside out as he did his own. I had a sense he was leading me to something. Mystical? Spiritual? We never talked. Only that sense pervaded the air. You're still lost in the fragrance of the jack-fruit, Yavakri. I have known what it is to grow heavy, burst open, drip and rot, to fill the world with one's innards. Then one day he received the invitation from the King. To be the Chief Priest of the fire sacrifice. And he left. The site of the fire sacrifice is only a couple of hours away from here. But in all these seven years he hasn't come back. I know he can't. But I look forward to having him home once the seven years are over. Alone, I have become dry like tinder. Ready to burst into flames at a breath. To burn things around me down at the slightest chance—

YAVAKRI: (*Looks up.*) Soon the sun will be overhead.

VISHAKHA: My husband and you! He left no pore in my body alone. And you. You think a woman is only a pair of half-formed breasts.

YAVAKRI: Enough now.

VISHAKHA: I'll give you the knowledge Indra couldn't give you. My body—it's light with speech now.

(*They go behind a dry champak tree on the bank. Long pause.* NITTILAI *and* ARVASU *enter.*)

NITTILAI: He's going to settle down here now, isn't he? So why can't you see him tomorrow? Surely a day isn't going to make a difference. If we are late, the elders will be angry with us and—

ARVASU: Let's give him five minutes. That's all, Nittilai. Please. You know there's always been a lot of bitterness between us cousins. Verging on hatred. Now he's made the gesture of asking me to meet him. Let me reciprocate. I'll touch his feet. As for his blessings. Then we go on.

NITTILAI: All right. But there's no one here. I hope he doesn't make us wait. (*Goes toward the stream. Stops. Suddenly she is transformed, from an innocent young girl into a consummate huntress. Silently, she beckons* ARVASU. *He goes near her. She points to something in the dry bed of the river. It is Vishakha's pot.*)

ARVASU: (*In a low voice.*) Our water pot! What's it doing here? Has sister-in-law forgotten to take it back?

NITTILAI: No one leaves a full pot of water behind.

ARVASU: That's true. (*Scared.*) They say a panther has strayed into these parts. If he was thirsty and . . .

NITTILAI: (*Inspects the river bed.*) No. Tracks of the barking deer. A couple of porcupines. A family of mongooses. No sign of a panther—or anything that big—not within the last three days.

ARVASU: (*Picks up a stick.*) Shall I go in and see?

NITTILAI: (*Smiles at the sight of the stick.*) No need. It's all here. Those footprints are obviously your sister-in-law's. She didn't drop the pot. She set it down, carefully. So as not to spill the water. And then—(*She freezes. Stares at the ground. Looks in the direction in which Vishakha and Yavakri have gone.*)

NITTILAI: Is your brother back?

ARVASU: Paravasu? Of course not. He can't leave the sacrifice.

NITTILAI: (*Gets up.*) Come, Arvasu. Let's go.

ARVASU: Where?

NITTILAI: Let's go. Please. To my village.

ARVASU: And leave sister-in-law to her fate?

NITTILAI: Listen to me. Nothing's happened to her.

ARVASU: I can't do that! I must know. I'll be back in a minute—

(ARVASU *goes behind the champak tree into the bushes. Suddenly exclamations, etc. He rushes out, followed by* VISHAKHA. *Her clothes are torn. Her back is covered with mud. She runs to the hermitage without even glancing at Nittilai.* ARVASU *stares uncomprehending. Then he sees the pot. Lifts it to his shoulder.*)

I'd better take it home. I'll be back . . .

(NITTILAI *nods. At this moment* YAVAKRI *steps out. He picks up a small metal pot with a snout and a handle, a* kamandalu, *which he has hidden behind a tree. He looks at the two, calmly walks to* ARVASU, *tips the pot on his shoulder to fill his kamandalu.* ARVASU *watches helplessly.*)

NITTILAI: (*Angry.*) Some people put the treacherous viper to shame.

YAVAKRI: (*Turns to her.*) Aren't you the whelp who was asking my old servant if I knew my moment of death?

NITTILAI: (*Taken aback.*) How did you know that?

YAVAKRI: (*Ignoring her question.*) I don't know when I'll die. But I promise you this: you'll be dead within the month.

NITTILAI: (*Recoils, shocked.*) Oh . . . I . . . I'm going home . . .

ARVASU: Nittilai . . . wait . . . I'll follow you—(*But* NITTILAI *disappears. He, with the pot on his shoulder, stands unable to follow.*)

YAVAKRI: (*Calmly.*) And you, Arvasu, you'll find me under the banyan tree, next to the black cliff. (*Exits.*)

(ARVASU, *confused, walks to his father's hermitage.*

   VISHAKHA *has gone to the hermitage ahead of Arvasu. She is about to enter the house when her father-in-law,* RAIBHYA, *steps out. He is thin and emaciated but physically active.* VISHAKHA *is horrified to see him. He scowls at her.*)

RAIBHYA: Where were you all this while?

VISHAKHA: I . . . I'd gone . . . to fetch water.

(*She has no pot with her.*)

RAIBHYA: Really?

(ARVASU *comes in with the pot of water and is startled to see Raibhya.*)

ARVASU: Father! I didn't know you were returning home today . . .

RAIBHYA: I didn't either. But perhaps I should give the two of you more such surprises.

(ARVASU *puts the pot down in a corner and retreats.*)

RAIBHYA: Wait! (*To* VISHAKHA.) You go to fetch water. And your brother-in-law carries it back for you. Strange! What is happening here? Why are you so filthy? You look like a buffalo that's been rolling in mud.

VISHAKHA: I suddenly felt faint. And fell down.

RAIBHYA: And he turned up, just at that moment to help you! Isn't that convenient! And you two have been taking a long time for just that. What were you up to?

ARVASU: (*Hurriedly.*) Nittilai was there too—

RAIBHYA: Who?

ARVASU: Nittilai. The hunter girl.

RAIBHYA: A savage! Was there anybody else?

(ARVASU, *taken unawares by the question, looks at* VISHAKHA. RAIBHYA *notices the look.*)

RAIBHYA: So there *was* someone else there, wasn't there? Who was it?

ARVASU: (*Finding it hard to lie.*) No one, Father. Nittilai and I went there—

RAIBHYA: (*Pointing to* VISHAKHA.) Was she alone? Or was there anybody else with her?

ARVASU: No, there was no one else. She was feeling faint . . . and fell down . . . so I helped her. I must go . . .

RAIBHYA: You want to run away, do you? All right. Go. But where will she go? (*To* VISHAKHA.) Tell me who was there. Tell me. (*He grabs her by her hair and starts beating her. Kicks her.* ARVASU *can't bear to see it. He rushes to her help. Holds* RAIBHYA *back.*)

ARVASU: Stop it, Father. Please. Go away, Sister-in-law. Go! Please—

RAIBHYA: Where can she go? I want the truth and I'll kill her if necessary. Let me go! I know how to handle her. (*Struggles to get out of Arvasu's hold.*)

VISHAKHA: Let him go, Arvasu. (*Calmly.*) Yes, there was somebody else there. Yavakri! And he had come to see me. Alone.

(*Long pause. They stare at each other.*)

RAIBHYA: You whore. You roving whore! I could reduce you to ashes— turn you into a fistful of dust—with a simple curse. But let that husband of yours handle you. Paravasu, Chief Priest of the sacrifice! Let him clean up his own shit! Yavakri! So this is what ten years of austerities amount to! So be it. So Yavakri, now it's between you and me. Where's that pot of water? Bring it here.

VISHAKHA: No, please! Don't do anything to him. It's my fault. Please don't harm Yavakri. I'm willing to face the consequences. Punish me, not him. Please.

RAIBHYA: Bring the water!

(*Sits cross-legged and sinks into deep meditation.* VISHAKHA *and* AR-VASU *watch him horrified, fascinated.* RAIBHYA *opens his eyes. Suddenly he is calm. There is no trace of anger in him.*)

Vishakha, go and tell your lover I accept his challenge. I shall invoke the *kritya* and send a *brahma rakshasa*, a demon soul, after him. Let Yavakri save himself. He need only go and hide in his father's hermitage. I loved my brother and will not desecrate his altar. Let Yavakri cower in there like a dog. If he steps out, he will be dead. Tell him this, too: if he can manage to stay alive for another twenty-four hours, I, Raibhya, shall accept defeat and enter fire. (*Sinks back into meditation.*)

VISHAKHA: (*Wakes up.*) Arvasu, we must warn Yavakri. Instantly. Go to your uncle's hermitage.

ARVASU: But Yavakri said he would be under the banyan tree near the black cliff—

VISHAKHA: I'll run there. It's nearby. You go to the hermitage in case he's there.

ARVASU: But . . . but . . .

VISHAKHA: Run, please. I've never asked anything of you till now. Just this once. Go. Run.

(*They run in opposite directions.* RAIBHYA *opens his eyes, pulls out a strand of hair from his head and throws it to the ground. The* BRAHMA RAKSHASA *appears. He is thin, almost naked and holds a trident. He runs in the direction of Yavakri as the lights fade out.*

ANDHAKA, *the blind man, is sitting at the gate of Yavakri's hermitage. He hears footsteps.*)

ANDHAKA: Ah, Arvasu!

(ARVASU *arrives.*)

Haven't you gone to the meeting?

ARVASU: I'm on my way. But has Yavakri come here?

ANDHAKA: Not since you and Nittilai left.

ARVASU: If he comes, tell him to stay inside the hermitage. Not to step out. Don't let him even peep out. His life's in danger.

ANDHAKA: What? How?

ARVASU: You don't move from here either. Wait for him. You must warn
him!

ANDHAKA: I will, but—

ARVASU: I have to go—Nittilai's waiting.

ANDHAKA: Listen, boy—

(ARVASU *runs away.* ANDHAKA *sits down, all ears.*

   YAVAKRI *is sitting cross-legged under the banyan tree next to the black cliff,*
murmuring incantations, his kamandalu in front of him. VISHAKHA *runs in,*
panting, sweating profusely. She heaves a sigh of relief when she sees YAVAKRI,
who briefly looks at her, nods encouragingly, and carries on meditating.)

VISHAKHA: You mustn't stay here, Yavakri. Go to your father's hermitage.
Immediately. Please! (*No reply.*) My father-in-law has found out everything, and he is bent on destroying you. (*Pause.*) Yavakri, he is calling
up the *kritya!*

YAVAKRI: He is? I am flattered. To invoke the *kritya* spell is to engage one's
full powers. That he should choose this instrument of death for me is
certainly an honor.

VISHAKHA: Go to your place, Yavakri. Father-in-law said you would be
safe there. Please. Hurry.

YAVAKRI: Don't be afraid, Vishakha, I was expecting something like this.
You see this water? I have consecrated it. (*He points to the water in the*
kamandalu.) A drop of this water, and the Brahma Rakshasa will become numb. Powerless. Uncle's entire threat will turn into a farce.
You needn't have bothered. But now that you're here, stay and see for
yourself.

VISHAKHA: But you don't need any of this. You only have to be in your
father's hermitage—the Brahma Rakshasa can't touch you *there!* Once
you are safe, I'll happily watch that living corpse burn—

YAVAKRI: Oh Vishakha! It's so wonderful to have you here. Because *you*
used to console me—don't you remember—when we were young? I
cried at the humiliations piled on my father. He was one of the most
learned men in the land. Probably the most brilliant mind. But he was
scorned while this unscrupulous brother of his grabbed all the honors.

VISHAKHA: Why are you bringing up all these grievances now, Yavakri? It's
hardly the time—

YAVAKRI: Grievances! You don't even flatter me with the word "hatred."

But it doesn't matter. What matters is that I hate your husband's family. My father deserved to be invited as the Chief Priest of the sacrifice. But that too went to Paravasu, your husband. Even in the midst of my austerities I wept when I heard the news. For I knew Father would refuse to take offense. I knew he would go and congratulate Paravasu on the honor, embrace and bless him.

VISHAKHA: Yes, he did that.

YAVAKRI: (*Enraged.*) Why? I hated him for it. *He* was one of the reasons I fled to the jungle.

VISHAKHA: Do we have to talk about it now? The past is gone.

YAVAKRI: The past *isn't* gone. It's here inside me. The time has come to show the world what my father's son is capable of. This is my moment.

VISHAKHA: But today your name's on every tongue in the land and they pronounce it with awe. Why do you need to—

YAVAKRI: The others don't matter, except as witnesses. (*Looks out.*) Where is that demon? Why is he late? (*To* VISHAKHA.) One night in the jungle, Indra came to me and said: "You are ready now to receive knowledge. But knowledge involves control of passions, serenity, objectivity." And I shouted back: "No, that's not the knowledge I want. That's not knowledge. That's suicide! This obsession. This hatred. This venom. All this is me. I'll not deny anything of myself. I want knowledge so I can be vicious, destructive!"

VISHAKHA: If anything happens to you, I'll never forgive myself. Go, go to your home altar. Please.

YAVAKRI: (*Incensed.*) Don't you understand anything? You want me to run away after issuing my challenge?

VISHAKHA: Challenge?

YAVAKRI: Do you think all this happened accidentally? You think I would leave anything to chance? How do you think Arvasu happened to arrive at the river bank at the right moment? Who called your father-in-law back?

VISHAKHA: (*Scared.*) Enough, Yavakri. Don't say anything more. I don't want to know. It's my fault. I shouldn't have yielded to you . . . I . . .

YAVAKRI: It was fortunate that you yielded. If you hadn't, I would have had to take you by force.

(VISHAKHA *stares at him in horror.*)

This is the moment toward which my entire life has rushed headlong. I will not let anything stand in its way. Your father-in-law will die, Vishakha. Let's see what your husband does then. Will he continue to hide like a bandicoot in his ritual world? Or will he commit sacrilege by stepping out to face me? Look, I am trembling. I am drenched in sweat. Because everything has worked out just right.

VISHAKHA: (*Under her breath.*) Oh, my God! . . . Yavakri!

YAVAKRI: Try to understand. They would have turned their backsides on me with contempt if I'd let them, as they did with Father! There was only one way to force them to confront me: catch Paravasu by his scrotum. Squeeze it so that he couldn't even squirm.

(*She is numbly staring at him.*)

I love you, Vishakha. I have not looked at another woman in my whole life. That you happened to marry Paravasu is not my fault! (*Pause. Paces restlessly, waiting for the* BRAHMA RAKSHASA.)

VISHAKHA: (*Quietly.*) I was so happy this morning. You were so good. So warm. I wanted to envelope you in everything I could give. It was more as a mother that I offered my breasts to you . . .

(*He is pacing restlessly, looking eagerly in the direction of Raibhya's hermitage. Quietly, she goes to the* kamandalu *and picks it up.*)

Why is life so contrary, Yavakri? One thinks one has stepped onto a bit of solid ground—a little haven—and the earth gives way—

YAVAKRI: Where's that shadow puppet?

(*Slowly, calmly,* VISHAKHA *starts pouring the water out. He looks at her and for a moment cannot comprehend what she is doing. He suddenly screams.*)

Oh God! What are you doing? The water—the sanctified water! My life! What are you doing?

(*He grabs the* kamandalu *from her hand. It's empty. He starts banging it on the ground.*)

Water, please! Just a drop. Oh gods! Only a drop . . . You devil. I trusted you . . . A drop of water.

(*Suddenly a very strange wail is heard from the distance, unearthly, terrifying and evil.* VISHAKHA *is frightened.*)

VISHAKHA: Yavakri, hurry. Go to your father's hermitage.

YAVAKRI: A drop . . . only a drop!

VISHAKHA: (*Pushing him.*) Go! Run!

YAVAKRI: I'm not here to run away. I've triumphed over Indra, the Lord of
Gods. Who are you to order me around?

VISHAKHA: Go! (*She pushes him. Suddenly* YAVAKRI *wakes up and starts to
run.*) Don't stop till you reach your father's house.

(YAVAKRI *runs.* VISHAKHA *stares after him, then heaves a sigh and turns. The*
BRAHMA RAKSHASA *has entered and is standing behind her. She sees him,
gasps, and falls down in a faint. The* BRAHMA RAKSHASA *runs after Yavakri.*

YAVAKRI *stops now and then, desperately digs for water, then not finding any
runs on. He comes to the hermitage, which is still being guarded by* ANDHAKA.
As YAVAKRI *comes running and is about to step into the hermitage,* ANDHAKA
jumps up and grabs him. Doesn't let him move.)

ANDHAKA: Who's that? Who—

YAVAKRI: Let me go! Let me—

(*The* BRAHMA RAKSHASA *comes and spears him.* YAVAKRI *collapses in*
ANDHAKA'S *arms. The demon pulls out the trident and goes away.*)

ANDHAKA: Who—Yavakri—? Yavakri . . . Son. (*He lowers* YAVAKRI'S *body to
the ground. Shakes him furiously as though to wake him up.* ARVASU *comes
running, stands frozen with horror.*) Yavakri! Child! What happened to
you? I didn't recognize your steps . . . Why, why couldn't I recognize
your steps?

(*It gets dark onstage.*)

Act Two

Evening. The village square. NITTILAI'S BROTHER *and a couple of his friends
are waiting under a tree. They talk in low tones. The* BROTHER *looks up and
sees* ARVASU *in the distance.*

BROTHER: He's come!

FRIENDS: Oh God! Now?

(*They fall silent as* ARVASU *comes running. He is sweating, panting. They do
not greet him. He tries to regain his breath. Looks around.*)

ARVASU: Hello! Isn't the Council of the Elders meeting here?

(*The* BROTHER *nods.*)

Then where . . . where is everybody?

BROTHER: Everyone's gone home.

ARVASU: Home? Oh God! But . . . but . . . the Elders . . .

BROTHER: The Elders waited for you all day. You did not come.

ARVASU: I know. I'm sorry. But I couldn't help it. What happened was—

BROTHER: It doesn't matter.

ARVASU: It does. It does. Please. I would like to explain to the Elders and apologize.

BROTHER: It's no—

ARVASU: (*Suppressing the mounting panic.*) You judge for yourself. I was on my way here when I saw Yavakri running. He was scared. I knew his life was in danger. I ran after him. When I got to his hermitage, he was lying there. Dead.

BROTHER: Dead?

ARVASU: Blood was still spurting from his back. Andhaka was there too, but had gone stone-deaf. He couldn't hear anything I said to him. Blind. Stunned. How could I leave the dead body with him there and come away?

(*The* BROTHER *listens intently.*)

The blood was fresh. It was gushing out. And wild animals had already started appearing in the bushes. Hyenas. Wolves. Ready to tear into Yavakri—into the old man, too. I had to cremate the body on the spot . . . What would you have done?

BROTHER: (*Guarded.*) You were perfectly right.

ARVASU: I knew you would understand. I know the Elders will too. I—

BROTHER: The Elders have all gone home.

ARVASU: I'll go to each one's house and explain. I'll touch their feet. I'll ask their forgiveness. Perhaps the Elders can meet again tomorrow—

BROTHER: Meet again? To do what?

ARVASU: To bless me and Nittilai!

BROTHER: Arvasu, since you failed to attend the Council meeting, the Elders decreed that Nittilai will marry another boy . . . of our own tribe.

ARVASU: (*Stares, stunned.*) What? Oh, no! No! No! No! That can't be . . .

BROTHER: That'll have to be, Arvasu. It's the decision of the Elders.

ARVASU: But it's not sunset yet! Nittilai said the Council would go on till sundown . . . I'm here well before then . . .

BROTHER: I agree. I'm afraid my father was a little hasty. But he was tired of waiting. He felt angry, humiliated. "This daughter of mine has made me a laughing stock in the eyes of the world," he said, "I'm willing to marry her off to anyone who'll take her." Fortunately, it was a nice young man, one of our relatives, who stepped forward. Nittilai will be happy. Console yourself with that thought.

ARVASU: No, no, you're making fun of me. I know you are—tell me you're making—

BROTHER: Nothing can be changed now. If only you'd come half an hour earlier.

ARVASU: Half an hour! Half an hour! Don't say that. Please, can I see the young man? I'll explain to him. Plead with him. I'll debase myself in front of him. Please, let me meet your father and the Elders. I'll go right now . . . I'll explain . . . It can't be . . .

BROTHER: Go home, Arvasu.

ARVASU: I'll offer chunks of my flesh to your gods as a penance . . .

BROTHER: It's no use.

ARVASU: (Shouts.) But I want my Nittilai . . . I . . .

(In one quick movement, the BROTHER knocks him down and plants his foot on his chest.)

BROTHER: You've caused enough trouble, Brahmin. Nittilai is to be married in the next couple of days. People are already sniggering about the two of you. Don't shame her further by shouting her name in public.

ARVASU: Can I . . . can I talk to her?

BROTHER: (Withdrawing.) No, you can't. Not till the wedding's over.

ARVASU: And after that?

BROTHER: That's up to her and her husband.

ARVASU: Please, tell me. How's she taken it?

BROTHER: It's been a terrible day for her. She is exhausted. Even now she is crying her heart out. You'll only make it worse for her by hanging around here. Go away.

ARVASU: (Starts to go, turns.) But listen. It's not my fault.

(*The* BROTHER *grabs him by the scruff of his neck.*)

BROTHER: Go!

(ARVASU *stumbles home.* RAIBHYA *is still awake.* ARVASU *throws himself down in a corner of the veranda.*

Footsteps. PARAVASU *enters in the dark. He is covered in a black rug. He carries a bow and quiver of arrows slung on his back.*)

RAIBHYA: Who's that? Who's that coming in the dead of night?

PARAVASU: It's me, Father. Paravasu.

RAIBHYA: (*Taken aback.*) Paravasu? (*Runs out of the house to make sure.*) Paravasu? It's not possible!

PARAVASU: (*Gently.*) Your blessings be on my head, Father. (*Prostrates himself in front of* RAIBHYA.)

RAIBHYA: (*Horrified.*) You? Here? What are you doing here? There's still a month left to go before the sacrifice ends. You are . . . you can't . . . you have broken the rules! You are *deliberately defying* the gods!

PARAVASU: I felt like coming home.

RAIBHYA: Felt? And just walked out? With the ritual bracelet on? As though the sacrifice were a marketplace? . . . Or have they thrown you out? Your wife's reputation must have reached there by now . . .

(*By now* ARVASU *and* VISHAKHA *have got up and are listening from a distance.*)

PARAVASU: (*Gently.*) Of course, they've heard the news. But they haven't chased me out.

RAIBHYA: So this is your usual insolence. Wilful transgression of the rules.

PARAVASU: If I am back there before dawn, no one need know.

RAIBHYA: (*Explodes.*) No one need know? The Chief Priest of the royal sacrifice sneaks out at night, crawls home, his face covered like a leper, and you think the gods won't know? They won't retaliate? How could I have fathered two such imbeciles? I told the King, "Mark my words, my son defecates wherever he goes. And he will defecate on your sacrifice—"

PARAVASU: The King often says he would have preferred you to be the Chief Priest. But it was a seven-year rite. They thought . . . a younger man safer.

RAIBHYA: I see. So you measured my lifespan, did you, you and your King?

Tested the strength of my lifeline? Well, the sacrifice is almost over and I'm still here. Still here. Alive and kicking. Tell the King I shall outlive my sons. I shall live long enough to feed their dead souls. Tell him the swarm of dogs sniffing around my daughter-in-law's bottom keeps me in good shape.

PARAVASU: I thought with your permission I would have a word with my wife.

RAIBHYA: You disgust me. You and that bitch of yours. I am going out . . .

PARAVASU: At this time of night, Father? Isn't it dangerous in the jungle? (*Calls.*) Arvasu—

ARVASU: Yes . . . (*Steps out.*)

RAIBHYA: If you want to be alone with your wife, send that fool somewhere else. I don't need him. It's not the wild beasts one has to watch out for, it's the human beings.

(PARAVASU *bows to his father.* RAIBHYA *walks off.* PARAVASU *turns to* ARVASU.)

PARAVASU: How are you?

ARVASU: I'm all right.

PARAVASU: (*Pause.*) Your eyes are bloodshot. I'm sorry if I've disturbed your sleep.

ARVASU: No, no.

PARAVASU: With your love of theater, I should have thought you would be quite used to late nights.

ARVASU: There haven't been any plays for ages, what with this famine. (PARAVASU *senses something is wrong but doesn't say anything.* ARVASU *is confused and tries to hide his confusion.*) I tell everyone: Let Brother's sacrifice conclude. It will rain. The players will come back . . .

PARAVASU: (*Smiles.*) And then you'll be able to act on stage again.

ARVASU: Me? I never act. I haven't done so since you asked me not to.

PARAVASU: I told you not to act?

ARVASU: Don't you remember? Long ago, before you left for the sacrifice, I was dancing with the hunters and you said: "If you value your Brahminhood, don't act on stage." I haven't since.

PARAVASU: Arvasu! How silly of you to have taken me at my word. You shouldn't have obeyed me!

ARVASU: I couldn't *disobey* you . . .

PARAVASU: Then you should have asked me again!

ARVASU: Again? How would that have helped?

PARAVASU: You asked a question. It evoked an answer. Suppose you repeated the same question—precisely—in the same words. You would
get the same answer. You ask again. Would that have helped? Yes,
certainly. Each time the question and the answer were repeated, a new
nuance would have arisen. Do you know, you could repeat a question
and an answer without altering a syllable, endlessly, and create a whole
new universe of meanings, more acceptable to you?

ARVASU: (*Looks at* PARAVASU, *uncomprehending. Then.*) I'll be on the tamarind hill. Call me if you need me. (*Runs away.*)

(PARAVASU *puts away his bow and arrows.* VISHAKHA *brings a pot of water and
silently places it near* PARAVASU, *who washes his hands and feet in total silence.
He sits down. Long pause.*)

VISHAKHA: (*In a low voice.*) How are you, Husband?
     (*No reply.*)
     Only occasional bits of news about you. When someone from here goes
     to the city and attends the sacrifice . . .
     (*No response.*)
     Are you well? Or do you still drive yourself to the point of illness, like a
     demon?
     (*No reply.*)
     I was sure you wouldn't come home even if I were on my deathbed.
     (*No reply.*)
     But my fornication was reason enough, wasn't it?
     (*No reply.*)
     Whatever you heard about Yavakri and me . . . was no rumor.
     (*No reply.*)
     Yavakri and you. How much you resemble each other. You both go
     away when you feel like it. Come back without an explanation. As
     though Indra is explanation enough! He isn't. Not for me. Why did you
     go away like that?

PARAVASU: One can practice austerities like your fool, Yavakri, to coerce
the gods to bend one's will. Stand in a circle of fire. Torture oneself. So
many techniques, all equally crass, to make the gods appear. And when

they give in, what do you do? Extend the begging bowl: "Give us rains. Cattle. Sons. Wealth." As though one defined human beings by their begging. I despise it. I went because the fire sacrifice is a formal rite. Structured. It involves no emotional acrobatics from the participants. The process itself will bring Indra to me. And if anything goes wrong, there's nothing the gods can do about it. It has to be set right by a man. By me. That's why when the moment comes I shall confront Indra in silence. As an equal. For that, it is essential that one shed all human weakness. Be alone. Absolutely on one's own to face that moment. Become a diamond. Unscratchable.

VISHAKHA: And become immortal?

PARAVASU: At least for that moment, yes.

VISHAKHA: And for that you must break all the rules?

PARAVASU: To say "all" is to make a rule. (*He gets up.*)

VISHAKHA: Will you come home once the fire sacrifice is over?

(*No answer.*)

I suppose that would be too human. But what's wrong with being human? What's wrong with being happy, as we were before you got Indra into you?

(*No answer.*)

I shouldn't ask. I should be silent. And you, in any case, will be silent. My silence again followed by yours. Silences endlessly repeated. Perhaps they too will describe a whole universe. But I am sick of silence.

(*No answer.*)

All right. Then do me a favor before you go back. Please. (*She takes his bow and arrow, puts them in his hands with the arrow pointing to herself. Then lies down on her back in front of him.*) I'll lay myself open to you as a devoted wife.

PARAVASU: You want me to kill you?

VISHAKHA: At last, a question from you. (*Pause.*) We're three of us here. Your brother's never home. That leaves me and your father. (*Pause.*) Something died inside your father the day the King invited you to be the Chief Priest. He's been drying up like a dead tree since then. No sap runs in him. (*Pause.*) On the one hand, there's his sense of being humiliated by you. On the other, there's lust. It consumes him. An old man's curdled lust. And there's no one else here to take his rage out on but me.

(*Pause.*) At least Yavakri was warm, gentle. For a few minutes, he made me forget the wizened body, the scratchy claws, and the blood, cold as ice. And he paid for it with his life.

(RAIBHYA's *steps are heard in the distance, as he returns.*)

Here it comes. The crab! Scuttling back to make sure I don't defile the Chief Priest as I did Yavakri. Grant me this favor, please. Kill me. For all your experiments you haven't yet tried the ultimate. Human sacrifice! You could now.

PARAVASU: You're right. I must. (*Pause.*) You are still my *guru.* (*He aims his arrow at her. A long silence as they wait. Then a low cough is heard from* RAIBHYA. *Instantly* PARAVASU *moves the arrow around so that it points in the direction of* RAIBHYA, *shoots an arrow.* RAIBHYA *collapses without a sound.* VISHAKHA *gasps. Pause.*)

VISHAKHA: Now you'll never know if I told you a lie.

(*Pause.*)

PARAVASU: You didn't need to. He deserved to die. He killed Yavakri to disturb me in the last stages of the sacrifice. Not to punish Yavakri, but to be even with me. I had to attend to him before he went any further.

(*Pause.*)

VISHAKHA: What's worrying you then?
       (*No answer.*)
     Something is, isn't it? I knew it the moment I saw you this evening. And it wasn't just your father. Something else you've come looking for?
       (*No answer.*)
     Yavakri would have poured out his woes. But you'd rather let the poison burn your insides than speak out. (*Takes his hand in her hand.*) Look at your hand. It's so tense. Your sinews are twisted like ropes—ready to snap. Tell me. What's bothering you?

PARAVASU: (*Looks in the direction of Raibhya.*) We must attend to the old man.

VISHAKHA: He's had a long life. Why should he be in a hurry now?

(*They look at each other. The stage darkens on them. We see* ARVASU *on the tamarind hill talking to himself.*)

ARVASU: Thorns! The wind has thorns now. The light too is nettled. Words . . . Even your name—Nittilai—has fangs that rip the skin off my mind and make it bleed. How can I punish myself enough? Half an hour! Half an hour! But I stopped to bathe on my way to your village . . . to dig for water so I could wash myself before coming to you. I knew it was getting late, but I had just cremated a dead body. I couldn't bear the thought of touching you with those unclean hands. An Untouchable wouldn't have cared. An outcaste wouldn't have cared. But my cursed caste wouldn't let me go . . . To think you would have been mine. Half an hour!

PARAVASU'S VOICE: Arvasu! Arvasu!

(ARVASU *gets up. Runs to the hermitage. He sees* PARAVASU *and* VISHAKHA *bending over something near a thicket.*)

PARAVASU: Arvasu—here! (*Plucks the arrow from Raibhya's body.*)

ARVASU: Where are you?

PARAVASU: Here, near the neem tree.

ARVASU: What are you doing there? (*He goes and finds* PARAVASU *and* VI-SHAKHA *kneeling over Raibhya's body.*) What is it? What's happened? Is that Father? What happened to him? Oh God! Blood! Blood . . . what's happened? Oh my God . . . I can't . . .

PARAVASU: In the dark, I . . . mistook him for a wild animal . . .

ARVASU: (*Almost hysterical.*) Is he all right? We must do something. He may still be alive. There. His eyelids . . . they're moving. Let's move him to—

PARAVASU: Take hold of yourself, Arvasu. He is dead.

(ARVASU *starts crying.* PARAVASU *slaps him.*)

Stop it. Don't be a child. There's no time to howl and wail now. I have to get back before I'm missed.

(ARVASU *and* VISHAKHA *react.*)

If anyone gets wind of what's happened here, the fire sacrifice is ruined. Do you follow me?

ARVASU: But . . . after all this . . . do you mean to go back? To the sacrifice?

PARAVASU: Yes, the sacrifice must go on. You know that. And only I can ensure that—

ARVASU: But the blood on your hands . . .

PARAVASU: Yes, that has to be washed. We must atone for Father's death. I know I should perform the rites of penitence. But I have to return. Immediately. So there's only one person who can do that. You. As his son, it's your prerogative and your duty.

(VISHAKHA *and* ARVASU *react in horror.*)

Cremate the body right now. And then concentrate on the penitential rites.

ARVASU: But, Brother—

PARAVASU: "But?" What do you mean "but?" Can't you see what is at stake? You must do it. (*He starts to leave.*)

VISHAKHA: Say "No," Arvasu.

ARVASU: Sister-in-law—

VISHAKHA: Refuse. He killed his father. Let him atone for it. Don't get involved in it.

ARVASU: But then—what about the sacrifice?

VISHAKHA: Let it go to ruin. Does it matter? There has been enough bloodshed already. Enough tears. Live your own life.

PARAVASU: (*As though she hasn't spoken.*) Don't rush through the rites. Perform them with care. Every detail has to be right.

ARVASU: (*Lost.*) Bless me, Brother.

(PARAVASU *blesses him by placing his right palm on his head and walks away.* VISHAKHA *stares dumbly after him and then walks mechanically back to the hermitage.* ARVASU *starts piling wood for the funeral pyre.*

PARAVASU *is walking back through the jungle when a figure jumps out of the shadows and stands in his path.* PARAVASU *and the* BRAHMA RAKSHASA *stare at each other for a brief moment.*)

PARAVASU: Ah! Not the Brahma Rakshasa himself! What a pleasure. (*Resume walking.*)

BRAHMA RAKSHASA: How did you recognize me?

PARAVASU: I was expecting you. Where else could you possibly go?

BRAHMA RAKSHASA: Help me. Please.

PARAVASU: Don't ask me. I don't help anyone.

BRAHMA RAKSHASA: Please, don't say that. I beg of you. You are my only hope.

PARAVASU: Hope of what?

BRAHMA RAKSHASA: I admire you. You aren't scared of me. You are tough. Your father gave me a new birth. We two are brothers.

PARAVASU: I don't need any more brothers.

BRAHMA RAKSHASA: You have no choice. Look, when lived my "human life," I . . . how shall I put it . . . I was bad. I'll spare you the details. But the result was that after my death I was not reborn, as any ordinary mortal would do. I became a *brahma rakshasa*. A soul locked in nothingness like a fetus stitched up inside its mother's sac. You can't imagine the horror of that existence. Nothing to look forward to. No birth, no death; nothingness stretching endlessly. Your father plucked me out and put me back in time, in order to kill Yavakri. I didn't want to, but I obeyed. And as a result, now I have something new. Hope. Of release— release from this state—

PARAVASU: You should have asked Father.

BRAHMA RAKSHASA: I would have. But you killed him before he'd recovered from his ordeal. *You* killed him. Now you have taken on his inheritance. Not that I mind. You may be more capable of getting me what I want.

PARAVASU: What do you want?

BRAHMA RAKSHASA: Free me from this pain. Liberate me. I want to fade away. To become nothing.

PARAVASU: (*Laughs.*) Yavakri asked for "all knowledge" in a begging bowl. You ask for the final release. *Moksha!* The demands seem to be escalating! I am not interested in your final release. I am not even interested in *my* final release. (*Mocking.*) "Liberate" you! How's one supposed to do that?

BRAHMA RAKSHASA: I wish I knew. I can only beg. Ask the gods when you face them.

PARAVASU: I will ask them for nothing.

BRAHMA RAKSHASA: You talk of immortality. Look, I have been immortal! And I long for death. Release me. You owe it to me.

PARAVASU: I don't owe anyone anything. Don't pester me. You'll get nothing.

(*They have reached the sacrificial site.*)

I must go in. Remember the sacrificial enclosures are protected against all unnatural spirits.

(*Goes in. The* BRAHMA RAKSHASA *watches him.*)

BRAHMA RAKSHASA: It's not so easy to get rid of a brother . . . Brother!

(*Disappears.*)

(ARVASU *completes the funeral rites. Comes home. Calls out to his sister-in-law. No reply. He goes in. The hermitage is empty. In a corner he sees the water pot, covered with cobwebs. He walks out of the house.*

ARVASU *comes to the sacrificial area. The fire sacrifice is going on. He enters the enclosure and goes and sits among the* BRAHMINS *watching the rituals.* PARAVASU, *initially engrossed in his work, notices him and suddenly freezes. His face turns pale. Words fail him. His unexpected silence draws everyone's attention. The hymns come to a stop. They all stare, uncomprehending, first at* PARAVASU *and then at* ARVASU. ARVASU *is baffled and embarrassed.*)

PARAVASU: You! (*Points to* ARVASU, *who gets up, puzzled, scared.*)
ARVASU: Me?
PARAVASU: Yes, you! Who are you?
ARVASU: Me? I . . .
PARAVASU: Yes. Tell us.
ARVASU: I'm Arvasu, son of Raibhya.
PARAVASU: And where have you come from?
ARVASU: My father died. I've just completed his obsequies . . . and the expiation.
PARAVASU: Why the expiation? Tell us. Why?
ARVASU: He was killed . . .

(*Consternation in the assembly.* PARAVASU *silences the* CROWDS.)

PARAVASU: At whose hands?

(*Long pause.*)

ARVASU: At the hands of his son.

(*The gathering breaks out into commotion.*)

PARAVASU: Patricide. patricide! What is he doing in these sanctified precincts? Throw him out. Out! Out! Demon!
ARVASU: But . . . but . . .

(*Three or four* BRAHMINS *pounce on* ARVASU *and drag him out. Dazed,* ARVASU *lets himself be dragged and pushed out of the sacrificial enclosure. Suddenly, he starts shouting.*)

ARVASU: But why, Brother, why? . . . Why?

(*A couple of* SOLDIERS *get hold of him and drag him away as he keeps shouting.*)

Why? Why? Tell me why . . . please.

(PARAVASU *looks at the assembly of priests and watchers.*)

PARAVASU: As the sacrifice approaches its completion, the demons come out. Rakshasas. Their sole aim is to disrupt the sacrifice. We must be on our guard.

(*At a sign from him, the rites begin again. The stage darkens.*)

Act Three

Night. The outskirts of the city. The stage is filled with bodies of people sleeping. NITTILAI *sleeps next to* ARVASU.

ARVASU *wakes up. Sits up. Looks around, and as though frightened by the night, begins to crawl across the sleeping bodies.* NITTILAI *stretches her hand out in her sleep to make sure Arvasu is next to her. He is not there. She sits up with a start, looks around, sees him and goes to him.*

NITTILAI: Arvasu—

(ARVASU *gasps and turns to her.*)

Where are you going?

(*He stares.*)

It's me, Nittilai—

(*She feels his forehead.*)

The fever has gone down. Thank God!

(*Feels his clothes.*)

You are soaking wet.

ARVASU: (*Unbelieving.*) Nittilai! You . . . ? It can't be . . . it isn't . . .

NITTILAI: (*Laughing.*) Yes, it is.

(*Suddenly* ARVASU *laughs happily like a child.*)

ARVASU: Nittilai! Nittilai! Am I dreaming? Or are you really here? You won't disappear again, will you? Nittilai! Where have you come from,

Nittilai? You *are* Nittilai, aren't you? Don't melt away. Please. Nittilai—
stay, now that you're here. (*Grabs her hand.*) I'll hold on to Nittilai now.
I won't let Nittilai go.

NITTILAI: Ssh! You'll wake them up!

ARVASU: (*Laughing.*) How did you come here?

NITTILAI: We can't talk in this place. Let's go over there. (*Helps him up. He
is light-headed and almost falls down again. She supports him. She also
carries a bundle of fruit with her. They move a little distance away.*) Be
careful! You're still light-headed.

ARVASU: (*Laughing.*) Light-headed. Light-footed. I'm flying—I'm floating
—I'm flowing down a torrent of wind—I feel happy. You are here! It's
beautiful. (*Tries to stand by himself. Reels. Clings to her. They both laugh.*)

NITTILAI: Wait! Don't be a child. Here. Let me tie your *dhoti* properly.
(*Unselfconsciously, she reties his dhoti, as though he were a child. Then
leads him along.*) Sit down here. (*She rekindles a dying fire as they talk.*)

ARVASU: Where are we?

NITTILAI: Outside the city gates.

ARVASU: And these people?

NITTILAI: Mostly starving villagers. They are here for the end of the fire
sacrifice. They are waiting for the concluding feast.

ARVASU: The fire sacrifice. Yes. I remember. (*He looks at her attentively.*)
You look so lovely. All those patterns on your hands and face. You're
like a bride. (*Suddenly.*) But . . . didn't you go home to sleep last night?

NITTILAI: (*Puts a fruit in his hand.*) Here. Eat this. I don't know when you
had a proper meal last.

ARVASU: How is it that you're here, Nittilai?

NITTILAI: I've run away.

ARVASU: From your husband?

NITTILAI: From my husband. From my family. From everything.

(*Pause.*)

ARVASU: Oh! (*Pause.*) Why? Didn't you like him? Did he beat you?

NITTILAI: I liked him. Very much. He's always smiling. I might have been
happy with him. (*Pause.*) If any other girl had done what I have done,
I'd be the first to thrash her in the village square. But when I heard
what'd happened to you—

ARVASU: What?

NITTILAI: We heard terrible stories.

ARVASU: (*Remembering.*) Yes, yes.

NITTILAI: I almost died when I heard they'd thrashed you. I got up and . . . ran all the way here.

ARVASU: (*Pause.*) And how did you find me?

NITTILAI: It didn't take much searching. Every stray pup here knows about you.

(*Long pause.*)

ARVASU: I went back to meet Paravasu. (*Excited.*) That night. I had to know why. What had I done? I thought he might tell me if I went to him secretly. So I went back at night. But he never came out . . .

NITTILAI: Arvasu, it's all right. All that's done with.

ARVASU: Soldiers pounced on me. Kicked me. Dragged me to some cemetery. Tore my sacred thread. I kept calling out to him. "Why, Brother, why?" They beat me.

NITTILAI: There now, don't excite yourself. Lie down.

ARVASU: Did he think I was married to you? Did he think I had become a low-caste actor? No, no. I remember. He clearly said: "Out! Out! Demon . . . Away with you!"

NITTILAI: Quiet now. Come, sleep for a while. It's still dark. (*She makes him lie down with his head on her lap.*)

ARVASU: I had such nightmares. And whenever I woke up I saw these bodies. Lying about, inert in the dark. I thought I was in the land of the dead. But I didn't see *you.* I wish I had. (*Stares at her.*) I worshiped my brother. And he betrayed me. I let you down, and you risk everything for my sake.

NITTILAI: (*Simply.*) I like you. (*Gives him another fruit.*) Here, I hid these for you. There are three children in the actor's family. Poor things! They're eternally famished—

ARVASU: Actors?

NITTILAI: Yes, it was they who saved your life.

ARVASU: (*Suddenly.*) Nittilai, how long is it since you left home?

NITTILAI: Three days.

ARVASU: (*Excited.*) Three days! Three days, she says calmly! And you've been moving around in this city for three days! Are you crazed?

NITTILAI: (*Lightly.*) I was only waiting for you to gain some strength.

ARVASU: (*Angry.*) Woman, have you no brains? You only think of others! I know your people. Hunters. Once they decide on vengeance . . . We must leave immediately.

NITTILAI: Let's. If your legs have gained as much strength as your voice, we should be able to cover a fair distance today! (*Suddenly they both burst out laughing. Then in a serious voice.*) Arvasu, when I say we should go together . . . I don't mean we have to live together . . . like lovers or like husband and wife. I have been vicious enough to my husband. I don't want to disgrace him further. Let's be together . . . like brother and sister. You marry any girl you like. Only please, Arvasu— spare a corner for me.

ARVASU: I won't marry. Ever. It's enough that you are here with me.

NITTILAI: (*Gets up.*) Take a little rest. I'll see you soon.

ARVASU: Where are you going?

NITTILAI: Let me arrange for something to eat on the way. Some meat. Fruit. The actor's family wants to go with us. Those poor starving babies—

ARVASU: (*Gently.*) Nittilai . . .

(NITTILAI *stops.*)

While you're away I think I'll make another attempt.

NITTILAI: Attempt?

ARVASU: To see my brother.

NITTILAI: How will you do that? Will he let you come anywhere near him?

ARVASU: No, he won't. But how can I go away without knowing why he acted as he did? I have to find out . . . I must . . .

NITTILAI: Will he tell you?

ARVASU: I don't think so. (*Pause.*) No . . . he won't.

NITTILAI: And suppose he did tell you? What will that do for you? Haven't you suffered enough?

ARVASU: If he can't justify his act, I'll . . . I'll push his face in it. I'll make him pay . . . I'll revenge myself on him—

NITTILAI: Arvasu!

ARVASU: I can't help it. I want to make them all pay. Yavakri. Father. Paravasu. It's a conspiracy, don't you see, it's all planned—because I wanted to marry you. Because I was ready to reject my caste, my birth. Can't you see it? I wanted to strike out on my own. So, first a corpse curls itself round my ankles. Yavakri. Then it's Father. Bodies drenched in blood. Like rats that pour out during the plague and die vomiting blood.

NITTILAI: Arvasu—

ARVASU: Listen. It's clear to me. Yavakri is dead. Father is dead. And Paravasu is alive. So he must know. He must be behind it all. My brother knew I would marry you even if he forbade it. So he—and his wife—and all those priests—yes, they planted those corpses in my way.

NITTILAI: You are talking nonsense.

ARVASU: You don't understand. You hunters—you only know minor spells and witchcrafts, spirits slithering in shallow caves or dangling on trees. But Yavakri and Father and Brother can bring out the terrors from the womb of the earth and play with them. They can set this foul nature against you. Can't you see the design in it all? Corpses pursuing me . . . evil, like a stink emanating from that sacrifice—

NITTILAI: Suppose you are right. What are you going to do about it?

ARVASU: I don't know. I don't know anything. Don't confuse me with questions. But if such an evil man continues as the Chief Priest of the sacrifice, it'll rain blood at the end—

NITTILAI: Leave that to the gods, Arvasu. Look at your family. Yavakri avenges his father's shame by attacking your sister-in-law. Your father avenges her by killing Yavakri. Your brother kills your father. And now you in your turn want vengeance. Where will it all end?

ARVASU: So what do I do? Sit in a corner with my hands crossed, like a eunuch?

NITTILAI: Do that. Better that than become the man you hate.

ARVASU: Become? What's there left for me to become? I am an unregenerate sinner in the eyes of the world, a killer.

NITTILAI: Then kick that world aside, Arvasu. Your hands are clean. Even I have wounded—betrayed—my husband. You have remained good. Stay that way. We don't need this world. We can find our own.

(He doesn't answer. A long tense pause. NITTILAI gets up.)

All right, let's go.

ARVASU: Go? Where?

NITTILAI: Let's go and face your brother. I don't want you to feel I'm depriving you.

ARVASU: (*Calms down.*) You are right. He won't let me come anywhere near him. I knew that from the beginning, didn't I? So what was I making such a fuss about? Do you think I'm going mad?

NITTILAI: You've been through so much, I'm surprised you're not worse.

(*The* ACTOR-MANAGER *comes.*)

ACTOR-MANAGER: Ahha! So the patient is better today?

NITTILAI: Yes, thank you. (*To* ARVASU.) He saved your life, Arvasu.

ARVASU: Thank you.

ACTOR-MANAGER: Hardly "saved." Our old man died. We went to bury him. And there you were in the burial grounds—stretched out stiff. Except that you weren't cold. You were burning hot. The bamboos we'd taken him out on served to carry you back. And you almost burned through them.

NITTILAI: I'm sorry your old man had to go. But it's lucky for us he chose that day. How's your brother?

ACTOR-MANAGER: His foot's much better, thank you. He can hobble about. Your magic touch again!

NITTILAI: (*Pleased.*) Good. I'll get him some fresh herbs.

ACTOR-MANAGER: (*Pointing to* ARVASU.) Now that he's well, do we start today?

NITTILAI: Within the next couple of hours. Let me go and arrange provisions for the trip. (*She goes.*)

ACTOR-MANAGER: What an extraordinary girl!

ARVASU: (*Distracted.*) Hm.

ACTOR-MANAGER: Lucky for you that she's here. Don't you ever forget that.

ARVASU: (*Startled.*) Why . . . why should I?

ACTOR-MANAGER: Listen, son. We actors are always on the move. Never stationary. And often along the way we see a scene. A bit of life. Only a tiny bit as we pass by. But enough to give us a sense of the rest of the story.

ARVASU: What do you mean?

ACTOR-MANAGER: I don't know what you are to her. Not that I want to know. Any fool can see you two belong to different worlds. Anything's possible in these troubled times. So I won't comment. But your name's on every tongue in this town, and they are mostly trying to spit it out. I didn't save your life. She did. I only found you. You were lucky that she turned up soon after, and it's she who's been nursing you. Mopping up your vomit, wiping your bottom. Like a baby. I'm grateful to her because my babies were starving when she came and now they get a bite to eat every day. Where she gets the food from I don't know, but she knows the woods. We would have moved out of this town the day the old man died, except that we've become dependent on her. For food. For nursing. For laughter. We're just waiting to leave with her, but she won't budge till you're better. (*Pause.*) Something about you worries me. She's a good girl. Don't hurt her.

ARVASU: (*Quietly.*) I won't hurt her.

(*While this scene is going on, in the background,* NITTILAI'S BROTHER *and* HUSBAND *enter, make a fire and sit near it, silent and immobile.* NITTILAI *enters, sees them, freezes and flees in panic. They haven't seen her. Long pause. The* ACTOR-MANAGER *hums a song.*)

ARVASU: You said you'd gone to bury your old man when you found me? You bury your dead? Not cremate them?

ACTOR-MANAGER: No, we are actors. We have been actors since the Lord of Creation entrusted the job to my ancestors. The earth gave us the body. When we are done, we hand over the job to our children and hand back the body to the earth.

ARVASU: But the body will rot in the earth, surely . . .

ACTOR-MANAGER: What were we in our mother's womb? Floating bits of flesh? Squiggly worms? To burn is to destroy. Neither the earth gets it, nor the wind. Well, to each his beliefs! My ancestors were actors and—

ARVASU: Then why are you leaving town?

ACTOR-MANAGER: We came here to perform a play for the sacrifice, but this town hasn't been good for us. The old man died. My brother's foot got infected—

ARVASU: (*Excited.*) How can you give up so easily? Surely you have a duty to your art.

ACTOR-MANAGER: Couldn't agree more. But a body needs to be fed before it can act. In fact, even the gods, who are bodiless, need to be fed before they will act. Hence all these oblations. But there are no oblations without a performance, and there's no performance without actors. I don't have enough actors, it's as simple as that.

ARVASU: (*Shyly.*) May I . . . may I . . . ask you something?

ACTOR-MANAGER: Go ahead.

ARVASU: You don't mind?

ACTOR-MANAGER: What is it?

ARVASU: Will you watch me?

ACTOR-MANAGER: Watch you?

ARVASU: I like dancing. If I dance now . . . will you tell me if I am any good?

ACTOR-MANAGER: You?

ARVASU: I realize . . . it sounds absurd . . .

ACTOR-MANAGER: But you are not an actor. You are a high-caste—

ARVASU: I used to be with the hunters most of the time. Dancing. Singing. I like dancing.

ACTOR-MANAGER: Well, some other time. We'll be traveling together, after all. I have other worries at the moment . . .

> (*But* ARVASU *has started dancing. Initially the* ACTOR-MANAGER *is only half-interested, but slowly, as he watches the dancing, his eyes light up. He keeps the beat.*)

Not bad. Not bad at all.

> (*He too stands up and starts dancing. Slowly first, then faster. He leads,* ARVASU *follows. The* ACTOR-MANAGER *occasionally tries to trick* ARVASU *with a complicated step, but* ARVASU *accepts the challenge.*)

Where did you learn all that?

> (ARVASU, *increasingly confident, laughs and taps his own skull in reply. He dances faster.*)

Enough. Enough now. Don't tire yourself. You've just got up from the sick-bed. Sit down.

> (*They both sit.*)

ARVASU: So—I'm not too bad then?

ACTOR-MANAGER: Bad? You're excellent. And that's what makes my stomach burn. It's just my cursed luck . . .

ARVASU: Why?

ACTOR-MANAGER: The fire sacrifice will be completed in the next few days. That's long enough for you to pick up a few bits of dialogue and half a dozen steps. We could have a show ready to celebrate the completion—but my evil stars have made sure that the one actor I could use can't go anywhere near the sacrificial precincts.

ARVASU: Actually, I don't think that would be a problem.

ACTOR-MANAGER: What do you mean?

ARVASU: I don't think Brother will stop me from acting. The problem is—I won't act—I can't.

ACTOR-MANAGER: But why not?

ARVASU: Nittilai and I must go away today.

ACTOR-MANAGER: We could all leave together, later—

ARVASU: No, we must leave today.

ACTOR-MANAGER: (*Disappointed.*) Oh! (*Hopefully.*) Perhaps we can have a show in some other town, on the way?

ARVASU: Perhaps. (*Pause.*) In a land far, far away! (*Pause.*)

ACTOR-MANAGER: Let me warn you. I never give up.

(NITTILAI *comes rushing in. She is frightened.*)

NITTILAI: Arvasu, Arvasu!

ARVASU: Nittilai!

ACTOR-MANAGER: What's happened?

NITTILAI: I was on my way, and I saw them. They were sitting round a fire . . . They didn't see me . . . in the dark . . .

ARVASU: Who?

NITTILAI: My brother. And husband.

ARVASU: Oh my God!

ACTOR-MANAGER: Ah!

NITTILAI: I just turned round and ran back—

ARVASU: (*Excited.*) We must leave then—immediately. Before it dawns, we must get out of the city—

NITTILAI: (*Desperate.*) No, no, we can't. Not now. Don't you see? It's too late—

ARVASU: Too late? Why?

NITTILAI: They don't know I'm here. That's why it's taken them three days to get here. They must have been searching among friends and relatives.

ARVASU: So?

NITTILAI: But everyone knows you're here. In this city. If you disappear now, they'll instantly realize we're together. Then they'll chase us—

ARVASU: So what do we do?

NITTILAI: I don't know!

ACTOR-MANAGER: Is this why you have been acting so mysterious, girl? Why didn't you tell me? I'm a wizard at disguise. With a little bit of make-up, I would have changed your entire appearance. Made you as good as invisible.

ARVASU: (*Exasperated.*) They are hunters. They don't need to see a quarry. They can smell it out. And once they are on the track, they'll run it to the ground.

NITTILAI: One thing's certain, Arvasu. You'll have to stay on in the city— be visible! Only that will throw them off the scent.

ACTOR-MANAGER: But won't they harm him?

ARVASU: No, I am an outsider. (*Bitterly.*) Everywhere.

NITTILAI: They're after me.

ARVASU: So what will you do?

NITTILAI: I'll disappear. Go and hide in the jungle.

ARVASU: (*Enraged.*) Hide? What do you mean hide? Are we playing games here? You there. Me here. No, I won't let you go.

NITTILAI: (*Flying into a temper.*) Do you think I want to die? You think I want to be hunted down by my brother and my husband? If they had come separately, it might have meant anything. But they're here to-gether! And they sat there by the fire—still. Alert. Listening. We never talk when we are on a hunt. We only listen. And my husband wasn't smiling. He looked . . . so sad. That scares me, Arvasu. I'm still young. I don't want to die. (*She starts weeping.*)

ARVASU: Don't cry. Please. It'll soon be light. And if you have to go you must. But what am I to do?

NITTILAI: (*Angry.*) Why do you keep asking me? Why don't *you* decide? Don't push everything onto my shoulders—

ARVASU: (*Quietly.*) I only meant—staying here in the city won't be easy . . . being spat upon, sneered at—

NITTILAI: Is that all you can think of when—

ACTOR-MANAGER: Act in my show.

ARVASU: (*Annoyed.*) Please, don't try to be funny.

ACTOR-MANAGER: I'm quite serious. If you are going to be here till the sacrifice is over, you might as well take part in my play.

ARVASU: Listen—

NITTILAI: What's that?

ACTOR-MANAGER: A moment ago he danced. He danced like a celestial being. With him I could stage a show in honor of the festival. But he won't agree . . .

NITTILAI: Paravasu will never let him—

ARVASU: (*Defiant.*) Paravasu himself has ostracized me. I'm an outcaste now. He can't stop me from acting . . . but how can I sing and dance while you're in mortal danger?

NITTILAI: I'll be safe enough. The jungle's like a home to me.

ACTOR-MANAGER: I am a selfish man. If this performance takes place, I'll be rich. We'll all be rich. My children will sleep on a full stomach for another two months. But that's not all. Think of yourself. If Arvasu has to be "visible," what better than rehearsing in the open, getting ready for a stage performance with the whole town in attendance? (*Pause. He waits for his words to sink in.*)

NITTILAI: Are you sure he'll be able to carry it off? He's never faced an audience before.

ACTOR-MANAGER: I am a professional, Sister. Do you think I would knowingly risk a failure? I even have a play ready. We'd just decided on it when the old man died. A perfect choice for this fire sacrifice. *The Triumph of Lord Indra.* A play about the struggle between Lord Indra and the demon Vritra.

NITTILAI: (*Laughs.*) Then Arvasu will want to play the demon. (*To AR-VASU.*) Aren't I right? (*To the* ACTOR-MANAGER.) He loves all that ghoulish make-up, the roaring and thumping, the acrobatics.

ARVASU: I never know whether you're going to laugh or cry.

ACTOR-MANAGER: He'll have to play Vritra. I, needless to say, will play the main role, Indra. The actor playing Vritra basically needs to dance. And my brother is in no state to dance. And the few speeches that are there won't be a problem to a Brahmin.

ARVASU: I am not a Brahmin.

ACTOR-MANAGER: Quite! Quite! But you won't need to be taught basic pronunciation. (*Pause.*) Think about it. I'll go and get the costumes for Vritra. If you're willing, we might as well start rehearsals right away. (*Exits.*)

ARVASU: What shall I do, Nittilai?

NITTILAI: I don't know. What do you want to do?

ARVASU: What he said made good sense. But . . .

NITTILAI: You've always wanted to act. As long as I can remember. What will you do otherwise? Brood over Paravasu? Whip yourself into a frenzy of anxiety over me?

ARVASU: I'm afraid.

NITTILAI: What's there to fear?

ARVASU: It's the nightmare I told you about. I am dying of thirst. But there's no water. Then I peer into a huge well. There's water there, but it has my reflection in it. I stare at it. And the reflection snarls: "Why are you staring, wretch? Go away." So I say: "You exist because I stare. You wouldn't be there if I went away." It says: "You think so, do you, you swollen-headed doll of flesh? I'll show you." And the reflection leaps out of the water. Gouges my eyes out. Chews up my face in its jaws. I scream, but I have no face . . . It keeps on returning, that nightmare, so that now I'm not at all sure it's me standing here and not my reflection, all ready to attack—

NITTILAI: How long are you going to turn your face away from it then? Face it. Face your brother as you wanted to.

(*He looks at her in surprise.*)

Not in hate, Arvasu. In the play. Show him how good you are. I'm sure the play will wash off the fear, the anger . . .

(*He nods.*)

ARVASU: All right.

NITTILAI: I'd better go. It's almost dawn.

ARVASU: Nittilai—

NITTILAI: What is it?

ARVASU: Isn't there any way you could watch the play that day? It would give me so much courage . . .

NITTILAI: I wish I could! But it's too dangerous. Come here after the play is over. At night. There'll be enormous crowds. We'll meet at this point . . . and fade away. (*She stands, reluctant to go.*) I'm glad you're not playing Indra. I don't like that god of yours.

ARVASU: Why?

NITTILAI: He is immortal. When someone doesn't die, can't die, what can he know about anything? He can't change himself. He can't . . . can't *create* anything. I like Vritra because even when he's triumphant he chooses death. I always wonder: if the flowers didn't know they were to fade and die, would they have ever blossomed? (*Gets up.*) I must leave.

ARVASU: Nittilai, I wish you could hide here—in the city somewhere.

NITTILAI: No. It's better than even you don't know where I am. (*Moves to go.*)

ARVASU: Don't I—

NITTILAI: Concentrate on your rehearsals. Learn. I am sure you'll be marvelous. I'm sure your dancing will bring the rains. Goodbye—

ARVASU: Nittilai—

(*She smiles and disappears. He stares dumbly after her. The* ACTOR-MANAGER *who's been waiting at a distance enters with the costumes and the mask of Vritra.*)

ACTOR-MANAGER: Here. This is the mask of Vritra the demon. Now surrender to the mask. Surrender and pour life into it. But remember, once you bring a mask to life you have to keep a tight control over it, otherwise it'll try to take over. It'll begin to dictate terms to you and you must never let that happen. Prostrate yourself before it. Pray to it. Enter it. Then control it.

(ARVASU *opens the bundle of clothes and dresses, almost in a trance. The stage darkens.* NITTILAI'S BROTHER *and* HUSBAND *melt away in the darkness. The audience, including* PARAVASU *and the* KING, *occupy their places and watch.*)

Epilogue

Slowly, ARVASU *puts on the mask. There is a roar of drums and then a sudden silence.* ARVASU *gives a wild roar and jumps up. He dances violently. The* AUDIENCE *responds with enthusiasm. The play is on. The* ACTOR-MANAGER (A-M) *dressed up as Indra enters from one side. The* ACTOR-MANAGER'S BROTHER *dressed as* VISHWARUPA *enters from the other.*

   VISHWARUPA *and* VRITRA *rush to each other, embrace.*

VISHWARUPA: Dear Brother Vritra—

VRITRA: Dear Brother Vishwarupa—

(*Since* VISHWARUPA *is limping,* VRITRA *dances, holding* VISHWARUPA'S *hands, emphasizing their affection for each other. The* AUDIENCE *reacts with pleasure.* A-M AS INDRA *watches from a distance, then talks to the* AUDIENCE.)

A-M AS INDRA: . . . After all, I am Indra, the King of the Gods. Should I then not be Supreme in the three worlds? Should not Brahma, the Father of All Creation, who gave me birth, have ensured that I stood unrivaled in all these domains? But alas! He fell in love with a mortal and produced a son by human womb, whom he crowned the King of Men. Vishwarupa! Everyone admires Vishwarupa. Everyone sings his praises. His wisdom and gentleness and mastery of the lores inspires a love which makes me feel like the eclipsed moon. It threatens my sovereignty of the worlds. But how can I destroy him?

For my father mated with a woman from the nether world and created a third son, a demon, Vritra. He made him the King of the Nether World and told him: "Vritra, protect your brother Vishwarupa, the King of Men, if necessary with your own life. For Indra is bound to try and harm him!"

And the two are inseparable. I sent, as you saw, the most enchanting of my celestial beauties to lure Vishwarupa to a lonely place. But he will not leave that infernal demon behind. How can I separate them? How can I isolate Vishwarupa? (*He reflects.*) Aha! I have it. I shall organize a fire sacrifice in honor of our father, Brahma, the Lord of All Creation . . . (*He adds with a wink.*) Whom incidentally I have already destroyed. I shall invite all the gods and men to this sacrifice. (*Goes round the stage and comes to* VISHWARUPA.) Vishwarupa, my dear brother—

VISHWARUPA: I bow to you, Brother Indra—

A-M AS INDRA: Vishwarupa, I am conducting a fire sacrifice in our father's memory. All the gods and the best of men have been invited. You must come too.

VISHWARUPA: Indeed, I shall. You are my elder brother. I don't need an invitation to attend a sacrifice conducted by you, I would have come on my own the moment I heard the news.

A-M AS INDRA: Your love for me is beyond description. Come, enter this sacrificial enclosure.

(VISHWARUPA *tries to enter, followed by* VRITRA.)

No, Vishwarupa. You are most welcome, but Vritra, who is accompanying you, may not enter the sacrificial precincts.

VISHWARUPA: And why is that?

A-M AS INDRA: Because he is a demon, a *rakshasa*.

VISHWARUPA: But, Brother, he is our father's son. Hence he is our brother and like our father, a Brahmin. Surely you will not forbid him entry?

A-M AS INDRA: His mother was a demoness and demon blood flows in his veins. A demon may not be permitted near the altar lest he is tempted to desecrate it. The rules are more ancient than us. We cannot tamper with them.

VISHWARUPA: So be it. (*To* VRITRA.) Dear Vritra, you have heard what Indra has to say. So please, wait here outside the enclosure while I go in.

VRITRA: Brother, my father gave me life so I could protect you. Let me come in with you. This Indra is treacherous . . .

VISHWARUPA: But, Vritra, you know that I have extracted from him a promise not to hurt me.

VRITRA: They say gods should never be trusted.

   (*Laughter from the* AUDIENCE.)

Indeed, it's said that when the gods speak to us, the meaning they attach to each word is quite different from the meaning we humans attach to it. Thus *their* side of their speech often denies what *our* side of their speech promises.

   (*Applause.*)

Even their silences have double meanings. Hence the saying, that the thirty-three gods occupying the heavens make for sixty-six silences.

   (*Laughter.*)

At least.

   (*Thunderous applause and laughter.*)

VISHWARUPA: But, dear Vritra, one must obey one's brother. So let me go.

VRITRA: Brother, I love you. But you'll not listen to me. So be it. I'll wait for you here outside.

(VRITRA *stamps in exasperation, goes and strikes a worried pose. The* AU-DIENCE *loves it. Applause.* VISHWARUPA *goes round the stage to indicate that he is covering a long distance.*)

ARVASU: (*Aside.*) Nittilai, I hadn't known it would be like this. I can feel the audience reaching out to me—their warmth coming in wave and wave, lapping against me. I'm good! Yet suddenly I don't care for this sea of smiling faces. I want yours. Where are you? Are you safe? My heart trembles to think of you.

(VISHWARUPA *finishes the round and arrives at Indra's fire sacrifice.*)

VISHWARUPA: Brother Indra, now I enter your sacrificial pavilion.

A-M AS INDRA: (*Laughs.*) Come, come. I shall welcome you properly. Come and sit by the altar and offer oblations to the gods.

(VISHWARUPA *mimes sitting down and pouring oblations in the fire.* A-M AS INDRA *laughing silently, moves behind him, takes up his thunderbolt, takes aim and plunges it into* VISHWARUPA'S *back.* VISHWARUPA *screams.* PARAVASU, *who has been watching impassively until now, jumps to his feet. The* BRAHMA RAKSHASA *appears next to him. The rest of the people on stage freeze.*)

PARAVASU: No. No. Wrong! That's wrong!

BRAHMA RAKSHASA: What's wrong?

PARAVASU: They understand nothing, the fools. Indra didn't mean to kill him—

BRAHMA RAKSHASA: Then what happened?

PARAVASU: He was panic-stricken.

BRAHMA RAKSHASA: Why?

PARAVASU: He saw a face by the altar. Whose face was it? The face of my dead father? Or of my brother, who is a simpleton, yet knows everything? Or was it my own face? Cold fear tore through him. He stood paralyzed. When he came to, he heard a voice asking: "Who are you?" His own voice. There was no choice now but to go on, to strike. But to think that the fear had lain coiled inside him and he wasn't even aware—

BRAHMA RAKSHASA: I see. Well, then. I must go.

PARAVASU: (*Startled.*) Go? Where?

BRAHMA RAKSHASA: I had better look elsewhere for help. You've enough problems of your own, Brother.

PARAVASU: I'll help you. I can.

BRAHMA RAKSHASA: Goodbye.

PARAVASU: Trust me. I'll help you—

(*The* BRAHMA RAKSHASA *disappears.* PARAVASU *shouts.*)

Come back! Come back, Demon!

(*The stage, frozen till then, leaps to life. The* AUDIENCE, *startled by Paravasu's shout, looks at him.* ARVASU *reacts to his brother's voice.* VISHWARUPA *screams, continuing his earlier scream. Rolls back.* A-M AS INDRA *strikes again.*)

VISHWARUPA: You, Brother? Why? I trusted you . . .

VRITRA: Whose voice is that? Familiar words!

(A-M AS INDRA *gives a villainous laugh.*)

VISHWARUPA: Brother, why this treachery?

VRITRA: Why, Brother? Why, why, why? Brother, why? Why? Indra's laughter—And why are the vultures, sparrows, kites, and eagles reeling in such frenzy over the sacrificial sanctum? Why are they ripping the skies with their shrill screams? Why is a wave of blood breaking out of the sacrificial enclosure like a flock of fear-crazed jungle fowl? (*He mimes entering the enclosure.* VISHWARUPA *is dying.*)

VRITRA: Another treachery! Another filthy death! How long will this go on? How long will these rats crawl around my feet vomiting blood? I must put an end to this conspiracy. Wait, Indra— (*Attacks* INDRA *with a ferocity that takes the* ACTOR-MANAGER *by surprise. They fight. The* ACTOR-MANAGER *is agile and well trained, but Vritra's violence shakes him and he runs.* VRITRA *chases him.*)

VRITRA: You can elude me, Indra. But you can't escape me. Even if you fly like a falcon across ninety-nine rivers I'll find you. I'll destroy you. I'll raze your befouled sacrifice to the ground. (*He pounces on a* GUARD *standing nearby and grabs a torch from his hand and rushes toward the real sacrificial enclosure.*) I'll burn down the sacrifice—

ACTOR-MANAGER: No, no! Not *that*—stop him! Stop him, for God's sake—

(*Two or three* GUARDS *try to stop* ARVASU *but he is uncontrollable. He swings his torch about and in a swift move, pulls out a dagger from a guard's belt. The* GUARDS, *half-scared, step back.*)

ARVASU: I am a Brahmin. If you try to stop me, I'll kill myself. And the sin of killing a Brahmin will be on your heads. I am a *rakshasa!* And I'll kill anyone who tries to stop me—(*He rushes into the sacrificial pavilion. The* GUARDS *rush in after him. There is commotion.*)

ACTOR-MANAGER: It's the mask—it's the mask come alive. Restrain him, or there'll be chaos.

KING: Stop him! Stop him!

GUARD: (*Rushes out of the sacrificial enclosure.*) But he is not human, sir. His feet don't touch the ground. He flies in the smoke like a *rakshasa*— he disappears in the flames—

(*Suddenly the weak and hungry* VILLAGERS *watching the scene from the crowds get up and start rushing into the burning pavilion. There is a stampede.*)

BRAHMINS: It's the tribals—the savages—they're desecrating the sacrifice—
Oh God! This is madness. The doomsday—they are eating and drinking the food kept for the gods. They're leveling the sacrifice to the
ground—

KING: Chief Priest! Paravasu! What shall we do?

(PARAVASU *has been watching the chaos, without so much as moving a muscle.
He gets up and without a word calmly walks into the blazing enclosure.*
NITTILAI *comes running.*)

NITTILAI: Arvasu! (*She rushes into the burning structure. The* CROWDS *mill
around. The structure, made of dry bamboo and wood, bursts into flames.*
NITTILAI *comes out, supporting* ARVASU. *She takes off his mask, throws it
away.*)

NITTILAI: It's all right. Don't worry now . . .

ARVASU: I don't know what came over me, Nittilai.

NITTILAI: It's all over. Thank God, you aren't hurt.

ARVASU: I lost, Nittilai. And Paravasu won. He went and sat there in front
of the altar, unafraid and carried on with the sacrifice. I couldn't destroy
him . . .

NITTILAI: You didn't mean to, Arvasu.

ARVASU: He went up in flames while I stood watching, untouched.

NITTILAI: It doesn't matter! Let's just go away from all this.

ARVASU: Yes, let us. Don't let go of me—please . . .

NITTILAI: Of course, I won't, silly boy. Come.

(*Suddenly* NITTILAI'S BROTHER *and* HUSBAND *step out of the crowd and bar
their way. She screams.*)

ARVASU: No! Listen—listen to me—

NITTILAI: Please, Brother . . . Husband . . . Please, don't—

(*The* BROTHER *knocks* ARVASU *down and pins him to the ground. The* HUS-
BAND *pulls out a knife, grabs* NITTILAI *by her hair, and slashes her throat in
one swift motion. He then lets her drop. The two go away.* ARVASU *gets up,
rushes to her, takes her in his arms. She lies there, her eyes open, bleeding,
dying like a sacrificial animal. The commotion dies away as* ARVASU *stares
numbly at* NITTILAI.)

ARVASU: (*Softly.*) Serves you right! Who asked you to meddle with this world? You plunge in—like a lamp into a hurricane. What do you expect? No one'll weep for you, Nittilai. Not even me. I'll sing no lullaby of hate for you. But I'll come with you. Where nothing matters, not your goodness, nor my stupidity, nor this world's evil. Where the fire will have reduced everything to ashes.

(ARVASU *lifts up her corpse, puts it on his shoulder and goes into the sacrificial pavilion which is still burning. The* CROWDS *watch in silence. He goes and stands inside the burning structure. The fire slowly dies out.*

Melodious music. The sunlight becomes soft and gentle. The entire atmosphere takes on an ethereal hue. The VOICE OF INDRA *is heard from the skies.*)

VOICE OF INDRA: Arvasu, son, do not grieve. We are pleased with you. Ask for any boon and it shall be granted.

ARVASU: (*Baffled.*) Who's that? Who's that?

VOICE OF INDRA: I am Indra, the Lord of Gods. Know that all the gods are pleased with you.

ARVASU: Indra? But what do I have to do with Indra? I didn't seek Indra, or any other god. Yavakri did. Paravasu did. I seek only Death. Why are you here?

VOICE OF INDRA: (*Laughs.*) You question the gods? Other mortals would be happy to receive—

ARVASU: But . . . what have I done to deserve this visit?

VOICE OF INDRA: We loved the way you challenged Indra, and then pursued him, in the play. But it could also be because of Paravasu's sacrifice or Nittilai's humanity. You humans are free to construe the acts of gods as you wish. The point is we are here and you can ask for anything you want—

CROWDS: Rain! Arvasu, ask for the rains! Water—

ARVASU: (*Slowly.*) Lord Indra, I want Nittilai back. Alive. That's all I want in my life. Grant me that. Nittilai . . . my gentle Nittilai . . . I killed her. I want her back—

CROWDS: Water, Arvasu, ask for the rains!

VOICE OF INDRA: It's no great matter to bring Nittilai back to life. But once the wheel of Time starts rolling back, there's no saying where it'll stop. Along with Nittilai, others too may return to life: your brother Paravasu, your father, even Yavakri . . .

ARVASU: Yes, let them. Let them.

(*Strange music fills the air. The souls of* NITTILAI, PARAVASU, RAIBHYA, YAVAKRI, ANDHAKA *as well as a host of* SOULS *enter the stage silently and come close to* ARVASU, *who looks at them and calls out.*)

ARVASU: (*Happily.*) Nittilai! Nittilai! Brother! Father—and who are all the others, Lord?

VOICE OF INDRA: Those who died all over the earth at the same time as your family. If the wheel of Time rolls back they come back to life too—

ARVASU: Yes. Yes. Let the world be as it was.

VOICE OF INDRA: But then won't the entire tragedy repeat itself, Arvasu? How will it help anyone to go through all that suffering again?

ARVASU: No, it won't. Lord, I have been an ignorant fool all my life. My stupidity contributed to that tragedy—fueled it on. But after all that I have been through, I'm wiser. I can now stop the tragedy from repeating itself. I can provide the missing sense to our lives . . .

VOICE OF INDRA: Are you sure?

ARVASU: Yes, I am.

VOICE OF INDRA: Well then—

(*At this moment a shout is heard from afar. It is the voice of the* BRAHMA RAKSHASA.)

BRAHMA RAKSHASA: Arvasu—

ARVASU: Who's that?

BRAHMA RAKSHASA: It's me. The *brahma rakshasa.* Your father invoked me. He ordered me to kill Yavakri and I did. I have done my duty and now I wander lost, and in torment. Help me, Arvasu.

ARVASU: What do you want?

BRAHMA RAKSHASA: I want release—release from this bondage. Your father gave me this life. We are brothers. So you must complete what your father couldn't. I want to melt away . . . I want peace, eternal peace . . . I beg of you . . . intercede on my behalf with the gods.

ARVASU: Lord Indra, you heard that. Could you—

VOICE OF INDRA: Arvasu, the wheel of Time must roll back if Nittilai is to return to life. It must roll forward for the *brahma rakshasa* to be released. You can't have it both ways. Choose.

ARVASU: (*Helplessly to the* BRAHMA RAKSHASA.) You see, there's nothing I can do.

BRAHMA RAKSHASA: You can, Arvasu. You can. Don't abandon me.

VOICE OF INDRA: There's another consideration, Arvasu. Not even the gods can guarantee a soul the ultimate release. That is a law beyond us. I may grant his release from birth and death because you ask for it. But there is every chance it may not work. In that case, his situation will remain unchanged and you'll lose Nittilai.

ARVASU: You heard that, Brahma Rakshasa. So forgive me—

(*The* SOULS *draw closer to* ARVASU, *their eyes pleading with him.*)

BRAHMA RAKSHASA: I don't forgive. I can't. But you are a human being. You are capable of mercy. You can understand pain and suffering as the gods can't—

ARVASU: I don't want to listen to you. Go away! Go away!

BRAHMA RAKSHASA: And when Nittilai comes back what will you tell her? Will you tell her that because of her a soul writhes in pain—

ARVASU: Shut up! She is not at fault—

BRAHMA RAKSHASA: Nittilai came to help you because she cared for you. She would have cared for me. Wept at the thought of my endless life in death. If you bring her back, you'll have destroyed what made her such a beautiful person—

ARVASU: That's not true.

BRAHMA RAKSHASA: Remember, Arvasu. If Nittilai lives again, she'll live a life as tormented as mine—tormented by the knowledge that her resurrection condemned me beyond salvation. And every moment of her life, she'll hear my screams. What you are asking for is not a boon. You are asking Indra to condemn Nittilai to a hellhole much worse than the one I'm in. Think, Arvasu. You're wiser now . . .

(ARVASU *is silent. The* SOULS *make a strange moaning noise.*)

VOICE OF INDRA: Arvasu, have you decided?

ARVASU: Lord Indra—

VOICE OF INDRA: Yes.

ARVASU: Grant this *brahma rakshasa* his release. Let him go.

VOICE OF INDRA: You're sure you want that?

ARVASU: Nittilai would have wanted it so.

VOICE OF INDRA: Well then, so be it!

(*The* BRAHMA RAKSHASA *cries out in triumph. A long pause. The host of* SOULS *gives a long, mournful sigh of disappointment and begins to withdraw.* NITTILAI'S *soul goes away with them.*)

ARVASU: Nittilai! (*Sits down and clutches Nittilai's corpse.*)

(*The* BRAHMA RAKSHASA *waits impatiently but nothing happens. He looks around baffled, scared. The world seems to stand still. The* CROWDS *of people begin to whisper.*)

CROWDS: What's that?—You smell that?—Yes. Yes. The smell of wet earth. Of fresh rains. It's raining. Somewhere. Nearby. The air is blossoming with the fragrance of earth. It's raining—It's raining—Rain! The rain!

(*Wind blows. Lightning. Thunder. People are shouting "Rain! It's raining!" Suddenly the* BRAHMA RAKSHASA *roars with laughter and melts away. Only his laughter can be heard for a few moments, reverberating, mixed with the rolling thunder. It pours. People dance with joy. They roll in the mud.* ARVASU *sits clutching Nittilai's body.*)

ARVASU: It's raining, Nittilai! It's raining!

Aramba Chekkan

by Kavalam Narayana Panikkar

TRANSLATED FROM MALAYALAM
BY THE AUTHOR AND ERIN B. MEE

CHARACTERS
(in order of appearance)

The characters in this play are not realistic people. They personify qualities, attitudes, or ideas.

ACTOR/ARAMBA CHEKKAN/ARAMBAN, a goatherd. *Aramban* means the one who begins; *chekkan* means boy or guy. Aramba Chekkan is not simply a goatherd, he represents mankind's discovery of nature, the beginning of man's relationship with nature. He is called simply Aramban by the other characters.

GOATS. Played by actors in masks

WILD ANIMALS (BEAR, LEOPARD, TIGER, WOLF). The wild animals represent the untamed, vicious, destructive side of nature.

CHEKKI. Chekki is the name of an orange forest flower found in Kerala. In this play, Chekki personifies the gentle spirit of the forest or of nature. She "blossoms" when she meets Aramban.

SNAKE. In Kerala mythology, snakes are the guardians of the soil and of all the treasures of the soil. In the play, Snake is the guardian of the forest, and he sees himself as the guardian of everything in it, including Chekki. Snake protects the forest from mankind, but he is also possessive of Chekki and causes her death.

THE SUN

A CROCODILE

PRANDAN. Kerala has a myth about eleven brothers, one of whom, Naranathuprandan, spends his time rolling a stone up a hill only to push it back down once he has reached the top. Prandan (which means madman) teaches us that life is precious: it takes a lot of time and effort to create something, but destroying what you have created is as easy as rolling a stone down a hill.

SERVANTS OF YAMA (2)

MARAPRABHU (Lord of the Trees), the owner and custodian of the trees. He therefore takes it upon himself to punish those who try to chop down the trees.

YAMADHARMA/YAMA, the god of death. Yama is not sure who deserves to go to hell and who deserves to go to heaven. Consequently, he is not sure how to judge the souls who come to him.

CHITRAGUPTAN, Yamadharma's assistant. He keeps records of the deeds of every person whose soul is being judged.

EXTRAS. People to hold the curtain.

A Note on Translation

We did not attempt to replicate the poetry of the Malayalam version. We have focused on conveying the meaning of the play rather than the flavor of the language, since too often it was impossible to do both. Because it is so difficult to distinguish Panikkar's texts from the way he envisions them in performance, we have followed what seems to be a new trend for publishing plays in India, which is to include in footnotes as much information as possible about the performance he envisions and his assumptions about performance that underlie and support the words.

The Sopanam theater company in a rehearsal of *Aramba Chekkan*
Photographs courtesy of Erin B. Mee

A bare stage. An ACTOR *enters, carrying a stick.*

ACTOR: (*Sung*)
   On a path
   through the village
   Comes a goatherd.

   A goatherd sets off
   on the village path
   driving his herd of goats
   to graze.

   Aramba Chekkan is his name
      (*Bowing to audience to acknowledge acceptance of his role, the* ACTOR
      transforms into the character ARAMBA CHEKKAN.)
   Aramba Chekkan is my name
      (*He gestures offstage for the* GOATS *to follow him.*)
   M . . . baa!

GOATS: (*Answering Aramba Chekkan as they enter in a neat formation—an
   orderly herd.*)
   M . . . baa!

ARAMBAN:
   M . . . baa!

GOATS:
   M . . . baa!

(ARAMBAN *then speaks about himself in the third person. He narrates his own
action.**)

---

*This is a convention that Panikkar has adapted from *kuttiyattam,* a particular way of performing Sanskrit drama in Kerala. In *kuttiyattam* the actor will elaborate on the text by making
political and social analogies, exploring emotional associations and telling related or background stories. Occasionally the character will step out of the "story" to comment, from the
character's point of view, on the story he is part of. These elaborations on the story can be
verbal, or they can be done through *mudras,* which are symbolic gestures, not unlike Ameri-

ARAMBAN: (*To the audience.*)

> Aramban went on
> Past the village
> along the winding way,
> into the forest.
>> (*Mimes climbing a hill with difficulty. The* GOATS *follow.*)
> The curved path which ascends
>> (*Mimes rushing downhill, with* GOATS *following.*)
> becomes the descending path.
> I follow the stick
> which leads my feet
>> (*Uses his stick to herd the* GOATS *in the right direction.*)
> Although Aramban has only two legs
> he is still one of the flock
>> (*Imitates the goats' walk.*)

GOATS:

> M . . . baa!

ARAMBAN:

> Goat language has only two syllables.

GOATS:

> M . . . baa!

ARAMBAN:

> M . . . baa!

GOATS:

> M . . . baa!

ARAMBAN: I speak this two-syllabled language, though I know a lot more than two syllables.

> (*Suddenly turning and seeing that the* GOATS *have begun to wander out of formation while he has been talking to the audience, he rushes up to them, waving his stick. Chants.*)

---

can Sign Language. Thus, in *kuttiyattam*, three lines of text can take three hours to perform, and the focus of the performance is on elaboration rather than interpretation. Panikkar expects directors to elaborate on his texts as well—although perhaps not to the same degree as in *kuttiyattam*. Aramban's journey is one place for the actor and director to elaborate. For example, Aramban can describe everything he sees in the village, and/or he can describe the flowers and trees he sees on the path and talk about their beauty.

Walk straight! Walk straight!
Walk, walk, he-goat,
Walk, walk, she-goat,
Small goat, tall goat, he-goat, she-goat
All of you walk straight!
Go! Go!

    (*Spoken.*)
If you don't walk straight
I'll beat you with my stick (*Hits first goat.*)
I'll kick you with my leg (*Kicks second goat.*)
I'll hit you with my hand (*Hits third goat.*)
It's for your own good (*Hits last goat.*)

(GOATS *react to being beaten by running wildly around the stage; then they circle* ARAMBAN *and advance on him.*)

GOATS: (*Yelling nonsense syllables that rhyme with Aramban's name.*)
    Arumba! Irumba! Urumba! Airumba! M . . . baa! M . . . baa!
FIRST GOAT: We are poor four-legged creatures with only two syllables, so
    why are you beating us?
ARAMBAN: It's not my job to domesticate you. I have a boss too, and I only
    get paid if I train you to behave.

(*He beats them.* GOATS *retreat to a corner of the stage where they regroup and advance on him again.*)

GOATS:
    Fine. Beat us if it makes you happy!
    Beat us until your stick breaks!
    Get out your knife, if you have one—
    a goatherd with a butcher's knife
    becomes the butcher himself!
      (*They stick their necks out, challenging him to chop their heads off.*)
ARAMBAN: (*Throwing the stick away.*)
    I'll get rid of the stick. I won't beat you, my children.
SECOND GOAT: (*Picks up the stick and gives it to* ARAMBAN.)
    The stick is innocent, what has it done?
    Take it, Father.

(*He refuses.*)

Take the stick, Father.

THIRD GOAT: Take us through the forest to graze in the meadow.

(ARAMBAN *takes the stick and leads the* GOATS *in a circle.**

As the GOATS *circle the stage on their way to the forest,* ARAMBAN *runs in and*

out among them.)

ARAMBAN:

Who leads whom?

Does the goatherd lead the goats, or

do the goats lead the goatherd?

Who is in front?

I'm in front, you're in front

I'm in front, you're in front

(*They leave the village and arrive in the forest.*)

Who is in front?

The village is in front

The forest is in front.

(*Sung. As he sings, he and the* GOATS *enact the song.*† *The verses of the*

song can be repeated.)

Along the forest's path

Under nature's lush canopy of

Jungle roots and wild fruits,

Savoring the taste of green,

Drinking water from the forest's stream.

(*Spoken.*)

Walk where you want.

Eat,

Sun yourselves,

Small goat, tall goat,

---

*Circling the stage is a theatrical convention that Panikkar borrows from *kuttiyattam* and
kathakali [classical dance-drama from Kerala]. It is used to denote a change of place and/or a
passage of time. One circle of the stage can represent a tremendous distance or the passage of
years.

† This is an opportunity for physical elaboration.

he-goat, she-goat.
Graze on the grass,
Bask in the sun.

But be careful. Don't attract the wolves' attention. Once your belly is full, hurry back home to the village—don't wander around alone. The forest is not a safe place. Take care of yourselves, I'll be back soon.

(ARAMBAN *walks through the forest and disappears; the* GOATS *play and graze. All of a sudden, the roar of* WILD ANIMALS *is heard.*)

WILD ANIMALS: (*Chanted.*)
The forest has shown only wildness.
The village has shown only fear.
The village is frightened of the forest.
These are the sounds of the forest:
BEAR:
The bear's growl!
TIGER:
The tiger's roar!
WOLF:
The wolf's howl!
WILD ANIMALS:
The wind's whistle!
What right do you have to enter our forest without permission?
    (*They advance toward the* GOATS *to tear them to pieces.*)
What are you doing in our forest? We are fierce beasts; you are domesticated animals. Domesticated by man.
GOATS:
Man is our savior.
WILD ANIMALS:
But who will save the savior from us?
Our forest's hunger wants you!
    (*They chase the* GOATS, *who run offstage. The* TIGER *catches* A GOAT *and tears him apart.*)
TIGER: (*Chanted.*)
My canine teeth snap under the spell of my desire
to tear this goat to pieces!

I don't want the hide,

I don't want the bones,

I don't want the teeth,

Mmm . . .

The flesh of this grass-eating goat is good.

LEOPARD:

I want goat's meat too.

I want to taste blood!

Give me a piece of this goat.

TIGER:

Kill your own goat. Or eat that goatherd.

(*The* TIGER *and* LEOPARD *fight. In the middle of their argument, the* WOLF *chases the other* GOATS *across the stage. The* TIGER *and* LEOPARD *join the chase, leaving the dead goat. All exit.* GOATS *re-enter, having escaped from the wild animals. Frightened, they approach the body of the dead goat. They sit around the dead body, keening.*)

GOATS:　(*Sung.*)

Oh friend, your two syllables have been silenced.

M . . . baa! M . . . baa!

Our friend is a victim of the forest's cruelty.

Where have you gone?

What we lose is lost forever.

(*The* WILD ANIMALS *re-enter with a collective roar; the* GOATS *start to run away.*)

WILD ANIMALS:　(*Chanted.*)

Stop right there!

We want village meat.

Our mouths water for your tender flesh.

GOATS:

Spare us!

(*The chase continues, and all exit. Blackout. Although there is a blackout, it indicates only a pause, not an intermission—the action should be continuous.*

　　ARAMBAN *walks through the forest enjoying its beauty.**)

---

*This is another chance for elaboration.

As ARAMBAN *walks, a hand-held curtain appears in his path. Underneath the curtain he can see a woman's feet.*

Behind the curtain, CHEKKI *sings and dances.*†

Attracted by the sound of Chekki's anklets, ARAMBAN *walks toward the two feet he sees beneath the curtain.)*

CHEKKI: (*Sung.*)

Can you hear the sound of the sympathetic forest?
Aramban?
Do you hear the sound of the benevolent forest?
Aramban?
Can you hear me?

Can I trust you, Aramban?
If so, I will give you the singing throat of the Koel bird.

Sing, sing, Aramban.
The melody I give you will flow,
Flow like the mountain stream.
Sing the song that has never been sung,
Sing, sing, Aramban.

Sing, sing, Aramban.
The melody I give you will flow,
Flow like the mountain stream.
Sing the song that has never been sung,
Sing, sing, Aramban.

ARAMBAN:

Sing? Can I sing?

---

*In *kathakali*, a curtain is used to "frame" the first entrance of every principal character. When the character enters, the plot stops, and the character is given an extended introduction to the audience, outside the context of the story. When the character has been thoroughly introduced, the curtain is taken away, the character joins the play, and the story continues.
†In the workshop production her dance was adapted from *Mohiniyattam*, which is sometimes called the dance of the enchantress. The arm movements are said to imitate the swaying palm tree and therefore to depict nature. True or not, this is now part of the mythology surrounding *Mohiniyattam* and is part of the reason Panikkar used it here. *Mohiniyattam* dancers tie bells around their ankles; whenever Aramban refers to "nature's rhythm" or to the sound of Chekki's steps, he is referring to the sound her ankle bells make when she walks or dances.

(He clears his throat.)

I don't know how to sing.

CHEKKI:

You can sing. Try.

ARAMBAN: *(Sings. As he sings,* CHEKKI *dances behind the curtain.)*

The mountains dance,

The forest rejoices.

My song makes the mountains dance,

which delights the forest.

Reflected in the water, I see

Bells tied to two beautiful ankles

Dancing down the forest path.

> *(The* WILD ANIMALS *enter, chasing the* GOATS. *They are enchanted by the music. They stop and listen.)*

This is the goatherd's song,

Your rhythm has made me sing.

Who put you on my path?

Who tied bells to your ankles?

> *(He can still see only her feet underneath the curtain.)*

Who, hidden, comes my way,

Beauty?

The mountains dance,

The forest rejoices.

My song makes the mountains dance,

which delights the forest.

CHEKKI: *(Sung.)*

Aramban. Beloved.

Beloved Aramban.

I am the forest.

I am the virgin forest.

Beloved Aramban,

Spring has waited for the Koel bird.

Spring, with flowers and honey,

blossoms and fruit,

has waited for you.

My Spring has waited for you.

Aramban. Beloved,

Singer.

Beloved Aramban.

ARAMBAN:

You have inspired a person with no knowledge of music to sing.

Inspiration, what is your name?

CHEKKI:

My name is Chekki.

I am the flower of the forest.

WILD ANIMALS: (*Who have been tamed by Aramban's song.*)

Aramban's song is the forest's song.

We have been tamed by the song of the forest.

(*They lie down and relax.*)

(*A venomous* SNAKE *enters, with its hood raised, hissing.*)

WILD ANIMALS:

What are you hissing about, Snake?

SNAKE: (*Angrily.*)

I own this forest!

I am the sentry of the soil!

You fierce forest-dwellers are forgetting yourselves!

By lying at the feet of this villager,

You are going against you own *dharma!*

LEOPARD: Listening to his music, I have completely forgotten myself.

BEAR: I feel only love.

WOLF: I usually like human meat, but I feel some unknown . . . some-thing . . . for this one.

TIGER: His music has tamed me.

SNAKE: When the village shows its real colors, the forest will pay. (*Continues to pace with his hood raised.*)

ARAMBAN: (*Who, oblivious to the interruption, has been watching Chekki's feet, sings.*)

The sky is above,

The forest below.

The leaves dance above
You dance here below.

The sky is above,
The forest below.
The leaves dance above
You dance here below.

Do you have a face?
I see nothing but a foot.
Does your root have a trunk?
Does it have a leaf?
Does it have a fruit?
Does it have a flower?
If it does, show it to me,
forest fantasy.

(CHEKKI *dances out from behind curtain;* SNAKE *follows her.*)

SNAKE: (*Sung to* ARAMBAN.)
Chekki is the flower of my branch,
the branch I wrap myself around,
In the tree that is my home.
Everything you see here is mine!
Chekki belongs to *me.*

ARAMBAN: (*Has been looking at* CHEKKI *so passionately he has not even heard the* SNAKE. *He sings.*)
Flower,
Soft flower,
Fragrant flower,
Blown by the mountain breeze,
The mountain's gift.

I saw this flower
I smelled this fragrance
Earlier,
in a dream
in my hut.

SNAKE: Listen, Aramban. The forest has plenty of flowers and plenty of
bees to dream about those flowers. *Your* flower-dreams aren't welcome
here. (*Moves around, looking for a chance to bite* ARAMBAN. *The* WILD
ANIMALS *notice this.*)

WILD ANIMALS:

Calm down, Snake!

Bite someone else.

This forest isn't yours,

And we are still fierce enough

To keep you in line.

(*They surround* SNAKE.)

SNAKE:

Some day

You will realize who Aramban is.

You will realize how dangerous he is.

Till then I will safeguard my *dharma,*

Till then I will guard the land.

Till then, insult the forest.

Till then, hate me.

(*Exits angrily.*)

ARAMBAN: (*Sung to* CHEKKI.)

In the forest

We will eat fruit,

We will drink honey.

In the forest's stream

We will splash,

We will play.

Follow me, Chekki.

(ARAMBAN *leads* CHEKKI *around the stage. The* GOATS *follow, but* ARAMBAN
pushes them away.)

GOATS:

Why can't we come with you?

Have you forgotten that we came here to be fed, Father?

Don't you want us?

ARAMBAN:

Rear yourselves.
Eat whatever you find:
Munch munch,
Swallow swallow.

Eat as much as you want.
The forest is inexhaustible.

GOATS:

Father, don't go!
If you go, you won't come back!
Who will protect us?
 (ARAMBAN *keeps going.*)
We'll only be able to eat if you sing us a song!

ARAMBAN:

A song?
Why do you need music to eat grass?

WILD ANIMALS: (*To* ARAMBAN.)

We want to hear a song too.
Have you forgotten about us?
Benevolence has given Aramban music,
and Aramban's song has tamed the untamable forest.

(ARAMBAN *disappears with* CHEKKI.)

GOATS:

Father has gone!
Tell him not to leave us all alone!
Do you see how cruel he is?

WILD ANIMALS:

Don't worry,
We'll take care of you.

(*The* WILD ANIMALS *exit with the* GOATS. ARAMBAN *re-enters with* CHEKKI.)

ARAMBAN:

Hearing me sing,
The flowering tree uproots itself

And dances.
The stones on the hill
Roll to the rhythm.

(THE SUN *enters and begins to cross the stage very slowly.*)

Who sparkles?

Is it a lamp?
Even in a storm this burning lamp is bright.
You can't touch it,
You can't blow it out.
Its heat is unbearable,
Not softened by leaves.

Aha!
It's the sun!
Sun, where are you going?
When will you return?
Light has gone with you.

(THE SUN *has set during this part of the song.*)

(*Spoken.*)
We are enclosed in darkness,
We can't see each other.
Oh, Chekki! Chekki!
After your dance inspired my song,
Have you gone?

(ARAMBAN *and* CHEKKI *exit. What follows is a dream sequence which takes place many months later.* CHEKKI *enters, followed by* ARAMBAN, *followed by the* SNAKE.)

SNAKE:

Aramban, look!
See who gives off half-light in full darkness—
The half-moon is peeking through the leaves.
Look at Chekki on whom the crescent shines.
Her walk is so beautiful,

Her hair is so beautiful.
Think how captivating she will be
If she belongs to you alone!

Don't let her go!
Make her yours.
Claim her before she disappears.
She gave you nature's song.
Break nature's cyclic rhythm.
Sing out of tune!

Nature doesn't want gentle caresses,
She needs the wild passion of the forest!
Possess her with your passion!
Attack her with your lust!

(*Goaded by the* SNAKE, ARAMBAN *grabs* CHEKKI. *Surprised by this unexpected behavior,* CHEKKI *runs away. The* SNAKE *disappears, and* ARAMBAN *is left alone in the dark. He calls out for a companion.*)

ARAMBAN:

Goats!
Wild animals!
Chekki!

(ARAMBAN *exits, forlorn.* SNAKE *and* CHEKKI *re-enter.*)

SNAKE: (*Sung.*)

Shouldn't we get to know each other?
You are the flower of the forest,
Shouldn't we get to know each other?
Your Snake is your root.
Shouldn't we get to know each other?
Can a flower ignore its roots?
We should get to know each other.

CHEKKI: (*Sung.*)

Days and nights will come and go
Without you.
The moon will play hide and seek with me
Without you.

I will feel the wind's caress
Without you.
I will grow in the sun's warmth
Without you.

SNAKE:

Is Aramban's crudeness your caress?
Is his attack your sun?
Is his lust your moon?
Don't forget, Chekki,
I am the Snake, the root of the forest.

CHEKKI:

You are not my root.
You are not the forest's root.
I am my own root.

SNAKE:

And Aramban? Where are his roots?
The village doesn't want him,
So why should the forest adopt him?
He tried to take advantage of you, didn't he?

CHEKKI:

And whose fault is that?

SNAKE:

You won't belong to anyone else, you are mine.
(*Rushes to embrace her, she moves away.*)
If you spurn me, I'll bite you.

(*The* SNAKE *starts to attack, and* CHEKKI *calls out for* ARAMBAN.)

CHEKKI:

Aramban!

(ARAMBAN *rushes to* CHEKKI. *The* SNAKE *transfers his anger to* ARAMBAN, *and goes after him. As the* SNAKE *tries to bite* ARAMBAN, CHEKKI *intervenes and is bitten.* CHEKKI *dies.* ARAMBAN *catches her as she falls. The* SNAKE *exits.*)

ARAMBAN: (*Sung, a keening song.*)

Mountain goddess,
Where have you gone?
Spirit of the Forest,

Which path have you taken?
Magical inspiration,
Traveling skyward,
When will you return?
Come back to life.
Come back as you are now.*
Only memory sees the unseeable.

Mountain goddess,
Where have you gone?
Spirit of the Forest,
Which path have you taken?

>(He searches for CHEKKI. He hears the sound of her ankle bells, and
>follows. He exits and re-enters in another part of the forest, walking to
>the rhythm of her ankle bells. Again he sings.)

Beautiful girl,
Graceful girl,
I follow the rhythm of your legs,
I come searching for your roots.
How do I reach the abyss,
the underworld you are in?
How do I descend to the depths?
Where did you disappear?

>(He is looking for the path to the underworld. He reaches a river which
>marks the boundary between the middle world and the underworld.)

The death-wind blows
The death-wind blows
I hear your bells on the other bank of the river
But my feet are stuck
On this side of the water.

>(A CROCODILE surfaces and looks threateningly at Aramban.)

---

*When Aramban says "come back as you are now," he refers to the cycle of death and rebirth. He wants Chekki to be reborn in the same body she now occupies, so he will be able to recognize her.

(*Spoken.*)

I see a whirlpool.

> (*He mimes entering a whirlpool and being spat out on the other bank of the river.*)

Conquering danger,

I have reached the other side.

(PRANDAN, *a madman, enters, laughing and pushing a big stone.* ARAMBAN *watches him from the side of the stage. Once Aramban reaches the underworld, the tone of the play changes drastically: the underworld is not the romantic world of the first half of the play; it is satirical. There is less poetry and more prose.*)

PRANDAN: (*Chanting a work song usually sung in Kerala villages.*)

E lassa, Elle lassa, E lassa!

Ai yai ya,

Elle lassa.

> (*He mimes pushing a huge rock up a hill.*)

Pushed by my hand,

Resting on my shoulder,

The stone goes up.

Elle lassa, E lassa.

Ascending the mountain,

Elle lassa

Is hard,

E lassa.

> (*He mimes reaching the top of the hill.*)

Then it is pushed down:

higgledy-piggledy falling,

the stone crashes down.

(PRANDAN *claps his hands and laughs. As he begins to push the stone back up the hill, an old man,* MARAPRABHU, *is brought onstage by two* SERVANTS OF YAMA, *with his hands tied.* PRANDAN *continues his scene in the background, silently. One of Yama's servants has a long stick with fruit at the end. The other servant carries a pot of water.*)

FIRST SERVANT: (*Holding fruit just out of reach of* MARAPRABHU'S *mouth.*) Have a banana, Maraprabhu! Don't you want a banana?

(MARAPRABHU *jumps toward the bananas, trying to catch one in his mouth, but before he can catch one, the* SERVANT *pulls the fruit away and laughs.*)

SECOND SERVANT: (*Bringing a pot of water close to* MARAPRABHU'S *mouth.*) Oh, isn't he giving you any bananas? Well, here's some water for you to drink, Maraprabhu!

(MARAPRABHU *leans in to drink the water but at the last second the* SERVANT *yanks it away. The* SERVANTS *laugh.* ARAMBAN *watches all this.* YAMA, *the god of death, enters with his accountant,* CHITRAGUPTAN.)

SERVANTS: (*Bowing to* YAMA.) This is Maraprabhu.

YAMA: So this is Maraprabhu! Why is he here? Chitraguptan, what sin has he committed?

CHITRAGUPTAN: (*Searching frantically in his account book.*) One minute.

PRANDAN: (*Stopping work for a minute.*) He punished the man who cut down a tree he planted.

YAMA: (*Referring to* PRANDAN.) Who is this?

CHITRAGUPTAN: He's just a madman.

PRANDAN: I am bored by people's endless ignorance, so I amuse myself by acting mad.

YAMA: I don't understand.

PRANDAN: That's your problem. I have to get back to work.

YAMA: I'll worry about you later. Your time will come.

PRANDAN: You should let Maraprabhu go. He's not a sinner.

YAMA: Oh! How do you know? Chitraguptan! What do the accounts say?

CHITRAGUPTAN: (*Searching frantically through the book.*) The accounts state that he has grown a tree.

PRANDAN: I'll tell you the rest of the story. (*Props his stone up so it doesn't roll downhill, and comes forward to talk to Yama.*) Maraprabhu planted a coconut tree. (MARAPRABHU *unties his hands and mimes planting a tree.*)

PRANDAN: The tree grew. Stout. Big. Maraprabhu took a coconut, broke it, and drank the milk. (MARAPRABHU *mimes breaking open a coconut and drinking milk.*) Maraprabhu gave the milk to the poor. (MARAPRABHU *mimes, with* SERVANTS *acting as the poor.*) Their thirst was quenched.

YAMA: Oh! That's good!

PRANDAN: One day, a woodcutter came. (PRANDAN *assumes the role of the woodcutter.* MARAPRABHU *transforms into a tree. They enact the story as* PRANDAN *tells it.*) He entered Maraprabhu's garden quietly, like a cat, and cut down the tree with his ax. (MARAPRABHU, *as the tree, falls down.*) Maraprabhu tied the woodcutter to the stump of the tree. (MARAPRABHU *now begins to play himself;* PRANDAN *continues to play the woodcutter.* MARAPRABHU *ties* PRANDAN's *hands. He takes the stick with bananas that Yama's servants were using to torture him and tortures* PRANDAN (*as woodcutter*) *in the same way.*)

YAMA: Stop! (*They all resume their own characters;* MARAPRABHU *ties himself back up with the rope.*) Chitraguptan! Where is that woodcutter? Why hasn't he been brought here?

CHITRAGUPTAN: (*Looking through book and not finding woodcutter.*) He's still alive. It's not yet time for him to die.

YAMA: I order Maraprabhu to be set free. (YAMA's TWO SERVANTS *untie him and take him off.*) Chitraguptan! Under Maraprabhu's name, wherever you see the word "sin," erase it and write "good works."

CHITRAGUPTAN: Okay. (*Erases and rewrites.*)

YAMA: (*To audience, frustrated.*) Why do the wrong souls end up here? Have they run out of space in heaven? Is heaven overrun by sinners? (*To* CHITRAGUPTAN.) Okay, now. What has this madman done wrong?

PRANDAN: (*Who has returned to work.*)
Elle lassa. E lassa.

CHITRAGUPTAN: He rolls stones up to the top of a hill with great difficulty.

YAMA: What's so sinful about that?

PRANDAN:
Higgledy-piggledy falling,
The stone crashes down.

CHITRAGUPTAN: Then he pushes the stones downhill.

YAMA: That doesn't seem so sinful either, Chitraguptan.

(PRANDAN *laughs and claps his hands.*)

CHITRAGUPTAN: (*Referring to laughter.*) That's the sin!

YAMA: What?

CHITRAGUPTAN: He laughs and claps his hands!

YAMA: Is that a sin?

CHITRAGUPTAN: It's not that he laughs, it's that he's making fun of us.

YAMA: How do you know that? Let him laugh if he wants. Chitraguptan, you don't understand this madman's act. You're really dumb. You're even dumber than the people whose souls you judge! What a shame, Chitraguptan! Your accounts are all wrong. Throw away your account book! Give that gentleman my seat, and offer him your prayers.

CHITRAGUPTAN: (Crossing to PRANDAN.) Yama is calling you.

PRANDAN: Tell him I'm busy.

YAMA: Don't trouble him, Chitraguptan. Does your book have any more cows that don't eat grass?*

CHITRAGUPTAN: There is a girl . . .

YAMA: Bring that cow here. (CHEKKI enters.) Who is she?

CHITRAGUPTAN: The book says she is a forest flower swinging in the wind.

YAMA: She isn't human?

CHITRAGUPTAN: (Looking at CHEKKI.) She doesn't look human.

YAMA: I didn't ask your opinion. What does your book say?

CHITRAGUPTAN: (Searching.) The book says . . . the book says . . .

YAMA: Chitraguptan, throw away your account book. (CHITRAGUPTAN closes it but holds on to it.) Oh, so you won't obey me? Give up that book!

CHITRAGUPTAN: She's a forest creature.

YAMA: Aha! Something like a tiger or a leopard?

CHITRAGUPTAN: She seems more like an antelope or a rabbit.

YAMA: Is that your own opinion?

CHITRAGUPTAN: Well, you told me to throw away the book . . .

YAMA: But you haven't thrown it away.

PRANDAN: This is a ridiculous argument about a senseless book. Aren't you supposed to be the Lord of Dharma who knows the truth without the help of a book?

YAMA: Tell me what to do, Prandan.

---

*There is a saying in Malayalam that the cow in the book won't eat grass, meaning it's not a practical cow, it can't do anything. Yama is asking if there are any genuine cases of sinfulness in Chitraguptan's book.

PRANDAN: If you're convinced that someone deserves punishment, then punish them without mercy. I don't understand why you can't make a simple decision.

YAMA: Why should I punish her? I can't punish her. I'm not even sure she's within my jurisdiction. When I say she's dead, that may just be a figure of speech. Another character appears in her story. He's the one who should be punished.

PRANDAN: Who is that?

YAMA: Bring him.

CHITRAGUPTAN: (*Looking in book.*) Let me see . . .

YAMA: Don't look in there! Look in the book of your mind.

CHITRAGUPTAN: Sir! He's already here!

(CHEKKI *dances, and in the rhythm she establishes,* ARAMBAN *sings from offstage.*)

ARAMBAN:

Forest flower.
Invisible one
who makes ankle-bells tinkle,
Where are you, where are you?
Where are you?

I walk an unending path
Searching for you
On and on
Through the spotted leopard's lair
Through the meadow where the frightened antelope treads
I walk an unending path
Searching for you.
On and on
I am coming
On and on
coming.

Where have you gone,
My sweet goat.
Where have you gone?

I am coming
On and on
searching.

(*Hearing Aramban's song,* YAMA *starts to dance.* PRANDAN, *seeing Yama dance, tries to control his laughter.* CHITRAGUPTAN *stands, uninterested.*)

ARAMBAN: (*Sings again.*)
Where are you hidden?
Only with you
Will I return
Only with you
Will I return

Where are you hidden,
little girl,
agile goat
who doesn't know how to graze.

I'll retrace my steps
Only with you
On this path
Only with you
Back to the middle world
Only with you

Where are you hidden?
Only with you
Will I return
Only with you
Will I return

YAMA: Is this the man who should be punished? What sin has he committed? Is singing a sin? His music is so beautiful and passionate, it has such depth of feeling, that I am completely overwhelmed by it.

CHITRAGUPTAN: He should still be punished.

YAMA: For what?

CHITRAGUPTAN: He has a sinful soul.

YAMA: But is he a soul already? He isn't dead. How can be become a soul without dying? He's only here because the beauty of his music has broken all the laws of this dead land.

CHITRAGUPTAN: He should still be punished. That's all I have to say. You can do what you want.

YAMA: This is my decision. Human being! Come here. Look at Chekki now, and sing. Let the melody of your song carry you harmoniously back to the middle world—on one condition.

PRANDAN: What's that?

YAMA: He must lead, and Chekki must follow. He may not look back.

PRANDAN: What if he does look back?

YAMA: I will have to rethink his punishment.

(ARAMBAN *walks, singing.* CHEKKI *dances behind him. They leave the under-world.* PRANDAN *continues his work with the stone.* YAMA *watches* ARAMBAN. CHITRAGUPTAN *holds his book and hangs his head.* YAMA, PRANDAN, *and* CHITRAGUPTAN *stay on stage to watch what happens with Aramban and Chekki.* ARAMBAN *literally retraces the steps he took to get to the underworld.*)

ARAMBAN: (*Sung.*)
    Up the descending path
    Without looking back.
    My mind is filled
    With the image of your face,
    the face that never disappears,
    the face that I imagine.

    Up the descending path
    Without looking back.
    My head is filled
    With the image of your face,
    in the face that never disappears,
    the face that I imagine.

(*The lights dim.* SNAKE *enters and tries to attack* ARAMBAN. ARAMBAN *ignores the* SNAKE *and continues singing. The* SNAKE *goes to* CHEKKI. *As he tries to catch her,* CHEKKI *stops moving, and the tinkling of her ankle bells stops.*)

Aramban's song is heard,
But not the ankle-bells' rhythm.
Chekki are you there?
My dear Chekki,
My small goat,
Have you forgotten me?
Have you forgotten my song?

(SNAKE *hisses, and* ARAMBAN *turns to save* CHEKKI *from the* SNAKE. *The minute he turns, she vanishes. Blackout.*

Dim light. ARAMBAN *gets up as if waking from sleep, searches for his stick and finds it. He tries to sing, but only "mbaa" comes out—the sound of the goats.*)

ARAMBAN:

I have found my stick,
But I have lost my melody.
Goats!
Small goat! Tall goat!
He-goat! She-goat!

(*The* WILD ANIMALS *enter and pounce on him. He tries to escape them but is caught and torn to pieces. The lights fade slowly. We hear* PRANDAN's *laughter.*)

Rudali

by Usha Ganguli

TRANSLATED FROM HINDI BY ANJUM KATYAL

CHARACTERS

(in order of appearance)

SOMRI, Sanichari's mother-in-law, an old woman

SANICHARI, a village woman

BUDHUA, Sanichari's son

HAROA (as a child), Sanichari's grandson

A CHILD, a little girl offstage

PARBATIA, Budhua's wife, Sanichari's daughter-in-law

DULAN'S WIFE, Lachmi (She is addressed as Dhatua's mother because it is the custom in rural Bihar to address a woman as the "mother of" her eldest son.)

A VAID, local Ayurvedic doctor

A VILLAGER

SECOND VILLAGER

DULAN, a village elder

BIJUA, the barber, a younger village male

WOMAN 1, a neighbor

WOMAN 2, a neighbor

WOMAN 3, a neighbor

DHATUA'S WIFE

DHATUA, Dulan's son

NATUA, a village man

HAROA (as a youth)

MISRI, Sanichari's neighbor

BIKHNI

SWEET-SELLER

MOHANLAL, a *pandit*

MADHO SINGH, a master of the villagers and peasants. The title *Singh* indicates their Rajput origin. They are settlers who own the land on which the villagers and peasants work. They are called *thakur* (master, idol) as a mark of respect.

BACHCHA SINGH, Madho Singh's brother

A BOY

PROSTITUTE 1

PROSTITUTE 2

PROSTITUTE 3

BACHANLAL, the landlord's retainer

SHANKAR, a young boy

LACHMAN SINGH, Madho Singh's uncle

OLD WOMAN, an attendant to the *thakurain*

THAKURAIN, wife of a *thakur*

BIKHNI'S NEPHEW

CHAMPA, a prostitute

GANGU, a prostitute

SUKHI, a prostitute

NASIBAN, an old maidservant to the prostitutes

NAILPOLISH WOMAN, a prostitute

GULBADAN, a prostitute

SAEEDA, a prostitute

GRAY-HAIRED WOMAN, a prostitute

A PANDIT

ZAMINDAR, a landowner

NATHUNI SINGH, a master of the villagers and peasants

GAJANAN

BHAGIRATH

RUDALIS

The Rangakarmee theater company performing *Rudali*
Photographs courtesy of Usha Ganguli

Scene One

Sanichari's home, a small hut with a courtyard, surrounded by a low boundary wall. At stage right, SANICHARI sits grinding wheat in the chakki. The monotonous creak of the chakki is the only sound. At stage left, her ailing son, BUDHUA, is lying on a charpoy. HAROA, Budhua's child, is stretched out on his stomach under the charpoy, absorbed in playing with a toy. Sanichari's old mother-in-law SOMRI is lying towards the back, wrapped in a tattered blanket.

SOMRI: I want food. Give me a *roti!* *Arre oh* Sanichari, give me a *roti*, won't you? (SANICHARI *continues to grind the* chakki.) Have you gone deaf or what? (SANICHARI *carries on grinding.* BUDHUA *coughs painfully, turns over.*) You *daain*, are you going to starve me to death?

SANICHARI: Parbatia will do the cooking when she gets back.

SOMRI: When will she come?

SANICHARI: I don't know.

SOMRI: You have the *atta*, why don't you make some *rotis*?

(*The* chakki *stops.*)

SANICHARI: Then who'll do the grinding? Wants *rotis* made from other people's *atta!* We can have *rotis* only after I get my payment in kind. (*The* chakki *resumes.* BUDHUA *coughs again.*) Budhua, Parbatia isn't back as yet. (*The* chakki *slows down.*)

BUDHUA: She'll come, why are you worried?

SANICHARI: I kept telling you, don't let her go to the market, don't let her go. Now she'll hang around there all day.

BUDHUA: What would she do sitting at home?

(*The* chakki *stops.*)

SANICHARI: Why, I stay at home, don't I? I grind wheat for others, make cowdung cakes, gather firewood from the jungle. Just say that she wouldn't be happy staying at home. (*The* chakki *starts up again.*)

BUDHUA: You know everything, Amma. You know that she steals from the money she makes selling vegetables, and buys all sorts of rubbish to eat.

SANICHARI: Don't I give her enough to eat?

BUDHUA: Her appetite is huge, Amma.

(*Pause. The* chakki *continues.*)

SOMRI: That whore will never return, and I'll never get my *rotis*.

(SANICHARI *turns around to glare at the old woman then resumes her grinding with renewed energy.*)

BUDHUA: Amma, Parbatia was saying that she wanted to go work for Lachman Singh.

(*The* chakki *stops.*)

SANICHARI: (*Looking at* BUDHUA.) Never.

BUDHUA: Why not?

SANICHARI: You're asking me why not? Once a young woman goes to work for Lachman Singh, the only place she's fit for is the whorehouse.

(*The* chakki *resumes. A little girl's voice is heard from outside.*)

CHILD: (*Off.*) Chachi, oh Chachi! May I have a few twigs of firewood? (SANICHARI *doesn't respond, continues to grind the* chakki.) Amma needs some to light the fire.

SANICHARI: (*Angrily.*) Last week your mother asked me to grind two and a half *sers* of *channa*. I got paid neither in cash nor kind—and now she wants firewood!

BUDHUA: Give it to her, Amma.

SANICHARI: Go on, Haroa. Give her four sticks.

(HAROA *crawls out from under the* charpoy *and leaves to give her the firewood. Their voices are heard offstage.*)

CHILD: Give it to me! Give it to me!

HAROA: Dadia, look, she's snatching my toy!

SANICHARI: Get lost, you wretch! (*To* HAROA.) Go, go to your father.

(HAROA *returns and sits beside* BUDHUA. *The* chakki *resumes.*)

SOMRI: The bitch won't give me a thing to eat.

BUDHUA: Amma, why don't you give her something?

SANICHARI: What do I give her? Do I feed her from the huge pile of *rotis* your wife so graciously prepared before leaving?

SOMRI: You bitch, just watch out. Jackals will eat your dead body.

SANICHARI: Yes, I'm a bitch, a *daain,* my corpse will be eaten by jackals—is there anything else you wish to say?

SOMRI: Yes there is. Give me some *roti.*

(*The* chakki *stops.*)

SANICHARI: *Hai Maiyya!*

(SANICHARI *rests her head on the* chakki *a moment, then gets up and starts grinding wheat from the second bag lying beside her.* BUDHUA *has a coughing fit.* SANICHARI *quickly rises and hands him some water.*)

BUDHUA: (*After drinking.*) Oh god!

SANICHARI: If there was a god your illness would have been given to me instead.

BUDHUA: Why do you say such things, Amma? As long as you're alive, my son has a chance . . .

SANICHARI: And I . . .

SOMRI: You'll kill off everyone else but you'll stay alive, you *daain.* As it is you've finished off your father-in-law, your brother-in-law, and your husband. Now you'll devour your son.

SANICHARI: Watch your mouth!

(*The* chakki *resumes.*)

SOMRI: Why shouldn't I say it? After all, you were born on an unlucky day, Saturday.* It's your destiny to devour everyone around you!

SANICHARI: And what great happiness did life bring you? You're Monday-born,† but you didn't get a better deal, did you? *Arre,* I've seen what lives

---

*Sanichari means one born on Sanichar, or Saturday.

†Somri means one born on Somvar, or Monday.

they all live, those born on Tuesday, Wednesday, Thursday. As for you, you do nothing but bitch, bitch, bitch, all day long. Behaving as though your father left you a pile of wealth! Another word out of you and I'll throttle you.

(SANICHARI *sits down and starts the* chakki *again. Her daughter-in-law,* PAR-BATIA, *enters and notices her son sitting beside his father on the* charpoy. *She grabs hold of him and dumps him angrily on the ground.*)

PARBATIA: Are you his father or his enemy?

SANICHARI: What's the problem?

PARBATIA: Problem? He's got an infectious disease and he's sitting there with the child clasped to his bosom!

SANICHARI: If you're so concerned about the child, then why were you living it up in the market place all day? The entire household is hungry, no one's eaten.

PARBATIA: Am I under contract to feed the whole household? I went to the market to sell vegetables.

SANICHARI: To sell vegetables, or . . . Anyway, go on, give me the money. (PARBATIA *hands her some money.*) What's this, only two *rupees*? You took a pile of *brinjals* and chillies to sell, and this is all you got for them? Or is there something more? Have a look, check—(*She moves towards the basket, but* PARBATIA *snatches it up. They wrestle with it, and some things fall out: a colorful hair ornament, some bangles.* SANICHARI *stares, aghast.*) *Hai, hai,* the whole household goes hungry, while her majesty preens and titillates! Where did you get these from, you bitch? Speak up!

PARBATIA: From the market, where else?

SANICHARI: Where did you get the money? Go on, tell me, you bitch, did you spend our vegetable money on this rubbish? (PARBATIA *doesn't answer.* SANICHARI *grabs her by the hair.*) Where did you get the money? Answer me! Who gave it to you?

BUDHUA: Let her go, Amma!

PARBATIA: (*Freeing herself.*) Don't you dare touch me! You can't even provide a few *rotis* for your family! And you think you can push me around, you bitch?

SANICHARI: I'll do it as often as I like! Her husband is lying there sick, and the whore preens in trashy trinkets!

PARBATIA: What's it got to do with you, oh mother of my husband? Huh! Husband indeed! Can't provide a square meal, but lays claim to being a husband.

SANICHARI: Look Parbatia, give me a straight answer. Who gave you all this?

PARBATIA: No one. I bought it out of my earnings. From the money I made splitting wood for Lachman Singh.

SANICHARI: (*Springing forward to hit her.*) You swine, you bitch, you went to Lachman Singh! When I've warned you over and over again to stay away from that devil!

PARBATIA: He may be a devil, but at least he's a man! Not like this one, coughing his lungs out all day!

SANICHARI: Parbatia, you'll get a thrashing for that!

(*The two of them fight, grappling with each other.* DULAN'S WIFE, *Dhatua's mother, enters.*)

DULAN'S WIFE: What's the matter, Sanichari? What's happened?

(PARBATIA *snatches up her trinkets and stomps off in a rage.*)

SANICHARI: Nothing. It's my *karma* that's to blame. (*She sits down at the* chakki.)

DULAN'S WIFE: Have you finished the grinding?

(SANICHARI *fills a bag with flour and hands it to her.*)

SANICHARI: Parbatia! Oh Parbatia! (*There's no reply.*) Haroa, please fetch the kneading dish from inside.

DULAN'S WIFE: Wait, I'll get it. (*She goes in, and returns with it. She uses it to remove a measure of flour from the bag and places it before* SANICHARI.) Here, this is your share. How's Budhua?

SANICHARI: Not good.

DULAN'S WIFE: Have you given him any medicine?

SANICHARI: (*Showing her the two* rupees.) Her highness came back with this. A measly two *rupees*. Do I spend it on medicine, or—

DULAN'S WIFE: Don't worry, Sanichari. I'm sure everything will work out all right. (*Handing over a sack.*) Here, Bisesar's mother sent this. Have it ground by tomorrow morning. (*Gets up.*) Okay, I'm off. (*Leaves.*)

SANICHARI: (*Angrily.*) Parbatia! Oh Parbatia!

PARBATIA: (*Off.*) What is it?

SANICHARI: Enough of your tantrums. Come on out.

PARBATIA: (*Storms in and stands facing her.*) What d'you want?

SANICHARI: Here, take this *atta* and make the *rotis*.

PARBATIA: I can't make the *rotis*.

SANICHARI: Why, you shameless hussy! Your child is starving, your husband is hungry, and you say you won't make *rotis*? Who'll make them, then? Your father? If you're living here, you'll have to do your share of work, understand?

PARBATIA: I'll do it today. But I'm telling you once and for all, I'm only staying here as long as he's alive. The moment he dies, I'm leaving—or I'm not my father's daughter.

(PARBATIA *picks up the full kneading dish and stalks off.* SANICHARI *looks after her, then casts a quick glance at Budhua and resumes grinding the* chakki *with a vengeance. The lights dim slowly.*)

Scene Two

Sanichari's home. Afternoon. SOMRI *is lying in her usual place.* BUDHUA *is on the* charpoy, *covered with a sheet. He breaks into painful, hacking coughing fits, then lies down again. Meanwhile, with the help of a mirror propped up against the wooden handle of the* chakki, PARBATIA *is busy arranging her hair.* HAROA *sits beside her, fiddling with her trinkets and make-up things. She slaps his hand away, then, when he touches them again, yells at him.*

PARBATIA: I told you not to touch, you bastard! Go on, get lost!

(HAROA, *chastened, goes to his great-grandmother.* SOMRI *consoles him and gathers him close.*)

SOMRI: Come, Beta, come to me. (*Muttering.*) Daain! (BUDHUA *is racked by a particularly violent fit.*) Hey Parbatia! Parbatia! Can't you hear?

PARBATIA: What is it?

SOMRI: Get up and give Budhua some water to drink.

PARBATIA: (*Plaiting her hair.*) What are you making such a fuss for? I'm just getting up.

(BUDHUA's *fit worsens.*)

SOMRI: *Arre,* you bitch, hurry up, can't you! The boy will die. Give him some water.

PARBATIA: (*Completes her plait.*) God! Bloody nuisance! (*She gets up, pours some water in a tumbler from the jar, then offers it to* BUDHUA.) Go on, drink. Let's get it over with. (*Continues to stand there, proffering the water.*) What's the problem? How long d'you expect me to keep standing here? (BUDHUA, *racked by coughs, extends his trembling hand for the tumbler, but knocks it out of her hand. At the sound of the clatter,* SOMRI *immediately calls out.*)

SOMRI: What happened, Parbatia? What's the matter? (PARBATIA *doesn't reply.*) *Arre* oh, you *daain,* will you tell me what's happened?

PARBATIA: (*In a flustered tone.*) N-nothing . . . the glass fell . . .

(*She continues to look searchingly at* BUDHUA, *then stands, thinking. She seems to come to a decision, picks up the fallen tumbler and goes into the hut. She emerges with a cloth bundle which she places near the* chakki. SOMRI *is lying quiet, with* HAROA *beside her. Feverishly,* PARBATIA *goes in once again, returns with some clothes and stuffs them into the bundle, then gets up, goes to the large storage pot and reaches for the pouch of money kept inside. All at once* SANICHARI's *voice is heard off stage.* PARBATIA *quickly shoves the pouch back in, snatches up a cloth, and begins to wipe up the spilled water.* SANICHARI *enters carrying a bundle of twigs and lowers it to the floor.*)

SANICHARI: What's the matter . . . couldn't you hear . . .

PARBATIA: Ask your son what the matter is.

SANICHARI *goes up to* BUDHUA *and turns him over. There is blood flowing from his mouth and his eyes are turned up. Seeing him in this terminal state* SANICHARI *loses her calm.*

SANICHARI: What's happened to you, Beta? (BUDHUA *utters broken sounds.*) Eh, Parbatia, run and fetch the *vaidji.* This doesn't look good at all.

PARBATIA: Can't you see I'm busy? Besides, my head aches in this afternoon heat.

SANICHARI: My son is dying, Parbatia.

PARBATIA: What can I do about it? I can't go anywhere.

SANICHARI: Are you a human being or an animal? Is this how your father brought you up?

PARBATIA: My father taught me well. He taught me to stay far away from the dying.

SANICHARI: (*Furious.*) You *daain*, how dare you? Come here and sit beside him. Don't move from here. I'll go fetch the *vaidji*. (*She leaves.*)

(PARBATIA *gets up, looks closely at* BUDHUA. *A pause. She casts a quick glance at the still* SOMRI, *then darts in and brings out her bundle. She takes the money pouch out, puts it into her bundle, and begins to hurry out. She catches sight of her son and stops. A pause. Then she abruptly runs out.*)

SOMRI: Parbatia, hasn't Sanichari returned yet? Is Budhua sleeping?

(HAROA *awakes as well.*)

HAROA: Maai . . .

SOMRI: Looks as if your mother's gone to the market.

HAROA: Maai, who'll make the *rotis*?

SOMRI: Are you hungry, Beta? Want to eat something? I have some pickle, do you want a little? Go, fetch a bit of *atta* in this bowl.

HAROA: Dadia will beat me.

SOMRI: No one will beat you. Go, fetch some.

(HAROA *fetches some* atta *in the small bowl.* SANICHARI *enters with the* VAID).

VAID: You people have no respect for time. Such impatience! Can't wait for even a minute. I was looking forward to my afternoon nap after a good meal, and you have to drag me here. Where's this son of yours?

SANICHARI: (*Going up to* BUDHUA.) Budhua, oh Budhua, wake up. Look, Vaidji's here.

(*The* VAID *approaches the* charpoy, *then stops. He frowns, places his hand under* BUDHUA's *nostrils.*)

VAID: Lower him to the ground and give me my fee.

SANICHARI: What's happened to him, Vaidji? Why don't you examine him?

VAID: You've dragged me all the way here in the afternoon heat to examine a corpse!

SANICHARI: What are you saying, Vaidji? My Budhua . . . check him carefully, Vaidji.

VAID: What am I to check? He's as stiff as a log. Come on, hand over my money, let me go home and rest.

SANICHARI: He was still breathing when I left to call you. (*Pleads.*) Just examine him once more, please . . .

VAID: What a nuisance this is! D'you think I'm lying? Feel him and see, he's cold all over.

SANICHARI: Budhua, oh Budhua.

VAID: He's not going to answer you. He's dead.

(*Hearing this,* SOMRI *breaks into loud wails.* A VILLAGER *enters, takes in the situation, and hurries out.*)

VAID: Hurry up and give me my money. It's getting late. And I'll have to cleanse myself in the river before going home. (SANICHARI *fixes him with an angry glare.*) What're you glaring at me for? Take out the money and pay up.

SANICHARI: What kind of man are you, Vaidji? My son is lying dead and all you can think of is your fee.

VAID: Did you hear that? Did you hear what this *daain* said? She's dragged me here by force, and now she's thumbing her nose at me! *Arre*, till I get my money I'm not moving an inch! All you low-caste people are the same—no knowledge of religion, no faith, no education!

(*Hearing the noise,* DULAN *enters with his* WIFE *and some other* VILLAGERS.)

DULAN: What's happened, Sanichari? Why all the commotion?

SANICHARI: Dulan . . . my Budhua . . .

DULAN'S WIFE: *Hai Ram,* what're you saying? Quick, lower him to the ground. (*She begins to wail in mourning.*) Budhua *re!*

A VILLAGER: *Arre* Bhaiya, he was all right this morning.

SECOND VILLAGER: Why don't you examine him one more time, Vaidji?

(BIJUA *enters on the run.*)

BIJUA: What's happened, Bhaiya, what's happened?

VILLAGER: *Arre* Bhaiya, Budhua's passed away.

BIJUA: *Arre,* how did this happen . . . smash the waterpot, brothers.*
Come, brothers, let's lower the corpse to the ground.

(*Several* VILLAGERS *move forward to lend a hand, but the* VAID *stops them.*)

VAID: Stop! I forbid you to touch the body. First, my fee.

SANICHARI: Just wait and see—when you die your corpse will be eaten by
jackals. I'm giving you your precious money!

(*She goes in. Some* NEIGHBOR WOMEN *enter wailing. They sit down by the dead
body. The body is lowered to the ground.* HAROA *comes and sits by it.*
SANICHARI *enters, stunned.*)

DULAN'S WIFE: What's the matter, Sanichari?

SANICHARI: I can't find Parbatia.

VAID: It's all over now, just give me my money.

DULAN: We're just giving it, Vaidji. (*He goes up to the stricken* SANICHARI.)
Come, give the money.

SANICHARI: Dulan, I'm finished. Parbatia has taken everything I had and
run off.

DULAN: What're you saying?

DULAN'S WIFE: No, no, Sanichari, it must be here somewhere.

SANICHARI: I'm sure she's run off.

VAID: *Arre,* now what's up?

DULAN: But . . . what about Vaidji's money?

DULAN'S WIFE: (*Untying a fifty-paise coin from the corner of her* sari.) Here,
give him this and let's get rid of him.

DULAN: (*Handing the* VAID *the coin.*) Vaidji, please accept this for now, we'll
send you the rest later.

VAID: Fifty *paise?* Do you take me for a beggar? I knew something like this
would happen! You low-caste people are all the same! Just you call me
again and see . . . *Daain* that you are!

(*The* VAID *leaves in a huff. The* NEIGHBOR WOMEN *whisper between themselves
then begin to wail again.*)

WOMAN 1:   *Hai,* Ram! To die at such a young age!

---

*Smashing the waterpot is a ritual performed in a household where there has been a death.

WOMAN 2:   Hey, Sanichari, where's your daughter-in-law gone?

DULAN'S WIFE: She's gone to the market, where else?

WOMAN 3:   Yes, I know exactly which market she's gone to!

WOMAN 2:   Her husband's lying dead and she's gone to the market!

WOMAN 1:   Parbatia's ways are hardly a secret in the village.

DULAN'S WIFE: This isn't the time or place to talk like this, Chachi.

WOMAN 2:   Why should I keep quiet? *Arre,* she used to live it up all day with that hefty young brown-eyed fellow—you know the one I'm talking about, the bangle-seller—using the market as an excuse to be out of the house . . .

WOMAN 3:   Gunni's father was saying that he treated her to *halwa-puri* all day long.

WOMAN 2:   Sanichari's luck is really bad.

WOMAN 1:   She has a heart like a stone, the *daain.* Not a single tear has she shed.

DULAN'S WIFE: Will you all shut up with your chatter? Dhatua's wife, come here. (*The girl goes to her.*) Take Haroa home, give him something to eat and drink, and put him to sleep. (*To* HAROA.) Go, Beta.

(HAROA *leaves with* DHATUA'S WIFE. BIJUA *detaches himself from the cluster of waiting men and moves forward.*)

BIJUA: Bhauji, better make some arrangements. The corpse can't just lie here like this.

DHATUA: Once the sun goes down there'll be a problem, Chacha.

DULAN: Don't worry about it, Sanichari, we'll manage everything. (*To* NATUA.) Hey Natua, listen here. Take Shankar and bring the firewood. (*To* BIJUA.) Now tell me, what else will we need?

BIJUA: *Arre,* there's lots to be done—do you think a *kriya* ceremony comes cheap? Mohanlal *pundit's* fee, *chivda, dahi, gur*—and won't you need to sacrifice a goat?

A VILLAGER: All this . . . ?

BIJUA: What else? On the fourth day one has to feed five Brahmins on *dahi* and *gur.* I tell you, living is tough for us poor people, but dying is even worse.

DULAN: Don't lose heart, Sanichari. One has to spend on such occasions, there's no way out. Is there anything you can sell?

SANICHARI: Whatever little bit I managed to put away, Parbatia's taken with her. I have nothing, Dulan, nothing.

DULAN: You can sell this *chakki* of yours.

SANICHARI: What are you saying, Dulan? If I sell this, how do I earn? What will I eat?

NATUA: I've arranged for the bamboo and firewood, Dulan *chacha*.

BIJUA: Now let's get moving, Bhai.

(SOMRI *begins her ritual wailing. The* OTHER WOMEN *join her.*)

DULAN'S WIFE: Cry, Sanichari, cry . . . it will make you feel better.

DULAN: Don't delay in sending the *chakki* off.

(*The* WOMEN *continue to wail.* SANICHARI *slowly sits down by the* chakki. *The lights dim.*)

Scene Three

Sanichari's home, eight or nine years later. Morning. HAROA *is now a youth. A cheap harmonica in his mouth, he blows away as he sits on the* charpoy, *tending his hair in front of a propped up mirror.* SANICHARI *enters carrying a basket of grain.*

SANICHARI: What's up, Haroa? Aren't you going to work?

HAROA: Don't feel like it today, Dadia.

SANICHARI: Why, Beta, what's the matter? (HAROA *doesn't respond.*) Eh, Haroa, say something.

HAROA: My stomach's paining . . . (*He glances at her.*)

SANICHARI: Don't make excuses. Nowadays your heart isn't in your work . . . *Arre oh*, you lordling. (HAROA *looks at her.*) Come here, sit next to me. (*He comes up to her.*) Now tell me, what's bothering you?

HAROA: I just don't feel like doing my work, Dadia.

SANICHARI: How I had to beg and plead to get you your job at Lachman Singh's, and now you say you don't feel like working. (*She keeps sorting the grain.*)

HAROA: I work like a donkey all day long, carrying heavy loads . . . I hate it.

SANICHARI: *Arre* Beta, if you don't work, how will you get money? (HAROA *is silent.*) Go, Beta, your employer will get annoyed.

HAROA: I'll do some other work.

SANICHARI: Where will you find another job? Who'll give you one? Look, Haroa, I'm getting on, now. I can't work the way I did before. It's up to you now, Beta . . . I'm relying on you. You're all I have, there's no one else to look out for me . . . You saw how Somri died, lying in her own filth. Do you want me to end up like that . . . ?

HAROA: Lachman Singh's son thrashes me with his shoe.

SANICHARI: If you don't work properly, of course he'll beat you! You don't get money for nothing, you have to work for it.

HAROA: He makes me slave all day and pays me a measly twenty *rupee*s a month.

SANICHARI: Plus a daily meal.

HAROA: Does that mean he can hit me when he likes, abuse me as he likes . . . ?

SANICHARI: That's a poor man's fate, Beta—the kicks of his master. Go on, Beta, go to work.

HAROA: Okay, I'll go; but Dadia, I want a colored vest from the market.

SANICHARI: Get your wages, and you'll get your vest. Now run along, you so-and-so.

(HAROA *gets up and prepares to leave for work. He combs his hair carefully before the mirror.* BIJUA *the barber enters.*)

BIJUA: (*On seeing Haroa.*) So, young man, how are things? (*He sits beside* SANICHARI.) Well, Bhauji, how's everything?

SANICHARI: Can't you see? I'm living in the lap of luxury, gorging on *halwa-puri!* (*She winnows* dal.) What brings you here so early in the morning?

BIJUA: Why? Can't I drop in to see my *bhauji* just like that?

SANICHARI: You wicked old so-and-so, you still haven't changed your ways . . . Go on, tell me why you've come.

BIJUA: I will, I will. First let me relax a bit.

HAROA: (*Ready to leave.*) Dadia, I'm hungry. Give me something to eat.

SANICHARI: Beta, there's nothing at the moment.

HAROA: But I'm hungry. How can I work on an empty stomach?

SANICHARI: There's nothing in the house . . . Once I finish winnowing this *dal* I'll get some *atta* in return. Only then will I be able to cook . . . Here (*Untying some money from the corner of her* sari.), take this twenty-five *paise,* pick up something on your way. (HAROA *is about to leave.*) Wait a bit, Beta! (*She gets up, goes to the urn, takes out a blessed charm and ties it on him.*)

HAROA: What's this?

SANICHARI: I got it from Mohanlal specially for you.

HAROA: I don't want to wear it!

SANICHARI: Don't say that, Beta, it's blessed by Shivji. Wear it, it'll be good for you. (*After tying it on him she strokes his head. His carefully combed locks are now displaced, so he combs his hair again and prepares to leave.*) Listen, Beta, there are lots of horned cattle in the market place. Be careful not to get too close to them.

HAROA: Okay.

SANICHARI: And listen, don't fall into bad company . . . all right?

HAROA: I've heard you.

SANICHARI: Don't touch cigarettes or *bidi*s.

HAROA: All right, all right!

(HAROA *leaves.* SANICHARI *sits down once again and takes up the winnowing tray.*)

SANICHARI: Now out with it, old man. What is it?

BIJUA: Hold on, old woman. We have time enough for work. First let me give you some ripe gossip.

SANICHARI: What?

BIJUA: Last week, I went to Tohri—

SANICHARI: So what's new? Ever since your wife passed away, you've been a regular visitor there, you rascal you.

BIJUA: Will you listen? In the whores' quarter there I came across Parbatia.

SANICHARI: Why're you telling me this?

BIJUA: What can I say, Bhauji? She's looking older than you. At first I didn't recognize her—

SANICHARI: Listen, Bijua, don't talk about her to me. I don't want to hear a word about her. Whether she lives as a whore or as someone's wife, that's her business. Why are you concerned? Let's talk about something useful.

BIJUA: Yes, yes . . . I was just talking casually. Actually, Lachman Singh's nephew Ratan Singh is having his *tilak* ceremony. The house is full of relatives. They need a lot of *dal* and wheat ground. So the *malik* has summoned you.

SANICHARI: What will I make out of it? I don't want to grind mounds of stuff and get just a fistful of grain in return.

BIJUA: *Arre* no, Bhauji. There's enough work for several days. The *malik* will pay you well.

SANICHARI: If that's true, then, old man, may you prosper!

BIJUA: And why not? Both of us will gain by it. (*They laugh.*)

SANICHARI: Haroa didn't tell me about this ceremony at Lachman Singh's.

BIJUA: You mean your grandson? How would he know?

SANICHARI: Why, he works in Lachman Singh's *godown*.

BIJUA: But I go there so often, I've never seen him there.

SANICHARI: What are you saying, Bijua? Doesn't Haroa go to Lachman Singh's?

BIJUA: *Arre* Bhauji, I've seen all Lachman Singh's employees, but I swear I've never once seen Haroa.

SANICHARI: Then where does he go when he says he's going to work?

BIJUA: He must be hanging around having a good time with the loafers in the market place, what else? (SANICHARI *is silent, suppressing her anger.*) These are dangerous years, Bhauji, when a boy is growing into a man. You should give him a little rein. (*He gets up.*) Okay, I'm off, Bhauji. Come across to Lachman Singh's this evening. If you earn some money, it will be a help.

(BIJUA *leaves.* SANICHARI *picks up the winnowing tray and begins to ply it with a vengeance.*)

Scene Four

Evening. A ray of the setting sun lights up Sanichari's house. DHATUA'S WIFE *is putting her child to sleep.* DULAN'S WIFE *is standing with a sack in each hand.* SANICHARI *is measuring flour into the sacks.* MISRI *is counting.*

MISRI: One, two, three, four, that makes one *ser*. One, two, three—what's this, one quarter less? I gave you a full two *sers*.

SANICHARI: Don't lie! How dare you claim you gave a full two *sers*—you gave me a quarter less!

MISRI: *Hai* Ram! First she steals, then she gets aggressive! She's swiped my *dal* and now she's acting innocent!

SANICHARI: (*To* DULAN'S WIFE.) Did you hear that? Why did I take on any work for this she-devil!

MISRI: Hey, Sanichari, watch your mouth! Call me a she-devil and I'll cut out your tongue!

DULAN'S WIFE: (*To* MISRI.) Why are you causing trouble? Take your *dal* and give her what's due to her.

MISRI: Why should I? She's already swiped a quarter of a *ser*, why should I give her anything extra?

SANICHARI: You're standing here in my house and calling me a thief! The whole village knows me for what I am! (*She thrusts the sack at her.*) Take your sack and get out! If you set foot in here again I'll break your head!

MISRI: You'll break my head, will you? I'll gouge out your eyes and shove you in the well, *daain* that you are! (*She takes her sack and stamps out.*)

DULAN'S WIFE: She makes everyone's life miserable.

DHATUA'S WIFE: And she didn't give you your share, Chachi.

SANICHARI: I spit on her! Nowadays you can't count on anyone!

(DULAN *enters.*)

DULAN: What's the matter, Sanichari?

SANICHARI: Nothing. Come and sit, Dulan. (*She readies the* charpoy *for him.*)

DULAN: (*Handing his wife a twist of paper.*) Here, here's some *ajwain*. Make it into a paste and give some to Dhatua.

(DULAN'S WIFE *hands it to* DHATUA'S WIFE, *who lifts up her child and leaves.*)

DHATUA'S WIFE: I'm going, Chachi.

DULAN: What's the matter, Sanichari, you look very disturbed.

SANICHARI: It's nothing.

DULAN: Why isn't Haroa going to work nowadays?

SANICHARI: Bijua was telling me the same thing.

DULAN: I've seen him with my own eyes, roaming around with the fair-ground magicians.

DULAN'S WIFE: *Hai* Ram, they have a terrible reputation. I hope they haven't enticed him by putting a spell on him or something!

SANICHARI: Just let him come! I'll break his legs! And as for you, Dulan, when you saw him misbehaving why didn't you give him two tight slaps?

DULAN'S WIFE: He's grown up now, you can't just slap him around.

(NATUA *enters.*)

NATUA: Ram Ram, Dulan *chacha.*

SANICHARI: How much did you sell?

NATUA: The *bhindi* sold well, but there're still some chillies left.

DULAN'S WIFE: (*Looking in the basket.*) What d'you mean "some"? There are lots of chillies left.

SANICHARI: Go, put it inside. (NATUA *goes inside to leave the basket.*) This Natua Dushad never manages to sell well.

DULAN: *Arre,* he must be swiping half the money, I'm sure of it!

(NATUA *returns.*)

NATUA: (*To* SANICHARI.) Here you are, four *rupees* eighty *paise.*

SANICHARI: Only four *rupees* eighty *paise?*

NATUA: What else?

SANICHARI: Look, Natua, you really fool around with the accounts—

NATUA: Fool around? Look here, if you don't trust me, get someone else to sell your vegetables. I'm not interested.

DULAN: Hey, you bastard, I'm wise to your sly ways. Hand over the rest of the money!

NATUA: Look Chachi, see what Dulan *chacha*'s saying—

DULAN'S WIFE: Why are you two quarrelling?

SANICHARI: Okay, okay, here—take your two *rupees,* and come nice and early on market day.

NATUA: Yes, of course I'll come early. If it wasn't for me, all your vegetables would rot . . . and you call me a thief! (*He leaves.*)

SANICHARI: It's true. If it wasn't for Natua Dushad, all my vegetables would go to waste. Budhua planted them with such love!

(HAROA *enters, playing his mouth organ. He stops when he sees the visitors.* SANICHARI *turns to look at him.*)

SANICHARI: Well, Mr. High-and-Mighty, where were you all day?

HAROA: Why? I was working in the *godown.*

SANICHARI: How many sacks did you stack?

HAROA: Umm... about...

SANICHARI: One more lie and I'll pull your tongue out, you bastard!

HAROA: What's the matter?

SANICHARI: It's been ten days since you went to work, and you're asking me what the matter is?

HAROA: Which swine tattled on me? (*He glances at* DULAN.)

SANICHARI: I'm telling you that you haven't been going to work.

HAROA: Yes, I haven't been going. I refuse to do that kind of work. He pays a pittance, and on top of that he kicks me around! Who's going to work in a job like that?

SANICHARI: *Arre,* you son of a bitch, is Lachman Singh your kith and kin, that he's going to pay you for doing nothing?

HAROA: I won't go to Lachman Singh's.

SANICHARI: Yes, I know, you prefer to hang out with those no-good magicians.

HAROA: Yes, I do.

SANICHARI: You'd better listen to me, Haroa. If you don't go back to work tomorrow, I'll throw you out of the house.

HAROA: You won't have to—I'm leaving.

SANICHARI: Go, then! Get out right now!

HAROA: I'm going, I'm going! Can't provide a square meal, and orders me around!

SANICHARI: What did you say? I don't feed you well? My whole life has gone in feeding and raising you, and now you turn around and say I don't give you enough to eat?!

HAROA: No you don't. You never gave anyone enough to eat. You starved my grandmother, you drove out my mother, you killed off my father...

SANICHARI: Haroa... (*In a fit of rage, she snatches his mouth organ out of his hand and flings it on the ground.*)

HAROA: Why did you throw away my mouth organ?

DULAN: Why are you talking to your grandmother like this, Haroa?

HAROA: I'll speak as I want! Who are you to interfere, you old sneak? She's a *daain,* she's finished off all the others, now she'll devour me—

SANICHARI: (*Picking up a stick.*) What did you say? I'm a *daain?* You called me a *daain?* You too? You're no different from your mother! (*She beats him.*) Take that! and that! Calling me a *daain!*

(DULAN *and* HIS WIFE *try to separate the two and prevent her from hitting him, saying "Don't hit him, let him go."*)

SANICHARI: No, today I won't let him get away with it. (*Continues to beat him.*) Leave this house, get out of here!

HAROA: (*Choked and tearful.*) I'm going! And I'll never come back! Can't provide for me, can't give me enough to eat! Why do you beat me? You've devoured everyone, you *daain!* I'll never come back! You'll have to stay here all alone.

SANICHARI: You get out right now, you swine!

(HAROA *takes his mouth organ and starts to walk out.*)

DULAN: (*Trying to stop him.*) Hey, Haroa, don't go—

HAROA: (*Shoving him aside.*) Out of my way, you stupid bastard!

(*He leaves.* SANICHARI *is as if stunned.*)

DULAN: That was not right, Sanichari. He's a young man now. You shouldn't have hit him.

DULAN'S WIFE: You could have explained things nicely. Why did you have to hit him? Suppose he takes it to heart?

DULAN: It doesn't look good to me at all . . .

DULAN'S WIFE: Then what are you standing here for? Go after him, calm him down, bring him back. (DULAN *leaves.*) You didn't do the right thing, Sanichari. (SANICHARI *remains silent.*) Well . . . I must be off, my daughter-in-law's on her own. You'd better light your lamps . . . (*She leaves.*)

(SANICHARI *remains standing, silent, for a while. She looks down at the stick in her hand, then flings it away. She starts to pick up the scattered grain from the floor. The light dims.*)

Scene Five

Evening. A roadside on the outskirts of a mela, or fair. A group of men and women are seated at the back, eating and drinking. Some children are running here and there, playing with carts. The hustle and bustle of a mela. Seated on the stump of a tree, BIKHNI *is eating a banana. She throws the skin on the ground and takes another banana from her cloth bundle. A* SWEET-SELLER *is on his way back from the* mela.

BIKHNI: Hey, you, come here . . . let's see what you've got.
SWEET-SELLER: Do you want to buy or just look?
BIKHNI: First I'll look, then I'll buy. Show me.

(*The* SWEET-SELLER *lowers his glass case to the ground.* BIKHNI *picks out a sweet from it and sniffs it.*)

SWEET-SELLER: Hey, old woman, what're you sniffing it for?
BIKHNI: Your mother may be an old woman, I'm not. Trying to pass off stale stuff and make a fool of me—
SWEET-SELLER: (*Laughs.*) He, he, he, I made them just this morning and you're calling them stale!
BIKHNI: So, how much?
SWEET-SELLER: Four for a *rupee.*
BIKHNI: What a crook! Just four! If you give me six for a *rupee,* I'll take some.
SWEET-SELLER: Impossible.
BIKHNI: Then go away. Scram!
SWEET-SELLER: (*After some thought.*) Okay, go on, take five.
BIKHNI: Give me a *rupee's* worth.

(*The* SWEET-SELLER *fills a paper bag with some sweets and hands it to her, taking the money in return. He leaves.* BIKHNI *tucks the packet away into her cloth bundle and continues to eat her banana. A weary* SANICHARI *enters, on her way back from the* mela, *carrying a bundle on her head. Her foot slips on the discarded banana peel. She falls.*)

SANICHARI: *Hai Maiyya!*

(BIKHNI *laughs out loud.* SANICHARI *picks herself up with difficulty. She glowers at* BIKHNI, *then stands up.* BIKHNI *keeps laughing loudly.*)

SANICHARI: Why, you idiot, does your father own this road or what? Chucking banana peels about like that!
BIKHNI: It doesn't belong to you either, for that matter! Don't you have eyes in your head to watch where you're going?

SANICHARI: You damned bitch, first you do something wrong, then you pick a fight about it!

BIKHNI: You're the bitch—and so's your mother! Comes prancing along and then wonders why she falls!

SANICHARI: Just listen to the whore! If you keep gobbling bananas and throwing peels left and right, won't people slip and fall?

BIKHNI: Let them fall! I'm going to continue eating as I like and chucking peels as I like. (*She throws the second skin on the ground.*)

SANICHARI: You wretch, I'll teach you a lesson.

(SANICHARI *slaps Bikhni hard.* BIKHNI *is momentarily taken aback, then she grabs hold of Sanichari's hair and they begin to fight. Suddenly* SANICHARI *looks searchingly at Bikhni's face and stops, astounded.*)

SANICHARI: (*Wonderingly.*) Kaali Kamli . . . aren't you Kaali Kamli?

BIKHNI: (*Taken aback.*) What did you say?

SANICHARI: Aren't you Bikhni? Kaali Kamli?

BIKHNI: Who're you?

SANICHARI: *Arre*, I'm Sanichari—Sanichari from Tohri.

(BIKHNI *is amazed. The two circle each other, staring at each other.*)

BIKHNI: Sanichari . . . you mean the daughter of Pipartala's Mangla *cha-cha*? The one with long, long nails? That Sanichari?

SANICHARI: Yes, yes, that very one.

BIKHNI: After all these years . . . in a *mela* . . . (*Words fail her. They embrace.*) Weren't you married to someone in Tahad village?

SANICHARI: Yes. And you?

BIKHNI: In Jujubhatu . . .

SANICHARI: You've changed so much . . . become an old woman . . .

BIKHNI: What d'you expect? I am old! Look at you, you're looking pretty old too. You still remember the Kaali Kamli bit?

SANICHARI: How could I forget? You'd walk around in that *ghagra* made out of a black quilt . . .

BIKHNI: And what about your catlike claws, with which you'd scratch us all the time . . .

SANICHARI: *Arre, dhat!* Look, see for yourself—no nails.

BIKHNI: Foolish creature, I no longer have that black *ghagra* either! (*They laugh.*) But tell me—how come you're at the *mela*?

SANICHARI: I came to look for my grandson.

BIKHNI: What happened to him?

SANICHARI: Let it rest. It's a long story.

BIKHNI: (*Lifting her bundle.*) You look as if you've been out since morning, and I bet you haven't eaten a thing all day.

SANICHARI: No, no, I had something at the *mela* . . .

BIKHNI: (*Taking out a* roti.) What're you acting so formal for? Here, sit yourself down and have this. Go on, eat it.

SANICHARI: You have some too.

BIKHNI: Oh, I'm full, I've been eating non-stop. Okay, tell me, who are the family members you live with?

SANICHARI: I'm completely alone.

BIKHNI: Alone? But your husband, children . . . ?

SANICHARI: Let's not talk about me, tell me all about yourself. Weren't you married off to some blacksmith in Jujubhatu?

BIKHNI: Yes. Tell me about your grandson. What happened to him?

SANICHARI: I have no one else in my life but him, Bikhni. They've all left me one by one. He was my only hope, my only comfort. And even he quarreled with me one day and ran away. I came here hoping to find him.

BIKHNI: *Arre* Sanichari, what can one do, it's all written in one's fate.

SANICHARI: I know he won't come back, but even then I keep looking for him here and there like a mad woman.

BIKHNI: Poor you. You're just unlucky, that's all.

SANICHARI: Tell me about yourself. What're you doing here?

BIKHNI: What can I say? My story's like yours, more or less. I have just the one son. He was born four years after my marriage, after so many wishes and prayers! He was just a baby when my husband died of a snake bite. It was a real struggle to get by—at first I reared other people's calves, then slowly managed to get four cows of my own, and two milk-yielding goats. Anyhow, I managed with great difficulty to raise my son, and finally gave him in marriage—

SANICHARI: Where?

BIKHNI: In Lohardanga. His in-laws are very well off. For his wedding, I took a loan from the *mahajan* and feasted the whole village on *dahi* and *chivda*.

SANICHARI: Then what happened?

BIKHNI: What else? The *mahajan* claimed my home and everything I had as repayment. And to my misfortune, my son, lured by the wealth of his in-laws, shifted in with them as a live-in son-in-law!

SANICHARI: Didn't you try to talk to him, explain . . .

BIKHNI: *Arre,* I did all that. I told him, "Beta, let's sell our cows and goats and repay the *mahajan's* loan." Instead, that thieving son of mine took my cattle with him and ran off to his in-laws!

SANICHARI: My god!

BIKHNI: But I'm not to be outdone that easily. I can be just as sly. I stole back two goats and sold them at the *mela.* I got thirty-two *rupee*s for them, and I took the money and set off.

SANICHARI: Where will you go now?

BIKHNI: Wherever chance takes me. Just as you have no son to call your own, I have a son who isn't really mine. I'll go off . . . to Daltongunj—Gomo—Bokaro—beg for alms on some railway station . . .

SANICHARI: You'll be a beggar?

BIKHNI: What else . . . ? (*A little* BOY *darts on and blows a whistle in Bikhni's ear.*) Scram, you little bastard! (*The* BOY *runs off.*)

SANICHARI: God knows what kind of unlucky star we were born under! You know, Bikhni, this is what happens when a woman doesn't have a man in her life. I tell you what—you come with me, Bikhni.

BIKHNI: Where?

SANICHARI: To my home. It's far too empty as it is . . . both of us will live there together.

BIKHNI: How can I . . . no, no, I can't go with you.

SANICHARI: *Arre,* come, please come. Don't make a fuss. Look, I live all alone. If you come and live with me, it'll cheer me up.

BIKHNI: All right. I'll come. Do you have enough water where you live? Any water problem?

SANICHARI: No, not at all—there's a whole river for our use.

BIKHNI: Okay, then let's go. But you keep these thirty *rupee*s with you.

SANICHARI: No, no—I want you stay with me, but I won't take your money. Keep it with you. This Sanichari is still capable of getting by on her own earnings!

BIKHNI: No. If you won't take this, then I won't go with you. Go on, keep these thirty *rupee*s with you.

(SANICHARI *takes the money. She hoists her bundle and stands up, then extends her hand to* BIKHNI.)

SANICHARI: Come, get up. Pick up your things.

BIKHNI: Yes, let's go. Tonight I'll miss my little granddaughter a lot . . .

SANICHARI: Come, let's go. Bit by bit you'll forget all that.

(*They leave. The lights dim slowly.*)

Scene Six

Evening. Sanichari's home. The hut is looking neat and cared for, with a freshly washed covering on the charpoy. BIKHNI, *seated on a low stool, is humming to herself as she carefully oils, combs, and plaits Sanichari's hair.*

BIKHNI: *Arre* you wretch, what a state your hair is in! Crawling with lice—whole fields of them!

SANICHARI: Nibbling away at me all day . . . and because of these damned lice even my nights were ruined—I couldn't sleep!

BIKHNI: You were messy even as a child. Those huge, long nails; oily, uncombed hair!

SANICHARI: And what about your black *ghagra!* Ram, Ram! It stank so much even dogs were scared away!

BIKHNI: Hold still, you black-tongued woman! Let me massage the oil in properly! Here, pass me the comb.

SANICHARI: Look beside you, it must be there. (BIKHNI *gets up and fetches the comb.*) We've used up so much oil, Bikhni!

BIKHNI: Shh, sit still.

SANICHARI: Where did I ever get the time to do my hair or dress up, Bikhni? My life has been nothing but the stove, the *chakki,* and outside jobs. If you had been in the same situation you would have realized—

BIKHNI: Oh I, of course, was lording it like a queen, feasting on sweetmeats all day! *Arre,* what can you do, such is a woman's lot.

SANICHARI: If my *bahu* had been half-way decent, I would have been better off. As it is, I divided my time between cleaning up my in-laws' shit and piss and tending to my Budhua. My son died, my daughter-in-law ran off . . . I brought up my grandson, looked after him till he was a young man, and then he went off with the no-good magic-men . . . My whole life has been spent working, working.

BIKHNI: What a life! Full of tears, sorrow—

SANICHARI: No, I never had the time to weep. They all died, one by one. My in-laws, my brother-in-law and his wife, my husband, my son. I didn't shed a single tear. They call me a *daain*—say it's as if I was born just to devour others.

BIKHNI: Which son of a bitch dares call you a *daain*? I'll scratch his eyes out! Don't worry, Sanichari, you'll see, everything will turn out fine. I'll get hold of some fertilizer from the government office and start growing vegetables once again, and I'll sell them myself in the market. (*Completes plaiting Sanichari's hair, and takes a look at her handiwork. Something strikes her. She fetches something from her bundle.*)

SANICHARI: What's happened?

BIKHNI: Wait a minute.

SANICHARI: What's this . . . ?

BIKHNI: Wait a bit . . . (*She puts a pair of earrings on* SANICHARI.) Let me put it on. I had bought them at the *mela* for myself. Just see how nice they look!

SANICHARI: Go on with you!

BIKHNI: Stop acting coy! (*She gets up and fetches the mirror.*) Go ahead, take a good look.

(SANICHARI *casts a quick glance at herself, then, embarrassed, puts the mirror away.*)

SANICHARI: This is the first time in my whole life that anyone has given me a gift . . . no, no, once my husband also . . . he took me to the Baisakhi *mela* at Tohri. He bought me lots of red and yellow bangles, and some *alta*, but . . .

BIKHNI: What happened?

SANICHARI: The next day I threw everything into the river, the bangles, the *alta*, my *sindoor* . . .

BIKHNI: Why?

SANICHARI: He paid a *rupee* and bought some of the milk that had been blessed by Shivji Maharaj. The milk was stale, it had gone sour . . .

within three hours he got severe cholera and died right there, in the government hospital . . .

BIKHNI: My god! Cholera from sacred offerings?

SANICHARI: What else d'you expect from a poor man's god? D'you know, because I was alone, I was forced to perform two *kriya* ceremonies for my dead husband?

BIKHNI: Really?

SANICHARI: Really. The Tohri *panda* told me that since you're here, you must make the *pinda* offering before you go. I paid a *rupee* and a quarter for an offering of sand and *sattu*. What a to-do there was in our village *panchayat* over this! That bastard Mohanlal said, how can a Tohri Brahmin know how we hold a *kriya* ceremony in Tahad village! He landed me with a second *kriya* ceremony. I had to feed the whole village on curds and *chivda* after taking a loan from Ramavatar.

BIKHNI: D'you mean to say that the Brahmins of Tohri village are different from the Brahmins of Tahad village?

SANICHARI: Who knows . . . the *thakur*s and Brahmins are all in this together. They control everything. It took me five years to pay off my debt to the *thakur*.

BIKHNI: All these bastards are the same!

(*They clean the dishes, put them away, and drink some water.*)

BIKHNI: Come, let's get some sleep.

SANICHARI: You haven't sat still a moment since you've come! You cleaned out the house, made cowdung cakes, picked the lice out of my hair, you want to plant the vegetable patch tomorrow morning—I'm telling you, Bikhni, in my whole life nobody has ever done so much for me. No one has even thought of me as a human being!

BIKHNI: Why are you keeping a tally? Whatever I've done is for us, after all—not for someone else. Go to sleep now.

SANICHARI: You know, when I was a girl my mother used to always tell me that a woman's worst enemy was other women . . .

BIKHNI: *Arre,* that's all stuff made up by men. Go on, go to sleep.

SANICHARI: Tonight I'll sleep peacefully . . .

(*They lie down beside each other and fall asleep. The lights dim slowly.*)

Scene Seven

Morning. Sanichari's home. SANICHARI *and* BIKHNI *are squatting and counting their money. A pot lies beside them.* SANICHARI *turns it upside down, and* BIKHNI *starts to sort out the money. The counting begins.*

SANICHARI: Twenty plus twenty makes forty, plus five makes forty-five and thirty and seventy-five *paise*—

BIKHNI: Not thirty, forty.

SANICHARI: How forty? Now look what you've done, you've mixed me up again.

BIKHNI: I've mixed you up? You've been counting all wrong from the start!

SANICHARI: Okay, wait, let me start again. Look, here's fifty *paise*, here's forty, that makes eighty—

BIKHNI: *Arre,* idiot, do forty and fifty make eighty?

SANICHARI: Yes—no, no, wait a bit. (*Counts on her fingers.*) Sixty, seventy, eighty, ninety—okay, ninety and thirty . . . that makes one *rupee* twenty *paise,* doesn't it?

BIKHNI: Yes . . .

SANICHARI: Five and five ten, plus five fifteen, and . . .

(MISRI *enters.*)

MISRI: So then, Sanichari, what's happening?

(*Sanichari's calculations get disturbed again.*)

SANICHARI: Oh, we're busy making sweetmeats for your wedding, that's all—come, join us!

MISRI: Why are you so badtempered? I just came to get news of your friend here. (*To* BIKHNI.) How are you, Sister?

SANICHARI: Got your news? Now you can leave.

MISRI: I heard that your friend brought a whole lot of money with her.

BIKHNI: Yes . . . a whole treasure-chest full! Can't you see? No matter how much we count, there's still more.

MISRI: Having fun, eh, Sanichari?

SANICHARI: Oh, yes, loads of fun. Tell you what, Misri—leave your husband and come live here with us. Then all three of us can have lots of fun.

MISRI: Why are you talking rubbish, Sanichari! You have a filthy mind! I just come here to ask you after your friend, and you start insulting me!

SANICHARI: Run along, now. All morning she's been hovering around us! (MISRI *leaves.*) She's an out-and-out bitch, that old hag! She's mixed me up completely . . . fifty and forty makes—

BIKHNI: That's enough, stop, you've done enough counting! (*She counts.*) Altogether it comes to two *rupees* and thirty *paise!*

SANICHARI: *Hai Maiyya!* Just two *rupees* thirty *paise!* That's all that's left!

BIKHNI: What do you expect? D'you think we can live a lifetime on thirty *rupees*?

SANICHARI: Now what will happen?

BIKHNI: We're in trouble . . . there aren't any vegetables in the yard either.

SANICHARI: We used up all your money, Bikhni.

BIKHNI: What's this "your" money business? The money was there, it got used up, that's all there is to it. (SANICHARI *is quiet.*) You still haven't accepted me as your own, Sanichari.

(DULAN'S WIFE's *voice is heard, off, raised in anger.*)

DULAN'S WIFE: *Hai,* may you die, you bastards! May you perish in flames! If I catch you, I'll roast you in the oven! *Arre,* why are you running away, you brats? If you have the guts come and face me! Come on!

BIKHNI: Sounds like Lachmi.

SANICHARI: (*Peering out.*) What's happened, oh mother of Dhatua?

DULAN'S WIFE: (*As she enters.*) Damn brats!

SANICHARI: Why were you screaming like that? Aren't you going to tell us?

DULAN'S WIFE: Should I sit quietly and let those bastards get away with it? The next time they enter my courtyard I'll break their legs!

SANICHARI: *Arre,* will you tell us what happened, or are you going to keep blathering on like this?

DULAN'S WIFE: I spent hours carefully grinding the *dal* to make *badi*s, and put them out into the sun to harden, and those bastards came and stole them all!

SANICHARI: Who? Who stole them?

DULAN'S WIFE: Hanumanji's descendants, those damned monkeys!

BIKHNI: Monkeys . . . ? You mean all this time you've been carrying on about monkeys! (*She laughs.*)

DULAN'S WIFE: What're you grinning about? If that marauding army of bastards had laid your vegetable patch to waste you would know how it feels.

DULAN: (*Entering.*) *Arre*, why are you cursing Ramji's disciples so roundly?

DULAN'S WIFE: Now don't you start! All my hard work . . .

SANICHARI: (*Arranging the* charpoy.) All right, now calm down.

BIKHNI: We'll make you some more *badi*s.

SANICHARI: Come, sit down, Dulan. It's good that you're here. Only you can help us.

DULAN: Now what's the matter?

SANICHARI: What can I say? All our savings are gone. There are no vegetables to sell. From tomorrow we'll have to starve.

DULAN: Why should you starve when there are so many ways to earn a living?

BIKHNI: It's the *malik-mahajan*s who have ways of earning open to them. Us *dushad*s and *ganju*s have to make our own openings.

DULAN: So go ahead and make them. Across the river there's a road being built for the Devi's temple. Dhatua was telling me that they're looking for laborers. Go there with your friend and set to work.

DULAN'S WIFE: In your dotage you're losing whatever little brains you had! You expect them to break stones at their age!

DULAN: *Arre*, if they can't break stones, they can pick one up, can't they?

SANICHARI: What do you mean?

DULAN: Early in the morning, when there's no one about, when everyone's sleeping, quietly make your way to the river and pick up a black stone from the riverbank.

SANICHARI: A black stone?

DULAN: Let me finish. Then you wash and bathe that stone, anoint it with oil, put *sindoor* on it, and take your place in the Tohri market place.

SANICHARI: Then?

DULAN: Then? Then you announce to everyone that Mahavirji visited you in your dreams and granted you a vision. Wait and see how the devout will throng to make offerings to your stone!

BIKHNI: This is a fine opening you've shown us, Dulan! We'll rake in the money!

SANICHARI: Quiet! Making mockery of the gods! All my life I've worked hard to earn my living—and now, in my old age, am I to fool around like this with something sacred?

DULAN: Well, you can consider it fooling around, or mockery, if you wish. But it just shows that you have a wicked mind. That's why you see something sinful wherever you look.

SANICHARI: How come?

DULAN: How come? I'll tell you. Now, you know Lachman's old mother has joint pains, don't you?

SANICHARI: Yes, she does.

DULAN: That old woman handed me ten *rupees* and said, "Dulan *bhaiya*, fetch me some of Deviji's oil from the market, won't you?" I said okay; but who's going to go haring off to the market just for that old hag? Two days later I took some oil from home and handed it to her. She applied that oil and a couple of days later that same bedridden old creature was hopping gaily all over the village on her own two legs.

BIKHNI: You save your tallest tales for us old women, huh, Dulan?

DULAN: I swear on Ram Bhagwan that every word is god's own truth. *Arre*, if your mind is pure then your actions are pure! I'm telling you, Sanichari, no god is more important than your belly. One does whatever it takes to feed one's stomach.

(*An agitated* BIJUA *enters.*)

BIJUA: Dulan *bhaiya, arre oh*, Dulan *bhaiya!*

DULAN: What's the matter? What's happened?

BIJUA: *Arre*, there's a big to-do in the village! Bhairo Singh of Barohi village has been murdered!

WOMEN: (*Together.*) *Hai* Ram!

DULAN: What're you saying . . . ?

BIJUA: Yes, Bhaiya. This morning at daybreak Bhairo Singh's corpse was found lying in the middle of the fields.

DULAN: What . . . ?

BIJUA: And the murderer is his son Madho Singh.

DULAN: Really?

BIJUA: That's what the villagers all say.

SANICHARI: *Hai Maiyya!*

BIKHNI: What a world this is—a son killing his father . . .

BIJUA: The world of the wealthy is different from ours. For the sake of money a mother can kill her son, a son his mother.

DULAN: *Achha*, has Madho Singh been caught yet?

BIJUA: Are you crazy? Will the police arrest someone like him? These people have the power of money—the law, the police, the government, are all firmly in their grasp.

SANICHARI: Bhairo Singh may have died, but your luck has blossomed.

BIJUA: Why not! Just wait and see what a fancy *kriya* ceremony Madho Singh will arrange for his father! Already two and a half mounds of sandalwood, pure *ghee* and incense have been sent for. Know what, Dulan *bhaiya*, he's even sent for whores to wail at the funeral!

DULAN: Really?

BIJUA: Okay, I'm off. I still have to inform Mohanlal—I thought I'd stop off on the way and tell you people first. Okay, I'm going now, Bhaiya. (*Leaves hastily.*)

SANICHARI: *Arre* Bijua, at least have a glass of water—

BIJUA: (*Over his shoulder.*) No, no, Bhauji, some other time.

DULAN: How about it, Sanichari?

SANICHARI: What . . . ?

DULAN: *Arre*, a *thakur* has died, mourners are bound to be required. Do one thing, the two of you present yourselves—

BIKHNI: Are there no family members to weep for him?

DULAN: Only the families of the poor mourn their dead. The rich households have to hire mourners. *Arre*, if you mourn for them you'll get money, grain, and the day after the *kriya* you'll even get clothes and a good meal.

SANICHARI: *Hai Maiyya*, are you suggesting that I should mourn? Me? I haven't been able to shed a tear, ever. When Budhua's father died, I thought at least then I would really cry hard. I even went and sat under a pipal tree and all day I kept thinking now I'll cry, now I'll cry—then it became evening and I hadn't shed a single tear.

DULAN: *Arre*, that's not the kind of crying I'm talking of. This is crying for money, crying as a business. Just do it the way you would grind wheat or carry bricks for the sake of a daily wage.

BIKHNI: Take me to them, Dulan, I can cry magnificently!

DULAN'S WIFE: Couldn't you think of some other work for them than sitting and mourning alongside cheap whores!

DULAN: Hold your tongue. A job's a job. You two come along, I'll take you there. The better the mourners, the more the *malik's* prestige increases.

SANICHARI: What will people say, Dulan?

BIKHNI: (*To* SANICHARI.) Are people going to come and feed us, support us? (*To* DULAN.) Come, Dulan, I'm ready to go.

SANICHARI: But . . . Bikhni . . .

BIKHNI: Shush. Go on, old man, tell us when you'll take us along.

DULAN: I'll come to fetch you in the afternoon. Be sure to wear black. And listen, Sanichari—I want my share of your earnings from any job I arrange for you.

SANICHARI: You so-and-so, you want a cut, do you?

DULAN: So what's wrong with that? Everyone from the Prime Minister down to the lowest Untouchable takes cuts.

BIKHNI: A hundred bastards must have died to give birth to a rascal like you.

(*The lights dim.*)

Scene Eight

Afternoon. The courtyard of Bhairo Singh's mansion. BACHANLAL *and* BIJUA *are occupied with chores in preparation for the funeral rites.* MOHANLAL *pandit is reciting from the* Bhagavad Gita. *On one side,* NATUA *and some boys are splitting bamboo and lashing the bamboo together with rope to form a stretcher on which the corpse will be carried to the cremation grounds. A cluster of* PROSTITUTES *is busy laughing and giggling. Bhairo Singh's corpse is laid out on the ground, covered with a white sheet.* BACHCHA SINGH *is seated by its feet.* MADHO SINGH *enters with a diya. He sits beside* MOHANLAL. *After completing his recitation of the shlokas,* MOHANLAL *begins the* pinda dan *ceremony.*

MOHANLAL: Now say after me: for the purity of my father's soul I make an offering to the Brahmin . . .

MADHO SINGH: I make an offering . . .

MOHANLAL: Of a set of clothes . . .

MADHO SINGH: A set of clothes . . .

MOHANLAL: Of grain . . .

MADHO SINGH: Of grain . . .

MOHANLAL: Now repeat after me: for the purity of my father's soul I gift the Brahmin a bed complete with bedclothes . . .

MADHO SINGH: I gift a bed . . .

(MOHANLAL *looks around him and gets annoyed when he doesn't see a bed.*)

MOHANLAL: *Arre,* where's the gift of a bed?

MADHO SINGH: (*Bounding to his feet.*) What the hell, Bijua, Bachanlal, where's the bed?

BIJUA: *Huzoor,* it's been loaded onto the bullock cart.

(*The* PROSTITUTES *laugh loudly.*)

MOHANLAL: Calm down, Madho Singhji, calm down. Come, sit. (MADHO SINGH *sits again.*) Now make the final offering. Say: for the purity of my father's soul I gift the Brahmin a cow . . .

MADHO SINGH: I gift a cow . . .

MOHANLAL: (*To* BIJUA.) Hey, Bijua, is the cow outside?

BIJUA: Why are you so worried, Panditji? Everything's there.

MOHANLAL: All right, all right. (*To* MADHO SINGH.) Now sprinkle holy water seven times to purify the dead soul. (MADHO SINGH *sprinkles the corpse with holy water while* MOHANLAL *recites the* shloka.) "*Om apavitraha pavitro va sarva vastahag todipva/yoh smaret pundri kakshayam sa brahma bhyantarah shuchiha.*"* The first *pinda dan* in this family now comes to an end. Now please get up, Madho Singhji, touch your father's feet and depart.

(MADHO SINGH *follows the instructions and leaves.*)

BACHANLAL: Is everything done, Panditji?

MOHANLAL: Yes, Bhaiya, everything's done.

---

*This is a *shloka* recited for the departed soul during death rites. It means, roughly, "You may be pure or impure, but if you pray to or call the name of the supreme deity, the Lotus-eyed One, you will be cleansed inside and out, rendered pure both spiritually and materially."

(BACHANLAL *also exits.* MOHANLAL *is busy gathering up his things. A* BOY *enters carrying a bundle of blankets on his head.*)

BOY: Where shall I put these blankets? They're meant to be donated to the *dom*s.

BIJUA: Put them inside, where else?

MOHANLAL: (*Busy gathering together his things.*) So, Bijua, have you arranged for the fresh milk?

BIJUA: Right away, Panditji.

(*He goes in. The* PROSTITUTES *begin to tease* MOHANLAL.)

PROSTITUTE 1:   Why, Panditji, that's a lot of stuff you've gathered . . .

PROSTITUTE 2:   Panditji, how come you didn't ask for a radio in your list of donations?

PROSTITUTE 3:   When you're sleeping beside your wife on that thousand *rupee* bed I hope you'll arrange for some song and dance as well!

(*They laugh raucously.* MOHANLAL *gets annoyed.*)

MOHANLAL: (*In anger.*) Quiet! How dare you! You've been brought here to mourn, and you sit there cackling your heads off!

(BIJUA *enters with milk. A* PROSTITUTE *tugs at his* dhoti *and addresses him.*)

PROSTITUTE 2:   Hey there, Bijua, how come we don't see you in the neighborhood nowadays? Found greener pastures, have you? (*They all laugh loudly.*)

BIJUA: *Dhat!* (*He frees his* dhoti *and approaches the* pandit.) Here, Panditji, here's the fresh milk.

MOHANLAL: Okay, leave it here.

(BACHANLAL *enters.*)

BACHANLAL: Panditji, here's fifty-one *rupee*s for the priest's fee. (MOHANLAL *takes the money and is about to leave.*) Bijua, load all Panditji's goods onto the cart. (BIJUA *picks up the things and prepares to follow the* pandit *out.* BACHANLAL *to the* pandit.) Be sure to come early for the fourth-day ceremony. Don't be late.

MOHANLAL: (*Turns as he is leaving.*) Don't worry about that, I'll be here for sure. But Bachanlalji, don't forget my button-down umbrella—

BACHANLAL: Okay, okay, it'll be arranged.

MOHANLAL: Fine.

(MOHANLAL *exits, with* BIJUA *behind him, carrying his things.*)

BACHANLAL: How much longer now?

NATUA: It's almost done, *sarkar.*

(*He finishes tying the rope on the bamboo stretcher. A boy,* SHANKAR, *enters with a tin of* ghee.)

SHANKAR: *Sarkar,* where should I put this?

BACHANLAL: On my head, you idiot!

SHANKAR: Oh . . .

BACHANLAL: Go inside and hand it to the young mistress. (*He looks at the prostitutes and notices that they aren't wailing.*) You haven't the least consideration for your master's honor! All your life you've been fed, clothed, and pampered by him! And now you shameless hussies can't shed a tear at his passing!

PROSTITUTE: Yes, yes, the master was like a god to us! He made whores of us, fed and clothed us, and on his death left us five whole *rupees*! How can we not mourn him! Come on, let's start! (*They begin to wail.*)

(BIJUA *enters.*)

BACHANLAL: Hey, Bijua, I asked you to organize ten or fifteen good *rudalis*, and all you could arrange was these three withered hags!

PROSTITUTE: The good ones can earn more than your measly five *rupees* on the job, why would they come here to beat their breasts!

BACHANLAL: You're getting too big for your boots—shut up and keep crying.

OLD PROSTITUTE: If you don't give us something to eat and drink how do you expect us to keep crying?

BACHANLAL: Shut up, old woman, first do your job!

(MADHO SINGH *enters.*)

MADHO SINGH: Well, Bachanlal—

BACHANLAL: Yes, *sarkar?*

MADHO SINGH: How much longer? Will the corpse be carried out before the sun goes down, or not? (*Looking at* BACHCHA SINGH.) What are you sitting here for, pulling a long face? Go, change your clothes and get ready.

BACHANLAL: We're only waiting for Lachman *babu, sarkar.*

MADHO SINGH: The sandalwood logs and *ghee* and so on are ready . . . ?

BACHANLAL: Yes, *sarkar.*

MADHO SINGH: When the pyre is set alight, I want it to be known for miles around that Madho Singh's father is being cremated.

BACHANLAL: Don't worry, *sarkar,* all the arrangements have been made perfectly.

MADHO SINGH: My father was the head of all the *thakur*s of Birohi village. His *kriya* ceremony should be as grand as an emperor's. Money's no problem—don't stint on anything. (*He turns to leave, then suddenly sees the three* rudalis. *He stops.*) What's this, only three *rudalis*? (*Loudly.*) *Arre,* Madho Singh's father dies and you arrange just three *rudalis*? Why didn't you get the whole whores' quarter here?

BACHANLAL: *Sarkar,* I kept telling Bijua the barber—

MADHO SINGH: Where's that son of a bitch? Send for the bastard!

BACHANLAL: Bijua!!

(BIJUA *comes running.*)

BIJUA: Yes, *sarkar* . . .

MADHO SINGH: What the hell, you fucker! D'you think it's your father who's dead, that you've picked up these three deadbeats?

BIJUA: *Huzoor,* they . . .

MADHO SINGH: Shut up, you shit! Not a word out of you! Send someone to the whores' quarter! I want the whole redlight district to report here, understand?

BIJUA: Yes, *sarkar.* (*He leaves.*)

MADHO SINGH: Madho Singh's father's funeral, and only three . . . (*He breaks down and sobs. Puts a hanky to his eyes.*) Babuji! (*He can't speak.*)

(NATUA *enters with the bamboo stretcher for the body.*)

PROSTITUTE: The bastard murders his own father and then weeps crocodile tears!

BIJUA: (*Entering on the run.*) *Sarkar,* Lachman *babu*'s here.

(LACHMAN SINGH *enters.*)

LACHMAN: Madho, my son!

MADHO SINGH: Chachaji! (*He touches the older man's feet.*)

PROSTITUTE 1: Lachman Singh of Tahad.

PROSTITUTE 2: Another one for the whores.

LACHMAN SINGH: Take yourself in hand, my son. People come, people go—that's the way of the world. I've had a word with the *Darogaji*, my son. Bachcha Singh, come here. (BACHCHA SINGH *gets up and goes to him. To* MADHO.) Now you'll have to look after him.

MADHO SINGH: You don't have to be concerned, Chachaji, he's my responsibility now.

BACHCHA SINGH: What's happened to my father?

LACHMAN SINGH: An enemy murdered him, my son.

BACHCHA SINGH: Will he kill me too?

LACHMAN SINGH: No, no, my son. Your brother will look after you well— isn't that so, Madho?

MADHO SINGH: Don't worry about a thing, Chachaji.

LACHMAN SINGH: Let me take a last look at my brother . . . (*He begins to remove the white sheet covering the corpse but* MADHO SINGH *hurriedly stops him.*)

MADHO SINGH: You won't be able to stand it, Chachaji. He's really been hacked up. Come, let's go. (*Leads him away.*)

LACHMAN SINGH: (*As he's led away.*) You come along as well, Bachcha Singh.

(*They exit.* BACHANLAL *goes up to scold the* rudalis.)

BACHANLAL: What the hell, have you been brought here to recite the scriptures? Go on, wail your loudest. Letting me down in front of the master!

(DULAN *enters with* SANICHARI *and* BIKHNI.)

DULAN: Ram Ram, Bachanlal *bhaiya!*

BACHANLAL: How are you, Dulan?

DULAN: I was so upset to hear that the old master was no more, that I decided to bring along two *rudalis*. After all, he deserves a really grand *kriya* ceremony!

(*The* PROSTITUTES *stop wailing and nudge each other.*)

BACHANLAL: All right, tell the two of them to sit beside them. (*Points to* PROSTITUTES. *To* SANICHARI *and* BIKHNI.) Here, sit.

DULAN: *Sarkar,* first the payment terms . . .

BACHANLAL: What terms do you expect for these old hags?

DULAN: *Sarkar,* these women may look old, but wait till you hear them mourn! You'll find yourself shedding tears!

BACHANLAL: Okay, they'll get some grain.

DULAN: That's not enough, *sarkar.* I've heard that a full two hundred *rupees* have been allocated just for *rudalis.*

BACHANLAL: Okay, okay, five *rupees* as well.

DULAN: Only five *rupees*! For women from decent homes! You must give them at least twenty *rupees* each, *sarkar.*

BACHANLAL: Are you mad? Twenty *rupees* each?! Okay, you can take thirty for the two of them. That's all.

DULAN: Thirty *rupees,* rice and clothes.

BACHANLAL: Not rice, wheat.

DULAN: Give them rice, *sarkar.* They've got good, strong voices.

BACHANLAL: Dulan, how many bastards died to give birth to you?

DULAN: Twenty-two, *sarkar* . . .

BACHANLAL: (*Calling offstage.*) Hey, Natua, is the bamboo stretcher ready or not?

PROSTITUTE: God knows where he picked up these two. Can these old hags cry?

(SANICHARI *and* BIKHNI *break into dramatic wails and cries as they approach the corpse. As they mourn loudly, people slowly begin to enter and gather around. As soon as* MADHO SINGH *comes in,* BACHANLAL *goes up to him.*)

BACHANLAL: Didn't I tell you not to worry, *sarkar*?

(*The crying and wailing reaches a climax. While crying,* SANICHARI *and* BIKHNI *fall on each others' necks.* BACHCHA SINGH, *affected by this, begins to cry aloud as he beats his head on his father's corpse.*)

BACHCHA SINGH: Bappa . . . Bappa!

(MADHO SINGH *tries to quieten him. The lights dim slowly.*)

Scene Nine

Sanichari's home. A winter evening. The house is looking a little more prosperous than before. There are a few additional household items. SANICHARI *and* BIKHNI *enter. They are dressed in black* ghagras. BIKHNI *is carrying a large bundle.* SANICHARI *has her head covered with a black cloth. As soon as they enter, they begin to take off the black clothing and drape it on the upended charpoy. They sit on the ground.*

BIKHNI: Is it still hurting?

SANICHARI: Less than before. Want to eat something?

BIKHNI: Don't I just, my stomach's growling with hunger. Go, fetch the thalis. (SANICHARI *fetches the plates while* BIKHNI *opens up the bundle.*) *Arre, baap re,* what a lot of *puris* and *laddus* they've given us!

SANICHARI: Eat your fill. It's not every day that Nathuni Singh's mother dies! Here. (*Hands* BIKHNI *some food.*)

BIKHNI: Again you've served me first . . .

SANICHARI: *Arre,* eat up! Just look at how much *chivda* and *gur* we've got!

BIKHNI: (*Takes a roll of black cloth from the bundle.*) The cloth is really good and soft, too.

SANICHARI: In these two months we've collected so much cloth! What shall we do with it, Bikhni?

BIKHNI: Don't worry about it. I'll take it to the market and sell it all off.

SANICHARI: There's so much food. Why don't we call Dhatua's mother and share some with her?

BIKHNI: (*Eating.*) Yes, let's do that.

SANICHARI: (*Going to the door.*) *Arre* oh, mother of Dhatua!

DULAN'S WIFE: (*From offstage.*) What is it?

SANICHARI: Just come here a moment . . . quick . . .

DULAN'S WIFE: Coming!

(SANICHARI *returns to her place and sits down.*)

SANICHARI: Nathuni Singh really spent generously on his mother's *kriya* ceremony. Sandalwood, pure *ghee,* donations of clothing for the poor . . . Bijua was saying he spent a full thirty thousand *rupees* on it all!

BIKHNI: Yes, he spent thirty thousand and got thirty *lakh*s in return—by way of inheritance.

DULAN'S WIFE: (*Entering.*) Why were you calling me?

SANICHARI: *Arre,* come and sit!

DULAN'S WIFE: (*Sitting down.*) So what did your fortune bring you today?

BIKHNI: What can it bring us? We split our foreheads open mourning at Nathuni Singh's.

SANICHARI: *Arre,* that's all part of the business. Here (*She gives* DULAN'S WIFE *some laddu.*), eat this.

DULAN'S WIFE: The *laddu* is good today. But Sanichari, that *laddu* you got day before yesterday was really stale! It stank!

BIKHNI: That's because this *laddu* is from the house of *thakur* Nathuni Singh, and that was from the house of Ganpathlal Lala. That bastard is the biggest miser going.

SANICHARI: Do you know what Lala's son Jaggilal did? In order to save money, he used *dalda* instead of real *ghee* to burn his father's corpse!

DULAN'S WIFE: *Hai Maiyya!*

SANICHARI: He also approached us to lower our rates, saying, take only five *rupees* from me, even though I know you take twenty *rupees* from the others! But you have to cry as well as you would for a *thakur* family! I told him straight, mourning a death is not like trading in oil or salt, that you can bargain and haggle! Huh! Trying to compete with the *thakur*s!

BIKHNI: We told him plainly—not a *paisa* less than fifty *rupees*!

DULAN'S WIFE: Well done! The stingy old miser!

(MISRI *comes up to the boundary wall.*)

MISRI: *Hai Maiyya!* Hogging *laddu*s, I see, mother of Dhatua!

(DHATUA'S WIFE *enters alongside.*)

DHATUA'S WIFE: *Maai,* Chachi's looking for you . . .

DULAN'S WIFE: What is it, Misri?

MISRI: Shall I come in so's I can tell you?

BIKHNI: No. You stay there. (*She gives* DHATUA'S WIFE *some* laddu.) Here, have some. (*She gets up and goes to* MISRI *with some* laddu *in her hand.*) Go on, your ladyship, you can hog some as well. (*She starts to give her some, then snatches back her hand.*) Oh, oh, wait, let me just ask Sanichari—(*Turns and asks* SANICHARI.) What d'you say, Sanichari, shall we give her some? (SANICHARI *inclines her head in assent.*)

MISRI: (*Taking the* laddu *from her.*) Sanichari, your luck has really turned! Feasting on *halwa-puri* every day!

BIKHNI: How does it bother you? Is it your father's wealth?

MISRI: *Arre,* when my father died, we really ate well! And this one—her father died, her husband died, but the woman never so much as shed a tear! Why should she, after all—there was no *halwa-puri* to be had, was there?

BIKHNI: You've eaten your *laddu,* now get out of here.

MISRI: I only came because my cow's giving birth, I'm not interested in anyone's *laddus!* (*She leaves.*)

DHATUA'S WIFE: Don't let her depress you, Chachi. Nothing can change her twisted mind.

(*An* OLD WOMAN *enters.*)

WOMAN: Does Sanichari live here?

(BIKHNI *gets up and goes to her. The* OLD WOMAN *whispers in her ear.*)

BIKHNI: Hey, Sanichari, just come here a moment.

(SANICHARI *goes up to them. The three of them talk softly, then the* OLD WOMAN *leaves.* DULAN'S WIFE *gestures to her daughter-in-law,* DHATUA'S WIFE.)

DULAN'S WIFE: *Arre oh,* Sanichari, what's up?

SANICHARI: Nathuni Singh's middle wife is here.

DULAN'S WIFE: What? Mohar Singh's daughter here, in your home? Okay, we'd better be off.

BIKHNI: *Arre,* sit for a while. Take some *chivda* with you.

DULAN'S WIFE: I'll take some in the evening. Besides, there's Misri's cow to be seen to. (*To her daughter-in-law.*) Come, let's go.

(*They leave.* SANICHARI *picks up the bundle and other things and goes in.* BIKHNI *arranges the* charpoy *for a visitor.* SANICHARI *brings out a covering and lays it on the* charpoy. *The* THAKURAIN *enters.*)

SANICHARI: Please sit down, Thakurain.

(BIKHNI *fetches a pot of water and a napkin. She washes the* THAKURAIN'S *feet and wipes them with the cloth, then touches her feet as a gesture of respect. The* OLD WOMAN *enters and seats herself at the back.*)

SANICHARI: Huzoorain, you here . . . ?

THAKURAIN: I have something urgent to tell you.

BIKHNI: You could have sent for us, why did you go to the trouble of coming here?

THAKURAIN: You'll have to take the early morning bus to Lohri village tomorrow.

SANICHARI: Why Lohri village, Thakurain?

THAKURAIN: My father Mohar Singh has been suffering from smallpox for a month. Since last night his condition has become very serious. There's no hope for him now.

BIKHNI: But I thought only the poor got that disease?

SANICHARI: Didn't he receive any treatment?

THAKURAIN: What can I say? My mother believes in prayers and *pujas*, nothing else. I have no one else but my father. Everyone in my in-laws' home is my enemy.

SANICHARI: But your father's still alive . . .

THAKURAIN: In name only. Such a pampered body, fed on milk and *ghee,* that his soul just doesn't want to leave it! Ten villages used to quake at the sound of my father Mohar Singh's name! When he dies, I'll show them all what a *kriya* ceremony is!

BIKHNI: But even Nathuni *babu* didn't spare any expense for his mother's *kriya*. That's what a son should be like! A real Sarvan Kumar.

THAKURAIN: Son my foot! Dispatched his mother to a wretched hut near the cowshed and left her there to die. All he did by way of treatment was to tether a goat beside her. No question of a *hakim* or *vaid* or doctor.

SANICHARI: To think that the daughter of Parakaram Singh was reduced to this!

THAKURAIN: All day long his old mother would lie rotting in her own piss and shit, while her son counted the days till the old woman popped off and he could lay his hands on all her wealth!

BIKHNI: Didn't he make any arrangements for her to be nursed or looked after?

THAKURAIN: Yes—Motiya Dushadin and Jagna Mehtar. Suddenly the question of her losing caste on being touched by *dushads* and *bhangis* was no longer a problem! *Arre,* it's all part of that older *bahu's* evil plan—as it is she swaggers around all day brandishing her thick bunch of keys and making everyone dance to her bidding.

BIKHNI: Why? Didn't you have some authority too? After all, you're the middle wife.

THAKURAIN: What authority would I have? Have I produced a son and heir for their family? I gave birth to a daughter, that was my big crime. When my mother-in-law died, thirty thousand *rupees* were spent on her *kriya*. Half of that money was given by my father, but even after that they treated me badly. I refuse to stay there any longer. I'll go to my father's house, and I'll organize such a magnificent *kriya* for him that the whole community will talk of nothing else. Tell me, how much do I pay you?

(BIKHNI *and* SANICHARI *exchange looks.* SANICHARI *gestures to* BIKHNI.)

BIKHNI: Well, if we're to prostrate ourselves on the ground while wailing, then it's fifty *rupees*, and if we're to beat our breasts all the way to the cremation ground then it'll be sixty-five, and—

THAKURAIN: I'll pay a full hundred *rupees*, but you must raise such a ruckus that the whole village gets to know of it.

SANICHARI: But the senior mistress gave us oil, salt, chillies, and *dal* as well.

THAKURAIN: I'll also give you rice, *dal, gur,* oil, salt, and a *thali* made of brass.

BIKHNI: Clothes . . . ?

THAKURAIN: Why are you so worried, you'll get everything. Just come along early in the morning. And no one should know that I came here today . . .

BIKHNI: Oh no, Huzoorain. Rest assured, no one will get to know.

(*They both touch her feet. The* THAKURAIN *leaves, along with the* OLD WOMAN.)

SANICHARI: The rich are really strange! Just see how she came running to us as soon as she needed us for something!

BIKHNI: *Arre* Sanichari, we've bruised our foreheads and rent our hair mourning for others; will there be anyone to mourn for us when we die?

SANICHARI: Of course there will be! The jackals will howl for us, the hyenas and dogs will howl for us . . . Come on, let's get our things together for tomorrow morning.

(SANICHARI *picks up the kneading dish and goes in.* BIKHNI *upends the* charpoy.)

BIKHNI: Oh, Sanichari!

SANICHARI: Yes?

BIKHNI: Nothing.

SANICHARI: (*Putting down the dish.*) *Arre,* what is it? Tell me.

BIKHNI: Early tomorrow morning we have to go to Mohar Singh's . . .

SANICHARI: So?

BIKHNI: Well, I was just thinking . . . from there I could take the Ranchi bus to Jujubhatu . . .

SANICHARI: What for?

BIKHNI: My brother-in-law's daughter is getting married. It's like this: yesterday when I went to the market, I happened to meet my brother-in-law. He was very insistent that I should go, and I also thought that this way I could get to see my grandchild once again . . .

SANICHARI: Two days have passed, and you didn't say a word to me.

BIKHNI: I thought it would upset you.

SANICHARI: You will come back, though . . . ?

BIKHNI: Why are you talking like this? This is my home, after all. How can I not come back!

SANICHARI: But . . . there's your grandchild . . .

BIKHNI: I'll just meet her and be back in two days, that's all.

SANICHARI: All right, go—but don't sit on a seat when you take the bus, they'll charge you eight *rupees.* Just sit on the floor and hand them two *rupees.* And listen, don't you stuff yourself full of rubbish on the way . . .

BIKHNI: Okay.

SANICHARI: Now go to sleep.

BIKHNI: And you . . . ?

SANICHARI: I have a lot of things to do.

(SANICHARI *goes into the hut, then covers* BIKHNI *with a sheet.* BIKHNI *hesitates, puzzled. The lights dim.*)

Scene Ten

SANICHARI *is seated on the floor, sorting clothes, with a big bundle of cloth beside her. She picks out some thin black cloth, gets up and fetches the sewing box, then stitches the cloth. She gets up, drinks some water, sits down again. The thread is used up. It is too dark for her to thread the needle. She gets up again, checks one of the old pots, then sits down again.* DULAN'S VOICE *is heard, off.*

DULAN: Sanichari! Oh, Sanichari!

(SANICHARI *gets up and opens the outer door.* DULAN *enters.*)

DULAN: The sun's gone down, how come you haven't lighted your stove?

SANICHARI: There's a *roti* still lying uneaten from this morning. I don't feel like cooking twice a day just for myself. (*Getting up.*) Come, sit down . . .

DULAN: Let it be. (*As he sits.*) Your friend seems to have disappeared.

SANICHARI: When she left she said she'd be back in two days. But it's been six days now, and there's no news of her.

DULAN: *Arre,* she won't be back. Why should she leave her son, her daughter-in-law, her grandchild, to come back here? What for?

SANICHARI: No, no, Dulan. She'll definitely come back. When she left she vowed she would. And she has a business here, why shouldn't she come back?

DULAN: *Arre,* if her son supports her why should she work? Anyway, I have some news for you. You've heard of *thakur* Gambhir Singh of Naugad, haven't you?

SANICHARI: Who hasn't? The long-nosed Gambhir Singh who used to parade through the *Diwali mela* on elephant-back!

DULAN: A big *zamindar*—lord of five villages. He really lived it up, drinking, womanizing—and now, in his old age, he's paying the price for it.

SANICHARI: Why, what's happened to him?

DULAN: What d'you expect? His entire body's rotted away. Swollen like a drum. He could drop dead any moment. Last night they even lowered his body to the ground, and this morning they found him breathing again! But the old man's time has come.

SANICHARI: So why're you telling me all this?

DULAN: Because you'll have to go when it's time to mourn. He's put it in writing that he wants a *lakh* of *rupees* to be spent on his death ceremonies. He wants to wash away all the sins of a lifetime with a *lakh* of *rupees*!

SANICHARI: But how can I go alone . . . ? Bikhni isn't here.

DULAN: *Arre*, if you sit around waiting for Bikhni you'll starve to death. I'm telling you, his *kriya* is going to be a really grand affair! Three different kinds of bands, horses, elephants, grain and cloth being distributed to the people of all five villages—Sanichari, you'll make enough to eat off for six months! And of course, I'll get something out of it . . .

SANICHARI: You've grown greedy for money, Dulan, you're not thinking about me. Bikhni isn't here, how can I go alone to mourn . . . ?

DULAN: Why? You can go to the whores' quarter in Tohri. At the sound of Gambhir Singh's name fifty whores will be willing to come along. And then your Parbatia is there as well . . .

SANICHARI: I? Go to the whores' quarter? To Parbatia?

DULAN: For the sake of money you can do anything. Besides, its Gambhir Singh's own wish that whores from the whores' quarter come to mourn him at his *kriya* ceremony.

SANICHARI: He expects the very women whose lives he ruined to cry over his corpse?!

DULAN: Don't concern yourself with all that! Just think about your own business. Tomorrow you should go to Tohri and fix it all up. I'll take you.

(DULAN *leaves.* SANICHARI *continues to sit silently. She starts to fold the black clothes. A voice is heard outside.*)

VOICE: (*Off.*) Is anyone home?

SANICHARI: Who is it?

VOICE: (*Off.*) I've come from Jujubhatu.

(SANICHARI *eagerly goes to the outer door.* BIKHNI'S NEPHEW *enters.*)

SANICHARI: Bikhni hasn't come . . . ?

BIKHNI'S NEPHEW: Well . . .

SANICHARI: What is it? Has something happened to her?

BIKHNI'S NEPHEW: On her way . . . in the bus . . . she ate some fritters . . . and even after the wedding, she ate a whole lot of stale tidbits.

SANICHARI: It was a bad habit of hers.

BIKHNI'S NEPHEW: Well, she got cholera from eating all that . . . she passed away two days later.

SANICHARI: Didn't you have her treated?

BIKHNI'S NEPHEW: We tried our best to persuade her to go to the hospital, but she just wouldn't agree.

SANICHARI: Is it that she wouldn't agree, or did fear of the expense keep you from taking her?

BIKHNI'S NEPHEW: Did my aunt leave any of her things here?

SANICHARI: Why d'you want to know?

BIKHNI'S NEPHEW: I'm her younger nephew . . . she was very fond of me, so I thought . . .

SANICHARI: When your aunt was roaming the streets alone with no one to help her, where were you then? (*Pause.*) Run along with you. If you leave now, you can catch the eight o'clock bus.

(*The* NEPHEW *glares at her angrily, then storms out.* SANICHARI *shuts the door behind him. She turns and begins to fold the black clothes and place them on the cot. All at once she breaks down. Harsh sobs tear through her. Gradually the intensity of the weeping eases. She gets up slowly and begins to fold the clothes again. The lights dim.*)

Scene Eleven

The whores' quarter. Morning. At stage left GANGU, CHAMPA, *and* SUKHI *are sitting, playing Snakes and Ladders, a board game. At stage right, another prostitute is seated, painting her nails. A transistor radio is blaring songs from a little stool. One woman is plucking out her gray hairs as she looks in a hand-held mirror. Two women are hanging saris up to dry.*

CHAMPA: Three . . . three . . . three . . . (*Rolls the dice.*) There, I got three! *Dhat*, it's four, not three!

GANGU: (*Yelling.*) Four means you're in the serpent's mouth! Go on, down you go, all the way do-ow-n!

CHAMPA: What d'you mean in the serpent's mouth, you cheat! Look, look properly—four moves bring me here!

GANGU: Rubbish! Gangu isn't a cheat like you! Here, it's my turn to roll.

(*She rolls the dice. From behind, one of the women hanging saris speaks up.*)

WOMAN: *Arre,* the water will finish, go and have your baths. You've been playing that game all morning!

SUKHI: Yes, yes, we're going, madam *pandit.* Why don't you finish washing your clothes first? (*She rolls the dice.*) There, I've reached a nice long ladder! Pitter patter pitter patter right to the top! Just like Kalua the pimp hoists Gulbadan right up to the sky!

GANGU: Jealous, are you? Go on, go on, it's your turn next.

(NASIBAN, *an old maidservant, enters, carrying a kettle of tea. She approaches the woman who is plucking out her gray hairs.*)

NASIBAN: *Arre,* how many can you remove? There'll be more tomorrow! Here, take your tea. And here's your twenty-five *paise.* Don't say later that I didn't return it to you!

(*She pours out tea for the women playing and sits down to watch the game.*)

CHAMPA: (*Yelling.*) That's it! I've won, I've reached Home! You two can carry on struggling, I'm off to have my bath.

(GULBADAN *enters.*)

GULBADAN: Hey, Nasiban, give me some tea.

(NASIBAN, *bringing her the tea, knocks against the mirror.*)

NASIBAN: *Arre,* why are you sitting right in the middle blocking the way? Go do this in your room.

NAILPOLISH WOMAN: So, Gulbadan, did you manage to get enough sleep?

GULBADAN: (*Stretching.*) No, how could I? Here, Nasiban, give me another cup.

NAILPOLISH WOMAN: When did the bastard leave?

GULBADAN: *Arre,* he brought me silver buttons and started begging and pleading . . . I took pity on him. Hey you, why're you raising such a ruckus?!

GANGU: There—there—there—straight into the longest snake's mouth!

CHAMPA: Down you go, all the way down!

GULBADAN: What's all the noise about? (*Suddenly her eye falls on the ribbon in* CHAMPA's *hair. She grabs hold of it.*) Why, you thief, you've been swiping things again!

CHAMPA: Swiping what?

GULBADAN: The bitch is always stealing from others and then acting innocent. This ribbon! Did your husband give it to you?

CHAMPA: Why you liar, I bought it in the market!

GULBADAN: Market my ass! Take it off this minute, you bitch! Go on, take it off!

(GULBADAN *grabs* CHAMPA *by the hair and drags her across the stage. The other women try to separate them. Meanwhile* SANICHARI *enters.*)

SANICHARI: Can someone tell me if Parbatia lives here?

GULBADAN: (*Noticing* SANICHARI.) What d'you want?

GANGU: *Arre*, I know you—weren't you one of the *rudali*s at Bhairo Singh's? Where's the other one, your friend?

SAEEDA: *Arre baap re baap*, how they cried! I still haven't forgotten it!

GULBADAN: No one's died here, what have you come here for?

SANICHARI: I want to meet Parbatia.

GULBADAN: There's no Parbatia here.

CHAMPA: Why are you lying? Doesn't that Parbatia from Tahad village stay here? Wait, I'll just call her.

GANGU: Why don't you sit down? (*Gives* SANICHARI *a stool.*) *Arre oh*, Nasiban, bring some tea! (*To* SANICHARI.) What's your name?

SANICHARI: Sanichari.

SAEEDA: What do you want with Parbatia?

(NASIBAN *brings the tea and hands it to* SANICHARI.)

GANGU: Here, have your tea.

(*As* NASIBAN *hands over the tea*, PARBATIA *enters, drying her long, wet hair.*)

PARBATIA: The bitch didn't even let me bathe in peace—who the hell is it? Showing up at this odd hour! (*As she throws back her hair she sees* SANICHARI.) What are you doing here?

SANICHARI: I have something urgent to talk to you about.

PARBATIA: There's nothing I want to hear from you. Go away.

SANICHARI: You haven't changed a bit! I came here to help you.

PARBATIA: I don't need your help! (*To the other women.*) This is my husband's mother . . . couldn't provide a square meal and says she wants to
help me! I'm not going anywhere with you, and that's final!

GANGU: What's all the fuss about? Why don't you at least hear her out?

SANICHARI: *Arre,* I haven't come here to take her home . . . Actually, I've
come here to help all of you . . . I'm here to offer you work as *rudalis.*

PARBATIA: I spit on your *rudali* work! *Arre,* you expect us to go and cry
over the bodies of the very men who've ruined us!

SANICHARI: At least hear what I have to say, Bahu—

PARBATIA: How dare you call me your *bahu!* I have a name—Parbatia. I
work as a whore and I'll continue in this line of work. I won't go off to
cry over someone's dead body! (*She exits.*)

GULBADAN: The old woman is crazy. Why the hell should we give up our
regular income to go cry over some dead man?!

SANICHARI: Why not? You stand in line for a measly fifty *paise. Arre,* does
this work of yours earn you enough to fill your stomach? Does it bring
you self-respect? Ask her. (*Gestures towards* GANGU.) Did she get to eat
two square meals yesterday? No clothes, no food, no self-respect . . .

CHAMPA: People don't die every day, do they? At least we work and earn
every day.

GRAY-HAIRED WOMAN: Listen to her! As if there's a queue of clients lined
up at her door!

CHAMPA: No, I won't go. This *rudali* work is too uncertain. There may be a
job today, but what happens tomorrow?

SANICHARI: You're still young today—what happens tomorrow? Look,
this is work, you hear me? Work. Better work than yours. Hard work
like grinding grain in the *chakki,* splitting logs of wood, digging the
earth . . .

SAEEDA: Any money in it?

SANICHARI: Yes, you make money, you get grain, clothes, the lot.

GANGU: Where do we have to go? Who's dead? Tell us that first . . .

SANICHARI: Gambhir Singh of Naugad.

GULBADAN: He's dead? Really?

SANICHARI: Yes, he passed away early this morning. His *kriya* will be held
in grand style. Money and gifts will flow like water. Come, all of you
come with me.

GRAY-HAIRED WOMAN: How much money will we make?

SANICHARI: Ten *rupees* a day, plus grain and clothes, and your meals as well.

GULBADAN: Whether anyone else goes or not, I'm definitely going. It's my father who's dead, you hear? My father! The man who ruined me, who ruined my mother! How can I not mourn at his funeral?

CHAMPA: Will we get colored cloth?

SANICHARI: Not colored, but definitely black cloth—

GANGU: *Arre,* you can sell it in the market and buy colored cloth instead.

(*They all come up and gather around* SANICHARI.)

SAEEDA: He's no kith and kin of mine, though.

CHAMPA: *Arre,* so what! Come on, we'll arrange that as well!

GANGU: Hey, I've never done anything like this before, why don't you show us how?

SANICHARI: When you start, weep as if you've lost someone close to you, someone dear to your heart. Beat your breast and cry out with such feeling that their blood runs cold! Give it everything you have, make their hair stand on end! (*She flings out her arms in demonstration, and lets out a loud, mournful wail.*) Hai re!

(*The rest of the women imitate her.*)

ALL: *Hai re!*

(*Lights dim.*)

Scene Twelve

A band is heard playing offstage. Hustle and bustle on stage. As the lights come on, Gambhir Singh's corpse is seen lying on a cot, heaped with flowers. Behind it, some people are burning incense. To the left chairs are arranged, on which the thakurs LACHMAN SINGH, MADHO SINGH, NATHUNI SINGH *and their relatives are seated. Behind Lachman Singh stands his armed* BODYGUARD. *The* pandit *is chanting* shlokas *and sprinkling everyone with holy water. One of the* zamindars *is laying a garland on the corpse.* BIJUA *and other* VILLAGERS *are present. There is a strong stench emanating from the body, which is affecting everyone. The* zamindar *covers his face with a hanky and goes to sit beside the others. Gambhir Singh's nephew and heir,* GAJANAN, *is directing the arrangements.* MADHO SINGH *is standing with him.*

PANDIT: Gambhir Singh took leave of this world at an auspicious time, during the waxing phase of the moon. His place in Paradise is assured.

LACHMAN SINGH: Panditji, a great soul like his is definitely destined for Paradise. After all, he spent his whole life in the service of our poorer brethren and the suffering multitudes.

MADHO SINGH: Naugad has been orphaned today! Don't distress yourself, Gajanan, we're all with you in your time of trouble. (*Pats* GAJANAN *on the back.*)

BIJUA: Our master had a splendid life, and an even more splendid death!

MAN: We're bereft at his passing. We've lost our main support. (*Shouts.*) Hey there! The incense has finished! Bring fresh incense!

GAJANAN: Here, Lachman *babu.*

(*He invites* LACHMAN SINGH *to lay a garland on the corpse.* LACHMAN *moves forward to do so. His gun-toting* BODYGUARD *follows him.* MADHO SINGH *moves to stand behind the* thakurs. *A* BOY *hands* LACHMAN *a garland. As he approaches the corpse, the stink of decomposing flesh hits him. He flinches.*)

LACHMAN SINGH: Gajanan, didn't you make arrangements to sprinkle some *attar* or something? My brother was so fond of perfumes! Go, someone, fetch four or five bottles of *attar.* (*Handing his garland to the bodyguard.*) Go on, you do it.

(LACHMAN SINGH *returns to his chair as his* BODYGUARD *places the garland on the corpse. He too winces at the smell, holding his nose, and then returns to his place. Meanwhile the band has stopped playing.*)

NATHUNI SINGH: *Arre,* Gajanan, why has the band stopped?

LACHMAN SINGH: Someone go and check. Have those bastards been paid to sit still?

GAJANAN: Hey, Bhagirath, you go and see.

MADHO SINGH: Your inheritance papers are all in order, I hope, Gajanan?

GAJANAN: Oh yes, that was all done while he was still alive. My *chacha* was very generous.

(BHAGIRATH *comes running in. The sound of several voices raised in mourning can be heard offstage.*)

BHAGIRATH: (*To* GAJANAN.) Malik, Malik! A whole mob of *rudalis* is coming this way, crying at the top of their voices!

(BIJUA *runs to the door with the incense burner in his hand. He peers out. There is an air of expectancy on stage. People start talking excitedly.* GAJANAN *tries to calm them down. A crowd of* RUDALIS *enters, swathed in black from head to toe. They circle the corpse, wailing dramatically. Then they grasp the cot and sit down. Pairing off, they hold each other and sit down stage left, and begin to beat their foreheads and breasts rhythmically in exaggerated, stylized movements. They stand up, beating their breasts and wailing in unison, enjoying the rapt attention they are getting. They sing in unison.*)

RUDALIS:

> *Hai re! Hai re!*
> *Hai,* the master! *Hai,* father of us all!
> *Hai, hai,* smash all your bangles!
> *Hai, hai,* take off your toe-rings!
> *Hai, hai,* wipe off your *alta!*
> *Hai, hai,* wipe off your *sindoor!*
> *Hai, hai,* Naugad *raja, hai, hai!**

(*While this is going on,* GULBADAN *shrugs the black cloth off her head and deliberately holds* MADHO SINGH's *eyes. He responds by getting up and surreptitiously making his way to her.* LACHMAN SINGH *notices this byplay and gets up, but then goes to the head of the corpse.*)

LACHMAN SINGH: Come on, come on, let's take the body out.

(MADHO SINGH *turns around. There is a stir on stage. The zamindars move forward to shoulder the body.* GAJANAN *is amongst them. Some people begin to shower the corpse with* khoi *and coins. They begin to chant "Ram nam satya hai." The chant mingles with the wailing of the* rudalis. LACHMAN SINGH *and*

---

*Each of these acts is a social ritual of widowhood. Since bangles, *sindoor, alta,* and toe-rings have traditionally been symbols of marriage, a woman breaks her bangles and removes her other ornaments on the death of her husband.

the PANDIT *lead the way, followed by the pall bearers, then the other people, with the wailing* RUDALIS *making up the rear. They move in procession across the stage.* SANICHARI *is standing at stage left.* GULBADAN *slips out of the group of rudalis and goes up to* MADHO SINGH, *who is lingering behind the others. The two of them exchange a few words, then leave together.* SANICHARI *looks at them and then down at the edibles left lying about. The procession exits.* DULAN *comes on, carrying a bundle of foodstuffs, which he places beside the silent* SANICHARI.)

DULAN: Here, take your stuff. Don't be late. I'm off to the cremation ground. You'll get the money later. (*He exits.*)

(SANICHARI *lifts the bundle and slowly begins to make her way out. An incense burner is lying overturned. She straightens it. She sees a coin lying beside it. She picks it up. Looks at it. Smiles sadly. Knots it decisively into her clothing. Faces the audience resolutely. Blackout.*)

The Wooden Cart

by Tripurari Sharma

TRANSLATED FROM HINDI BY MOHIT SATYANAND

CHARACTERS
(in order of appearance)

SWEEPER

WATER CARRIER

KASIM

MADAN

PROCESSIONISTS

GUARD

COIN CHANGER

PRIEST

MAN

WOMAN

NARRATOR

NARAYAN

ANNAY-MA

ACTOR 1

ACTOR 2

AUDIENCE MEMBER

KANU

RAMA

CRONE

DAUGHTER-IN-LAW

OLD MAN

VILLAGERS

KANU'S HUSBAND

MIRA

ORDERLY

ASTROLOGER 1

ASTROLOGER 2

ANUJ

ROSHAN

PRABHA

POLICE OFFICER

POLICE SERGEANT

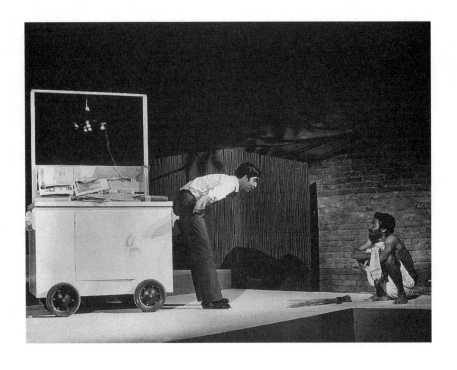

Actors from the National School of Drama in *The Wooden Cart*
Photographs courtesy of the National School of Drama, Delhi

Scene One

An open stage with three or four spectators. Between them, several paths lead to the stage, in particular, a large one, which a SWEEPER *is sweeping. A* WATER CARRIER *moves out of the sweeper's way with his load. Loknath temple in the background. Early morning.* KASIM, *a leper, spreads thin white garments on the floor, anchoring them with stones. Hidden inside a thick blanket, but inwardly excited,* MADAN *slowly makes his appearance.*

MADAN: Isn't this where the procession begins?

SWEEPER: That's right, sir.

(MADAN *moves off. Meanwhile, people are collecting. The temple* GUARD *appears.*)

GUARD: The place isn't swept yet? People are here; it's time for the procession, and—

SWEEPER: At least I'm making myself useful. Unlike your lordship.

GUARD: Shaddup and get to work. Get it? (*To* KASIM.) And you! You think we clean the place so you can beg for alms? (KASIM *collects his clothes and moves away. After a while, begins laying them out again.*) Didn't you hear me? Beat it. (*To himself.*) If they had their way, they'd walk right into the temple.

SWEEPER: What's the matter? Didn't you collect last week?

GUARD: You think I'd touch their money? If I had my way—

SWEEPER: (*To* KASIM. *Laughing.*) Hey, I'm untouchable too. He won't take water from me, but he'll sure take his cut of my wages. (*To* GUARD, *who is glowering.*) Come on, hit me. Hit me. But then you'll have to touch me.

(KASIM *laughs.*)

GUARD: People like you should be lined up and shot. Like useless horses.

SWEEPER: Yeah! But the poor pious souls—to whom will they give their alms?

(*Meanwhile, more people have gathered on stage. Among them, a* COIN CHANGER. KASIM *gives him some coins and collects bills in exchange. Others change paper currency for coins. A* PRIEST *appears.*)

PRIEST: An audience, sir? Only fifty-one *rupees*! An excellent audience, sir—real close to God. No problem. So close you can touch his feet.

GUARD: (*To* KASIM.) Changed your coins? (KASIM *pretends not to hear, but the* GUARD *pursues him and extracts his weekly turf fee.*)

PRIEST: (*To* MAN.) Where are you from, sir? Just need your father's name, and the town you're from, and I'll tell you all the rest.

MAN: I'm in a hurry.

(*Clamor of flower sellers and sweet-merchants.*)

PRIEST: (*Muttering.*) It's time for the morning prayers, and God's still asleep.

WOMAN: When's the procession?

PRIEST: Who knows?

(*Just then, a hubbub. A small crowd, singing a hymn in procession, pull a temple chariot carrying Loknath [an incarnation of Shiva] through the audience. They are followed by a lone man, who is* NARRATOR *of the play and producer-director of the theater company.*)

PROCESSIONISTS:

Baba Loknath, we serve at your feet.

Yea—Kailashnath, we serve at your feet.

Hail, hail, Mahadev, hail, hail, hail.

Bholeydev, at your feet we serve.

Hail, hail, hail Mahadev, hail, hail Bholey Baba.

He'll grant us Grace, Bholey Baba, grant us Grace.

Hail, hail, hail Mahadev, hail, hail, hail.

(*As conch shells sound, drums are beaten, and voices chant, the religious fervor rises. Some circumambulate the chariot; others prostrate themselves before it.*

From a distance, NARAYAN *propels himself through the audience in a cart re-peatedly proclaiming, "Jai Mahadev." The cart is one-and-a-half feet long, a homemade affair of wooden planks, mounted on wheels that are three to four inches high.** ANNAY-MA *follows. Both are aged lepers.* KASIM *moves toward them, ringing his little aluminum bowls on the ground. The crowd is trans-ported.* ANNAY-MA *is swaying, repeatedly banging her head on the ground.* MADAN, *who is watching quietly, takes off his shoes and tries to peer up at the Shivling on top of the chariot.)*

GUARD: *(Glares at Madan's shoes; then, understanding.)* Hey! Catch him! A leper's come in—the chariot—catch him!

(A commotion results. MADAN *scurries here and there. He hides inside the chariot, while people are looking for him outside.* TWO ACTORS *stand in a cor-ner of the stage area and make fun of the audience's reactions.)*

ACTOR 1:   Look! Look how they've screwed up their noses.

ACTOR 2:   Are they dusting off their shirts yet? Look—how tightly she's pulling her *sari* around herself.

ACTOR 1:   Look at this one—he's going green around the gills.

ACTOR 2:   And he's looking at his watch. Seems the play isn't going to pack the halls. *(To* NARRATOR.*)* Sir, please clear the stage.

NARRATOR: What for?

ACTOR 1:   The audience is getting restless.

NARRATOR: *(Scolding.)* You've really screwed it up, haven't you? *(To audi-ence.)* Well, the play's begun: you've seen how Madan wanted to touch the feet of Loknath, but had to hide because of the crowd.

ACTOR 1:   What a hero—a leper!

NARRATOR: Just take the word—*leper.* How it reeks of hatred and fear.

ACTOR 2:   Be careful! These are Delhi folk—refined and squeaky clean.

NARRATOR: The worst kind! *(To audience.)* Let's hear it from you, folks. What is your opinion of the happenings on stage?

ACTOR 1:   They've seen this scene—every day of their lives. And ignored it. Doesn't that tell you what they think?

ACTOR 2:   Hey—you don't call an audience in to insult them.

---

*Once a leper's feet are wasted, he transports himself in such a cart, usually with the help of a block of wood in each hand; the blocks also serve to protect his hands.

NARRATOR: Our audience, our honored guests.

(*An* AUDIENCE MEMBER *rises and comes forward.*)

AUDIENCE MEMBER: Excuse me. Why all the praying and chanting?

ACTOR 1: Because!

AUDIENCE MEMBER: What is the motivation for it? (*Points to the play program.*) On the one hand you talk of presenting a scientific point of view, and on the other, you shove in all this mumbo-jumbo.

ACTOR 2: It's a matter of form. All modern plays begin like this. It's the contemporary style.

AUDIENCE MEMBER: Forget about style; I'm talking about substance.

NARRATOR: The eternal question! From where do we begin? From our English education or our own tradition?

AUDIENCE MEMBER: Tradition or superstition?

NARRATOR: Whatever. But, are we to forget those forms of behavior that are the product of our milieu?

ACTOR 1: (*To* AUDIENCE MEMBER.) Save it for after the show.

ACTOR 2: (*To* NARRATOR.) Yeah—you're wasting our time. And the audience's.

NARRATOR: We have nothing to hide from our audience. Are we not creatures of the same world? Friends! My story is a few years old. The setting: a small town. The home: my own. The money: tight. And then, this confounded theater bug. You get the drift. Anyway, I got myself a part-time job as a medical assistant—in the field of leprosy. Yeah—at first I found it a little weird too. All those notions about leprosy—I had them too. But, as I learned about the disease, and its patients, things changed.

I want to tell you about some of the people I met at the time—about Madan and Kanu. After one bout with the disease, they're both well now. Madan you've already seen in a somewhat peculiar situation. And here's Kanu.

(KANU *rises from the audience; draped in a shawl, she comes on stage.*)

NARRATOR: How's your mother? Happy to see you?

KANU: Ye-e-es . . .

NARRATOR: (*Trying to lessen the embarrassment.*) Husband? Kid?

KANU: I didn't make it there—didn't have the time.

NARRATOR: Well, you've made it here. (*Indicates the audience.*) Won't you talk to them?

KANU: You want me to blubber in front of all these people? Oh, I get it! It's to be a colorful drama, bursting with tears and human feeling.

NARRATOR: I won't force you, but what's the point of silence? There's no harm in their knowing.

KANU: (*Hesitating.*) It's all so hard. And I don't want to cry.

NARRATOR: Take it nice and easy. They'll figure out the rest.

KANU: (*To audience.*) I live at home now—with my parents . . . Those days, my friends, they still mean a lot to me. It's all so confusing . . . Where do I begin?

NARRATOR: Let's begin with Kanu, the second character in our presentation. She lived in a remote village in Bengal. Married a few years, babe in arms, a home full of daughters and daughters-in-law.

(*Some actors drag the chariot off stage. The others prepare the stage for the next scene, using a few props, such as a child's cradle. KANU takes off her shawl and, handing it to an actor, enters the scene.*)

Scene Two

The home of a middle-class peasant family. The men are away. A tableau of women: preparing a beauty paste, folding clothes, a CRONE massaging the elder DAUGHTER-IN-LAW. KANU peers into the cradle then turns to RAMA, her sister-in-law, and begins to wet her hair.

RAMA: Wow! That feels great. My head was feeling so heavy.

CRONE: (*Telling a story.*) The king would pay no attention to the queen. He'd come home, eat his fill, and snore his head off. The poor queen couldn't figure it out.

ALL: I'd rather go home to my parents.

DAUGHTER-IN-LAW: (*Calling offstage.*) Shyamu! Hurry up with the water. Haven't you finished your work yet?

KANU: I hope you're going to leave some water for us.

DAUGHTER-IN-LAW: Me? First we'll all have to wait for Rama to make herself beautiful. (*To* CRONE.) Why have you stopped? I haven't got all day.

CRONE: Why are you chattering so much? (*To* KANU.) Come on, your turn now. (RAMA *tosses her hair back; we see her face.*) Attagirl. Now she looks like a bride.

KANU: Mind which village she'll be entering.

CRONE: I was the one who was told "give the girl the once over."

RAMA: Go ahead—look for all you're worth. Pass me a towel. (*Dries her hair.*)

DAUGHTER-IN-LAW: Shyamu! Are you dead? Do you hear me? (*Gets up and collects her things.*)

CRONE: (*To* KANU.) Why are you avoiding me? Come and sit. I won't gobble you up.

KANU: Pamma first. What do you say, Pamma?

CRONE: You're getting too big for your boots—he doesn't need no massage. (*Yanks her down, places a hand on her neck.* KANU *screams.*) See? You're all knotted up. Good Lord—you gotta take care of yourself. Your arms are so loose, in a few months the flesh will be swinging from them.

KANU: Enough!

CRONE: Now you lay there—quiet like. (*Resumes her tale.*) He was just getting up, when the queen said . . . (*Suddenly.*) What's this?

KANU: On my back? I must have hurt myself.

CRONE: Uh unh. Anyplace else? (KANU *shows her arm. The others crowd around.*)

ONE OF THEM: Hurt yourself?

DAUGHTER-IN-LAW: (*With a grimace.*) Poor you! Does it pain?

KANU: No, not at all. (*Laughs.*)

CRONE: (*A little harshly.*) It must pain a little. Here! (*Takes a pin from her hair and jabs.*)

KANU: No.

CRONE: (*Touching her torso.*) Now?

KANU: Yes. (*Looking at her.*)

CRONE: Didn't feel nothing there? (*Touches her arm, disbelieving.*)

ONE OF THEM: Her blood's gone rotten.

DAUGHTER-IN-LAW: Us folks don't care for these spots. They're the sign of the devil.

(*Whispering, the women move to the side.* CRONE *makes to leave.*)

KANU: (*Loudly.*) What's happened to me?

CRONE: Seeing's we're from the same village, I won't say nothing. Now, you keep quiet about it.

KANU: There's little chance, now. But nothing's going to happen.

CRONE: Ssh! There's no telling when trouble boils over. Look, I'll give you a powerful charm. But it'll cost—these are hard times.

(KANU *removes the bracelet from her child, Pamma, and hands it over.*)

CRONE: And seeing as you love Pamma, I wouldn't go near him.

KANU: Won't I get found out?

CRONE: Such a charm I'll give you . . . quick, get me a bowl and some rice.

KANU: Don't tell my husband.

CRONE: Hasn't he noticed?

KANU: Must have touched . . .

CRONE: Don't stop him, or he'll figure something's the matter. Now look up and pray to the great god Loknath. Touch your forehead to the ground twenty-one times.

(KANU *follows her instructions. The other women look on with interest.*)

RAMA: What's happened to her?

DAUGHTER-IN-LAW: I told you—stay away from her. She's no good.

RAMA: Isn't it enough, her feeling poorly? You don't have to bad-mouth her.

DAUGHTER-IN-LAW: It's us the world is going to be bad-mouthing soon. (*Hotly picks up a bucket and moves off.*)

CRONE: (*Looking carefully at* KANU.) So young and sweet-faced!

KANU: (*Looking down.*) If these spots have a name, tell me. I've not hidden them from you—please, tell me. Do you know? (*Now looks up at the old woman, intent.*) Tell me.

CRONE: Ever been to that hill, the old landlord's place? The one whose hands have rotted away? He'll tell you.

KANU: I'm not going there. He's a leper. (CRONE *laughs lightly.*) Lord knows what sins he's paying for. I'll find what I need in this house.

CRONE: These gentle eyes—like a she-deer's. Who can tell what they've seen. (*Leaves.*)

KANU: (*Moving towards her child.*) You don't have them, do you? (*About to touch the baby, then withdraws.*) Oh, Ma, didn't you see? Or did you think to pass me on to another family?

(*To audience.*) The days passed, the spots spread. My hands were still strong—they could do anything, except tell me what they felt. (*Laughing.*) Like Ma and Pa—anything he wanted, she'd do. (*Pause. To her hands.*) Speak. Why don't you speak? When you keep quiet, the hurt goes deeper. (*Getting lost in her own thoughts.*) My finger is getting crooked . . . should I go ask that . . . thing . . . on the hill?

(KANU *moves across stage to an open shack, in which sits a bundle of an* OLD MAN, *draped in a torn blanket, his hands and feet hidden from view. Battered old pots and pans lie at a distance. Still some distance from him,* KANU *hesitates. She is holding a pan and some cloth. Silence, then the* OLD MAN *senses someone.*)

OLD MAN: That's the path to the village.

KANU: That's the path I took. (*Steps forward.*) I brought some rice and white cloth.

OLD MAN: Leave it outside.

KANU: The crows will get it . . . Why not bring it in?

OLD MAN: I will. When you leave.

KANU: Now, while I'm here.

OLD MAN: Have mercy. . . . Please leave.

KANU: My sister-in-law is about to be engaged, but . . . (*Coming forward.*) Do you know these spots? Have you ever seen them before?

OLD MAN: On many bodies.

KANU: Your own?

OLD MAN: How could I see my own back? Anyhow, now I'm like the bark of a tree.

KANU: Show me! I want to see.

OLD MAN: You're a strange one, wanting to see an old man's wounds.

KANU: Why did the crone tell me to come here? What secrets do you know?

OLD MAN: Don't you smell the rotting flesh? (*Laughs.*) In time, you'll know it well.

KANU: Be quiet. (*Makes to go.*)

OLD MAN: (*Quietly picking up the cloth.*) White cloth? For this body?

Praised be the great god Loknath. (*Drapes the cloth around himself; it flutters in the breeze.*) You've forgiven this sinner.

KANU: What?

OLD MAN: (*Lost to himself.*) He's heard me. Now . . . (*Turns his head up to the sky.*)

KANU: Why aren't you dead yet?

OLD MAN: (*To himself.*) Now he will come—into this body. I will shed this dead skin. And on this stump will grow pink fingers. Baby pink, too small for this man's hand, but whole fingers. And on my palm he'll draw a Line of Fate. (KANU *laughs.*) You have no faith. He said He would call me. Lay His hand upon my back. Then, every pore of my body will come alive, dance with the tongues of fire.

KANU: Who will prepare your funeral pyre?*

OLD MAN: I need no one. He loves me. On this hill he will stand and open his arms. I'll melt into his light, pass through the fire as though it were water. What peace! Like taking off a dirty bandage and putting on a fresh one. The pyre is ready. I climb on it, light as a cloud. He said he'd send for me—soon. You'll see, all of you—he'll stand on the edge, and take me in. The sky will open, snow will fall, melted gold will flow down the hill . . .

(*Religious music swells.* KANU *exits. Excitement in the village.* VILLAGERS *shout to one another.*)

FIRST VILLAGER: The old geezer wants wood to burn himself.

SECOND: Burn his hut. That'll send him directly to heaven.

FIRST: It's his brothers he should be asking. Bastards took all his land.

SECOND: Them! You won't even get a funeral feast out of them.

THIRD: How did the old bugger feed himself all these years?

FIRST: He must have stashed something away. Let's kill some goats.

SECOND: And get hold of some booze.

THIRD: Shame on you. A soul is passing over to the Lord.

FOURTH: D'you really think he'll burn alive? Won't he run?

FIRST: Let him try. Look at this stick. If he moves, I'll . . . (*Wields his stick.*)

---

*There have been cases of lepers preparing their own funeral pyres and immolating themselves, convinced that Loknath, the god of lepers, has sent for them. When Kanu brings the old leper some white cloth, he interprets this as a call from Loknath.

FOURTH: Poor chap—doesn't stand a chance.

SECOND: He had it coming—whoring around all night.

THIRD: Next morning, you'd find him in a gutter, frothing at the mouth, feet all cut up.

FIRST: He'd get drunk and roar like a wild elephant.

FOURTH: I've heard he stole cows from the temple.

SECOND: Stole them, and slaughtered them. My father caught him red-handed; made him spit out the bones. A sinner if there was one. No wonder he has stumps for hands.

FOURTH: And then? Did the cow come alive? (*The others glare at him.*) Maybe there'll be a feast today . . .

THIRD: Better be, if he wants our blessings. And if there's booze, he can take my share of heaven too!

KANU: (*Listening from a corner of the house.*) They're just waiting for him to die to set their tongues loose—all the filth of their minds, smeared on him. What they won't say about me. (*Imagining others talking about her.*) A whore! She'd go with any man. Heaven knows, she'd put a spell on her husband. She lay in bed all day, getting fat. Her sister-in-law was all set to marry her lover. That's why she drank poison. (*Getting excited.*) Let them bark. I'm clean; I can hide the spots. But, this finger? Between these two, like this, if I sit like a madam? (*Conceals the bent finger under her chin, and sits down in a sprawl.*)

(RAMA *and the* DAUGHTER-IN-LAW *enter, with an oil-lamp.*)

DAUGHTER-IN-LAW: Aren't you going to watch him burn?

KANU: Are you going all dressed up like that?

DAUGHTER-IN-LAW: Who knows, her in-laws may show up. We don't have circuses like this every day.

RAMA: Come with us! It's better than being here alone.

DAUGHTER-IN-LAW: Not alone—your brother'll be back. Anyways, she scares so easy!

RAMA: Why don't you come after dinner? You can smell the fire all the way here!

KANU: (*Disgusted and agitated.*) Why don't you go?

DAUGHTER-IN-LAW: (*Leaving, but loud enough for Kanu to hear.*) She can't hide it any longer—everybody knows. (*To* RAMA.) I always said he should have married my cousin, but no! He wanted this one. Well, I hope he's having fun now.

(*Hubbub of crowds heading for the funeral fire.* KANU *leans against the child's cradle and sings a lullaby, her voice agitated, as if to drown the noise outside. Then, in an effort to change her mood, she settles her clothes and lets her hair loose. Then she turns down the lamp, lights an incense stick, moves to the mirror, puts her hair in a bun, and adds some flowers. Her* HUSBAND *enters.* KANU *smiles and proffers water for him to wash his hands. He doesn't move. Though taken aback, she hides her feelings and continues to do her hair.*)

HUSBAND: (*Staring.*) They were asking about you.

KANU: They're taking a girl. There's going to be questions. (*Moves to the mirror.*)

HUSBAND: That old woman from your village—she said something.

KANU: (*Changing her tone.*) You must be tired.

HUSBAND: I was, till I went to the hill. There's booze aplenty, and folks coming and going. (*Coming to her.*) You didn't go? Rama looked like she was getting married, and now it's off. How did you hide it? (*Turns up the lamp.*) I can't touch you; might as well look at you. (*Noise outside.*) They're burning him.

KANU: He's burning himself.

HUSBAND: You can see the firelight. It must be getting dark on the hill . . . So what if my sister's marriage is off . . . I'll make your fire with sandalwood. Come, I'll take you there.

KANU: No. They're not good people.

HUSBAND: Oh! And you're good? Let me see . . . where've you hidden your disease? (KANU *moves away.*) Others got to know before me.

KANU: You never had time.

HUSBAND: So you wanted me to rot too? You look so innocent.

KANU: I haven't changed.

HUSBAND: You'll still be saying that when you dish the food out with your stumps. I'm not going to die. What did your father have against us? We didn't do him any harm. And you—have you no shame—living here like a queen?

KANU: What's happened to you? How can you change like this?

HUSBAND: Couldn't you take your hell elsewhere?

KANU: If something happened to you, do you think I'd turn away?

HUSBAND: If I wanted, I could push you into that fire. Nobody could stop me. (*Noise outside.*) Must've burned—there's lots of folks. He won't be saved.

KANU: Maybe it'll rain. Why don't you find out? Maybe there's a cure.

HUSBAND: Tomorrow, you go back to your folks, or rot someplace else. Folks're going to be asking why this happened to us.

KANU: Pamma . . .

HUSBAND: Is he your father's son for him to rear?

KANU: But he's my child—I'm not going to eat him up. (*Silence.*) When Rama's married, can I come back then?

HUSBAND: Why?

KANU: These spots'll go, I promise. Can I come back then?

HUSBAND: They're not going to go.

KANU: I can still do everything myself: sweep the floor, scrub the pots, split the wood . . .

HUSBAND: A woman it makes me sick to touch—I've no use for her.

KANU: Will Pamma have a new mother?

HUSBAND: Don't you have old friends, whom you left behind when you got married? We'll see how friendly they are now. Should I take you home now, all dressed up like this?

(RAMA *and the* DAUGHTER-IN-LAW *enter.*)

HUSBAND: Has he burned?

DAUGHTER-IN-LAW: We couldn't stay to the end. Folks're saying Rama's wedding's off!

HUSBAND: They've fixed themselves up for elsewhere.

DAUGHTER-IN-LAW: That's why I kept saying the wedding should be soon. Didn't you ask what's to become of this poor thing?

HUSBAND: They heard something about us that . . .

(KANU *moves away; all three glower at her as if she's committed a crime.*)

DAUGHTER-IN-LAW: What terrible folks.

HUSBAND: I'll go back to them.

(*They exit, leaving* KANU *alone.*)

KANU: (*To audience.*) If I went home, Ma and Pa'd just look at each other, quiet like. The neighbors'd come. I didn't want no more shame. I left that night—didn't tell a soul. It's not as if they'd come after me—everyone's happy when a storm clears. (*Leaves.*)

Scene Three

Loknath's chariot. Night. Soft background sounds of people praying—"Bholey Baba, grant us Grace." The voices of the GUARD *and the* SWEEPER, *apparently looking for* MADAN. *He peeps out of the chariot, then emerges.*

MADAN: Way to go, Loknath—I love your style. (*Examines his wounds.*) With all these new followers hounding you, what's a poor tramp like me to do. (*Thinks for a bit.*) Strange folks—to be scared of me. If only they knew how scared I am—LEPER! APEMAN! (*Looks for his shoes, but they aren't there.*) They stole my shoes as well? Make your pile guys, this here is the bottomless vault of the great Loknath. And what am I to do with these feet of mine? When I die, I'm going to hack them off and leave them on your altar. (*Gestures to Loknath.*) But how do I keep them going till then? (*Takes out a gold bracelet from his pocket.*) Still got the gold, haven't lost my mind, haven't gone blind—I guess that's enough. I can figure things out, even move about. Is there a chemist someplace? I need to tidy these up before I feed my face. My trusty fellow travelers, these feet that never tire!

(*Enter the* SWEEPER. *He casts the beam from his flashlight about and catches* MADAN *in the beam.* MADAN *cowers and tosses him a coin.*)

GUARD: (*Off.*) Find him yet?
SWEEPER: (*Gestures to* MADAN *for more money, which he gets. Then.*) No. No one here. (*To* MADAN.) This is the leper colony. The hospital's that way.
MADAN: Hospital? (*The* SWEEPER *is gone.*) Whom to ask? (*He is alone on the stage. Addresses the audience.*) Brother! Is there a hospital here some-place? A first-aid center? A doctor's clinic? I don't mind if it's pricey. Don't think I'm broke. I may be starving, I may be bleeding, but that's something else. Brother! I'm not pan-handling. Uh-unh, I don't need

your tears. Got a wristwatch, got some gold. Stop and listen to me, hear what I need! Sirs! I'm a stranger in these parts, I don't know these streets! (*Voice rising, gets more aggressive.*)

NARRATOR: (*Rushing in.*) Don't shout.

MADAN: Can't you see—I can't walk anymore.

NARRATOR: (*Calling offstage.*) Send the doctor! He should have been here already. Doctor?

ACTOR: (*Pokes his head in briefly from offstage.*) No doctor. You'll have to do without. I think he's gone to a convention.

NARRATOR: Now what? See, that's how it is—gone when you need them most. Make them responsible, and they're off to a convention.

MADAN: Can't you hear me? I need help.

NARRATOR: (*Picking up a first-aid box.*) OK. I'm going to help you.

MADAN: That's your job. I don't need no pity, and you won't get no thanks.

NARRATOR: Sure! (*Smiling.*) You coulda come earlier. (*Looks at his hands.*)

MADAN: Don't touch. Don't you know?

NARRATOR: Sure I know. (*The two look at each other.*) You're not half as fearsome as you make out.

MADAN: I became that way—the filth, these charms, this hair. "Apeman!" they call me.

NARRATOR: You've gotta cut your hair.

MADAN: No, only after . . . (*Then, disappointed.*) I don't know when.

NARRATOR: (*Laughing.*) OK brother, I'm going to cure you.

MADAN: Been drinking too much? Go find another sucker.

NARRATOR: I'll drink now, to your health. OK? (*Begins bandaging him.*)

MADAN: I'll do it myself. (*Tries, but gets into a tangle.*) Kinda got used to rags, I guess.

NARRATOR: That's a love you'll have to leave. (*Snips bandages with scissors.*) Got something to eat?

MADAN: Got lotsa rocks.

NARRATOR: Do they taste good? (MADAN *gets angry;* NARRATOR *laughs.*) See—no pity from me. (MADAN *reddens; tears well up.*) You must have seen a lot of that—pity.

MADAN: I ran from it. It's not enough . . .

NARRATOR: You set them free.

MADAN: It wasn't them—I stole away. He made me leave school—my Pa did. Four years they kept me locked away, so visitors wouldn't see me. Ma just had to see me and she'd burst into tears. Night after night, her crying would keep me awake. First the stench, and then . . .

NARRATOR: You'll sleep well tonight. She's crying, but you won't hear her.

MADAN: I was like the snake god: feed it milk, but keep it in it's hole.

NARRATOR: You want to come home with me?

MADAN: You have space?

NARRATOR: Enough for you.

MADAN: You're really not scared?

NARRATOR: Of what?

MADAN: It's infectious.

NARRATOR: Are you a doctor?

MADAN: Well that's what they say.

NARRATOR: And you believe it?

MADAN: Yes . . . no . . . but how can I come over? We're not related, not even friends. And I'm in no shape to go visiting. I stopped calling on people, stopped being called.

NARRATOR: Stand up. Let's see if you're comfortable walking. (MADAN *does so easily.*)

MADAN: The treatment you were talking about . . . does it work?

NARRATOR: If you want it to.

MADAN: (*Perplexed.*) Will folks start calling me over? I won't hesitate . . .

NARRATOR: You could have come earlier.

MADAN: And now?

NARRATOR: You've come now. That's enough. The past is gone forever. What's lost cannot be found—like money that's spent.

MADAN: (*Looking at his hands and feet.*) What's gone is gone?

NARRATOR: The treatment will clear the infection inside you—the sores, the patches, the bacteria—they'll all be gone.

MADAN: But will people believe me when I tell them? How will I make them understand? Most won't come near.

NARRATOR: So if your neighbors don't like the smell, you stop cooking fish?

MADAN: I want to live among other people. But if they don't want me to . . .

NARRATOR: Live in a cave, for all I care—but your hands and feet—they're yours alone. Look after them, and you'll have their use forever. But if they become stumps, no one's going to be happy feeding you. Then, you'll need all the pity you can find.

MADAN: I've had it with talking to myself.

NARRATOR: Try me. Imagine I'm a friend. (*They look at each other.*)

MADAN: If the disease was the crime, then the sentence should be its cure. (*To* NARRATOR.) Tell me about this treatment of yours. Tomorrow and the day after—that's all the time I'll give it.

NARRATOR: Four years for the great Loknath, and I don't even get four days? (*Laughs. A footfall. The* GUARD'S *whistle.* MADAN *hides. The* NARRATOR *smiles. Then the whistling stops, and* MADAN *emerges.*)

MADAN: I feel like a thief. Maybe I should've thanked my family for locking me away—saving me from the likes of this man. Watch out! A snake's been let loose—be careful!

NARRATOR: So what do you know about snakes? Most are not poisonous.

MADAN: You won't have me caught? Look, I'm not a leper. Just . . . these. (*Helplessly shows his hands and feet.*) Not in a leper's colony. I'll live here, with you.

NARRATOR: That's just what I said. Let's go. (*They leave.*)

MADAN: Have you cured anyone else?

NARRATOR: No one the way I'm going to cure you. You're the first patient I've heard ask for a hospital.

MADAN: Will I be able to play tennis? Does this town have a club? Will they make me a member? I'll hold a pen—my first letter—"Respected Father," this to you in my own hand. (*Holds up his hand.*) Lies—you're telling lies . . . Don't get me wrong. It's years since I've talked to someone like this—normal like. It's as if the war's over and I've come back home.

NARRATOR: The war is still on. Look, you'll have to be a little careful. People don't understand.

MADAN: Will I have to hide?

NARRATOR: Till the sores heal. Then you can do what you want—maybe start a business, or—

MADAN: Yeah, I've even got some money. What do you think—what can I do in this little town?

(*Both laugh.*)

NARRATOR: (*To audience.*) We did the tests, and began the treatment. I didn't want to hide anything from him. And he wanted to know it all. I showed him the smear slide,* and . . .

MADAN: (*Peering through a microscope, observing the leprosy bacterium on his smear.*) So! This is the cruel god, germ of so much shame and hatred. How Gerhard Hansen must have felt when he first saw it! How vexed he must have been. But then, he did something—that's really living. I'm ready to do something too, if only to be a guinea pig. You pinned down the germ, and showed it to us; why couldn't you find a quicker way of finishing it off? This long treatment is like a penance, sometimes it never ends. But I'm already feeling lighter, restless to go out, do something, see something. Find a wide open road, and something will happen—I'll pick up speed . . .

Scene Four

KANU: (*To audience.*) Madan got lucky. He found a friend who advised him well. For me, the road was narrow and crooked. Soon, I found myself in a lepers' home. No light, no air—the breath would stick in your throat.

(*A scene from a home for lepers. In a corner* MIRA *is embroidering a tablecloth.* KANU *enters and stops at a distance.*)

MIRA: Did the doctor come? Why are you looking like that? Like you're hurt.

KANU: I don't like it here.

MIRA: Then leave. Who's stopping you?

KANU: (*Coming close.*) Still at it?

MIRA: Yeah! They'd have done well to keep me at home—an obedient slave for free, and my thanks till kingdom come!

KANU: I told Nirmala to get a sheet, but—

MIRA: (*Sharply.*) She's gone? With whom? Who was here?

---

*When a patch appears on the skin that is suspected to be leprous, it is scraped, and the resultant smear microscopically examined for the presence of the leprosy bacillus. Gerhard Hansen, referred to in the next speech, was the scientist who identified the bacterium that causes leprosy.

KANU: The same man who was here yesterday—next to you.

MIRA: Don't worry, you'll get your chance. They love your helpless kind— for one night or two, or three—all night long.

KANU: Hush. I'm not that kind.

MIRA: When they whistle, everyone follows, wagging their tails. Who wants to starve?

KANU: If I do that, how will I face folks at home?

MIRA: When you go home cured, you really think your man's going to set you in his lap?

KANU: He'll have another woman for sure.

MIRA: You just keep taking your pills. You're here for good.

KANU: I don't know why I came here. They give you nothing. I don't even have a bar of soap. (*Moves toward a passing* ORDERLY.)

MIRA: (*Stopping her.*) Have you gone mad? Sit tight now.

KANU: It's easy for you. Only thing you have on your mind is men.

MIRA: If only one would keep me. I keep popping my pills, but they still don't want me at work. I'm well, but I'm still here.

KANU: They'll take me back.

MIRA: You think you're an angel from heaven? Look here. (*Takes out a photograph.*) He looks like a sweet, respectable husband doesn't he? In six months he was going to be mine. He visited me every day. I went home, and he was courting my girlfriend. The shit. I came back, to these drooling dogs.

KANU: Don't ruin your life.

MIRA: There's nothing left of it, just this rotten body.

KANU: You're not sick.* Your hands and feet are fine.

MIRA: Don't say that. Say, "You're rotten. Thrown in the gutter—and it was the right thing to do." They should've burned me alive. (*Sobs.*)

KANU: You don't need them to live.

MIRA: I'm going to leave. I'll roll on the pavement, cover myself in muck, and lick it off. Then I'll throw myself on everyone: "Give, in the name of the Lord. Give, give. You swine, I'll scratch your eyes out." (*Her voice breaks.*) I'm not going to stay here.

---

*If identified in time, leprosy can be cured. Mira is perfectly healthy, tainted only by the *stigma* of leprosy.

KANU: You believe in God, don't you?

MIRA: Will God give me a home? A good man? Free me from this prison? What did my fiancé think, that no one else will touch me? Wait till I find my man. He'll look after me, put me in a swing, push the hair from my brow . . .

KANU: Nirmala's coming back, without a sheet. They don't care about you here. Get up, it's late.

MIRA: If you want to escape, this is the time. A moonless night is best.

KANU: But . . .

MIRA: What's bothering you? Kanu, they won't even notice. Let's leave.

(After a few moments of hesitation, they leave the home.)

KANU: *(To audience.)* Heaven knows what we had in mind, but once we were out, we just looked at each other. *(To MIRA.)* Now what?

MIRA: We'll figure something out in the morning.

KANU: Just remember, Mira, we're out on the streets now. If you wink at one man, you're on your own.

MIRA: Hey, not so loud. I come from a good home, too.

KANU: Let's find a poorer area, so we look real good.

MIRA: As long as the windows open, so we get something to eat.

(They walk a bit, then come upon a rubbish dump.)

KANU: Look, food. *(Points at the dump and picks up a roti.)*

MIRA: It's a little stale, but it'll do. Look, there's more.

KANU: Best of all, there's no dogs.

MIRA: If your husband's family fed you food like this, just think what you'd tell your parents.

KANU: That I've left him for good! *(Laughing, they pick out the food.)*

(Enter the SWEEPER, carrying an empty basket. He's come to raid the dump himself. Surprised to see them, he slams the basket down on the ground.)

MIRA: Where'd he turn up from?

KANU: Who knows. Forget about him.

SWEEPER: *(After some hesitation.)* Come in the morning, and the kids have cleaned out the paper and plastic. Now this! *(To KANU and MIRA.)* Who said you could be here? D'you hear?

KANU: (*Looking at* MIRA.) We hear you.

SWEEPER: Get lost.

KANU: This is no one's home. We're eating.

SWEEPER: Yeah? And who's going to feed my kids? How'd you come by the whole neighborhood's leftovers? I'll set the cops on you.

MIRA: We have no home, no money.

KANU: Ssh!

SWEEPER: Then go find a place. There's a poorhouse there, and a whorehouse over there. There's no room for you here. Get lost.

(*Intimidated, they move away. The* SWEEPER *rummages through the trash.*)

KANU: Now what?

MIRA: Let's go find a real run-down neighborhood. We'll think there.

(*They exit.*)

Scene Five

Enter MADAN, *pulling a stall on wheels. He is almost unrecognizable—clean-shaven, well-scrubbed, and wearing shoes. Books and magazines are neatly arranged on his stall, and it is decorated with pretty bells.*

MADAN: (*To audience.*) The days passed, and I became well enough for this. (*Pulls a rope that rings the bells; he takes delight in their tinkling.*) It's not the kind of work I'd really like to do—I am a graduate. But it couldn't be helped—nobody would give me a job. Anyhow, I've made a start, so something new will come of it. Now I'm well and truly in your world. (*The* SWEEPER *enters and starts wielding his broom in the exact spot where* MADAN *intended to park.*) Hey! You're raising the dust!

SWEEPER: Am I upsetting you, sir?

MADAN: The dust will spoil the books.

SWEEPER: You should have said so earlier—I wouldn't have swept at all. (*Starts dusting the books.*)

MADAN: It's all right, I'll do it myself. Leave it be.

SWEEPER: It's my job. If you want, I'll come in even earlier. It'll cost you only five *rupees* a month.

MADAN: There's no telling where I'll park my stall.

SWEEPER: Oh, if you want, I'll sweep the whole place, just for you.

MADAN: OK, OK! (*The* SWEEPER *is attracted by the bells.*) Go ahead, pull.

(*The* SWEEPER *rings the bells and is fascinated. Rings them again.* MADAN *extends his left hand to ring the bells too.*)

SWEEPER: How'd you lose your finger? (*With a jerk,* MADAN *hides his hand. The* SWEEPER *suppresses his suspicion.*) Have to sweep it all—I'll do it on your account. Just five *rupees.*

(*From now on* MADAN *constantly hides his left hand, the one with the cut-off finger, in his pocket.*)

MADAN: OK, OK. Go ahead. (*To audience.*) We had help at home too—but not like this.

(*Enter* NARAYAN, ANNAY-MA, *and* KASIM, *all lepers and beggars.*)

NARAYAN: (*Propelling his cart with his hands.*) Praise Govinda, Hail Govinda, chant the name of Hari-oh! (*Suddenly sees* MADAN, *halts just in front of him.* MADAN *steers his stall away, but* NARAYAN *follows, singing all the while. Confronted with this face of leprosy,* MADAN *breaks into a cold sweat.*)
   Hail Govinda. Praise Govinda,
   Chant Govinda's name.
   Chant with me the name Govinda,
   Our lives are all the same.
   Sir—Bholey Baba will bless you—Sir, ten *paise*—Sir

SWEEPER: Don't trouble the poor chap. He's just set up his stall. Go to the temple, there're enough pious souls there.

NARAYAN: (*Ignoring the* SWEEPER.) Loknath will bless you, sir.

MADAN: (*Moving away from* NARAYAN.) No, no, go away. Let me make my first sale.*

NARAYAN: Yours will be my first sale too, sir.

(TWO ASTROLOGERS *enter and are surprised to see Madan's stall.*)

---

*In India, the first sale of the day is considered auspicious, and every trader (and beggar) pays obeisance to the cash received from the day's first transaction.

ASTROLOGER 1:   What's this shop doing here? Who's taken this place? It's mine.

ASTROLOGER 2:   Do you have a license?

MADAN: (*To* ASTROLOGER 1.) What do you mean? I've spoken to the guard there. I give him five *rupees* a week.

ASTROLOGER 1:   Move your stall.

MADAN: No. When the guard comes, I'll talk to him.

ASTROLOGER 1:   You've taken my place. I don't want to hear any more nonsense. Move your stall.

MADAN: Look, I have a license.

ASTROLOGER 1:   Move your stall. Move your stall.

ASTROLOGER 2:   Forget it. Don't let him scare you. He can't do a thing. You keep sitting right there. Let's see if he can make you move.

ASTROLOGER 1:   Hey, I pay my turf fee every week.

ASTROLOGER 2:   And that makes you special? Everybody pays up.

ASTROLOGER 1:   You keep out of it. Buzz off.

ASTROLOGER 2:   Why don't you go back to where you used to sit? All this screaming and shouting . . .

(*They fight with each other. The* GUARD's *whistle is heard, followed by his appearance.*)

ASTROLOGER 1:   Good morning, sir. Am I happy to see you!

GUARD: What's with all this noise first thing in the morning? Get lost. (*Notices the* SWEEPER.) What are you doing here?

SWEEPER: (*Who's been enjoying the goings-on between the two astrologers.*) Sir, I was on my way, if only they'd let me—

NARAYAN: A pleasure to meet you, sir, after all these days. May Loknath bless you.

GUARD: What's this stall doing here?

ASTROLOGER 1:   My words exactly, sir. This is my place.

GUARD: You think this land belongs to your father? Shove off.

ASTROLOGER 2:   It's your land, sir.

GUARD: Get outta here.

ASTROLOGER 1:   I've been paying you every week, sir!

GUARD: Are you going to move? Five sniveling *rupees* a week . . . Go find a place in the other market. Get lost.

(ASTROLOGER 1 *starts moving. The* SWEEPER *starts to pick up his broom.*)

ASTROLOGER 2:   So much for his astrology—it didn't tell him he'd have to move shop today. Didn't I say you should sit pretty? It's your place now.

GUARD: You think it's your turf, huh? Go—join your pal.

ASTROLOGER 2:   Hey, I've been paying up every week.

GUARD: Yeah, I know. Get lost. I'll meet you in the next alley.

ASTROLOGER 2:   Look, I've been paying you more than anyone else . . .

SWEEPER: Do what he says today. Come back tomorrow.

(ASTROLOGER 2 *starts to leave. Meanwhile, the* GUARD's *attention has shifted to the book stall.*)

GUARD: You too, pal. Let's go.

MADAN: (*To* GUARD.) Fond of reading, sir?

GUARD: Yeah.

MADAN: That's a good book. A little expensive—twelve *rupees*.

GUARD: Parking here—it'll cost you thirty *rupees* a month.

MADAN: Yeah?

GUARD: That low-life used to give me twenty *rupees*.

MADAN: But I have a license.

GUARD: Good. You need one. I'll read this and tell you what I think.

(GUARD *turns to leave, but finds his path blocked by* NARAYAN *and* ANNAY-MA.)

NARAYAN: (*To passers-by.*) Kind sir, madam. Lord bless your children, sir—

GUARD: How many times have I told you, you old bastard—if you want to visit the temple, you better be prepared to scrape the skin off of your knees. But no—you gotta ride in your Cadillac, with the missus by your side. Bugger off! (*Without a word,* NARAYAN *and* ANNAY-MA *move out of his way.*)

KASIM: I'm gonna build him a new car, sir.

GUARD: You too. Get lost.

NARAYAN: Let's go, Kasim.
          Hail Govinda. Praise Govinda,
          Chant the name Govinda-oh . . .

(*All three leave.*)

MADAN: (*To himself.*) Why couldn't I have gotten treated in my hometown, found work there? (*People pass by, show no interest in his books; he looks on. Begins to read a newspaper.*)

(*Enter two young men,* ANUJ *and* ROSHAN, *and a young woman,* PRABHA. *They look about.*)

ANUJ: Some guys were saying let's can the play and have a fancy dress pageant instead, or a string of song and dance numbers.

ROSHAN: Some guys, hunh? Sure you're not speaking for yourself?

ANUJ: Not me. Catch me singing some old-fashioned love song.

ROSHAN: You shoulda said so then.

ANUJ: I would have, but I kept my mouth shut because of Prabha.

ROSHAN: But she always does what you want.

PRABHA: Either way, the decision is yours, Roshan.

ROSHAN: Don't kid me.

(*Still talking, they stop at Madan's stall.* MADAN *is obviously extremely pleased.*)

ROSHAN: If it's to be a fancy dress, that's what Prabha can do.

(KANU *runs on. Her hands are bandaged, and she has a large envelope under her arm. She's alarmed and looking for a place to hide. Her arrival creates a peculiar atmosphere.*)

PRABHA: (*To* MADAN.) What was she hiding?

MADAN: No idea. Something, I guess.

PRABHA: Does she come by often?

MADAN: Who knows? Are you guys planning a fancy dress parade?

PRABHA: We're still deciding.

ROSHAN: (*Who has meanwhile started reading the papers.*) There was this famous poet, Shamshad Hussain. He'd've been a hundred this year—he was born in this town.

PRABHA: Now what?

ROSHAN: Why not do something around him?

ANUJ: (*Looking at the paper too.*) There are lotsa books listed here. Have you read them?

PRABHA: (*To* MADAN.) Do you have any of his books?

MADAN: (*Reading the paper.*) Maybe . . . (*Pulling some ragged old books out of the stall.*) I've heard the name, and anyway I'm quite into poetry.

PRABHA: Let's go with this poet thing.

MADAN: Here, have a look. (*Puts a pile of books in front of them.*)

PRABHA: This says his tomb's in a bad way. Why not try and fix it? That's charity too.

ANUJ: These books are expensive.

ROSHAN: (*To* MADAN.) Can't you bring the price down?

MADAN: That's kinda difficult. But you guys can read them here.

ANUJ: There's others who'll have to read them too.

MADAN: If you like something, copy it out. I can help—my handwriting's not bad.

PRABHA: He must've had a home here as well.

ANUJ: If his tomb's in bad shape, the house—

PRABHA: Whatever we do, we've got to learn more about him. It would be great if we could tell people how he began writing, the hassles he had— the poor guy must always've been broke. (ANUJ *laughs.*)

MADAN: I'll find out.

PRABHA: I love sitting around tombs. It gives me a strange kind of peace.

ROSHAN: Great. That's enough for one day. (*Gathers his things to leave.*) You guys read these and fill me in. (*Leaves.*)

PRABHA: Man, is he lazy!

ANUJ: Let's go too. There's no reason for us to kill ourselves.

PRABHA: (*To* MADAN.) Then, you'll find out for us? (MADAN *nods.*)

(ANUJ *and* PRABHA *leave.*)

MADAN: College kids! The same joys everywhere, even in this little town. For me, it's like something inside has died.

(KANU *returns.*)

KANU: I hope no one was here. The temple guard's after me.

MADAN: No one comes here. When you need to hide, you're welcome.

KANU: The bottle . . . ?

MADAN: Oh, I'll get it! (*Opens the envelope and takes out a bottle.*) A little sip . . .

KANU: I've got to get it to the shop—they'll give me fifty *paise*.

MADAN: And if you get caught? (KANU *laughs it off and reaches for the bottle. He begins scolding her.*) Show me your hand . . . take off the bandage. (KANU *is amazed.*) Your hand seems OK. Take it off . . . don't worry . . . show me . . . I'm not a guard. (*Slowly,* KANU *begins to remove the bandage.*) A little bent. You shouldn't do these things—that's how we, er you, get a bad reputation. There's a hospital close by. Have you been there?

KANU: They threw me out.

MADAN: OK, I'll bring you the drugs.

KANU: And some money too . . . I don't even have a place to live.

MADAN: Where is home?

KANU: Was. My husband's. Before that, my father's. Now, nothing. (*Picks up the bottle.*) As long as I get some work—even this, I won't beg. (MIRA *enters; signals to* KANU, *who goes over; they whisper.*)

MADAN: (*To himself.*) Does pity make us wretched, or bring pain? (*To audience.*) Just because we look different, does that make us inferior?

KANU: (*To* MIRA.) Where is he?

MIRA: Who, Kasim? He's gone home. Wanted to clean up. He said, "How can I take you to a dirty place?" He lives in the graveyard. An old couple live there too. You can stay with them.

KANU: Me! Really?

MIRA: Sure! They have some land too. And chickens. He's going to teach me to farm. He even knows how you can light a fire without burning your hand.

KANU: You sure he won't leave you?

MIRA: You tell me: was your marriage for keeps? No, Kanu, I think he needs someone as well. He's all alone . . . just a few fingers missing.

KANU: You know what this means?

MIRA: But, without a home . . .

KANU: And if you can't stand it?

MIRA: Come, have a look.

KANU: (*To* MADAN.) It looks like I've found a home. I won't be needing your help.

(*They leave. At one end of the stage, a small group of performers begins making music in preparation for Mira and Kasim's wedding. The* NARRATOR *and two* ACTORS *enter.*)

NARRATOR: Where are you lot off to?

ACTOR: It's time for the wedding scene!

NARRATOR: Whose wedding?

ACTOR: Mira and Kasim's.

NARRATOR: Get lost. You must be loony.

ACTOR 2: Sir, is the scene canceled?

ACTOR 1: The one scene that was working so well, and you had to cut it.

NARRATOR: We'd have had the scene for sure, if we could've gotten the priests for Mira and Kasim's wedding. But there was no way—not for lepers. The decision to live together—that's all the ritual they'll get.

MADAN: What about our scene?

NARRATOR: Just a minute. (MADAN *quietly sits down in a corner of the stage. To audience.*)

No bridal veil for the girl,
No turban for the man.
If two of you can get along,
Then you can make a couple.
Find a roof where you can,
A place to call your own.
A companion is what you need,
Not prayers or dowry treasure.
Find a mind that meets your own,
And lead your lives together.

(*The actors assembled on stage applaud enthusiastically then exit.*)

NARRATOR: So Mira and Kasim began to live together. And what is to become of Kanu? She isn't even getting treated.

MADAN: I told her she should, but all she wants is money.

NARRATOR: Did you show her your foot? Tell her about yourself? Perhaps . . .

MADAN: I'd get caught out. As it is, I feel like a spy on foreign soil.

NARRATOR: Why don't you go home?

MADAN: Why don't you understand? I'd get no respect.

NARRATOR: Set up home with Kanu.

MADAN: With an illiterate village girl?

NARRATOR: There's no meeting ground?

MADAN: We share a disease. That doesn't mean we're from the same tribe.

NARRATOR: Why not take a trip to their little colony. You'll feel less alone. It would make them happy too.

MADAN: You want me to go there? I'm not filthy, I'm not a beggar, I haven't given up on life.

NARRATOR: I think I'll walk across and see how they're doing. I haven't been there in a long time. (*Begins to leave.*)

MADAN: Go—see how little they are satisfied with. I know what I'm losing: calling on people, arguing about the news, a trip to the river with friends, the buzz of alcohol, fights about a football game on the bus ride home, getting angry with my mother when she worried about me . . . these trifling pleasures. Would Kanu understand them? Can our shared disease shoulder our whole life together? Someone will come—sky-blue *sari,* wide-eyed, round face. I'll have swept the room, put flowers in a vase, laid out the best china. A necktie? Maybe. The bell . . . Do come in, this is my room. I'll smile. Do sit. An expensive cigarette. Care for one? Read the papers? Some localities are absolutely quiet; the ones you don't get any news of, that's where things are in turmoil—some politics the disease teaches you. Do you enjoy poetry? Why not, one should relish life. Yes, of course we'll go to the poet's grave—wherever you want. Will you hold my hand as we walk? (*Glowers at his hands, at their numbness.*) No, not here. (*Puts a hand on his shoulder.*) Here, this is where I can feel something.

Scene Six

Evening. The graveyard colony. KASIM, MIRA, *and* ANNAY-MA *are busy with their chores. Enter* NARAYAN *on his cart. Goes up to* KANU.

NARAYAN: Kanu, Kanu. (KANU *is looking ill. He comes closer.*) See what I got today. (*Shows her a blanket.*) Money too—two *rupees.*

KANU: So soft. And no holes anywhere.

NARAYAN: It's election time. Did you know we get to vote too? Even after the world throws you out, you're still tied to it. It's for our own good our families threw us out, so Loknath can take us in.

ANNAY-MA: Seems you're the only one he took in. No one else got a blanket.

NARAYAN: It all comes from Him, direct to you. I am nothing.

KANU: How lovely it is! How easy your winters will be.

NARAYAN: You like it? You're always sick. Come, wrap yourself in it.

(MIRA *looks at* KASIM.)

KANU: No. How can I? . . . They gave it to you . . .

NARAYAN: Who needs it now? You or I? If you have something, you might as well put it to use. No sense in it sitting around wasting. (*Hesitating,* KANU *takes it.*)

ANNAY-MA: The old beggar'll find himself another one. Won't you?

NARAYAN: Begging doesn't make me less of a man.

KANU: It's so warm! Mira, look! Isn't it nice?

MIRA: Shame on you, asking the old man for it!

KANU: I didn't ask!

MIRA: She can't stop talking when she's with us. But on the street, she won't open her mouth. We do all the begging, and you have all the fun!

NARAYAN: Why are you getting so angry? Go ask for one yourself.

MIRA: I'm not up to fighting. If I can sit in one place . . .

ANNAY-MA: If your mind's someplace else, you won't get a thing.

MIRA: I never get a thing. Everybody knows that.

KASIM: You gotta have a manner. If you want to sell something, you need to have a manner.

NARAYAN: If you want them to feel pain, you've got to become wretched.

KASIM: It's a free market—someone's selling cloth, someone gold. There's the bangle man, the vegetable man, the religion man, and there's us . . .

MIRA: (*To* KASIM.) The rest've got bags full of the stuff. And you?

KASIM: I can only sell what I've got to sell.

MIRA: If that's the case, then I've got the best goods of all. (*Stands tall and runs her hands over her body.*)

KANU: Mira! You're talking too much.

MIRA: Easy for you to say—you got a blanket without shifting your butt. All nice and new. Sitting around in it, all wrapped up like a lady. Been sick all week—and we've got to feed you.

KANU: It's not my fault.

MIRA: Instead of lying around here, you should've lain down in the market—you could have got a lot more money that way.

KANU: When we ran from the home, we shared everything.

MIRA: Instead of wearing your blanket, why don't you sell it, so we all get something.

KANU: (*Tossing down the blanket.*) Do what you want with it. I don't like folks shouting at me.

MIRA: My! Isn't she touchy.

ANNAY-MA: Come on, it's not worth fighting about.

MIRA: (*Frenzied.*) Then what's wrong with me? Why should I beg?

KASIM: Don't, if you don't want to.

NARAYAN: Wanting, not wanting—we can't chose. You're talking rot.

MIRA: (*Breaks down.*) I don't want to beg. I'm trapped. You saw his picture, didn't you? So good-looking . . .

ANNAY-MA: You decided to live here.

MIRA: In this home. So why should I wander about?

KASIM: She's found a roof; now she wants a mansion.

MIRA: I thought . . . there'd be two of us—more money . . .

ANNAY-MA: It's not pity that gets her money. It's her face.

KASIM: (*Looking at* MIRA *as if for the first time.*) My house isn't good enough for her. Not that I can't do anything else, but . . . (*Starts rummaging around in some junk for a tool box. The others look on, surprised.*)

NARAYAN: Looking for your tools?

KASIM: Yes, Pa. If she hadn't reminded me . . .

ANNAY-MA: Just setting up home brings so much respect.

(*All laugh. Lights dim.*)

KANU: (*Talking to herself.*) That day I got really mad. I'd never felt so rotten, not even when they threw me out of my house. Mad with Mira, mad with myself—why did I go with her? I could've kept rotting in the home. Why did you listen to her, Kanu? Always letting others tell you how to live. You left your village because your husband told you to, you left the home because of her . . . You're always stuck to someone . . . That's why you keep getting sick, keep getting hurt.

NARAYAN: (*Moving his cart towards her.*) Here, Kanu. Instead of shivering in the cold, put it on.

KANU: I don't want it. I'm leaving.

NARAYAN: You can't leave now—don't be stubborn. If I could stand, I'd wrap it round you myself.

KANU: You should never go by what others tell you.

NARAYAN: Maybe, but there's nothing wrong with what she said. Here everyone's got to look out for themselves.

KANU: But I can't beg.

NARAYAN: You'll have to swallow your pride.

KANU: It's not pride. I've never asked for anything—not from my Pa, not from my Ma, not even a powder puff from my husband.

NARAYAN: Know what my kids asked for? "Pa, if you want to see us happy, go away."

KANU: I have no right to ask for anything.

NARAYAN: Did they have a right to ask for this, to send me into this living grave? They threw me upon the mercy of the Lord. Everything I get comes from Him.

KANU: Can't you find me some work? Any kind . . .

NARAYAN: (*Taking out the money he'd hidden.*) Don't talk like a child. I can give you this. Have the roof repaired so you don't feel so cold.

KANU: How can I . . . it's yours.

NARAYAN: It all comes from the Lord above. How can I call it mine?

KANU: If you ever need . . .

NARAYAN: Tomorrow is another day.

KANU: If things get bad . . .

NARAYAN: I'll raise my price!

KANU: This money will finish in a month. Then . . .

NARAYAN: If Loknath wanted me to work, would he have taken away my hands and feet?

KANU: I don't set any store by him.

NARAYAN: Think anyone'll buy goods your hands have touched? Anyone at all?

KANU: That's true, (*To audience.*) You tell us. Would you like to? Anything we've made? You're reasonable folks, educated. You'll still think twice, won't you?

NARRATOR: (*From the side of the stage.*) There are moments when you need to make a fresh start. At such times, you need some support, a gentle push to get the cart rolling . . . During this time, I went to their colony. (*Sounds of the leper colony . . . "the doctor is here" . . . the residents come onto the stage, and the* NARRATOR *dispenses medicine.*)

MIRA: Good morning!

NARRATOR: Ah, Mira! Could I have a drink of water? (*To* KANU.) You're not looking after yourself. Don't you want to go home? Here, will you tie this bandage, or should I?

KANU: I'll do it.

NARRATOR: Are you sure?

(KASIM *enters. He's had his tools repaired.*)

KASIM: Good morning, sir!

NARRATOR: Morning, morning. I saw you dancing outside the temple that morning.

KASIM: You remember? Well, I can do most things, sir.

NARRATOR: And you still beg for a living?

KASIM: I tell you, sir, nothing I can't do. I belong to the weaver caste. I can make better cloth than this.

ANNAY-MA: He has a brother in this very town—

KASIM: Leave it be. When Luck leaves you, she's gone for good. After I left home, I did all kinds of things: was at a cycle shop for six months, with a shoemaker for three years. Then I made toys for a year. Had myself treated too. But when these started showing on my hands, that was it—I came here, to these old folks.

MIRA: Hey, I can make toys too.

KASIM: Will you start making them again? With me?

NARRATOR: Ah, yes—now you've set up home.

(MIRA *and* KASIM *are embarrassed.*)

KANU: Could I do something too?

NARRATOR: You certainly should.

(NARAYAN *rapidly wheels his cart towards them.*)

NARAYAN: Why are you misguiding them, sir? We're doing fine as we are.

ANNAY-MA: Keep quiet. I'll handle the old man; you do exactly as you please. But, sir, who's going to buy their toys?

NARRATOR: If they're well made, folks'll buy them.

KASIM: They won't even let us sit on the sidewalk.

NARRATOR: You don't have to sell them. I will. We already have a shop, where everything will get sold. Have you seen the new book stall?

KASIM: That gent's?

NARRATOR: Seen his hands and feet? Ask him sometime, though, how he kept his face from getting scarred.

KANU: You mean—he too?

(*They all laugh.*)

KASIM: Hey, I can do something too. I'll make . . .

NARRATOR: Yes? What?

KASIM: Slippers . . . Will you get us some leather? I'm going to make some stuff. That's for sure!

NARRATOR: But they shouldn't be expensive.

KASIM: Don't give me a thing, sir—only what they cost. Just get me the leather, that's enough. And, sir, if you like them, will you place an order? You came here of your own accord, talked to us . . . And sir, if folks start buying them, will you give me a decent share—me and my woman—there's two of us now.

KANU: Make them colorful. I'll wear the first pair. Make them tough, so's they don't break. With soft soles—my feet have to keep me company, don't they? One day they'll take me back to the village. Folks will look at me, but they won't see the patch. It'll have gone, won't it? (*Laughs.*)

(*A wave of hope washes over the stage.* MIRA *and* ANNAY-MA *gaze at* KANU *with affection.*)

Scene Seven

After intermission. As the third bell rings, stage lights come up, but the actors are not ready: a couple of ACTORS *are collecting their props. The* NARRATOR *looks on, harassed. Madan's stall stands center stage. Instead of books it now carries toys, footwear, brooms, etc.*

ACTOR: That's the third bell. Hurry up!

ACTRESS: Lord, I didn't hear . . .

NARRATOR: Can't you guys hurry up?

(*The* NARRATOR *takes up position near Madan's stall and starts the play. Prescribed postintermission music swells.*)

NARRATOR: (*To the audience.*) Friends, the tree of hope bears early fruit. As it did with Kanu, Mira, and Kasim. They started making things—simple things, honestly crafted. Hungry people, folks'll call them, hollow people. But that's not telling it like it is. At that time, another question started troubling me, maybe because finding separate work for a few people, keeping them going, selling—all this was tough enough. So the question—why do we separate them, make lives so much more difficult—our lives and theirs? Why do we take away their jobs, make them live in these colonies? It's a strange game. They got thrown out of their homes, hence these colonies. If they get taken back, the colonies will empty, . . . and many do want to go home. (*Waits for the play to start, but the actors are not yet on stage. Shouts.*) Shetty! Move it! Why aren't you in position?

ACTOR: I'm looking for my prop!

NARRATOR: So you're looking for a prop. And where's Madan?

ACTOR: I don't know. (*Calling.*) Madan, hey Madan!

NARRATOR: (*To musicians.*) Cut the noise. The actors aren't on stage yet, and you've already begun your caterwauling.

(MADAN *comes running on.* KANU *enters downstage and addresses him. Tightly wrapped around her is the shawl she had on when the play began.*)

KANU: You're having a lot of fun aren't you? Telling the whole world your story?

MADAN: Yes, now that it's in the open.

KANU: Some things I don't even know myself!

MADAN: Some things you're still hiding.

KANU: What?

MADAN: (*Changing topic of conversation.*) So, how does it feel to stay at home and look after a sick mother?

KANU: She needs me.

MADAN: Others needed you too, but you ran away.

KANU: I'm back where I belong. To tell you the truth, folks aren't that bad.

MADAN: You always believed that.

KANU: I wanted to. See, you got to start someplace. Things are gonna happen—move faster.

MADAN: My own words—and I have to hear them from you?

KANU: Do they still sound like yours when you hear them repeated?

NARRATOR: I can't figure out what's happening.

KANU: Is it true what I've heard? That you're in love with Prabha?

MADAN: My feelings are none of your business.

KANU: Am I glad I didn't go with you!

MADAN: Why? I'd have stuck by you.

(*Voices of other actors, eager to start the play.*)

KANU: (*Off.*) Just a minute! (*To* MADAN.) And if you got tired of me? You'd've run off—and found a good excuse too, wouldn't you?

MADAN: You didn't try it, so you'll never know!

KANU: You're always running, aren't you? You ran away from home, had one fight with the guard, and came running here.

MADAN: I always had a reason.

KANU: Yeah.

MADAN: Like you had a reason for going home—your sick mother. You did as you saw fit. So, I'm doing as I see fit.

KANU: I'm not complaining.

MADAN: (*Sarcastically.*) It's always the same thing—we aren't complaining, we don't know how! Everything's just fine as it is. Right?

(SWEEPER *enters.*)

SWEEPER: That's how the sweeper thinks, which is what this scene is supposed to establish!

MADAN: Do we have to—

SWEEPER: We're all ready for our entrances. Come on now!

(*Voices of other actors, now quite angry.*)

NARRATOR: (*To* MADAN *and* KANU.) C'mon guys, you're screwing it all up.

MADAN: I can't go on with it.

SWEEPER: Why don't you do the scene with me?

MADAN: I can't do it.

NARRATOR: (*Beside himself with rage.*) Do *something!*

SWEEPER: C'mon, grab your prop and go for it. (*Hands* KANU *a wooden toy horse.*)

KANU: I made one like this myself. Remember where it went?

MADAN: I've kept it. I've kept it.

KANU: I stayed up all night making it—brought it here first thing in the morning.

NARRATOR: I'm sure you did. But how does that concern us now?

MADAN: I feel weird doing this scene.

NARRATOR: Well do *something!*

ACTOR: We'll stop after a bit—they'll figure out the rest.

NARRATOR: Shut up!

MADAN: I tell you, the audience is going to find this childish.

SWEEPER: If you worry about them, you'll get nowhere. Though, mind you, I understand. Come here. I don't like doing this role either. Yesterday some folks wouldn't shake hands with me.

NARRATOR: I've had enough! *KANU!* You're not on stage yet. Get off! Let's start the action.

(KANU *leaves.* NARRATOR *moves to one side.* MADAN *and the* SWEEPER *start painting the stall.*)

MADAN: Looks good, doesn't it?

SWEEPER: It would have looked better if I did it by myself.

MADAN: (*Hastily.*) I'm still learning.

(*Temple bells ring.*)

SWEEPER: Better learn fast. (*Bells still ringing.*) It's gonna be morning.

MADAN: Come back at night. We'll finish it. (*Starts collecting paint, etc.*)

SWEEPER: Yup. (*Hesitantly.*) Er, do you have a minute? I got a letter from home a few days ago. Could you read it to me?

MADAN: A letter? Yes, of course. (*Takes the letter from the* SWEEPER, *and his face falls.*) I think you better send some money home. Or, if you can take time off . . .

SWEEPER: What's it say?

MADAN: They set fire to your area. Your home got burned down, and maybe your kid too.

SWEEPER: I kinda figured something like that . . . Well . . .

MADAN: Why not send for them? Or make a trip yourself?

SWEEPER: It's best to leave things alone, sir. Doesn't do to go against the will of Lord Loknath.

MADAN: Always the same answer! Use your brain, man. That fire was no mistake.

SWEEPER: Nothing happens unless He wills it so.

MADAN: Saying that doesn't help any.

SWEEPER: And if I listen to you, are things gonna get any better?

MADAN: At least they won't get worse. You'll move on.

SWEEPER: Unh! If you go to the temple, make a wish for me.*

MADAN: I don't go there.

SWEEPER: Why? Everyone goes. How nice it must feel—the hymns, the scriptures, God . . .

MADAN: All bunkum. If you want to enjoy life, you have to face reality, not run from it.

SWEEPER: There must be a God; only God could have made me an Untouchable.

MADAN: Man has infinite strength, but that Loknath of yours, he robs it from us. Your child has been burned, and that doesn't trouble you?

SWEEPER: It does, but my job is here, and—

MADAN: Do you recognize me?

(SWEEPER *looks at him intently.* NARAYAN *enters.*)

NARAYAN: Loknath's blessings upon you, sir. See how I got left all alone! Even the old bird won't come back till her work is done.

MADAN: You're a stubborn man.

NARAYAN: I can't help it, sir. Got to do what feels good and right. Makes life more exciting. Helps the day go easier too.

MADAN: Sure, but just once you should try putting everything into a job. You might find you don't need any excitement.

NARAYAN: It's an age, sir, since I've done any work. Your shop is doing well, I haven't got anything out of it though.

MADAN: (*Looking at* NARAYAN.) Acceptance! It takes the strength of a rock, but it doesn't get you anywhere. (NARAYAN *exits.*)

(*Enter* MIRA, KASIM, *and* KANU, *carrying their wares.*)

MIRA: Just you see—all my toys are gonna sell today.

---

*As an Untouchable, the sweeper would traditionally not be allowed in a temple.

MADAN: C'mon, let's have your stuff.

MIRA: Sold three brooms.

KANU: Two pairs of slippers.

MIRA: And that horse as well—I didn't think anyone would buy it.

MADAN: The gent who took it wanted more of the same.

MIRA: If it keeps going like this, we'll be able to get ourselves a loom.

KASIM: But first I'm gonna build a cart for the old man.

KANU: This is the toy you wanted—isn't it? (*Shows* MADAN *the wooden horse.*)

MADAN: Did you make that all by yourself? Wheels and all? It's excellent. I'll buy this one. How much?

KANU: I paid ten *rupees* for the wood and things.

MADAN: (*Thinking.*) I'll give it to you later. I've got to pay Kasim right now. Here you go Kasim—ninety *rupees* for those slippers. You do a good job with them.

KASIM: They're selling, aren't they?

MADAN: Folks come and take them away!

KASIM: Ninety *rupees*, at one go! (*Laughs with joy.*) I only got fifty *rupees* a month at the shoemaker's. Used to give it to my mother. It was enough to make her happy. Now . . . (*Drifts into thought.*)

MADAN: (*To* KANU.) You have such lovely hands, why don't you look after them? You shouldn't be too greedy—do only as much as you can.

MIRA: She's raring to go home. (*To* KANU.) Why? Don't you feel easy with us?

KASIM: (*To* MADAN.) Is there any way you can get this money to my mother? She lives right here, in this town.

MADAN: No, I don't have the time. Send her a money order.

KASIM: You have to pay extra, and she could use every bit.

MADAN: I don't have the time. (*Tenderly.*) Make the cart first. (*To* KANU.) Why are you worried? You'll be fine.

KANU: Leave me alone.

KASIM: The sun is rising.

MIRA: We're all done. Let's go.

(MIRA, KASIM, *and* KANU *collect their things.* MIRA *and* KASIM *exit. The* SWEEPER, *who has been watching, begins sweeping again as* MADAN *turns.*)

MADAN: (*Tormented.*) Mother of God!

SWEEPER: Sir, is all the stuff made by them?

MADAN: By them and by a few others too.

SWEEPER: You shouldn't get stuff from them, sir, or let them near your shop.

MADAN: Because they're sick, is that why? Everybody gets sick.

SWEEPER: I don't know, sir—I don't have the answers. But if folks get to know, they're going to stay away. Most folks don't want to get within sniffing distance. (*Pause.*) Sir, aren't you the guy was hiding in the temple?

MADAN: Yes. So?

SWEEPER: Just asking. I won't ask again.

PRABHA: (*Entering.*) Has Anuj come yet?

MADAN: Last evening.

PRABHA: He's never around when he's needed.

MADAN: He's your friend.

SWEEPER: Excuse me.

PRABHA: Yes?

SWEEPER: Not you. Him.

MADAN: (*Pulling him aside.*) What is it?

SWEEPER: I need my money, sir. I figure you should start paying me more now. I need to send some home as well.

MADAN: (*Giving him money.*) Go—go on.

(SWEEPER *leaves.*)

PRABHA: Why don't you report him?

MADAN: (*Sarcastically.*) Report? Come, sit—let me show you the new toy I had made.

(*Shows off the toy.* KANU *is watching carefully, draped in her shawl.*)

PRABHA: Nice. It rolls too.

MADAN: Even toys need to move.

PRABHA: Can I try? (*Pushes the horse around.*) Will you come this evening? I can't say how good the program will be!

(*They roll the horse back and forth from one to the other.*)

MADAN: With you in it, I'm sure it'll be great. (PRABHA *laughs.*) Your friend is nice.

PRABHA: Anuj? (*Laughs.*) I want to marry him.

MADAN: I can see that.

PRABHA: How?

MADAN: Seeing as how he loves you.

PRABHA: But if my father finds out . . .

MADAN: Don't keep it hidden. That's hard on you guys, and dangerous, too.

PRABHA: But he won't understand. That's why there're so many things I don't write to him about.

MADAN: I guess—it's best to let things ride for now. Deal with it when you have to.

(PRABHA *suddenly loses her balance and falls on the horse, cutting her foot.*)

MADAN: Careful! (*She sits up.*) Did you get hurt? It must be a thorn. Pull it out.

PRABHA: Have a look.

MADAN: If I look . . . (*Extremely ill at ease.*) Where's your friend gone?

PRABHA: It looks like iron.

MADAN: Yes, it may be a nail. It's bleeding. Here, tie this around it. (*Offers a handkerchief.* PRABHA *waves it away.*)

PRABHA: I should take it out first, or I won't make the show tonight.

MADAN: You're right. (*Takes out a blade.*) Use a blade—you may be able to get it out. (PRABHA *is speechless.*) Hurts, this little cut? You're lucky— your wounds will never fester. They took rocks and nails out of my feet, and I just sat there, watching quietly.

PRABHA: Can't you take it out?

(MADAN *looks at her, then turns away and gets up.*)

MADAN: If you knew, would you still be asking? If you come to know, you're going to be so scared.

(ANUJ *arrives.*)

ANUJ: Why did you want to go to the tomb?

PRABHA: Oh shut up!

ANUJ: What are you doing here? I've been looking for you all over town . . . haven't put the posters up . . . If it goes on like this, nothing's gonna get done.

PRABHA: Look—I've cut my foot.

ANUJ: You really should be more—

PRABHA: Careful, it hurts.

ANUJ: Sure it's gonna hurt. You need a shot too.

MADAN: Yeah, you better get it seen to. I'll put the posters up.

ANUJ: I know what I need to do. (*Takes hold of* PRABHA *and leaves.*)

PRABHA: (*As they exit.*) Anuj, you're always taking off without telling me. I don't like it one bit.

MADAN: The many aspects of love! Don't stop coming by, though. (*Picks up a poster to paste it on the wall. Suddenly.*) And what if my father finds out? (*Mocking, plays the role of his father.*) My son pasting posters on the street to impress some girl? Impossible! Catch him by the ear and bring him to me! He needs a good hiding. If I don't watch out, he'll be rioting tomorrow, painting movie hoardings the day after, failing his exams. Vagabond! What'll they say? What will they think about us, about the whole family? (*Tired.*) No, Father, it's not as bad as you think. The fact is, when you live at home, there's a right way to behave. Without a home, got to live differently. I'm trying to get into the new mode . . . Love is a luxury I can't afford. (*Sits down; tries to write a letter.*) Should I write home? What to write? How I'm doing in this town? Should I write the truth, or something to make sure you don't think I'm unemployed and destitute?

KANU: Going downhill from here, eh?

NARRATOR: Please! Let him finish. Why are you interrupting?

KANU: (*Highly emotional.*) Is your father really such a monster, or is this your bitterness speaking?

MADAN: This is between me and my father. Keep out of it.

KANU: But you're making such a big thing of it.

MADAN: I can say what I want.

KANU: 'Cause no one knows you here? If this had been your hometown, and your father were in the audience?

MADAN: In your case it wouldn't have mattered either way—'cause you're still hiding it.

KANU: And you—would you speak out?

MADAN: Yes—most likely. And ask him a few questions too.

KANU: I'm sure you'd want to; but you'd get scared, like you just were with Prabha. (*Pause.*) You never told me about this.

MADAN: Did you want to know?

KANU: How come you thought of us living together?

MADAN: I thought we could make it work.

KANU: Before coming to our colony with Prabha, or after?

NARRATOR: We were just getting to that scene. If you guys would stop messing things up . . .

KANU: (*To* NARRATOR.) But why did he want to become a gentleman?

NARRATOR: If you keep interrupting, you're going to kill the rhythm of the play. (*Voices of other actors in support, saying, "Keep the play going."*) Let's get on with the events. (*To audience.*) So friends, what happened between Kanu and Madan—

MADAN: No! What's the point of doing that scene?

ACTOR: Bring a real character into a play and this is what happens! (*Other actors laugh.*)

NARRATOR: When you've gotten this far, you might as well do what's left.

MADAN: I've already said too much.

KANU: Why not come clean—you'd rather not repeat what happened after this?

NARRATOR: Kanu, please! Try and help. Don't get so emotional!

MADAN: I'm not going to do any more scenes with you.

KANU: Why? Because what happened was the exact opposite of what you wanted?

NARRATOR: Christ! Is this the only chance you've ever gotten to speak?

KANU: (*Moving to* MADAN.) I want to do that scene. Let's do it.

MADAN: Why? Are you having fun now?

NARRATOR: Let's go guys. Let's change the set.

MADAN: No—I'm telling you I can't do it.

NARRATOR: Now you're behaving like a kid. If you want to work in the theater, you've got to have commitment.

(*The actors bring on the sets for the leper's colony, while the* NARRATOR *tries to persuade* MADAN.)

KANU: (*To audience.*) What Madan said that day . . . it was a strange sort of day . . . I don't know whether to laugh or to cry. I suppose, wherever you are, there's some joy and some sorrow; some things just have to be done.

(KANU *takes off her shawl and hands it to an actor. Takes a bucket from him and enters the leper's colony. Music.*)

Scene Eight

The graveyard colony. KANU *takes some clothes out of the bucket and puts them out to dry.* MIRA *is painting toys.* KASIM *is working on a half-finished cart.* ANNAY-MA *is lying to one side, weak and ill.*

KANU: How is she now?

MIRA: She won't live. (*To* ANNAY-MA.) How does it feel to be out in the open? (ANNAY-MA *tries to sit up;* KANU *comes to her.*)

KANU: Can you eat something? (ANNAY-MA *declines.*) You should eat something . . .

MIRA: How d'you like this toy?

KANU: Is there someone you want to meet? Should I send for anybody?

KASIM: Look, I made this cart for your old man. Like it? (ANNAY-MA *tries to nod.*)

KANU: What's your home address? Do you have it written somewhere?

ANNAY-MA: (*With great difficulty.*) Want to go to the temple.

KANU: In your condition? No way.

ANNAY-MA: Don't know . . . will God forgive me . . . or not. (*She communicates through a mixture of words and gestures.*)

KANU: Narayan'll ask it for you. (ANNAY-MA *shakes her head then whispers something in* KANU's *ear.*) There's nothing he doesn't know.

KASIM: There's no money for firewood. We'll have to bury her. It's not something one man can do alone . . . I'll get going soon as I finish this. (*Returns to weaving the rope seat of* NARAYAN's *cart.*) Should I get Madan?

KANU: (*To* MIRA.) You know what she said? "My husband was alive, but I was a widow and a beggar."

MIRA: So?

KANU: How can I explain? (*Exits.*)

NARAYAN: (*Entering.*) He knows everything. Lord Loknath sees everything.

MIRA: Off again? Today, you could—

KASIM: He thinks only of himself. (KANU *brings a stone and sets it down near* ANNAY-MA.) Good idea, Kanu. (*To* ANNAY-MA.) If you have to ask forgiveness, do it right here. (KANU *helps her sit up. As she touches her head to the stone,* ANNAY-MA *bursts into tears.*) See, you've got to touch it! Actually, Mira and I aren't married either.

NARAYAN: How does that change anything?

KASIM: Try sitting on this.

NARAYAN: No way. I've been making do with this for thirty years, and now you want me to sit on that?

KASIM: Six months savings went into it. (KASIM, MIRA, *and* KANU *pick him up and put him into the new cart.* NARAYAN *is fidgety and makes it more difficult.*)

NARAYAN: 'Stead of this, you should have made me crutches or something. I could've stood up straight. Keep sitting, the gas fills up in your guts. Don't feel hungry.

KASIM: Feed him.

(*By now* NARAYAN *is sitting in his new cart.*)

NARAYAN: This is great, Kasim—it's so roomy. I can move around without even getting out. (KASIM *pushes the cart.*) Hey, that's enough—I'll fall. (KASIM *pushes faster.*) You're going to kill me! I was better off in the old—

KASIM: If you keep babbling, I'm going to make sure you fall.

(NARAYAN *sprawls comfortably inside the cart.*)

NARAYAN: All right, all right. It's great—feels like Loknath's chariot. (*Moves about.*) Listen to her—she keeps crying. Sit her here. (ANNAY-MA *refuses.* KASIM *pushes the cart some more.*) What do you think, Kanu, sitting like a king, aren't I? Takes me back to the days when I rode a bicycle. Mira, my child, get me a mirror. After all these years, I'm feeling gutsy enough to look at my face.

(MIRA *brings a mirror.*)

KASIM: Have a look. They say the face is the mirror of the soul.

NARAYAN: Not us—the uglier our mugs get, the more virtuous we become. I know it all boy: exactly how much money you stashed away, what you saved in six months, and all I earned too. And all gone into this. Sure, I know it all. That's why you built this cart you can't use yourself. (*To* ANNAY-MA.) See—he wants that I should stay with you forever. (*Pause.*) She's going. Feel like I'm half gone too, after years of trial. My mind's jumping all over the place, saying, "you're almost done now." The little that's left—I guess that will pass in the same way too. (*Takes hold of* ANNAY-MA's *arm.*)

(PRABHA, MADAN, ROSHAN, *and* ANUJ *enter from one side of the stage, in search of the tomb.* KANU, MIRA, KASIM, *and* NARAYAN *watch them.*)

PRABHA: You better tell us soon where this tomb is, Madan.

MADAN: You tire real fast! See those old buildings? Near there.

ROSHAN: Near the *pipal* tree?

PRABHA: You mean we have to walk that far? It's so hot in the sun, and my feet are aching.

MADAN: You want to visit a poor poet's grave, you better be prepared for tired feet!

KANU: Are they looking for something?

MIRA: I think they're coming here.

KASIM: Why here?

PRABHA: That smoke there—where's it from?

ANUJ: Must be some little factory.

PRABHA: But . . . this is . . .

MADAN: It's a settlement, some people live here.

PRABHA: What kind of people?

MADAN: Half-dead.

ROSHAN: You're speaking in riddles.

PRABHA: Let's go have a look.

ANUJ: No way—I've got to drink some water first.

PRABHA: You can drink some there. (*Heads towards the colony.*)

KASIM: I don't want to meet anyone.

NARAYAN: It doesn't work like that. If there's folks around, they're gonna come.

KASIM: This ain't a place to visit—there's no circus here!

NARAYAN: OK—go inside.

MIRA: (*To* ANNAY-MA.) Look, see how many people are coming to visit you? They got word in your village—all your sons and daughters. (*By now* MADAN, PRABHA, *etc. have reached the colony.*)

KANU: (*To* MADAN.) You too?

MADAN: Yes—we're out for a walk, felt thirsty. Is there water?

KANU: Of course. Come in.

NARAYAN: Welcome, Madan, do come. (KASIM *goes off to one side and busies himself.*) Mira, child, give me a push. (MIRA *pushes* NARAYAN *towards* MADAN.) Don't worry. I won't ask for a handout.

PRABHA: (*Gesturing towards* KANU.) That's the same girl, isn't it?

ANUJ: (*To* PRABHA.) Let's go there as well—there's a bit of shade.

MADAN: These are my friends. They go to college here, they do plays as well.

ROSHAN: (*Intrigued by the stumps of Narayan's hands.*) Anuj—what interesting hands! I should photograph them. (*Takes out a camera.*)

NARAYAN: Mira, push my cart back. I said—push my cart back!

KANU: (*Bringing water.*) Water?

ANUJ: We had some before we left.

NARAYAN: Everyone who comes here has had some before they left.

KANU: (*To* MADAN.) You?

MADAN: I'm not thirsty. (KANU *stares at him.*)

NARAYAN: (*To* MIRA.) I told you, didn't I—push my cart back? But, no, you love being photographed. Go on in and make yourself useful.

(MIRA *goes to* ANNAY-MA.)

ROSHAN: There's no need to get mad.

ANUJ: We don't want to trouble you; we were just passing this way, so . . .

NARAYAN: How come? (ROSHAN *gives him a cigarette, they talk.*)

PRABHA: (*To* KANU.) You live here?

KANU: Yes.

PRABHA: How old are you?

KANU: I don't remember.

PRABHA: Are you married?

KANU: Yes, but not here; there . . .

NARAYAN: Whatever's ours is here. You folks may not want to look around, but . . . (*Looks helplessly at his cart. After some hesitation,* MADAN *starts pushing him.*) That bit of land you see there—that's ours. We farm it. These chickens are ours as well. And look at this, son, we make these toys here too.

ANUJ: Hey that's great. What lovely toys.

MIRA: (*To* PRABHA.) You and he . . . ?

PRABHA: He's my steady, er . . . friend.

MIRA: And that's my friend. (*Pointing to* KASIM.)

PRABHA: And he? (*Referring to* MADAN.)

KANU: One of us—but makes as if he isn't. (PRABHA *is stunned.*)

NARAYAN: Yes—we paint them as well.

MIRA: And this old lady here is mother to us all. But she's in a bad way now.

PRABHA: Haven't you sent for a doctor?

(KANU *and* MIRA *are silent.* MADAN *wants to say something, but* PRABHA *turns her head away.*)

KANU: (*To* ANNAY-MA.) Look—so many people to see you.

ROSHAN: You folks are so talented. Do you perform as well? Sing or something?

NARAYAN: You want to hear a song?

ANUJ: Will you sing?

NARAYAN: Sure.

ANUJ: Prabha, this gentleman is going to sing for us.

NARAYAN: Yes, come sit.

(ANUJ, ROSHAN, *and* PRABHA *spread handkerchieves on the ground and sit.*)

NARAYAN: (*A devotional song.*) Krishna Murari, Gopi Manhari . . .

(MIRA *and* KANU *join hands and start dancing.*)

KASIM: Stop this. What nonsense is this? (*Everybody is stunned. In a rage he comes towards them.*) What is it you want to see? You really want to see something? Lay some nails on the ground and watch me walk on them.

PRABHA: Really! That's great—he can perform at our next show.

KASIM: Yeah, light a match—it won't do anything to me.

PRABHA: (*All excited.*) Roshan—you have matches!

ANUJ: Don't be silly—he'll burn his hand.

(ROSHAN *lights a match, and* KASIM *extends his hand.*)

MADAN: Stop it. (*Pushes* ROSHAN.)

ROSHAN: (*Innocently.*) What?

MADAN: He can't feel, but he can get wounded.

KASIM: There are many things I can do, from making slippers to making toys (*Shows him.*) I want a job. Will you get me one? A regular job. Me

and my wife, we'd both work, and be grateful, too. You gonna help? I'm
sure not.

MADAN: Is this some kind of joke? Who's going to give you a job?

KASIM: Don't you know . . . (*Indicates* ANNAY-MA.) she's dying, and . . .

NARAYAN: (*To* ANUJ.) Take me to her, son; she's gasping. (ANUJ *hesitates*.)
Hey, it's not like I'm asking you to dig her grave.

KASIM: You don't need to ask him. I'm still around.

(MADAN *was about to take hold of the cart, but stops*.)

PRABHA: We should leave; it's getting late.

NARAYAN: Did we upset you?

ANUJ: That's not it. We weren't meant to come here at all. We were headed
to the poet's grave.

NARAYAN: Yes, it's close by. Kasim goes there. On days when we have oil,
he lights a lamp there.

KASIM: There's nothing to see. Why do you want to go?

ANUJ: It's just something I like doing. We'll come again.

MIRA: You must, when we're less tied up.

(KASIM *glares at her.* ANUJ, PRABHA, *and* ROSHAN *start to leave*.)

ANUJ: Interesting, hunh.

PRABHA: I was scared. But Anuj, we have to do something for them.

ANUJ: Next year, definitely . . .

PRABHA: Give them some money? (*Hands* MADAN *some money*.) Here—it'll
come in handy.

ANUJ: Take it. Don't feel shy.

MADAN: So, now you know.

PRABHA: Yes, and it's helped get rid of my prejudice.

(MADAN *reaches with his left hand and takes the money in a flash.* PRABHA *is
taken aback by his unfriendly manner*.)

ANUJ: I was thinking, Prabha, if someone in my family got the disease,
would I be able to let go of them?

PRABHA: And if you got it? (*Laughs, and then quietly wipes her hand with
the fabric of her* sari.)

ANUJ: You tell me.

PRABHA: I don't know about you, but if I got it, you'd leave me for sure—there's so many other girls around, aren't there?

(*They leave.* MADAN *remains.*)

NARAYAN: If folks keep coming by, we won't feel so alone.

KASIM: They just happened to pass by. They're not going to come back. We don't need tourists; we need folks who'll help.

NARAYAN: It's not their fault, son. They haven't had a chance to get to know us.

MADAN: (*Softly.*) Kanu, can I come live with you?

KANU: Why, didn't it work out with her?

MADAN: "Work out"—do you know what that means?

KANU: I haven't been on that road.

MADAN: Will you?

KANU: Why should I? You wanted to play the gentleman, didn't you? Remember how you took off my bandage? Did you stop to think how I felt? If somebody talked about your feet in a public place . . . ?

MADAN: They have.

KANU: So, time to get real, hunh? I'm a married woman.

MADAN: But he didn't stick by you.

KANU: Why are you interested? Couldn't find anyone else?

MADAN: Don't you need someone?

KANU: I've lived alone an age.

MADAN: Loneliness—that's the real reason why. Look, we'll only get close when we live together, when we share our joys and sorrows.

KANU: I can't handle you.

MADAN: You won't know till you try it.

KANU: You've been to college and all. How will we get on?

MADAN: The important thing is, will you be able to give all your love?

KANU: (*Smiling.*) I'd like to go home and find out.

MADAN: Still fooling yourself!

KANU: I just want to make sure. When I go, I don't want to have anything left to hide.

MADAN: As long as you hide nothing from your God.

KANU: Hey, isn't that what the old man just said?

MADAN: Look Kanu, I really want—

KANU: (*Putting it off.*) Come back; we'll see. It'll work out if it has to. (*Laughs reluctantly.*)

(MIRA *leaves* ANNAY-MA's *side and turns.*)

MIRA: She's gone.

NARAYAN: Well, it's for the best. She went smiling—not everyone's so lucky.

KASIM: I'll go start digging. Come with me, Madan? To dig the grave?

MADAN: I don't know how to dig.

KASIM: I'll teach you.

(MADAN *and* KASIM *pick up shovels and leave.*)

KANU: Alone again.

NARAYAN: You'll find someone. But with her gone, I'll never . . . (*His eyes fill with tears of unbounded grief.* KANU *turns his cart around and wheels him off.*)

Scene Nine

NARRATOR: Annay-ma passed on. The others became objects of public curiosity. Donations were raised for Madan, making some young people feel good. A relationship started building up between the town's citizenry and the residents of the colony. There were some clashes too, but things slowly got back to normal.

MADAN: (*Standing by his stall.*) How could life get back to normal? I never met my new friends again. I wasn't the same either, after I dug that grave—for an old woman I didn't really know.

(*Enter the* GUARD.)

GUARD: Changed your place?

MADAN: Yes.

GUARD: Didn't like it in the middle of the market? Too much of a crush?

MADAN: Whatever.

GUARD: It became a hang-out for those college kids.

MADAN: That's their business.

GUARD: Nice slippers. (*Picks them up.*)

MADAN: Don't touch them. They cost thirty-five *rupees*. I own this shop. You want a pair of slippers, tell me.

GUARD: You call this stall a shop?

MADAN: If you want to shop here, you'd better learn how.

GUARD: I'm just looking.

MADAN: This is not a museum. I've had it with your freeloading—those sandals, some books, a bundle of rope—eighty *rupees* in all. When're you gonna pay?

GUARD: Where d'you live, anyway? (MADAN *gets a little worried.*) Tell me. (*Grabs his hand, but* MADAN *feels no pain. The* GUARD *is amazed.*)

MADAN: Anyhow, pay me soon as you can. (KASIM *enters. He wasn't expecting to see the Guard here.*) What brings you here? Want to buy something?

GUARD: (*Taking goods out of Kasim's basket.*) He brought stuff for you to sell. (KASIM *is anxious.*) How come you're all shy now? (MADAN *calmly takes the merchandise, though the tension is rising.*) I hear you got hitched.

KASIM: Yes.

GUARD: Is that why you stopped coming to the temple?

KASIM: Sell anything today Madan?

GUARD: What's she like?

KASIM: If you want, I'll make sure you get paid every week. (*Starts to leave.*)

GUARD: Singing a different tune, now that you're making money, aren't you? Wouldn't open your mouth then. And that woman of yours—what an operation she runs! She's got customers that bring other customers.

KASIM: That kind of talk makes you no better.

GUARD: Better! And who said you could come here? (*To* MADAN.) How did these things get here? When? He made these sandals. Couldn't find anyone else to make them! His wife must have made this broom. Great stuff. (*Starts flinging things around.*)

MADAN: Don't touch those things.

GUARD: Yeah? (*Gives the stall a violent shove, scattering the merchandise.*)

MADAN: Please leave; I need to close the shop.

GUARD: I want to know how you're selling this stuff!

MADAN: It was made to be sold.

GUARD: If I want—

MADAN: (*Enraged.*) There're no burglars here, no gambling going on. You can't behave like you own the place! (*Catches hold of the* GUARD *and yanks him.*) I've had it with your foul mouth. You're just a bully! (*In his rage, he uses both hands. Surprised at first, the* GUARD *examines* MADAN's *left hand.*)

GUARD: What happened to your hand? Your feet—these shoes, the workers, this stuff—you think I haven't figured it out? Hiding it all, and acting tough, too!

MADAN: I'm hiding nothing. If you'd asked me like a human being, I wouldn't have lied. There's nothing you can do, in any case.

(*Enter the* SWEEPER.)

SWEEPER: Caught between these two. And I'm the third. Got you this time. Try getting out of this one!

(*Cornered, the* GUARD *looks around.*)

GUARD: Bastards!

KASIM: Here. I won't touch you.

(*Still afraid, the* GUARD *begins to leave. The* SWEEPER *hits him from behind and laughs.*)

GUARD: You can laugh now, but you'll pay for this, sure as I got balls. I'll show these bastards where they get off. One low-caste pig, and these two—standing up to me? (*Leaves in a hurry.*)

KASIM: Shouldn't have done that. I know the guy, he's gonna make hell for us. Working on the sly, we should lie low. (*Gathers the merchandise.*)

MADAN: There's nothing he can do to us. I'm cured now—the bug's gone—there's no call for isolation. He's the guilty party. He broke all our stuff.

KASIM: You didn't have to speak! Didn't I keep shut? And I'm the guy who made all this stuff, worked day and night . . .

SWEEPER: Maybe he won't do anything. He got quite a scare.

(*The* GUARD *enters with some* POLICE OFFICERS. *They advance towards Madan's stall.* MADAN *watches from a corner. The* SWEEPER *runs off.*)

GUARD: Here he is.

MADAN: What is it?

OFFICER: Shut up.

SERGEANT: Nice stuff.

GUARD: Doesn't have a license.

MADAN: That's not true. I have a license.

OFFICER: Shut up and sit down. (*Threatens* MADAN *with a cane.*)

SERGEANT: This stuff's not bad!

GUARD: From the lepers' colony. And the guy who sells it—a real bum, not from these parts. Don't know his father's name or whereabouts.

SERGEANT: Take it away. The stuff ain't bad. (*Gets the* OFFICER *to start moving it.* MADAN *tries to stop him, but they don't let him speak.*)

GUARD: Yeah, it's pretty good—it's made by lepers, but guys who're cured now.

OFFICER: I guess we can sell it!

SERGEANT: It's bad enough we let them into town. They think they can set up shop . . . Take him away!

MADAN: Hey—don't take my cart away . . .

OFFICER: Shut up, you leper bastard. Want to run a shop, eh? Go *beg* for your food somewhere! (*Gives the cart a rough shove.*)

MADAN: I have a license for it . . . you can't take it away.

OFFICER: We'll have a look at your license down at the police station. (*Gives the cart another shove. It topples, and the bells ring.*)

(MADAN *looks on, angry and helpless. Chokes a cry and looks away. The* NARRATOR *enters.*)

NARRATOR: They took it away, and you looked on!

MADAN: Shut up.

NARRATOR: Now you'll have to go to the police station.

MADAN: No. They'll keep me there!

NARRATOR: Are you crazy or something? It's not as if you've stolen anything.

MADAN: Maybe I have—not in this life, but in an earlier one. I'm a stranger in this town—I don't know what they're gonna ask.

NARRATOR: Simple stuff—your name, father's name, date of birth . . .

MADAN: No! Not my father's name. If they check with him, he'll deny it, disown me.

NARRATOR: No way.

MADAN: He will—he never liked me. I wouldn't bow my head when he scolded. Even when he hit me . . .

NARRATOR: It's not a big deal. You can't get hassled by this kind of stuff.

MADAN: The guard came, tried to bully me. All I wanted was to run my shop like a shop. He told me where I could get off. You should have told me earlier. My roaming around freely—it's dangerous for you guys.

NARRATOR: You're imagining things. It's all in your head.

MADAN: It's all because of you. What you say gets me into trouble. I bet the sweeper never asked how come he's Untouchable. If I hadn't met you, maybe I'd have accepted things as they are—found a reason . . . (MADAN *is really scared. Begins to revert to the furtiveness and fear we saw before he became friends with the Narrator.*)

NARRATOR: No one ever got anywhere by giving up.

MADAN: You're misleading me. Who knows what lies you've been feeding me. If what you said was true, then how come the law—

NARRATOR: The law! The law is nothing but a code of behavior. What you're doing doesn't seem natural to them. We're gonna have to—

MADAN: 'Cause I'm ill, or 'cause I'm an inferior being?

NARRATOR: You're not ill.

MADAN: Try telling that to them. What they believe becomes the law.

NARRATOR: That's why I keep saying go home. Tell them you're fine now.

MADAN: Home—yeah! Easy for you to say. I wrote to them. Got back a letter, dripping with love. "You're well, stay well. We're glad you're earning your keep now. I've retired. Your two brothers are sending home four hundred *rupees* a month. I don't think of you as being any different from my other children. Sad, though, that because of your illness, I can't leave you anything in my will. Your Ma and I plan to go on a pilgrimage this winter. We could all meet at the train station. We'll work out the train schedules and fix a time . . . our blessings will always be with you."

But where are you now, when I need you to prove I am whole? No, Pa—not at the station. If you want to meet me, you've gotta come to where the lepers live. If you've got shame, I've got pride!

NARRATOR: You feel like running away even before you're done? Fighting is difficult, but not impossible. If you stand up and fight, you'll help a lot of people. Think of the cause.

MADAN: This is a weird fight—and I don't have long to live. The first part of my life—it's been hard enough. I don't want a cause now, I just want some peace. Isn't that enough of a cause?

NARRATOR: You want to worm back into that slum and live without any dignity, waiting for the next handout?

MADAN: Dignity can wait. First I need a place, a roof. I can't hide any longer. When I hide, something dies inside. Keeping that alive—that's enough for someone who's already half-dead. (*Goes and sits in a corner of the stage.*)

NARRATOR: You've lost your nerve; you're trying to run.

(*To audience.*) Most important, he stopped believing me. He left. I wanted to stop him. The one thing I couldn't say was, "I'll fight your fight." He had to fight for himself. Maybe there is an age when you look for challenges. Then a time comes when you think, "just living, that's enough." That thought, it's like some intoxicating drug that pulls you— all the way to the big sleep of your grave. I guess that's what happened to Madan. He fought the case, won it, got his shop back. Then he went back to the colony, started work again, but he cut himself off. What could I tell him? They've got work today, but they've cut themselves off—from me, from you, from the world. Meanwhile, I met Kanu. (KANU *enters from the other side.*) She said . . .

KANU: I'm well now. The smear test was negative. Remember what they used to say in the village? I feel sorry for them. I wrote to my friend. She wrote back: my father's passed on, my husband's gotten a new wife, and my mother's had a stroke. She's got no one to look after her. My friend wrote, "You're well now, come back, you're needed." I'm gonna go.

NARRATOR: You're needed here . . .

KANU: (*Turning to audience.*) I've gotta go . . . I'm coming Ma. Will you still welcome me? Same as when I still had a home and a husband? Or just 'cause you've got no one else? Anyhow, till I get there, look after yourself. I'll handle the rest; I've still got my hands and feet.

NARRATOR: It's best to have a look for yourself. Which is exactly what Kanu did. Madan must have gotten more and more lonely. Mira and Kasim must have told him, "Go home. Go and meet your folks." I'm sure he didn't listen. The Madan I used to know—so playful, so full of fun —he got lost somewhere. Maybe it's better he remains lost. Stories like this don't have an end. Their characters get lost somewhere, in some narrow, twisted alleyway. Halfway through, the story loses its thread. But you know that. Just like the friends you lose along the way.

(*The actors come on for the curtain call.* KANU *takes her shawl from one of them.*)

MADAN: (*Getting up from the corner.*) Just a minute! And suppose one day that friend finds you on this stage and starts to think, "why did it happen this way?"

NARRATOR: What do you think, Madan? Do you think you did right?

MADAN: What do you think? Do you think I was treated right? If Kanu and I had got together, maybe . . .

KANU: (*Wrapping the shawl around herself.*) Then what? You would have held me back too . . .

MADAN: See—she doesn't believe me either. (*Smiles, turns to the audience.*) It's true—I didn't try too hard to lead a normal life—I gave up too soon. But how much does anyone try? Was I really good for nothing? So far gone that, in my own land, I didn't have the right to lead the life of an ordinary citizen?

Tara

by Mahesh Dattani

CHARACTERS
(in order of appearance)

DAN. The older Chandan. Early twenties. Walks with a limp.

TARA. Chandan's twin sister. Fifteen. Walks with a noticeable limp because of an artificial leg.

CHANDAN. Fifteen, but could look younger than Tara. He wears an artificial leg on the opposite side of Tara's.

BHARATI. Tara and Chandan's mother. Early forties.

PATEL. Tara and Chandan's father. Mid-forties. An executive director in a large multinational firm.

ROOPA. The girl next door. Fourteen or fifteen.

DR. THAKKAR. The surgeon who separated the conjoined twins. Mid-fifties.

The Scene Stealers' production, in Delhi, of *Tara*
Photographs courtesy of Vivek Mansukhani

Act One

A multilevel set. One level represents the older Chandan's bedsitter in a suburb of London. We see a small bed, and, in the foreground, a small writing table with a typewriter and a sheaf of papers. Perhaps we see a part of a wall covered with faded wallpaper. This is the only realistic level. Behind, on a higher level, is a chair on which sits DR. THAKKAR. *He remains seated throughout the play. Although he doesn't watch the action of the play, his connection is made certain by his sheer, godlike, presence. The lowest level occupies a major portion of the stage. It represents the house of the Patels. It is seen only in memory and may be kept as stark as possible. On the stage level, running along the cyclorama and, in an* L*-shape, downstage right, is the gali outside the Patels' house, which can be suggested by crosslighting. The older* CHANDAN *will be referred to as* DAN *for clarity. The play starts without any music. A spot picks up* DAN *at his writing table.* DAN *is typing furiously. He stops and removes the sheet from his typewriter. He looks up and speaks to the audience.*

DAN: In poetry even the most turbulent emotions can be recollected when one is half-asleep. But in drama! Ah! Even tranquility has to be recalled with emotion. Like touching a bare, live wire. Try distancing yourself from that experience and writing about it! A mere description will be hopelessly inadequate. And for me . . . I have to relive that charge over and over again. (*Pause.*) Excuse me while I recharge myself. (*He hobbles to a cabinet, pulls out a bottle of liquor, and pours into a glass. He drinks.*) Yes. I have my memories. Locking myself in a bedsitter in a seedy suburb of London, thousands of miles from home hasn't put enough distance between us. (*Holding up his glass.*) My battery charger helps on some occasions. But now I want them to come back. To masticate my memories in my mind and spit out the result to the world in anger. (*Picking up the sheet he has typed.*) My progress, so far, I must admit, has been zero. But I persist with the comforting thought that things can't get any worse. I keep staring at my typewriter every day, wondering how best to turn my anguish into drama. All I find every day, without fail, is one typewritten sheet with the title of the play, my name and address, and the date. Nothing changes—except the date. (*Reading from the sheet.*) "Twinkle Tara. A drama in two acts by Chandan Patel. Copyright, Chandan Patel, 93, Fishpond's Road, Tooting, London SWI177LJ." Today I made some progress. I even typed my phone number. (*Putting down the sheet.*) Not to say that I don't have anything to show to the world yet. I do. For instance, these. (*Picking up a manuscript.*) *Random Raj.* Short stories on the British Raj. Still hounding publishers. The publishers here ignore them because none of them deal with *sati,* dowry deaths, or child marriages—all subjects guaranteed to raise the interest of the average Western intellectual. And back home, of course, Indo-Anglian literature isn't worth toilet paper. (*Throwing the manuscript away.*) But that's all done with. Tonight I drop everything I've desperately wanted to be in my years in England. (*Mimes removing masks and throwing them away.*) The handicapped intellectual's mask. (*Removing another one.*) The desperate immigrant. (*Removing yet another.*) The mysterious Brown with the phoney accent. The last being the hardest to drop, having spent two whole years in acquiring it. And what remains is what I intend making capital of. My freakishness. I am a freak. (*Pause.*) Now, a freak doesn't have to look very far for inspiration. (*He moves to his table.*) But what is hard is to let go. Allow the memories to flood in. (*He winds another sheet on the typewriter. He stops.*) To tell you the truth, I had even forgotten I had a twin sister.

    (*Music fades in slowly.*)

Until I thought of her as subject matter for my next literary attempt. Or maybe I didn't forget her. She was lying deep inside, out of reach . . .

    (*A spot on the stage level.* CHANDAN *and* TARA *walk into it. They both
    have a limp, like Dan. Tara's is on the opposite leg.*)

Tara. And me. Maybe we still are, like we've always been, inseparable. The way we started in life. Two lives and one body, in one comfortable womb. Till we were forced out.

    (PATEL *and* BHARATI *are seen.*)

And separated.

(*The lights cross-fade to the Patels' living room.* CHANDAN *and* TARA *are play-ing a game of cards. It is obvious* TARA *is winning.* BHARATI *has finished her morning puja.* PATEL *is checking the contents of his briefcase and is ready to leave for work.*)

BHARATI: Tara, drink your milk!

TARA: Sorry, new places slow down my peristalsis.

CHANDAN: New pinch for a new word.

TARA: Where are Thatha's brass tumblers?

BHARATI: They have yet to be unpacked.

PATEL: It's getting late for me. (*Gets up and moves to the children to pat them goodbye.*)

BHARATI: Your father doesn't want us to use them. (PATEL *looks at her.*) He doesn't want us to use any of your grandfather's things.

PATEL: What are you saying, Bharati?

BHARATI: Now that we've moved out of his house, he doesn't—

PATEL: Just a minute. It was you who didn't want to unpack them. You said so yourself. You said—

BHARATI: Me? Why would I not want to use my own father's gifts to us?

(*Pause.*)

PATEL: (*Quietly, controlling himself.*) Let me make this clear. I have no reason to tell you not to use your late father's—gifts. You're free to do as you please. In fact it was you who didn't want to unpack them, so why are you—

BHARATI: (*To* TARA.) Finish your milk.

TARA: I won't! Stop shoving it down my throat.

BHARATI: Tara!

PATEL: (*To* BHARATI.) Why d'you serve her so much if she doesn't want to—

BHARATI: But she must put on more weight!

PATEL: She's fine.

BHARATI: No! She's much too thin! She—she must put on more weight. This morning at the clinic, Dr. Kapoor checked their charts. She's lost half a pound in one week.

PATEL: Half a pound isn't much.

BHARATI: (*Over him.*) In one month she will lose a kilo! (*Getting worked *up.*) If I don't force her to eat, how will she gain weight? She will keep getting thinner till she's all shriveled and she is only—skin and bones! It's bad enough that she—they . . . (*Moving to* TARA.) Tara. Please!

PATEL: Tara will be fine. They are both going to—they'll be fine.

BHARATI: The doctors are concerned about—

PATEL: (*Testy.*) I know what the doctors said! (*Calmer.*) Dr. Kapoor was surprised at their progress and—

BHARATI: Surprised? Did you say—

PATEL: I meant to say he was happy to note—.

BHARATI: You said surprised!

PATEL: (*Testy again.*) I know I did but I meant he was happy—

CHANDAN: (*Offering.*) Or happily surprised?

TARA: Now don't start on your sidey jokes!*

CHANDAN: Or he was surprised that he was happy.

TARA: Enough, enough!

PATEL: (*Quietly, after a while.*) He was *pleased* with their progress. Beyond everyone's expectations. He is going to mention them in a medical journal.

BHARATI: No! I don't want my children being mentioned in any medical journal!

PATEL: Why, what's the harm? It will only be read by other doctors. It might help them with other such—

BHARATI: I just don't, that's all! I don't want all that publicity to start again.

PATEL: It's only a journal. It won't . . . (*Resigning.*) All right.

BHARATI: You *will* put on more weight, won't you Tara?

TARA: I'll do anything you say, Mummy. Except drink this milk.

BHARATI: (*Vaguely.*) Anything you say, Tara. Anything.

(*The lights cross-fade to the street. We see a girl of fifteen. She calls towards a house.*)

ROOPA: Prema! Premaa! (*No response.*) Premaa! Oh, hello Aunty. (*In Gujarati.*) *Kem chcho? Majhjha ma?* Is Prema in? (*Listens.*) Good. May she come out? Oh, nowhere special. I thought we could maybe go over to Yankee Doodle's for an ice cream or something. (*Listens.*) A cold? That's

---

Sidey joke is a slang term meaning a cheap joke.

okay. I'll come up and keep her company. (*Listens. Mock surprise.*) She told you that I was taking her to see *Fatal Attraction?* No, that's not true at all! Well, I did say we will see the movie at Eros, but I meant *Snow White and the Seven Dwarfs.* What? (*Listens.*) Oh, *Fatal Attraction* is playing there. Well you see, they show *Snow White* in the mornings. Well, I didn't want to tell you, you see. After all she is my best friend and all that, but actually it was her idea to see both. Look, I'm sorry she has a cold. On second thought, I'd better not see her. I might catch it myself. So, if you don't mind, I won't come up. Tell her not to feel bad. So sorry. Thank you. *Avjo.* (*She keeps grinning until presumably Aunty is out of sight. Then she sticks her rear out in Aunty's direction and makes a rude sound. She hesitantly walks towards the Patels' house, calling.*) Hello. (*No response, then louder.*) Hello. Tara!

(*The lights cross-fade again to the living room.* BHARATI *has exited to the kitchen.*)

PATEL: Chandan.

CHANDAN: (*Dealing the cards.*) Ya.

PATEL: I was just thinking—it may be a good idea for you to come to the office with me. (*Surreptitiously glances towards the kitchen.*)

CHANDAN: What for?

PATEL: Just to get a feel of it.

CHANDAN: You can take Tara. She'll make a great business woman.

TARA: How do you know?

CHANDAN: Because you always cheat at cards!

TARA: (*Cross, throwing her cards at* CHANDAN.) Just because I win doesn't mean I cheat, okay!

PATEL: (*Firmly.*) Chandan, I think I must insist that you come.

CHANDAN: We'll both come with you.

PATEL: No! (TARA *looks at* PATEL, *slightly hurt.* PATEL *softens.*) Yes. You may both come—if you want to.

(ROOPA *has been listening at the door.*)

ROOPA: Hello!

TARA: Oh, hi Roopa. Come on in.

ROOPA: (*False.*) Sorry! Hello Uncle. Sorry! Am I disturbing you?

TARA: Not at all. The men in the house were deciding on whether they were going to go hunting while the women looked after the cave.

CHANDAN: I haven't decided yet. (*Looking at* PATEL.) I might stay back in the cave and do my jigsaw puzzle.

TARA: Or carve another story on the walls. (*To* ROOPA.) He's a writer you know.

ROOPA: Ooh! How nice. What kind of writing? I love stories with ghosts and monsters.

PATEL: (*To* BHARATI.) Is there anything you need?

BHARATI: (*Off.*) No. Nothing you can get. (PATEL *picks up his briefcase on the coffee table.*)

PATEL: (*To* CHANDAN.) Well. Take care. If you two need to go out anywhere just call the office. I'll send the car. (*Patting* TARA.) Take care.

(PATEL *exits to street. He is fixed in a spotlight. He converses as if with a neighbor.*)

ROOPA: Oh good, at least you two are at home. Let's all sit down. Maybe we can watch a movie.

(*She makes herself comfortable on the sofa.* TARA *and* CHANDAN *stand beside her. Spot on them.*)

PATEL: Hello, Narayan *saab*. How is your health, today? Dr. Kapoor was inquiring after you.

ROOPA: (*To* CHANDAN.) Or tell us one of your stories. A monster story. You know, like oglers.

TARA: Oglers?

ROOPA: You know. Those monsters with one big eye in the middle of their foreheads.

CHANDAN: Ogres.

ROOPA: (*Defensively.*) Well, they *look* like they are ogling.

PATEL: I don't look well because I'm not—frankly I'm worried—about her.

CHANDAN: I haven't written any story about monsters—yet.

ROOPA: Really? How disappointing. What do you write about?

TARA: He writes about people he knows.

ROOPA: Really? How interesting.

TARA: Yes, he is going to write a story—about me.

PATEL: She needs help. I am not so sure—maybe some kind of therapy—or counseling.

TARA: About me. Strong. Healthy. Beautiful.

ROOPA: That's not you! That's me! He is writing a story about me. Aren't you, Chandan?

CHANDAN: (*Serious.*) Yes. You will be in the story too. As the Ogler.

PATEL: Maybe *I* need some advice—or counseling. I don't know—whether I am prepared for the worst.

TARA: I *am* strong. My mother has made me strong.

(*Spot on the three fades out.*)

PATEL: Maybe I'm expecting the worst. It may never happen—no. Things are getting out of hand. I *must* worry about her. Yes. I am worried— about my wife.

(*Cross-cut to* DAN, *who suddenly jerks as if woken from a nightmare.*)

DAN: No! No! That won't do. I can't have all that just swimming in my mind. The mind wanders too much. Unnecessary details, irrelevant characters which do not figure anywhere. I've got to put it all down. I've got to make a start. (*He goes to the cabinet for a refill. After a swig.*) Now steady, Dan boy. One thing at a time. Get to the desk. (*He moves to the table.*) Sit on the chair. (*He sits.*) Put your fingers on the keys. (*He does so.*) And type. (*He cannot.*) Well, you can't have everything. No wait—let me think. What is Tara? Kind, gentle, strong, her mother has given her strength. And Daddy? Silent? Angry? And—Mummy. (*Breaking away from his thoughts.*) This isn't fair to Tara. She deserves something better. She never got a fair deal. Not even from Nature. Neither of us did. Maybe God never wanted us to be separated. Destiny desires strange things. We were meant to die and our mortal remains preserved in formalin for future generations to study. Our purpose in life was maybe that. Only that. But even God does not always get what he wants. Conflict is the crux of life. A duel to the death between God and Nature on one side and on the other—the amazing Dr. Thakkar. (*Smiles.*) Yes. You will be pleased to know that I have found my beginning.

(*A television show–type signature tune fades in while the spot fades out. Although* DAN *is interviewing* DR. THAKKAR, *he remains where he is, in darkness.*)

The tune ends and a spot picks up DR. THAKKAR, *seated as if being interviewed in a studio.*)

DAN: (*Mock cheerful.*) Good evening, viewers and welcome to another edition of *Marvels in the World of Medicine.* We have with us this evening at our studio Dr. Umakant Thakkar, who has been in the news lately for his outstanding work at the Queen Victoria Memorial Hospital in Bombay. Dr. Thakkar has been associated with many major hospitals in the U.S.A., most notably the Children's Hospital in Philadelphia. During his stay at the Queen Victoria Hospital, he was surgeon-in-chief to a most unique and complex surgery, the first of its kind in India. Dr. Thakkar, could you tell us what was so special about this surgery?

DR. THAKKAR: To start with, the patients were only a few months old and—

DAN: How old were they exactly?

DR. THAKKAR: Oh, three months.

DAN: (*Mock surprise.*) Three months? Was the surgery really necessary?

DR. THAKKAR: Yes, absolutely. Surgery was their only chance of survival. You see, they were twins, conjoined from the chest down.

DAN: Siamese twins?

DR. THAKKAR: Yes. That is the common term used for them.

DAN: Is it a rare phenomenon?

DR. THAKKAR: Twins as such are not so rare, the chances—

DAN: What about Siamese twins?

DR. THAKKAR: Conjoined twins are quite rare. I think one in every fifty thousand twin conceptions could have a probability of containing this—defect.

DAN: How does it happen?

DR. THAKKAR: Sometimes, we don't know why, a fertilized egg, destined to separate and develop into two different embryos, fails to do so fully. The result is a conjoinment—in this case from the breastbone down through the pelvic area. It is indeed a miracle that they were born alive. Twins with a conjunction of such complexity are, in most cases, still-born.

DAN: How many twins of this kind have actually survived through birth?

DR. THAKKAR: There are, I think, seven recorded cases in medical literature, but—

DAN: And how many are still alive?

DR. THAKKAR: In all cases, so far, one twin has always died by the age of four.

DAN: Dr. Thakkar, what is your opinion on the Patel twins? Will they survive?

DR. THAKKAR: You see, there is something even more remarkable about this case.

DAN: And what is that?

DR. THAKKAR: Conjoined twins—your Siamese twins—developing from one fertilized ovum are invariably of the same sex. Well, almost invariably. But these two were obviously from different fertilized eggs.

DAN: So?

DR. THAKKAR: The twins are of different sexes. Very, very rare.

DAN: (*Aside.*) A freak among freaks. Now I know I'll be a really brilliant writer.

(*Spot fades out on* DR. THAKKAR *as we hear the explosive opening of Brahms' first piano concerto. The street area is lit.* TARA *enters street. She mimes meeting someone and smiling, starting a conversation. After a while she slowly lifts the leg of her trouser to reveal her artificial limb. She laughs in an ugly way. Then she says goodbye and enters the living room as the lights cross-fade.* CHANDAN *is lying on his back on the floor listening to the music, conducting an imaginary orchestra in the heavens.*)

TARA: Oh, I hate those girls!

CHANDAN: (*Waving his hands to the music.*) What? Made friends already?

TARA: You must be joking. (*Listening to the music.*) Oh! I love this part.

CHANDAN: How was physio?

TARA: Nice doctor. Rotten nurse. Not like Bangalore.

CHANDAN: (*Jovial.*) Doctors. Nurses. A painful necessity in our lives. (*Referring to the music.*) Now comes the best part.

TARA: Mind you. Some of the doctors aren't so painful to look at. This one's called Dr. Gokhale. He's handsome in a *Ghati* sort of way. I love Maharashtrians!

CHANDAN: In London you swore you were going to marry that Irish doctor, what's-his-name. And we were only twelve then.

TARA: That was London. This is Bombay. One learns to love the natives. I know.

CHANDAN: How can you know at twelve? How can you know at sixteen?

TARA: We women mature fast. Speaking of maturity, you better not skip any physiotherapy sessions. Daddy wants you to be big and sturdy. He will find out from the hospital and—this music is so—I don't know.

CHANDAN: It has passion.

TARA: Yes. Beethoven must have been a passionate man.

CHANDAN: Brahms.

TARA: Yes and—what?

CHANDAN: Brahms. Not Beethoven. Brahms' first piano concerto.

TARA: Are you sure?

CHANDAN: Of course. His very first.

TARA: Stop it. Turn it off. I thought that was Beethoven.

CHANDAN: (*He stops the music.*) You've heard this so often.

TARA: Yes. But I always thought it was Beethoven.

CHANDAN: Well, they do sound similar. But this one is unmistakably Brahms. It has his quality of high tragedy and romance—of youth bursting forth in the world with all its claim. A spring-like freshness—

TARA: Do me a favor. When you become a writer, stay away from poetry.

CHANDAN: It's written on the record cover.

TARA: You mean you can feel all that in the music?

CHANDAN: (*Thinking about it.*) Well, his music is so—I don't know.

(*They both laugh.*)

TARA: Where's Mummy?

CHANDAN: In the kitchen, where else? Showing the new cook how to make your favorite dishes.

TARA: I think I'm going to like Bombay. It's all so new and different!

CHANDAN: We've been here before.

TARA: When? Oh, you mean—

CHANDAN: Yes. The surgery was done here.

(TARA *giggles.*)

CHANDAN: What's so funny?

TARA: You could say that we were "separated" when we were babies in Bombay.

CHANDAN: Separated? (*Understanding.*) Oh—right! And we find each other again in Bombay.

TARA: (*Mock "filmi" style.*)* Bhaiya! (*She hugs him.*)

CHANDAN: Careful, we are in Bombay. You just called me a *doodhwalla.*

TARA: Oh Chandu. What would I do without you?

CHANDAN: Tara, stop saying such things.

TARA: (*Slapping his back.*) I'd probably have a ball, that's what I would do. Having both Mummy and Daddy dancing around me. "Yes, Tara!" "No, Tara!" "Anything you say Tara!"

CHANDAN: They do that now.

TARA: Well, Mummy, yes. It's all right. I can take it. I'm a big girl now.

CHANDAN: No it's not all right. You can't take it, you're still a little girl with a wild imagination.

TARA: Women have an instinct for these things.

CHANDAN: Women, not girls.

TARA: It's *innate!* We are born with it!

CHANDAN: (*Easing off.*) Okay, okay! I leave you with your instincts. The world of Brahms awaits me.

(*He leans over and plays it softly. They both listen to the music. After a while* TARA *speaks.*)

TARA: You know who I met? The ugliest girls in the whole world. Prema and Nalini. They live in the building opposite. They had a friend with them. Equally ugly. They were all running across the street laughing their ugly heads off over something. When they saw me get off the car, they stopped. They stopped running and they stopped laughing. And they waited, watching me get off and walk across the footpath towards them. Embarrassing me, making me go slower than I would. When I reached them they grinned. Nalini whispered something to her ugly friend. I knew what was coming. Might as well play along, I thought. I smiled and introduced myself. We exchanged names. Nalini and Prema. The other one just tittered. I smile to her as well. Then I showed it to them. The duckling couldn't believe her eyes. She stared at my leg. She felt it and knocked on it. Silly as well as ugly, I thought. "The very

---

*"Filmi": Imitating a cliché scene in Indian films.

best from Jaipur," I said. "We get them in pairs. My twin brother wears the other one."

CHANDAN: (*Laughing.*) You didn't.

TARA: Then they ran off. Pleased with themselves, laughing even harder. Their day was made. One of these days I'm going to tell them exactly how frightful they look.

CHANDAN: Maybe they already know.

TARA: Still, it would be nice to see their reaction. Oh, play the music real loud. Beethoven was never as good as this.

(CHANDAN *turns up the volume. With the next phase of music* ROOPA *is seen at the street as she hesitantly walks towards the Patels' house. She enters and stands near the door not knowing what to do.* CHANDAN *notices her first. He stops the music.*)

TARA: Why did you do that? I was just enjoying—

CHANDAN: Hello.

TARA: (*Turning around.*) Oh, hello.

ROOPA: Hello.

TARA: Won't you come in? We were just talking about you.

ROOPA: (*Gushing.*) Oh, really? We've only just met!

TARA: Yes. I was just telling Chandu about how you were admiring my leg.

ROOPA: Oh that! I'm sorry, I hope you didn't mind.

TARA: Mind? Why should I mind?

ROOPA: Oh it's just that—I thought you might feel—you know.

TARA: Hurt? Embarrassed? Not at all. You can say it sort of "runs" in the family—this leg. Chandu—show her yours.

(CHANDAN *proudly shows his Jaipur leg to her.*)

ROOPA: Oh, wow! I can't believe it. *Both* of you! I don't get it. How? When?

TARA: We don't get it either. And we didn't get your name.

ROOPA: Oh. Didn't I tell you? Nalini and Prema didn't give me half a chance. You know, those two love to gas about. If I were you I would stay away from them. They'll talk behind your back and all that. Real bitches. They'll think of all kinds of names to call you. That Bugs Bunny and that drumstick. Some people are like that. You know.

TARA: Yes. I know. I still haven't got your name.

ROOPA: Oh—oh. I'm Roopa. Hi, you're Tara, I know and—

TARA: This is Chandan.

CHANDAN: Hi.

ROOPA: Hi. And you're twins? Funny, you don't resemble each other.

CHANDAN: Not all twins are peas in pods.

ROOPA: (*Not understanding.*) Huh?

CHANDAN: Two peas in a pod. That's something we aren't.

ROOPA: Uh, yes. Yes. Very funny.

CHANDAN: Is it? I didn't think so.

ROOPA: You know—two peas in a pot. Isn't that funny?

TARA: (*Observing she hasn't understood.*) Oh, yes of course. (*Nudging* CHANDAN.) Very funny. Two peas in a (*Distinctly.*) pot.

CHANDAN: (*Catching on.*) Yes. Very funny.

(ROOPA *and* CHANDAN *laugh.*)

TARA: (*Laughing as well.*) Hysterical.

(TARA *and* CHANDAN *burst into genuine laughter.* ROOPA *realizes that things aren't quite as lucid as they seem. She stops laughing.*)

ROOPA: Well. I didn't think it was *that* funny.

CHANDAN: (*Controlling his laughter.*) Excuse me. (*He gets up.*) I think I must write something down.

(*He moves towards his room. He can't control himself and bursts out laughing. He exits muttering "two peas in a pot!"*)

ROOPA: (*Visibly annoyed.*) Well!

TARA: Oh, don't mind. It's just some silly family joke.

ROOPA: Very silly if you ask me.

TARA: Yes. Yes. So tell me about yourself. Which standard are you in?

ROOPA: I've finished my ninth. And you?

TARA: We've just completed our tenth. The results aren't out yet.

ROOPA: Where are you from?

TARA: Bangalore.

ROOPA: Oh really? We're Kannadigas too. My mum's from Bangalore.

TARA: Which part?

ROOPA: (*A little crushed.*) Well, Tumkur really. But I was born here.

TARA: My mother is from Bangalore. My dad's Gujarati.

ROOPA: Oh, an intercaste marriage! Was it a love marriage? Tell. Tell.

TARA: Yes. My father had to leave his parents because of the marriage, if you really want to know.

ROOPA: No! I didn't mean to be nosy or anything! But don't stop now.

TARA: There's nothing much to tell. My grandfather, my mother's father, was a very influential person. But my dad didn't take any help from him. Today my dad is the General Manager of Indo-Swede Pharmacia, the biggest pharmaceutical company in the country. Heard of it?

ROOPA: Yes. I love their cough syrup!

TARA: He will soon be one of the directors.

ROOPA: Oh, that's great. So you're going to do your plus two here in Bombay.

TARA: (*Pause.*) Well. I don't know.

ROOPA: What d'you mean? Aren't you going to live here?

TARA: Yes. But I will soon be going in for surgery.

ROOPA: Oh, how sad! On your leg.

TARA: No. A kidney transplant.

ROOPA: Gosh!

TARA: We knew it was going to happen. I was prepared.

ROOPA: And your brother? Will he also . . . ?

TARA: Oh, no. He's fine. Thank God for that.

ROOPA: Don't you need someone to—you know—give you a kidney.

TARA: A donor. Yes. I've got one.

ROOPA: Your brother?

TARA: No.

ROOPA: Your dad?

TARA: No.

ROOPA: Then your—?

(BHARATI *enters.*)

BHARATI: Tara, I hope you'll like Chinese for dinner. Ida says chow mein is her speciality. Oh, how I miss Gopi. Maybe I should call Vadivu *akka* and ask her to send him after all. Hello—I see you've made friends already.

ROOPA: (*Grinning. Speaking in her best Kannada.*) Hello, Aunty. *Heg iddira?*

BHARATI: Oh, we have a Kannadiga for a neighbor in Bombay. How refreshing! Specially since we had all those Gujarati neighbors in Bangalore.

ROOPA: Oh, we have them here too.

(*Pause, while* BHARATI *beams and observes* ROOPA.)

BHARATI: Sit down—er . . .

TARA: Roopa.

BHARATI: Roopa. (*Pause.*) I—I mustn't interrupt you two from . . . Tara what's Chandan up to?

TARA: I think he's writing.

BHARATI: That boy! Let me see if he needs anything.

(*She exits to* CHANDAN's *room.*)

ROOPA: I think I better get going.

TARA: Well, I'll see you later. If you need my old notes or textbooks or anything, just ask.

ROOPA: Right. And remember to stay away from that Prema and Nalini. They will be nasty to you.

TARA: That's okay. I can handle them.

ROOPA: That's what you think. Besides, they are not really our standard you know. Their English isn't that good. They won't understand your jokes like peas in pots and all that.

TARA: (*Smiling.*) Well, we'll teach them.

ROOPA: You will be wasting your time on them. They are—you know (*Crinkling her nose in disgust.*) *wandh tarah.*

TARA: One *tarah?*

ROOPA: Odd types. Don't you know Kannada?

TARA: (*Understanding.*) Oh! *Wandu tarah!* (*Meaningfully.*) Yes, I know what you mean.

ROOPA: Well forewarned is forehanded. So. Take care. Bye.

(BHARATI *enters.*)

BHARATI: Tara! You haven't finished unpacking. The green suitcase is still lying there.

TARA: It's got all my old things, I don't—

BHARATI: Do it now!

(TARA *moves to her room.*)

TARA: That will take the whole day! Okay, bye Roopa. Come any time.

ROOPA: Bye! (TARA *exits. There is an awkward moment between* BHARATI *and* ROOPA. *After a while* ROOPA *speaks.*) Well, *bartheeni* Aunty.

BHARATI: No. No. Stay for a while. Please.

ROOPA: No. You must be having a lot of work to do.

BHARATI: Sit down.

ROOPA: (*Grinning embarrassedly.*) No. It's okay.

BHARATI: (*With an element of sternness.*) Sit down.

ROOPA: (*Laughing uncomfortably.*) If you say so. (*She sits.*)

BHARATI: Tara is a very nice girl.

(ROOPA *is stunned at first. Then—.*)

ROOPA: Yes! An extremely nice girl.

BHARATI: Good. I'm glad you think so.

ROOPA: (*Nervous.*) Yes.

BHARATI: And you will be her friend?

ROOPA: Yes. Yes! Certainly. Such a nice girl.

BHARATI: She—she must make more friends. Chandan is all right—he has his writing, but she—he is different, he is sort of *self-contained,* but Tara—she can be very good company and she has her talents. She can be very witty and, of course, she is intelligent. I have seen to it that she . . . more than makes up in some ways for what she . . . doesn't have.

ROOPA: (*Nodding violently.*) Oh yes! That she does.

BHARATI: You will be her friend?

ROOPA: (*Hesitantly.*) Well, yes. If you say so.

BHARATI: You will be her best friend?

ROOPA: (*Now playing hard to get.*) Well, I don't know. Nalini and Prema are my best friends.

BHARATI: If you promise to be her best friend—what I mean is if you would like to be her friend—I will be most grateful to you and I will show it—in whatever way you want me to.

ROOPA: I don't think I . . . understand.

(*Pause.*)

BHARATI: (*Suddenly.*) Do you have a VCR at home?

ROOPA: (*Puzzled.*) Yes.

BHARATI: (*Disappointed.*) Oh. And you see a lot of films?

ROOPA: Not a lot. My mother only allows me to watch a movie on Sunday afternoons.

BHARATI: So—there must be a lot of films you are dying to see.

ROOPA: Yes. Plenty.

BHARATI: You can see them here, any time you want to. No restrictions.

ROOPA: (*Guarded.*) I don't know what my mother would say.

BHARATI: How will she know?

ROOPA: (*Thinking about it. Then—.*) Can I watch *Fatal Attraction?*

BHARATI: (*Sharply.*) You can watch whatever you want! (*More subdued.*) Just be my Tara's friend.

ROOPA: Yes. May I go now?

BHARATI: Yes. First promise me that you will be her friend.

ROOPA: I don't know. Can I think about it?

BHARATI: (*Hissing.*) Promise me now!

ROOPA: Look, I—I will come back later. Okay?

BHARATI: (*Recovering.*) Yes. Of course. I'm sorry I didn't mean to . . . force anything on you.

ROOPA: (*Backing towards the door.*) It's okay. I understand. I will come again.

BHARATI: Yes. Please! Do come!

ROOPA: I will. Bye.

(*She scoots down to the street. Spot on* BHARATI. ROOPA *calls to her friends.*)

ROOPA: (*Urgently.*) Prema! Premaa! Come quick! Where's Nalini? Never mind, you come here! My God! Oh, my God! Guess what? I went to her house! Yes. Right inside! I met everyone there. She is a real freak of Nature all right, but wait till you see her mother! Oh God! I can't tell you—she is *really—wandh tarah.* Oh God! I'll never go there again.

(*Spot off on street and* BHARATI, *cross-fade to* DR. THAKKAR, *who is still in the middle of his interview.*)

DR. THAKKAR: The parents were warned of the odds against survival. They were, understandably, totally disheartened in the beginning. But, soon, even the remotest chance for survival was received with hope once they were made aware of the facilities offered by modern technology. I had a conference with the resident doctors at the Victoria Hospital. A very efficient and competent team of doctors. I was shown the test reports. X-rays, scan results from the Bangalore hospital. There were many points to be reconfirmed and further observations were necessary before any decision on surgery could be taken. The twins were flown in from Bangalore and were moved immediately to the intensive care unit for observation and tests. It was two weeks of exhaustive work. The results were encouraging. The twins did not share any vital organ. There were two hearts clearly indicated by two electrocardiograms. There were two livers, although joined. Each twin would have one kidney—all this meant that there was a very strong possibility of both twins surviving. What we needed to know more about was the pelvic region and the extent of conjoinment there—

(*Light cross-fades to* PATEL *on the phone.* BHARATI *is tense and listens to him intently.*)

PATEL: Yes, Dr. Kapoor. I am happy to hear that . . . Indeed she is a very lucky girl . . . Yes. As soon as possible. Well, after what she has been through so far . . . anyway, he will be glad she won't have to go for her dialysis after the surgery. Don't worry doctor, she is a very high-spirited girl. Knowing her, she will probably joke about it. And her brother gives her enough moral support. Yes, I will call you tomorrow. Thank you, doctor. Thank you.

BHARATI: (*Excited.*) So? Everything is all right? We are compatible? I think God wanted it this way—

PATEL: (*Quietly.*) Bharati. You cannot give her your kidney.

BHARATI: But just now—on the phone—you were making preparations.

PATEL: Tara is very lucky. She has found another donor.

BHARATI: A commercial donor?

PATEL: Yes.

BHARATI: Why? What is wrong if—why can't she have mine?

PATEL: You can't, that's all.

BHARATI: You won't let me! I am going to call Dr. Kapoor right away and tell him to make the—

PATEL: It's no use Bharati.

BHARATI: You can't stop me from doing what I want! (*Dialing.*) 6438—

PATEL: Bharati put down that phone!

BHARATI: How dare you run my life!

PATEL: Oh, for God's sake! You are getting out of hand!

BHARATI: Oh, God! What's his number? 64 . . .

PATEL: Bharati calm down.

BHARATI: His number! (*Hysterical.*) Give me his phone number!

PATEL: I will not.

BHARATI: Very well. I will look it up in the—

PATEL: You don't even know his full name.

BHARATI: I—I can call . . .

PATEL: Who? Bharati, stop pretending. You are in no condition to be taking major decisions.

BHARATI: (*Quietening down.*) Give me his number.

PATEL: I can give you his number. But I will not let you donate your kidney
to her.

BHARATI: The tests showed that I could do it. There—there is nothing
wrong in it.

PATEL: Yes. It is wrong. Now that we have a donor, I will not let you do it.

BHARATI: Think of the expenses involved.

PATEL: When have expenses ever bothered you? Your father's wealth has
always been your strength against me. Don't talk about expenses to me!

BHARATI: (*Pleading.*) Why won't you let me do it?

PATEL: (*Controlling.*) *Because*—need I tell you? Because I do not want you
to have the satisfaction of doing it.

BHARATI: I will do it!

PATEL: You will have to obey me. It's *my* turn now.

BHARATI: I want to give her a part of me!

PATEL: (*Holding her roughly.*) Now listen! You need help. I'm going to
arrange for a doctor to examine you thoroughly.

BHARATI: I am fine. I don't need a doctor. My blood pressure is under
control and—

PATEL: I meant a psychiatrist.

BHARATI: I don't need one!

PATEL: It can't do you any harm.

BHARATI: I tell you I don't need one! You—you are wasting your time.
Think about Tara and Chandan.

PATEL: I am thinking about them. That's why I need to make you more stable.

BHARATI: (*Calming down.*) Look. Don't worry about me. I am perfectly all right.

PATEL: I cannot handle your moods any longer. Have you looked at yourself recently? Look at the way you behave, the way you react to—

BHARATI: I promise to control myself in future. Just—

PATEL: I know you want to, but can you?

BHARATI: Just—just let me do what I want to.

PATEL: Anything but allow you to—

BHARATI: Who are you to stop me? Just who do you think you are?

PATEL: Sit down, Bharati.

BHARATI: This is no way to treat me.

PATEL: (*Pushing her down.*) Sit down. Now listen. I am going to fix an appointment for you and you are going to see that doctor.

BHARATI: I don't want to. I don't *need* to!

PATEL: You will. I *demand* it from you.

BHARATI: All right! You want me to be all right? Yes. I will do it.

PATEL: Good. I will call him right now.

BHARATI: I will tell her.

(PATEL *stops.*)

BHARATI: I will tell them everything.

(PATEL *goes to her and slaps her. The moment* BHARATI *recovers, she looks at him with some triumph.*)

PATEL: You wouldn't dare tell them. Not you. Please, don't! Not yet!

BHARATI: Then let me do what I want to do.

PATEL: (*Defeated.*) You cannot tell them. For their sake, don't! (PATEL *looks at her suddenly with determination.*) If at all they must know, it will be from me. Not from you.

(*Cross-fade to* DAN *who is busy typing. He stops and reads out his last line.*)

DAN: "If at all they must know, it will be from me. Not from you."

(DAN *continues to type as the lights cross-fade to the living room.* ROOPA, TARA, *and* CHANDAN *are watching a movie.* BHARATI *is knitting. As the movie ends—*)

ROOPA: Oh, that was wonderful! Wasn't it? I love surprise endings.

CHANDAN: It was very predictable.

TARA: I didn't think so. I feel sorry for that woman.

ROOPA: What a nice title: *The Mirror Cracked*. Very dramatic.

TARA: Imagine not being able to have children because somebody gave her German measles when she was pregnant.

ROOPA: How does the poem go?

CHANDAN:

The curse has come upon me!
Cried the Lady of Shallot.

ROOPA: I feel sorry for the Lady of Shallot. Locked up. Not being able to see the world, you know. Just sitting and weaving a tapestry or something. And having a cracked mirror.

TARA: The mirror cracks later.

ROOPA: But still. Seven years' bad luck and all that.

BHARATI: More coffee for you, Roopa? (BHARATI *picks up their mugs.*)

ROOPA: No, thank you Aunty. (*To* CHANDAN.) Your mother's coffee is really something.

(BHARATI *exits to kitchen.*)

CHANDAN: Ida makes it.

ROOPA: Really? But it has that typical Southie flavor. I think it's the—you know—concoction.

CHANDAN: Concoction?

TARA: She means decoction.

ROOPA: Decoction—yes of course! How silly of me. A concoction is something you have when you get hit on the head. Anyway, I'm glad I can have coffee here. My mother only gives me milk. (*To* TARA.) You would have had plenty of milk being a Patel and all that. (*Laughing as if she has made a joke.*)

TARA: (*To* CHANDAN.) Did you get that?

CHANDAN: No. Did she?

ROOPA: You mean you don't know about Patels?

TARA: Don't know what?

ROOPA: Oh, so you don't know!

CHANDAN: Unless you tell us what it is, how will we know whether we know?

ROOPA: It's probably not true. It's just an old saying. Prema told me when she came to know you were Patels. It's about milk.

(BHARATI *enters.*)

TARA: What is?

ROOPA: They drown them in milk.

BHARATI: (*Tense.*) Are you sure you wouldn't like another cup of coffee?

ROOPA: (*In Kannada.*) *Beda,* Aunty, thanks.

TARA: They drown what in milk?

BHARATI: Well then, don't you think its time you went home? Your mother might be worried

ROOPA: Oh, I don't think she will be.

BHARATI: She might be concerned about how much video you are watching here.

ROOPA: (*Understanding.*) Oh. Yes, I didn't think of that. Well, I better go home then.

TARA: I'll come out with you.

(*They both move to the door.*)

ROOPA: (*To* BHARATI.) Well, thanks for the coffee, Aunty—and the movies.

BHARATI: (*Loaded.*) Don't mention it!

ROOPA: Bye, Chandan. Let me read your story sometime. I hope I'm in it.

CHANDAN: Don't worry. You are.

(TARA *and* ROOPA *go out to the street.* BHARATI *joins* CHANDAN *on the sofa.*)

BHARATI: Chandan. What's your story about?

CHANDAN: It's called "The Ogler Next Door."

BHARATI: It's—it's not about anything else?

CHANDAN: Like what?

TARA: (*On the street with* ROOPA.) Well, Roopa, what's all this about drowning them in milk?

ROOPA: Oh—nothing. I don't think I will tell you.

TARA: Well—all right.

ROOPA: Aren't you dying to know?

BHARATI: I wish your father would pay more attention to Tara.

CHANDAN: He does. He doesn't like to show his affection.

BHARATI: Don't tell me about your father. He is more worried about your career than hers.

CHANDAN: That's because I'm more sure of what I want. She is just . . . playing it cool.

TARA: Yes, I am. But you don't have to tell me if you don't want to.

ROOPA: I don't want to!

TARA: Rubbish! You are dying to tell me.

BHARATI: It's time Tara decided what she wants to be. Women have to do that as well these days. She must have a career.

CHANDAN: She can do whatever she wants. Grandfather's trust will leave us both money, isn't it?

BHARATI: Yes. But she must have *something to do!* She can't be—aimless all her life.

CHANDAN: There is nothing aimless about Tara's life.

TARA: Go home! It's probably something you haven't fully understood yourself.

ROOPA: I beg your pardon! Don't think you are very smart.

TARA: Only in comparison.

BHARATI: It's all right while she is young. It's all very cute and comfortable when she makes witty remarks. But let her grow up. Yes, Chandan. The world will tolerate you. The world will accept you—but not her! Oh, the pain she is going to feel when she sees herself at eighteen or twenty. Thirty is unthinkable. And what about forty and fifty! Oh, God!

CHANDAN: Mummy. Tara is my sister. Everything will be fine.

ROOPA: Since you insist, I will tell you. It may not be true. But this is what I have heard. The Patels in the old days were unhappy with getting girl babies—you know dowry and things like that—so they used to drown them in milk.

(*Pause.*)

TARA: In *milk?*

ROOPA: So when people asked about how the baby died, they could say that she choked while drinking her milk.

(*Pause.* TARA *suddenly laughs.*)

TARA: How absurd!

ROOPA: (*Laughing.*) Silly, isn't it?

TARA: (*Laughing.*) Absolutely hilarious.

ROOPA: What a waste of milk!

TARA: Is *that* what Mummy was trying to stop you from telling me?

BHARATI: Your father has a lot of plans for you.

CHANDAN: I have a lot of plans for me.

BHARATI: And Tara?

CHANDAN: I'll always be there if she needs my help. But I don't think she will.

BHARATI: She will. She doesn't know it, but she will.

CHANDAN: Do you have plans for her?

BHARATI: Yes. I plan for her happiness. I mean to give her all the love and affection which I can give. It's what she—deserves. *Love can make up for a lot.*

TARA: Mummy is so cute—sometimes.

ROOPA: (*Disagreeing.*) Yes.

TARA: When we were young, I used to be quite a sick child.

ROOPA: What with all your problems.

TARA: And it was always I who got her attention and care.

ROOPA: That must have made Chandan quite jealous.

TARA: A little bit I suppose. But he has always been so . . . he has never really asked for much. *He is so happy with so little.* I have always demanded more and more.

ROOPA: It pays sometimes to be the sickly one.

TARA: I really used to play hard to get. Sulking all the time. And when I smiled, it made everyone quite . . . relieved! As if, if I didn't smile I would just curl up and die! Mummy said my eyes really twinkled when I smiled.

ROOPA: (*Not happy at hearing such a cheerful story.*) Twinkle Tara—that's really cute. And what about your father? Did he spoil you just as much?

TARA: (*After a while.*) I don't remember.

(*Spot fades out on* TARA *and* ROOPA.)

CHANDAN: Is that a sweater you are knitting for Tara?

BHARATI: Yes.

CHANDAN: You've dropped a stitch.

(*Lights cross-fade to street.* ROOPA *has gone.* TARA *talks to* PATEL *as they come home.*)

TARA: Oh, nothing much, we've been watching movies the whole day.

PATEL: The whole day? And Chandan?

TARA: Him too.

PATEL: And your mother?

TARA: Well, you know how she is. You can't tell exactly what she is doing.

(*They enter. Both* BHARATI *and* CHANDAN *are busy unraveling the knitting.* CHANDAN *is trying to keep the wool in order.* BHARATI *is a bit more frantic.*)

PATEL: Hello.

CHANDAN: Hi, Daddy.

PATEL: What are you two doing?

CHANDAN: Mummy's knitting and I'm helping her sort out her mistake.

PATEL: Let Tara do it.

CHANDAN: It's okay.

PATEL: Give it to her.

CHANDAN: Why?

BHARATI: It's all right, I'll manage. Leave it.

CHANDAN: I will just roll all this and—

PATEL: Chandan, leave that damn thing alone!

BHARATI: (*Frantic.*) Go! Chandan, just go!

PATEL: (*To* BHARATI.) How dare you do this to him?

CHANDAN: Wait a minute, Daddy, she never asked me to do any—

PATEL: Can't you even look after the children?

CHANDAN: Look Daddy, it's—

PATEL: What did you do the whole day, huh? Watch video?

BHARATI: I can't think of things for them to do all the time!

PATEL: But you can think of turning him into a sissy—teaching him to knit!

CHANDAN: Daddy, that's unfair.

BHARATI: Chandan, *please* go to your room!

CHANDAN: All I'm doing is helping Mummy to—

PATEL: I am disappointed in you. From now on you are coming to the office with me. I can't see you rotting at home!

CHANDAN: I don't want to go to the office!

PATEL: You will come with me to the office until your college starts.

CHANDAN: I don't want to go to college! (*Fighting his tears.*) Not without Tara! If she is going in for surgery, I'll miss a year too!

PATEL: You will not. I won't allow it.

CHANDAN: I will not go to college without Tara!

PATEL: That would make me very unhappy.

CHANDAN: (*Shouting.*) Well, that's too bad! (*Backing off to his room.*) That's just too bad!

(CHANDAN *exits.*)

BHARATI: Say it! Go on, say it—that it's all my fault! That I am turning the children against you.

(TARA *stands back frightened.*)

PATEL: You are turning them against the whole world.

BHARATI: *I* am doing that?

PATEL: Yes! Look at the way you treat Tara. As if she is made of glass. You coddle her, you pet her, you spoil her. She's grown up feeling she doesn't need anyone but you!

BHARATI: What d'you want me to do? Just tell me in plain, simple words what you want me to do and I'll do it!

PATEL: Let go. Just let go. And let me handle them.

BHARATI: All right. You stay at home then! You stay at home and watch what they can do and what they can't. You remind them of what they can't be. It's easy for you to talk about their future and your plans. But tell them what they should do now. This day, this hour, this minute. Tell them! I want to hear!

PATEL: Chandan is going to study further and he will go abroad for his higher studies.

BHARATI: And Tara?

PATEL: When have you ever allowed me to make any plans for her?

BHARATI: I'm stopping you from making plans for my daughter?

PATEL: Don't lie. Bharati! You don't want me to, and you know it. You have told me so a dozen times.

BHARATI: That's not true!

PATEL: You have to face it. You want her to believe you are the only one who loves her!

BHARATI: Why? Why would I want that!

PATEL: (*Quietly.*) You don't want me to say it, do you? And you threaten me that you will tell them. But you won't. You can't. You don't know what you want.

BHARATI: Just leave me alone, with my daughter.

PATEL: Is that what you want? To love her. You said your love will make up for a lot, didn't you?

BHARATI: Ask her! Ask her what she wants and give it to her!

PATEL: You know she loves you. You're sure of that. Don't make her choose between us, for God's sake! You're ruining her life because you are sick. I want to help you Bharati, please allow me to help you.

BHARATI: I don't need your help.

PATEL: Look at you. Do you ever go out? No. Have you made any friends? We've been here for two months and you haven't even talked to anyone. You just sit here rotting.

BHARATI: I don't need anyone!

PATEL: Exactly! That's what I want from you. Don't make my children say that.

BHARATI: I'm not doing that! I've always made sure that Tara has had friends. I go out of my way to—why that Roopa . . . she . . . she—what you're saying just isn't true! You—you can't lie about me like that in front of my children. Now that they are at an impressionable age and might take your words very seriously.

PATEL: (*Angry.*) Oh! How deviously clever you are! I'm the liar and I'm the one who is feeding them with lies when they're at an impressionable age? I am the violent one and you are the "victim" of my wrath. You don't go out because I don't let you. Go on, say it.

BHARATI: Stop it! Stop this madness and let me live in peace!

PATEL: How can I? Not now, when you are turning my own children against me.

BHARATI: You said it! (*Laughing. Almost demented.*) I knew you would say it! Say it again. I don't care—after all these lies you've said about me!

PATEL: Yes, call me a liar, a wife beater, a child abuser. It's what you want me to be! And *you.* You want them to believe you love them very much.

BHARATI: Yes!

PATEL: (*Grabs* TARA.) Look at her, Bharati. And tell her that you love her very much.

BHARATI: Tara knows it. Leave her alone!

TARA: Daddy—

PATEL: Tara, please believe me when I say that I love you very much and *I have never in all my life loved you less or more than I have loved your brother.* But your mother—

BHARATI: (*Hysterical.*) Stop it! Don't fill her with nonsense about me.

PATEL: But your mother would like you to believe that it's not true. I love you. (*Looking at* BHARATI.) We both do.

TARA: I never doubted it, Daddy. I . . . I don't feel too . . .

(TARA *slumps like a rag doll into* PATEL's *arms.*)

PATEL: Oh God! Her insulin. No! Get the sugar!

BHARATI: (*Rooted to her spot.*) She is dying! My Tara is dying!

PATEL: (*Shouts.*) Get the sugar! (BHARATI *doesn't move.*) Didn't you hear me? Get me some sugar before she—(*He realizes he will have to do it himself. He carries* TARA *to the kitchen.*)

(BHARATI *is dazed. She sits on the sofa and sobs. Spot on her. The spot on* DAN *fades in as he unwinds the sheet on his typewriter. He reads aloud.*)

DAN: "Bharati sobs. Patel brings in the revived Tara. Patel picks up the phone and dials the hospital. The act ends with the explosive opening of Brahms' first piano concerto."

(DAN *stretches himself while the concerto plays. Slow fade out on* BHARATI.)

Act Two

Spot on BHARATI *and* TARA. *Music. There is a certain beatitude in* BHARATI's *demonstration of affection for* TARA.

BHARATI: Tara! My beautiful baby! You are my most beautiful baby! I love you very much.

TARA: (*Enjoying this affection.*) Yes, Mummy. I know that.

BHARATI: I want you to remember that, Tara.

TARA: I will.

BHARATI: Everything will be all right. Now that I am giving you a part of me. Everything will be all right.

TARA: Do you really want to do that, Mummy?

BHARATI: Very much.

TARA: Because you love me so much.

BHARATI: Yes. That's why. Don't worry. You will be fine. After the operations, we will all be happy together. And I will make up for . . . for . . . your father, and I will make up for all the things God hasn't given you.

TARA: I have plenty. I have you.

BHARATI: Yes. Thank you, Tara! Thank you.

(BHARATI *is overwhelmed and they embrace. Cross-fade to* DAN, *who is looking at a book.*)

DAN: I was looking through this old scrap book. A present Daddy gave me just before I left. It's got all our news cuttings. Dr. Thakkar is in the headlines. Then there are interviews with my Mom and Dad. And worst of all a hideous photograph of us. Before and after. I don't think the Elephant Man got so much publicity. Two tiny, smaller-than-life babies, hugging each other. Only a closer look . . . Here's the one I'm looking for. "Patel twins still twinkling. The Patel twins made medical history today by being the longest surviving pair of Siamese twins—Tara Patel, who underwent her seventh prosthesis and a kidney transplant in the same month, was smiling and jovial within hours of a complex surgery. Surgery for us is like brushing our teeth, joke the twins. Tara Patel, whose recovery was nothing less than a miracle, states that her source of strength was her mother, and of course her brother and father. Mrs. Bharati Patel, however, was too indisposed to give an interview. A distraught Mr. Patel explained that this has been a trying time for her. For, in spite of the brave façade put up by her, Tara has far too many complications to be completely out of danger. However, the will to survive has proved to work more miracles than the greatest of Science" . . . etc., etc. (*Thinking about it.*) Poor Tara. Even Nature gave her a raw deal.

(*Cross-fade to* DR. THAKKAR.)

DR. THAKKAR: Complications were expected. Our team of doctors were aware of that. The pelvic region, as I had mentioned before, was a problem. There was only one bladder and it belonged to the boy. So did the rectum. We would have to have an artificial one made for the girl. Later on, when she grows up, we can fashion one from her intestinal tissues. And the boy's lungs aren't fully developed. However, considering the magnitude of the work involved, this was a minor detail. The prognosis, on the whole, was favorable for both. Nature had done a near complete job. Medical science could finish it for her. Theoretically, the separation was possible.

(*We hear the second movement of Brahms' first piano concerto. The lights come up on the* gali *as* PATEL *slowly walks in with* TARA. *Again we can identify the beauty of a special bond between parent and child created by their movements, the lighting, and the music. As they enter, their living room is flooded with light and* CHANDAN *and* ROOPA *spring from behind the sofa. They have modest bouquets with them. The music stops.*)

CHANDAN: Welcome back!

ROOPA: Welcome back, Tara!

(*They give her the flowers. She accepts grandly.*)

TARA: Thank you, good people. (*Imitating an Oscar winner.*) First of all I would like to thank my agent. And those wonderful people, my mum and dad. And my wonderful brother (*hugging him*) without whose glorious presence this operation would never have been made.

ROOPA: (*Gleefully.*) How true! How true!

TARA: (*Turning to* ROOPA.) And to my friend out there, Roopa. (*Waving the bouquet.*) I am winning this Oscar for you!

PATEL: Careful! I have an allergy to your Oscar!

ROOPA: As a special treat for you, I got *Children of a Lesser God.* I'll go get it.

PATEL: Oh, no thanks. Video services have been terminated—

ROOPA and CHANDAN: (*Disappointed.*) Oh!

PATEL: For the day.

CHANDAN: Oh great! We'll watch something better tomorrow like *Twins.*

TARA: Where's Mummy? Still after Ida, I suppose, making something special for us.

PATEL: (*Giving* TARA *her bag.*) Now take this to your room and wash up. You can chat with your friend later.

TARA: My, oh my! You sound just like Mummy! (*Exiting.*) You men can imitate us so well if you want to. Pity we can't return the compliment.

(TARA *exits.*)

PATEL: We'll tell her after she settles down.

ROOPA: Oh! You mean she doesn't know?

CHANDAN: We haven't told her yet.

ROOPA: Surely she must have asked for her.

CHANDAN: It happened while she was undergoing surgery.

PATEL: Roopa. I think it will be better if you left. Just for now. You are most welcome to come back later.

ROOPA: Oh, *sure!* If she needs my company just give me a shout. Or send her over, I'll comfort her.

CHANDAN: Thanks.

ROOPA: Bye. (*To* PATEL.) Bye bye, Uncle.

PATEL: Bye.

(ROOPA *exits. Street lights. She scoots towards Prema's house.*)

ROOPA: Pst! Prema! Are you there?

TARA: (*Coming out of her room.*) Oh this is terrific. Mummy doesn't even come to say hello.

PATEL: Tara. (PATEL *leads her to the sofa. She sits down. Spot on them. Their conversation and* TARA's *reaction are mimed over* ROOPA's *speech.*)

ROOPA: (*As if to* PREMA.) Yes. She is back. Can you believe it? They haven't told her about her mother, yet. Well, they are telling her now.

(TARA *looks up at her father. A look of pain.*)

I tell you that whole family is crazy. And I always knew that mother of hers was bonkers. They say she had a nervous breakdown. I think she has finally gone completely looney. Stark naked mad.

(PATEL *comforts* TARA. CHANDAN *sits beside her.*)

This is no surprise to me. I had told you she was really *wandh tarah*.

(*Spot fades out. The spot on* TARA *lingers just a little longer. The spot on* DR. THAKKAR *fades in.*)

DR. THAKKAR: . . . It took us a further ten days just for planning. We couldn't afford to make any miscalculations. There would be separate teams for each twin. Two operation tables were to be joined together. When the separation was done, the tables would be pushed apart and each twin was to receive individual attention.

(*Cross-fade to living room.* TARA *is seated looking very depressed.* CHANDAN *is trying to cheer her up.*)

CHANDAN: . . . And then this socialite lady at the physio tells me that she had worked with mobility-impaired children before. "Mobility impaired?" I asked. She pointed to my leg and shrugged her shoulders. And you know what I said? (*No response.*) Come on, take a guess! (*Tapping her.*) Go on, guess.

TARA: (*Irritated.*) I don't want to guess.

CHANDAN: I said, "Well, I haven't worked with brain cells impaired people, so I'm sorry, we cannot have a true cultural exchange." (CHANDAN *laughs.* TARA *remains silent.* CHANDAN *shrugs his shoulders.*)

(PATEL *enters from kitchen.*)

PATEL: Tara, what would you like for dinner? (*No response.*) Will Kanchipuram *idlis* do? (*No response.*) Tara! Ida is waiting.

CHANDAN: Knock, knock!

TARA: (*Suddenly putting on an act of cheerfulness.*) Right! Let's get the act going. Come on Chandu, let's hear some more of your gags. I promise to laugh at all of them, even if I've heard them before. I promise to be cheerful all the time. I promise I will eat whatever Ida cooks for us, and I promise, I promise not to mention Mummy at all.

CHANDAN: You don't have to do anything you don't want to do.

TARA: (*In tears.*) Very well. I don't want to go to college. I don't want to listen to your wisecracks. And I don't want to eat dinner. All I want is to stay with Mummy at the hospital.

PATEL: No.

TARA: Why not?

(*Pause.*)

PATEL: There will be no more discussion on that. Now, I do hope you plan
    to go to physiotherapy tomorrow.

CHANDAN: If she isn't, I'm not going either.

TARA: It doesn't make any difference to me whether you go or not.

CHANDAN: Very well. (*Getting up and going to her.*) We will both stay at
    home as usual. Watch video and turn into blobs of nothing. Or maybe
    the Bodysnatchers will invade this house and get our bodies.

TARA: They won't get much will they?

PATEL: (*to* CHANDAN.) You filled up your forms?

CHANDAN: Tara?

TARA: Of course not. There's no point in my going to college if I have to
    drop out half-way through or stay away for days not knowing when—
    no!

PATEL: I understand. (*Going to* TARA.) But we have a problem here. Chan-
    dan refuses to join college without you.

TARA: Look, I'm not going to go to college for his sake. So tell him not to
    not go to college for my sake.

CHANDAN: Don't be ridiculous. I just don't feel like joining without you.
    I'm not doing anything for your sake.

TARA: Oh, for God's sake!

PATEL: You two are old enough to sort this out amongst yourselves. I won't
    interfere. But this is certain, Chandan has to join. I have plans for him.
    Your Praful uncle will help him get into a good university in England. I
    know he can get a scholarship on his own if he tries. But Praful will take
    care of the . . . special requirements for him. With a solid education you
    just can't fail. Not to say that Chandan will have to work for a living.
    Your grandfather has left all his wealth to you. Since your mother was
    his only child, you and Tara inherit their home in Bangalore.

CHANDAN: That huge house. It gave me the creeps, I remember.

PATEL: He left you a lot of money.

CHANDAN: And Tara?

PATEL: Nothing.

CHANDAN: Why?

PATEL: It was his money. He could do what he wanted with it.

TARA: And the house? Are we going to live there later on?

PATEL: (*Pause.*) Do me a favor. Both of you. Don't ever go there. Just lock it up. Or better still, burn the whole place down!

(PATEL *exits to bedroom.*)

CHANDAN: Poor Daddy.

TARA: Chandu. Why?

CHANDAN: He must have had some misunderstanding—

TARA: No. I mean, why don't you join college?

CHANDAN: Without you?

TARA: Yes!

CHANDAN: (*Getting up.*) Goodnight.

TARA: You're scared. You're scared you'll find out you can't do very much on your own!

CHANDAN: Nice try.

TARA: Oh, you can't hide behind your jokes all the time! Face it. You're a coward.

CHANDAN: (*Angry.*) Well I'm sorry. Not everyone has your strength!

TARA: You are afraid. Afraid of meeting new people. People who don't know you. Who won't know how clever you are. You are afraid they won't see beyond your—

CHANDAN: That's not true!

TARA: Who do you know in this city? Except that silly Roopa?

CHANDAN: Who do you know?

TARA: I don't. It's all the same. You. Me. There's no difference.

CHANDAN: No difference between you and me?

TARA: No! Why should there be?

CHANDAN: That's the nicest thing you've ever said to me.

TARA: I'm scared as hell too! I wish I was back with our schoolmates. It took me years to show them how stupid they were!

CHANDAN: So we'll start all over again in college! You will join!

TARA: (*Laughing.*) Bastard!

CHANDAN: Vulgar girl! Calling yourself names!

(*They both laugh.* CHANDAN *moves towards the main door.*)

TARA: Where are you going?

CHANDAN: Come!

TARA: You're going out?

CHANDAN: (*Going to her and taking her hand in his.*) For some fresh air.

(*He takes her out on the street. The lights cross-fade.*)

TARA: You might get an infection. Wear a muffler. (*He leads her down the street.*) At least take your bronchodilator.

CHANDAN: If I need it, you can run and get if for me.

TARA: Very funny.

(*They stop, facing the audience. Spot on them.*)

CHANDAN: The oglers are all asleep. Nalini, Roopa, Prema.

TARA: Oh, quite a clear sky. No moon, no—

CHANDAN: No shooting stars to make wishes on!

TARA: How true. Oh, I wish there was one!

CHANDAN: Make your wish anyway.

TARA: What would you wish for?

CHANDAN: Oh, I would wish for the stars! And you?

(*Music: Chopin's Prelude no. 2 in A Minor.*)

TARA: Me?

CHANDAN: Yes.

(*Pause.*)

TARA: I would wish for both . . . I would wish for two of them.

CHANDAN: Two Jaipur legs?

TARA: No, silly, the real ones.

(*Pause.*)

CHANDAN: Tara?

TARA: Yes?

CHANDAN: Don't cry.

(*Pause.*)

TARA: I miss Mummy so much.

(*They stand arm in arm while the spot slowly fades out. The music carries on while the spot comes on DAN.*)

DAN: (*Making notes.*) Chopin's Prelude no. 2 in A Minor. If possible Dinu Lipatti's version. (*To audience.*) People who know they are dying have such a deep understanding of life. And a sense of attachment to it.

(*Music stops. Cross-fade to* DR. THAKKAR.)

THAKKAR: The separation itself was quite complicated. The pelvis had to be fractured in several places to facilitate separation. Cutting the two livers apart was an extremely delicate job. We had to be careful not to damage the bile ducts. We had had about six rehearsals with dummies to make sure that every detail was considered. In terms of the physical movements of the surgeons during the operation as well as surgical procedure.

(*Cross-fade to* CHANDAN *listening to music.* ROOPA *is at the door. She steps in very slowly, watching* CHANDAN *lost in the music. She has a video cassette with her. She sneaks up behind him.*)

ROOPA: Boo!

CHANDAN: (*Looking up at her. In mock horror.*) Aaagh. The ogler has come to get me! Help!

ROOPA: (*Annoyed.*) Very funny! (CHANDAN *has turned down the music.*) It's okay. Listen to your music. I'll go if you don't want me around. (*Pause.*) But since you are all alone, I'll stay and keep you company.

CHANDAN: Where would we be without you?

ROOPA: I'm glad you appreciate my coming here. Nalini and Prema always crib that I spend less time with them now.

CHANDAN: How heartless of you.

ROOPA: Anyway, who cares. I've got a lovely film we can watch. Don't worry. It's not *Fatal Attraction* or anything like that. It's one of those class films with Meryl Streep.

CHANDAN: *She-Devil?*

ROOPA: No, one of her older ones, *Sophie's Choice.* Have you seen it?

CHANDAN: Yes.

ROOPA: (*Disappointed.*) Oh! You don't mind seeing it again?

CHANDAN: I do.

ROOPA: Oh. Well tell me what it's about.

CHANDAN: I can't remember.

ROOPA: (*Brightening.*) Then shall we see it? Just to jog your memory?

CHANDAN: No, I think I remember. It's about this Polish immigrant.

ROOPA: Sophie.

CHANDAN: Yes.

ROOPA: And?

CHANDAN: That's it.

ROOPA: Well, what's her choice?

CHANDAN: She didn't have a choice, you see.

ROOPA: Oh. Then why is it called *Sophie's Choice?*

CHANDAN: It sounds better than *Sophie Had No Choice.*

ROOPA: Yes. I see what you mean. But what was the choice she didn't have?

CHANDAN: (*Thinking about it.*) Actually, she did have a choice. (*Suddenly.*) What would you do if you had to choose between a boy and a girl? Who would you choose?

ROOPA: A boy definitely!

CHANDAN: Definitely?

ROOPA: Yes. It's bad enough studying in an all-girl's school. I would definitely want a boyfriend.

CHANDAN: No. No. I didn't mean that!

ROOPA: Then what did you mean?

CHANDAN: I meant a son and a daughter.

ROOPA: Oh, boy child and girl child. Say that!

CHANDAN: What would your choice be?

ROOPA: Mmm . . . I would be happy with either one.

CHANDAN: That's not the point. In the film I mean. The Nazis will only allow her to keep one child. The other one would be taken away to a concentration camp or something.

ROOPA: How nasty of the Nazis!

CHANDAN: Would you send your girl child to the concentration camp?

ROOPA: Definitely not! I think it's more civilized to drown her in milk, if you ask me. Anyway, there's plenty of time to think about all that. I'm only fifteen, you know. For now I would settle for a boyfriend. Chandan, do you have any girlfriends?

CHANDAN: No.

ROOPA: Would you want one?

CHANDAN: I don't know. What will I do with one?

ROOPA: I don't believe this! Didn't you go to a co-ed school in Bangalore?

CHANDAN: Yes.

ROOPA: Well, wasn't there any one girl you were close to? Someone whom you shared homework with? Or someone you sat next to in class?

CHANDAN: Yes.

ROOPA: Yes, you did?

CHANDAN: Of course, Tara!

ROOPA: She doesn't count.

CHANDAN: What did you say?

ROOPA: I said she doesn't count. She is your sister. What I mean is she doesn't count in this department.

CHANDAN: I understand.

ROOPA: For a minute I was wondering—(*Pause.*) Where *is* she?

CHANDAN: She has gone for her physiotherapy.

ROOPA: What about you? Don't you need to go as well?

CHANDAN: I do. But I don't.

ROOPA: Why?

CHANDAN: I just don't, that's all. (*Pause.*) Hospitals depress me.

(CHANDAN *goes to the music system. He changes the record or the cassette on the player.*)

ROOPA: I know what you mean. My cousin Saraswati had her appendix removed. I had to spend the night with her at the hospital, you know. Her mum was tired and that's the least I could do. God! The smells! The chloroform and DDT and what not. I just threw up. Poor Saraswati, she had to help *me* go to the bathroom. After that I swore I will never go to a hospital.

(CHANDAN *has inserted a cassette and plays it.*)

How's your mother?

(*Chopin's Prelude no. 25 Opus 45 in A Flat plays from half-way through.*)

When is she coming back?

(*No reply.*)

Is she going to be all right?

CHANDAN: (*Vaguely.*) I hate hospitals. The smells. The people. The sterility.

(*He lies on the ground or on a gadda near the music system. He is soon engrossed in the music.* ROOPA *slowly comes to him and lies down or sits beside*

him. She slyly looks at him. He feels her presence. He looks at her. She pretends
to be with the music. He cannot ignore her now. He slowly puts his hand on her
shoulder. She freezes. He very awkwardly moves his hand till it is almost on her
breast. The music ends.)

ROOPA: (*Rises immediately.*) Aagh! Stay away from me! Stay away from me
   you horrible thing!

CHANDAN: You led me on!

ROOPA: How dare you say that!

(TARA *enters in street.*)

CHANDAN: (*Fighting tears.*) You were leading me on all the time!

ROOPA: You actually believe that I would want you to—you have some
   hopes!

CHANDAN: You are a cheat! A fraud!

(TARA *is at the door.*)

ROOPA: (*Tearfully.*) Oh, Tara! You've come just in time!

CHANDAN: Tara, don't listen to anything she—

ROOPA: Oh my God! How can I even begin to—?

CHANDAN: Shut up!

ROOPA: Your brother is a real—a real *monster!*

CHANDAN: Stop cooking up lies!

ROOPA: He—he, why he practically raped me! He's a raper.

TARA: Rapist.

CHANDAN: Don't listen to her. She's lying!

ROOPA: How dare you call me a liar!

CHANDAN: How dare you call me a rapist!

ROOPA: You are. You—you creepy thing!

CHANDAN: Get lost! You wanted me to do it!

ROOPA: What rubbish! I only wanted to keep you company but you took
   advantage—you, you . . . (*At a loss.*) Oh! All men are like that.

TARA: Like what?

ROOPA: Like *that!* You know—after one thing.

CHANDAN: I wasn't after one thing.

ROOPA: Well I'm sorry. I'm just not that type. And personally I don't think
   we are, you know—combatible. If you get what I mean.

CHANDAN: You're right we aren't—combatible.

ROOPA: And if you really want someone who is—you should meet Freni Narangiwalla. I think you will get along fine. She is mentally retarded!

(*Pause.*)

TARA: You are right. They would be quite—combatible.

(CHANDAN *who has been suppressing his laughter, giggles a little.* ROOPA *looks at him. Then she looks at* TARA. TARA *giggles.* CHANDAN *bursts out laughing.* TARA *laughs too.* ROOPA *thinks it is another joke she has missed. She shifts uncomfortably.*)

ROOPA: Well, I better get going.

TARA: No stay. Keep us company.

CHANDAN: Yes. Please stay.

ROOPA: Well, if you need me, how can I say no?

TARA: Sit down.

ROOPA: (*Sitting down.*) What shall we do? See a movie? (*To* TARA.) I've got this great cassette—

TARA: No. Let me tell you a story, about my friend Deepa.

ROOPA: Deepa?

TARA: My classmate in school.

CHANDAN: (*To* ROOPA.) Standard 8. Her best friend.

TARA: (*There is a harshness in* TARA *we haven't seen before.*) Not in the beginning, she wasn't. Used to sit next to me in class because Mrs. Ramanathan—our science teacher, told her to. Never talked to me. Until Ratbag—Mrs. Ramanathan—paired us off for some stupid project. Wanted us to make a model of the solar system or something as our homework. I decided I would rather go over to her house than call her home. She didn't like the idea, but Ratbag decided for us. So Deepa had to take me home with her. We sat on her bed, making our model with rubber balls and wires. Her bed felt different somehow. I put my hand under the cover, and guess what?

ROOPA: What?

TARA: There was a rubber sheet underneath! Imagine. Thirteen years old and she was wetting her bed. I laughed. I laughed out loud. She went red.

ROOPA: (*Sarcastic.*) And she became your best friend?

TARA: I never told anyone at school. But she knew I could easily have done so—at the slightest provocation. I soon had her doing all my homework.

ROOPA: (*Uneasy.*) I don't think that's—why are you telling me this.

TARA: (*Looking at her.*) It's good to know what hurts other people.

ROOPA: (*Laughing nervously.*) I suppose so.

TARA: Comes in handy.

ROOPA: Well—yes.

TARA: Knowing their secrets is useful.

ROOPA: I suppose so.

(*Pause.*)

TARA: So how does it feel having one tit smaller than the other? (ROOPA *is stunned. She rises, her mouth open.*) Don't worry—it's not very noticeable, except from a certain angle. Then it's *very* noticeable.

ROOPA: How dare you! You one-legged thing!

TARA: I'd sooner be one-eyed, one-armed *and* one-legged than be an imbecile like you. An imbecile with uneven tits.

ROOPA: And to think I pitied you. Oh! I think you are disgusting! I only come here because your mother asked me to. No, she didn't ask me, she *bribed* me to be your best friend. Yes, your loony mother used to give me things. Charlie bottles, lipsticks, magazines. Now that she's finally gone crazy, I guess she won't be giving me much. So goodbye.

(ROOPA *exits.* TARA *shouts after her.*)

TARA: Get lost! And please ask Nalini and Prema to come here. I have something to say to them—about you! Oh, wait till they hear this! They will love it. They are going to look at your tits the same way they looked at my leg! Let me see how *you* can face them ogling at you! You won't be able to come out of your house, you horrible creature! You are ugly and I don't want ugly people in my house! So get lost!

(*She enters, gasping. She moves to the sofa.* CHANDAN *speaks after a while.*)

CHANDAN: They are not the ugly ones. We are. Horrible one-legged creatures.

TARA: (*Angry.*) Yes, but you don't have to say it!

CHANDAN: (*Moving to her.*) I'm sorry. You mustn't mind very much.

TARA: What?

CHANDAN: Being one-legged.

TARA: What makes you think I mind?

CHANDAN: (*Softly.*) I feel your pain.

TARA: Yes, I do mind. I mind very much.

(*Cross-fade to* DR. THAKKAR.)

DR. THAKKAR: That's a very interesting question. You see, due to the complex conjoinment at the pelvis, it is very difficult to say how their reproductive organs will develop. A lot depends on the hormone levels their bodies will be able to produce. Imbalances are highly probable. But enough research has been made on the subject. With the necessary supplements it isn't unreasonable to expect them to have a fairly normal growth otherwise. Of course, it would be impossible for either of them to be able to reproduce. They are completely sterile.

(*Cross-fade to* TARA *and* CHANDAN.)

TARA: Oh, what a waste! A waste of money. Why spend all the money to keep me alive? It cannot matter whether I live or die. There are thousands of poor, sick people on the roads who could be given care and attention, and I think I know what I will make of myself. I will be a carer for those people. I . . . I will spend the rest of my life feeding and clothing those—starving, naked millions everyone is talking about. Maybe I can start an institution that will—do all that. Or I could join Mother Teresa and sacrifice myself to a great cause. That may give— purpose to my—existence. I can do it. I can do it, can't I? I will be very happy if I could, because that is really what I want. That is really . . . Oh, bullshit! I don't care! I don't care for anyone except Mummy!

(*Pause.*)

CHANDAN: It's somehow wrong.

TARA: I don't care!

CHANDAN: You should. You should care—for people around you.

TARA: How do you expect me to feel anything for anyone if they don't give me any feeling to begin with? Why is it wrong for *me* to be without feeling? Why are you asking me to do something that nobody has done for me?

CHANDAN: I don't know. Somehow, it is wrong, to be so—selfish.

TARA: Selfish? Yes. I am. I have the right to be selfish, like everyone else!

CHANDAN: No you don't! We don't. We are not everyone else.

TARA: I think that bothers you more than it bothers me.

CHANDAN: I'm not being bothered by anything.

TARA: But it bothers me to hear you preaching to me what's wrong and what isn't.

CHANDAN: All right, I won't! You can do whatever you want and—just—maybe—I will help you do whatever you want. Okay?

TARA: Oh, don't bother. You're not my big brother, okay? I can teach you a trick or two if I want to.

CHANDAN: (*Annoyed.*) Oh, sure! Women mature faster!

TARA: (*Emotional.*) Yes! We do. We do! And we are more sensitive, more intelligent, more compassionate human beings than creeps like you and—and . . .

CHANDAN: And?

TARA: Daddy!

(*Cross-cut to* DAN. *He is on the telephone.*)

DAN: Hello. (*Louder.*) Hello. Dad? Can you hear me? *Dad?* (*The line is cut.* DAN *dials again.*) Hello? Operator, I'm having trouble getting to Bombay. Could you give me India 0226574423 please? . . . I will hold, thank you. (*Pause.*) Hello? Dad? This is Chandan. Praful uncle called me. I believe you had called him . . . Yes I received your letter. Mummy was admitted again, I know. If you have anything to say to me, you should call me and not uncle . . . Well sometimes I take it off the hook, when I'm writing . . . What is it Dad? How is Mummy, now? (*Pause.*) How? . . . (*Pause.*) When was this . . . Oh, was it—sudden? . . . I'm sorry, Dad. But I can't help but feel—relieved that it's all over . . . No. No. I don't think I can come. I'm sorry. Look. I can understand how you feel and I know I should be with you now—but please Dad, don't ask me to come back . . . Well I'm in the middle of writing something, but that's not it, it's just that I don't think I can face life there anymore . . . Why don't you come here? . . . I just thought that now since you are all alone. You've got your brothers over here. And me. Not that I would be able to give you much. I never was a giver . . . You misunderstood Dad; I never held you responsible for what happened . . . How can you feel that it was your fault? No. Don't talk about her. It's not fair to me . . . Tara has been dead for six years and now that Mummy has gone as well, there's nothing left for me to come back to . . . yes, maybe I'm hurting you deliberately, I don't know why, but I can't help the way I feel . . . Either you come here or you live in Bombay all by yourself . . . Well, that's too bad! That's just too bad! (*He hangs up.*)

(*Cross-fade to twins.*)

TARA: When did you last visit Mummy? You didn't come with us last Sunday.

CHANDAN: I don't like hospitals.

TARA: (*Sarcastic.*) I know. They depress you!

CHANDAN: I'll go. Soon.

TARA: You've only come with us once.

CHANDAN: I will come this Sunday. She isn't any better I know. You can visit her more often if you want to.

TARA: I want to.

CHANDAN: Who's stopping you?

(*Pause.*)

TARA: Daddy.

CHANDAN: Why? (*No reply.*) I think you're being unfair.

TARA: You are always defending him.

CHANDAN: I'm not. He's not what you make him out to be.

TARA: You say that because he's nice to you.

CHANDAN: He's nice to you.

TARA: He talks to you more often.

CHANDAN: All right. He talks to me, but he's nice to you.

TARA: I tell you, he hates me!

CHANDAN: Nobody hates you.

(*Pause.*)

TARA: I hate him.

CHANDAN: Why?

(*Pause.*)

TARA: Chandan. I did not go to the physiotherapist today.

CHANDAN: Where did you go then?

TARA: To the hospital.

CHANDAN: What? Why didn't you tell me?

TARA: I just decided on the way. I asked the driver to take me there instead . . . I wanted to meet her. Alone.

CHANDAN: Well? What happened?

TARA: Chandan I *must* meet her alone.

CHANDAN: Didn't you meet her?

TARA: They wouldn't let me!

CHANDAN: They who?

TARA: The hospital staff. At the reception, they asked me who I wanted to see. I told them. They asked me to wait. One of the nurses passing by recognized me. She drew the receptionist aside and spoke to her in a low voice. She thought I couldn't hear what she was saying. But I heard! She told her that she had received strict instructions from our father that I shouldn't on any account be allowed to see Mummy on my own. (*Pause.*) Now tell me I'm imagining things. Tell me that he doesn't hate me!

CHANDAN: Don't be stupid. There must be a reason. Maybe he feels that your presence upsets Mummy some way—

TARA: *I* would upset Mummy?

CHANDAN: Just a possibility. I didn't mean—

TARA: Oh, so it's me, is it? I'm the one upsetting her. Your daddy is blameless. Maybe I am stupid. I must be, complaining to the allied party!

CHANDAN: Maybe *you* should be the writer, with your wild imagination!

TARA: Chandan, I need your help.

CHANDAN: Don't expect me to take your side and quarrel on your behalf. I don't think I should encourage you.

TARA: Okay, don't believe me. All I want is your help in getting me alone with Mummy so I can talk to her!

CHANDAN: How can I do that?

TARA: I don't know. Maybe next time we visit her you could distract Daddy. Pretend you are getting another attack or something.

CHANDAN: Hmm. And then she will disclose her dark secret to you. What do you think she will tell you?

TARA: She will tell me about him.

(*Pause.*)

CHANDAN: I don't think I can do it. Maybe it's all for the best.

TARA: What?

CHANDAN: If Daddy wants to stop her from saying something to us, maybe it's not good for us to hear it.

TARA: And who decides what's good for us to hear and what isn't?

CHANDAN: Whatever it is, if at all it exists, he will tell us himself when he thinks we are good and ready.

TARA: Will he?

CHANDAN: Trust him. He will.

TARA: What if the secret concerns him? Will he tell us then? Chandan, she is *desperately* trying to tell me something, and I want to know!

CHANDAN: I don't understand. It's not like Daddy to withhold anything from us. I think, you are just—well, making a mountain of it.

TARA: I don't think you care for us!

CHANDAN: Wait a minute. That's silly!

TARA: You don't care about me, you don't care about Mummy. You don't even want to see her. As far as you are concerned she is already dead!

CHANDAN: That's not true!

(*Cross-fade to* DR. THAKKAR.)

DR. THAKKAR: Postoperative care needed just as much planning. Other operations may have to be made when the twins grow up. But, the important thing is—the separation was a complete success.

(*Cross-fade to twins.* PATEL *is coming up the* gali.)

CHANDAN: Not now please, we will ask him tomorrow.

TARA: Tomorrow may be too late!

CHANDAN: Don't. He's disturbed enough by Mummy's—

TARA: I'm disturbed! How dare he stop us?

(PATEL *has entered.*)

TARA: Daddy—

CHANDAN: You look tired, dad.

PATEL: Oh, it's just the heat, and the traffic, nothing to—

CHANDAN: Are you feeling all right?

PATEL: (*Sitting down.*) Oh, don't worry about me. Did you two go to physiotherapy?

CHANDAN: Well I didn't. Sorry.

PATEL: And Tara?

CHANDAN: She—she did go. I think.

PATEL: Did she or didn't she? I had sent the car for both of you.

CHANDAN: Oh, yes. The car came, she went.

PATEL: What's wrong with her? Can't she speak for herself? (*No response.*) Did you go to physiotherapy? (*No response.*) Tara, I'm talking to you.

TARA: No. I didn't go. I went to the hospital.

PATEL: Don't ever go there without my permission.

TARA: Very well. I'm asking for your permission to go tomorrow.

PATEL: We will all go.

TARA: On my own.

PATEL: Never.

TARA: Oh, it's no use! I'm going to hate you anyway!

(*Lights on street.* ROOPA *is already there. The lights are dim, perhaps one-sided, creating a grotesque shadow of* ROOPA.)

ROOPA: Prema! Nalini! Are you ready? Let's teach that bitch a lesson!

(*The lights remain on* ROOPA *until she exits.*)

TARA: We will go without your permission.

PATEL: You will not!

TARA: Chandan, will you come with me?

PATEL: Chandan, you can't!

TARA: Chandan?

PATEL: No! Don't go!

TARA: Will you come with me or do I have to go alone?

(*Pause.*)

CHANDAN: We'll both go.

(*Lights on* DR. THAKKAR. *Dim light remains on him till the end.*)

DR. THAKKAR: Our greatest challenge would be to keep the girl alive. Nature wanted to kill her. We couldn't allow it.

ROOPA: (*Shouting.*) Tara! Come on out! We want to talk to you!

PATEL: All right.

CHANDAN: You mean we can go?

PATEL: No. I don't want to give her the satisfaction of—confessing. Oh, why didn't I have the strength to stop her then?

ROOPA: What's the matter? Are you scared? Come on out!

PATEL: I suppose we were both to blame. Your mother and I. And your grandfather. Her father was a wealthy man. An industrialist, and an M.L.A. He might have become Chief Minister if he had lived. He had power. My parents were more—orthodox, and didn't approve of our marriage. I broke away from them. Ours was a happy marriage. We were all overjoyed when we came to know Bharati would have twins. Until certain tests revealed the—complications.

ROOPA: You can't hide in your house forever! You have to come out!

PATEL: We didn't expect you to survive. But you did. When I first saw you—you looked like two babies hugging each other. It was only at a closer look. We were now prepared for the worst. Until we came to know of Dr. Thakkar, who was visiting India. He had done research abroad on such—cases. I came here to Bombay to meet him—and discussed your case. There was hope.

DR. THAKKAR: Both twins have only one leg each. The Artificial Limb Centre at Jaipur was contacted and suitable, flexible legs will be provided when they are slightly older. They will have to be changed from time to time as the twins grow up . . .

ROOPA: (*Shouting.*) What's the matter you freak? Are you deaf as well?

PATEL: Your grandfather got involved personally in our discussions with the doctor. The separation would be done in Bombay, it was decided. Some tests had to be carried out immediately. There were problems, you know them. But there was one complication which hadn't been discussed. There were three legs.

ROOPA: All right. Stay inside! We're going to get a present for you!

(ROOPA *exits. Street lights fade out.*)

PATEL: A scan showed that a major part of the blood supply to the third leg was provided by the girl. Your mother asked for a reconfirmation. The result was the same. The chances were slightly better that the leg would survive—on the girl. Your grandfather and your mother had a private meeting with Dr. Thakkar. I wasn't asked to come. That same evening, your mother told me of her decision. Everything will be done as planned. Except—I couldn't believe what she told me—that they would risk giving both legs to the boy . . . Maybe if I had protested more strongly! I tried to reason with her that it wasn't right and that even the doctor would realize it was unethical! The doctor had agreed, I was told. It was only later I came to know of his intention of starting a large nursing home—the largest in Bangalore. He had acquired three acres of prime land—in the heart of the city—from the state. Your grandfather's political influence had been used. A few days later the surgery was done. As planned by them, Chandan had two legs—for two days. It didn't take them very long to realize what a grave mistake they had made. The leg was amputated. A piece of dead flesh which could have— might have been Tara. Because of the unusual nature of the operation, it was easy to pass it off as a natural rejection. I—I was meaning to tell you both when you were older, but . . .

(*A special spot on* BHARATI. *Music. She talks as if to an infant in her arms.*)

BHARATI: Tara! My beautiful little girl. Look at her smile! Smile, Tara. Smile again for me! Oh! See how her eyes twinkle. You are my most beautiful baby!

(*Her spot fades out with the music. Silence. The street area is lit.* ROOPA *has brought on a poster which says "*WE DON'T WANT FREAKS.*" She places it prominently against a wall or post.*)

ROOPA: (*Shouting.*) There. At least you are not blind! Do you get the message? Freaks!

(ROOPA *exits.* TARA *stands alone in a spot, in a daze.* CHANDAN *moves to her and gestures to her to hold his hand.* TARA *turns away from him.* CHANDAN *is crushed.*)

TARA: And she called me her star!

(*Lights off* TARA, PATEL, *and* CHANDAN. *The poster remains lit.*)

DR. THAKKAR: Yes. Indeed, it was a complete case. But modern technology has made many things possible, and we are not very far behind the rest of the world. In fact, in ten year's time we should be on par with the best in the West.

(DAN's *area is lit.* DAN *makes mock applause.*)

DAN: Thank you very much Dr. Thakkar! It has been a *real* pleasure. Now go, just—go away. (*Breaking down.*) Get out of my mind you horrible creature! You are ugly and I don't want ugly people in my memories! (*Pause.* DR. THAKKAR's *spot fades out.*) Give me a moment and the pain will subside. Then I can function again. (*Pause. Much more controlled now.*) Yes. The material is there. But the craft is yet to come. Like the amazing Dr. Thakkar, I must take something from Tara—and give it to myself. Make capital of my trauma, my anguish, and make it my tragedy. To masticate them in my mind and spit out the result to the world, in anger. (*Slowly, as if in a trance, he picks up his typed sheets and starts tearing them as he speaks.*) My progress so far—I must admit—has been zero—but I persist with the comforting thought that things can't get any worse. All I find every day is one typewritten sheet . . . with the title of the play, my name and address, and the date. Nothing changes—except the date . . .

(*The voice-over fades in as the spot fades out.*)

DAN'S VOICE: Someday, after I die, a stranger will find this recording and play it. The voice is all that will remain. No writing. No masterpiece. Only a voice—that once belonged to an object. An object like other objects in a cosmos, whose orbits are determined by those around. Moving in a forced harmony. Those who survive are those who do not defy the gravity of others. And those who desire even a moment of freedom, find themselves hurled into space, doomed to crash with some unknown force. (*Pause.*) I no longer desire that freedom. I move. Just move. Without meaning. I forget Tara. I forget that I had a sister— with whom I had shared a body. In one comfortable womb. Till we were forced out—and separated.

   (*A spot fades in—empty.*)

But somewhere, sometime, I look up at a shooting star—and wish. I wish that a long-forgotten person would forgive me. Wherever she is.

(TARA *walks into the spot without limping.* DAN *also appears without the limp.*)

And will hug me. Once again.

(*They kneel. Face to face.*)

Forgive me, Tara. Forgive me for making it my tragedy.

(TARA *embraces* DAN *as the music starts. The explosive opening of Brahms' first piano concerto. They hug each other tightly. Slow fade out.*)

Routes and Escape Routes

by Datta Bhagat

TRANSLATED FROM MARATHI BY MAYA PANDIT

CHARACTERS

(in order of appearance)

KAKA GODGHATE, Satish's uncle, between 50 and 60

HEMA GODGHATE, Satish's wife

DASRAO JOSHI, headmaster of a school

PROFESSOR SATISH GODGHATE, a teacher

ARJUN JADHAV, Satish's student

POLICE INSPECTOR NAYAK

SONAL JOSHI, Dasrao Joshi's daughter

SUBHAN, a party worker

FIRST STUDENT

SECOND STUDENT

THIRD STUDENT

The premiere, in Pune, of *Routes and Escape Routes*
Photographs courtesy of Sudhir Mungi

Act One
SCENE ONE

The drawing room of Professor Satish Godghate's house. A portrait of Dr.
Babasaheb Ambedkar and a Sewadal calendar on the wall. A study table in the
corner with some books. The drawing room has a sofa with a teapoy. A shoe
stand in another corner. The arrangement is neat and simple. When the curtain
goes up, it is evening. KAKA—*age between fifty and sixty—sitting in a chair, try-*
ing with considerable effort to read a newspaper.

KAKA: (*Stops reading in the middle.*) Sunbai . . .

HEMA: (*From the kitchen.*) Coming . . . (*Enters.*) Yes, what?

KAKA: (*Angry.*) What do you mean "what"? How many times do I have to
tell you? Never say "what" when I call you. Say "*ji.*" That's proper. Can't
you be a bit polite?

HEMA: I am sorry.

KAKA: (*Brightens up.*) That's better! You know, when I was young, I, too,
used to say "what," whenever my mother called me. And then she
would get furious and shout, without even stopping for breath, "Bastard, don't you say 'what'; either say 'ji,' or go rot." (*Laughs loudly.*) Since
then I've got this habit of saying "*ji.*" Whenever someone calls me, I
always say "*ji*" in reply. Even a baby. (*Stops. Then in a strict tone.*) Always
remember to say "*ji.*" Understand?

HEMA: *Ji.*

KAKA: That's better.

HEMA: I don't mind as much if you scold me when we are alone. But you
shouldn't insult me when there are people around.

KAKA: Then you should learn how to speak and behave properly. But who
am I to teach you that? After all, we are merely Buddhists! But you are a
Brahmin! On top of everything else you are educated.

HEMA: (*Furious.*) Stop referring to my caste, Kaka, in every other sentence.

KAKA: (*A bit crestfallen, but without showing it.*) You want me to stop? Okay, I will. (*Pauses.*) But tell me, does caste disappear if I stop talking about it? Babasaheb used to say, what you can't cast off is caste.

HEMA: But I absolutely don't like it!

KAKA: What? Caste, or my talking about it?

HEMA: Both. We broke away from our castes and got married. In the face of stiff opposition. Who supported us? No one. Our parents, relatives, no one! Not even you!

KAKA: Okay, okay! I accept.

HEMA: We didn't have jobs. Used to go hungry for days. But who came forward to help? Not a single soul! Neither relatives nor people from our castes. Even you refused to see us! For one and a half years! Because we got married against your wishes.

KAKA: Now, now. Let bygones be bygones!

HEMA: Exactly! That's what I say too. But you aren't ready to forget. It's almost six months since you came to stay with us, but hardly a day has passed without your referring to my caste.

KAKA: Oh, well! How can I help it if the truth slips out like this? (*Plainly nettled by her attack.*) Who likes caste? Tell me, who does? I have worked with Babasaheb for more than forty years against the caste system. But has it disappeared? No. How many years has it been since your marriage? Five. Why, it's more than three years since Satish came here, to this town, to take up this job. But what do people say even now? Tell me: Satish Godghate, professor, a Buddhist, and his wife, a Brahmin! And there is no dearth of peeping Toms around us, let me tell you. Even small girls bend over backwards just to see what's happening in our house. Tell me why?

HEMA: Let people do what they want. But you are not people! You are his own uncle!

KAKA: Of course I am! Not a grafted one, but a real one, his own father's brother!

HEMA: You are, aren't you? Then at least you should stop talking in this manner.

KAKA: (*Accepting that the tables have been turned on him.*) Hmm. Okay. I'll try. (*Pause.*) Did Satish do it?

HEMA: What?

KAKA: What I had asked him to do. Don't tell me you, too, have forgotten!

HEMA: Oh, about Shewanta's certificate?

KAKA: So you do remember after all!

HEMA: He said he wouldn't do it.

KAKA: Why?

HEMA: Kaka, Shewanta has never worked in any school. How can they issue her a false certificate of experience?

KAKA: Did he ask anyone at all?

HEMA: I don't know!

KAKA: I'm sure he never asked anyone!

HEMA: That's right! He didn't!

KAKA: And why not, pray? He knows that headmaster, doesn't he? Dasrao Joshi. Or did he say no?

HEMA: Satish is against asking for such false certificates, Kaka!

KAKA: Why? How does it harm anyone? In what way? The poor girl wants to learn. She's a widow. Shouldn't we help? She's even got admission to that course. B.Ed. or D.Ed., whatever they call it.

HEMA: Maybe you are right. But Satish has absolutely refused to do it.

KAKA: Who the hell does he think he is? The God of Truth? Why did he get educated if he didn't want to help his own people? Ha! I would have procured ten such certificates had I been in my own village!

HEMA: Well, I did try to reason with him, but he wouldn't listen, he was angry! Maybe if you try talking to him . . . !

KAKA: Me? I can, of course, talk to him! Who's scared of him? I asked you because I thought you might be able to convince him better. But why should I talk to him? I'll talk directly to Dasrao Joshi himself. I know him quite well. I'll ask him straightaway. Let me see how he dares to refuse! (*Starts towards the door with his walking stick.*)

HEMA: Now, where are you going?

KAKA: Blast you! Did you have to ask that? How many times do I have to tell you? Never ask me where I am going, when I am going out on some important work! I am going to Joshi Master's school.

HEMA: Now? At this time?

KAKA: Yes. Now. At this time. The school probably isn't over yet. I'll collect the certificate and take it immediately to Shewanta.

HEMA: When will you be back?

KAKA: Damn you and your questions! My wife never had this habit of asking questions. But you? The moment I decide to go out, there you go bang with your question, "Where are you going?"

HEMA: You know, Kaka, he waits for you at mealtimes. And if you aren't around, I get scolded for letting you go out at mealtimes.

KAKA: Sunbai, once we step out of the house in the name of Babasaheb Ambedkar, who knows when we will be back? Ah, now that you ask me about meals, I remember, I am eating at Bhim Nagar today.

HEMA: At Bhim Nagar? At whose place?

KAKA: Some *Upasakas* had gone on a pilgrimage to Bodh Gaya. They returned yesterday. They've collected money for a community dinner. (HEMA *is perplexed.*) Well, think of it as *mavanda.*

HEMA: *Mavanda?*

KAKA: What else can you call it, then? I'll be back late.

HEMA: Why?

KAKA: There's a meeting of the Bharatiya Bodh Mahasabha to discuss the construction of a Bodh Vihara. But what's the point of telling you all this? You have neither religion nor God.

HEMA: Where are you planning to build this Bodh Vihara?

KAKA: Suppose I want to build it right here, in Sivaji Nagar! Would it be allowed?

HEMA: But . . . are you sure the meeting is just to discuss the Bodh Vihara? Or . . .

KAKA: (*Guardedly.*) Then what else is it for?

HEMA: We've heard some rumors . . .

KAKA: What?

HEMA: What is cooking at Milind Nagar, Kaka?

KAKA: Milind Nagar? Nothing that I know of.

HEMA: And how is Arjun connected with that?

KAKA: How do I know?

HEMA: Arjun hasn't turned up here for quite a few days. Does he ever see you?

KAKA: Oh yes. We meet when I go to Bhim Nagar.

HEMA: I've heard he's collecting subscriptions.

KAKA: Yes, he is.

HEMA: He is? What for?

KAKA: (*Confused, but then recovering.*) For the Vihara.

HEMA: For the Vihara, or for acquiring by force houses built for people affected by the flood?

KAKA: For both. He has submitted an application to the *tehsildar* with signatures of all the people.

HEMA: It is rumored that he's going to break the locks open and allot the houses to all slum dwellers in case the government refuses to give them the houses. Is that true?

KAKA: What's wrong in doing that?

HEMA: That means, Kaka, you know perfectly well what's cooking at Milind Nagar. But Kaka, are you aware that doing any such thing would be illegal? Arjun's hiding it even from Satish. Please ask him at least to talk to Satish before he does any such thing.

KAKA: Why should I ask him to talk to Satish? As if Satish would allow it! He isn't even prepared to ask anyone for Shewanta's certificate. What's the point of asking him?

HEMA: Are you in it, too?

KAKA: Me? Why should I be? And what do I need a house for, now?

HEMA: You don't. But what about the Dalits in Bhim Nagar . . . ?

KAKA: Of course they want houses. And why shouldn't they? As if Satish intends to do anything . . .

HEMA: Well, he is trying to form a housing society, isn't he?

KAKA: Housing society! That's what I have been hearing for the last six months! He's been trying . . . for ages! The *rickshawala*s have set up hutments as if they are nomadic tribes. Aren't they human beings too? Bungalow after bungalow is coming up. But for whom? Housing society, she says! And who are you trying to scare with the law? Us? Who made the laws? Babasaheb. For whom? For us. And you dare to scare us with the law? Your father is a judge, isn't he? Go ask him. I'll wait till then. By the time they get their housing society, these people will be dead and gone!

HEMA: (*Pacifying him.*) Kaka, don't I understand your agony? After all, am I not your daughter-in-law?

KAKA: Eh? Of course. You know, you have a way about you. You speak so sweetly sometimes that I forget my anger. All right, so what do you suggest?

HEMA: Kaka, could you do one thing? Bring Arjun along with you here. Do you seriously believe that Satish will do anything to harm the interests of the Dalits? He's better educated than Arjun. Besides, he's Arjun's teacher. Now, if Arjun's decision is to be accepted by all, hadn't we better consider all the pros and cons?

KAKA: Now you're talking sense. Where's our register?

HEMA: Which one?

KAKA: Bharatiya Bodhsabha.

HEMA: Ah, that's in his cupboard. Just a minute. I'll fetch it for you.

KAKA: Okay. I'll wait. (HEMA *brings the register from the cupboard and gives it to him.*) Don't worry. I'll definitely bring Arjuya with me after the meeting.

HEMA: And what's this, Kaka? Forgotten your medicine again, haven't you.

KAKA: Plain forgot about it! All right, give it to me. I'll gulp it down.

HEMA: (*Giving him a tablet from a bottle on the stool and some water in a glass.*) And you have an appointment with the doctor today, remember?

KAKA: How do you remember every detail? And what's wrong with me? That silly doctor has got nothing to do, so he calls me and whiles away his time, counting my heartbeats!

HEMA: Kaka . . .

KAKA: Okay, okay. I am off. But I know I won't escape him. He'll leave me alone only when my heart stops beating.

HEMA: Now, now, that's no way to talk! As if the doctor has nothing better to do! See him first and then go to Bhim Nagar.

(HEMA *goes in to the kitchen.* KAKA *is flipping through the register when* DASRAO JOSHI *enters.*)

DASRAO: Is Godghate Sir at home?

KAKA: Oh, Dasrao Guruji?

DASRAO: *Namaskar*, Kaka.

KAKA: (*Looks straight into* DASRAO's *eyes.*) *Jai Bhim.* That's how we greet people, you know.

DASRAO: Eh? Oh yes! You just won't give up anything, will you?

KAKA: And what about you? You also say "*Namaskar*" when you see me, don't you? (*Both laugh.*) Ah, but what a godsend that you came! I was about to come and see you myself.

DASRAO: See me?

KAKA: Why? Shouldn't I?

DASRAO: About what?

KAKA: Easy, easy. I'll explain everything at length, but first sit down and relax. (*He sits down himself, relaxed.*) Sunbai.

HEMA: *Ji.*

KAKA: Bring some first-class tea for this esteemed relative of mine by marriage. You won't mind, Guruji, will you?

DASRAO: No. Why should I?

KAKA: Taking our tea, you know, in our company, sitting next to us—well of course, now our Satish is half Brahmin himself! Still . . . you know . . . sure you don't mind?

DASRAO: (*Understands the taunt.*) Kaka, what's wrong in taking tea in anybody's company? And anyway, it's Hematai who's going to make the tea! So . . . Right?

KAKA: Quite! That's exactly the point I was explaining to my daughter-in-law just now. That come what may, people just won't forget caste. By the way, I hope you aren't angry, Guruji!

DASRAO: What for?

KAKA: I said you were a relative by marriage.

DASRAO: What's there to be angry about, Kaka? We consider Hema to be our own daughter, older than our Sonal.

KAKA: Ahha! Agreed.

DASRAO: Good, now tell me, where does caste come in?

KAKA: Wait! Not so fast, not so fast. Let me proceed systematically. Now, see, you are a Joshi, I a Godghate. (*Pauses deliberately.*) So? . . . Get it? That's why. Get the difference now?

DASRAO: (*In the same taunting spirit.*) You bet I do. And why not? So what if we are related by marriage?

KAKA: Now you are talking.

DASRAO: Yes. So what if we are related by marriage! You won't give us any place in your thirty-three percent would you, Kaka? Tell me seriously, would you?

KAKA: (*Understands the taunt.*) Oh, oh, oh! A sharp eye, indeed, on our reservation!

DASRAO: So you won't give us any place, Kaka, right? You won't! Right! Let it pass.

KAKA: Guruji, aren't you a freedom fighter? You, too, have your own green pasture, don't you, thanks to Mother Indira! How much does it come to a year? Surely not less than twelve hundred? No? Concessions in railway fares, bus fares, college fees, plus several other perks of various kinds. Then why look enviously, sir, at our reservations?* Our kids have started getting an education only recently. Let them learn a bit, enjoy good posts, be DSPs and collectors. Then you can have it all for yourselves.

DASRAO: But I don't object, Kaka!

KAKA: Oh yes, you don't object, but then you want to eat the cake and have it too, you know.

DASRAO: How?

KAKA: Take this girl, Hema, for instance! My daughter-in-law. Our God of Truth, Lord Sattyawan, brought her into this house. Sattyawan is our Satish you know. Sattyawan is what I call him, because he yaps about Truth a lot.

DASRAO: Okay, so?

KAKA: She's a gem of a girl really. So what if she's a Brahmin! But suppose he hadn't married her . . . wouldn't a girl from one of our own poor families have lived like a queen in this house? This is what I call eating the cake and having it too. Of course, I don't blame her. Our own boy was a bad coin, so it couldn't be helped. (*Turns to* DASRAO.) We, as a people, are ready a hundred times over to forget caste, but are you people ready to forget it, Guruji? You consider Hema to be your own daughter. Agreed. But Shewanta? Do you consider her your own daughter too?

DASRAO: Shewanta? Who?

KAKA: Gopya's wife. That *rickshawala*, you know.

DASRAO: Ah. What about her?

KAKA: Gopya died last year. Was run over by a truck. She's a widow now. Has no relatives. She has passed metric.

DASRAO: Oh yes. She passed last year. She sat for the examination in my school. Her number was in my school.

KAKA: She says she wants to do D.Ed. or B.Ed.

DASRAO: That's good. At least she can earn her own livelihood.

KAKA: Guruji, tell me, what's this D.Ed. or B.Ed.?

---

*This refers to the reservation of seats in the legislature and the apportionment of job positions for former Untouchables.

DASRAO: Oh, D.Ed? It's a kind of training, you know. To become a teacher. After matriculation. It's equivalent to the eleventh standard.

KAKA: She's even got admission for that course, you know.

DASRAO: Good for her.

KAKA: Yes, isn't it? But her headmaster, you see, is creating problems.

DASRAO: Why?

KAKA: Because she doesn't have a certificate of teaching experience.

DASRAO: Oh yes. That certificate is a must, you know, Kaka. For a period of at least three months.

KAKA: (*Eagerly pouncing on him.*) Then give it, why don't you?

DASRAO: Who, me?

KAKA: Why not? Yours would do fine.

DASRAO: But Kaka, she has never worked in my school.

KAKA: Had she really worked in your school, where was the need for me to come and plead with you?

DASRAO: But Kaka, a false certificate?

KAKA: What the hell do you think she's going to use it for? A highway robbery? That poor thing will get a job at least.

DASRAO: Yes . . . but a false certificate! Right here in this town, where people know . . .

(HEMA *brings tea.* KAKA *relaxes on the couch.* HEMA *serves tea and returns to the kitchen.*)

KAKA: Ah, here's tea. Have it. (*Pause.*) That's what I said. You don't consider Shewanta to be your daughter like Hema. Well, never mind. Have tea.

DASRAO: Kaka, you know, a false record has to be prepared for that. And doing that here in the same town as she is in . . .

KAKA: (*His hopes rising now.*) What's the problem with that? Show that she's worked during somebody's leave period and write the certificate. Actually, I have asked our own Satish. But he considers himself to be the very God of Truth. How can he ever tell a lie? I suppose he never even approached you!

DASRAO: Kaka, I'll tell you what. Shewanta's doing her D.Ed. from here. So it wouldn't look nice to arrange for a certificate from around here. What I'll do is this: I'll get her a certificate from the school at Kasarkhed.

KAKA: (*Enthusiastically.*) Shall we go tomorrow?

DASRAO: No, no. You don't come with me. I'll get it myself the day after tomorrow.

KAKA: (*Nodding.*) Okay. As you wish.

DASRAO: The headmaster of the school at Kasarkhed is a good friend of mine.

KAKA: Wonderful! That ends the matter. Yours is what I call a Brahmin brain. Guruji, it wasn't for nothing that you had a pen in your hand! I knew you would find a way out.

DASRAO: Happy?

KAKA: Very. Well, I'll be getting along now. (*Calling off to* HEMA.) Sunbai, inform my Lord Sattyawan it's been taken care of. Dasrao Guruji did it.

DASRAO: Why tell him?

(HEMA *enters.*)

KAKA: Why, he must know how to get things done! Now if you'll allow me, I'll push off.

DASRAO: Going for a walk?

KAKA: Hah! I have no taste for the idle antics of the Brahmins.

HEMA: (*Scolding.*) Kaka!

KAKA: Sorry! Today there's a meeting of the Bharatiya Bodhsabha, in Bhim Nagar. Now Guruji, tell me, there are so many Buddhists in this town, but is there even a single Bodh Vihara around? But our Lord Sattyawan doesn't approve of any such thing, you know.

DASRAO: So you want to build a Bodh Vihara!

KAKA: Well, they have collected some money—a thousand *rupee*s or so. However learned the Brahmins be, they'll always build a temple of Lord Ganesha in their locality. Then what's wrong with our building a Bodh Vihara?

HEMA: Kaka!

KAKA: Oh, caste! There it comes up again! Sorry. High time I went. (*Getting up.*) Can anyone do without religion, Guruji? Can you point out even one person on this earth who doesn't have religion? You tell me. Tell this girl here and her husband, our Sattyawan. Okay. Don't believe in God, if you don't want to. Say what you please when on stage. But help, you must, when it's a question of building a Vihara. Well, leave it. I, at least, won't sit idle, Guruji. I'll continue to do something or the other wherever I go. We were comrades of Babasaheb Ambedkar, Guruji, in the movement. Fought along with him, shoulder to shoulder. We didn't understand Babasaheb like these people, by reading only his books. Well, see you. (*Leaves.*)

HEMA: (*Following* KAKA *with her eyes.*) Don't mind what he says. He's got a caustic tongue, but his heart is pure and simple. Doesn't nurse any bitterness, you know.

DASRAO: Does he always talk like that to you too?

HEMA: Oh, I'm used to it by now.

DASRAO: Poor you. What else can you do now, anyway?

HEMA: What do you think Guruji? Am I saying all this because I am unhappy?

DASRAO: Oh well, he is always sarcastic, isn't he? It's only you who can put up with it. No one else could have, in your place.

HEMA: Oh no! It absolutely isn't like that, Guruji. He barks all right, but he doesn't bite like you.

DASRAO: Like me? What do you mean, Hematai?

HEMA: Since you've asked, let me tell you something. Satish was going to rent rooms in your house, Guruji, after getting a job in this town. Remember? And you had even collected your rent from him in advance! But when you came to know his caste, what did you do? You simply told him that the house had already been rented; that your wife had taken an advance from someone else without informing you! That was your pretext, remember? And you returned his money.

DASRAO: So you did finally come to know about it! These women! Can't keep anything secret!

HEMA: Now go ahead and blame your wife. But I came to know about it two years back. I was furious at the time. It was Satish who consoled me. And now you, of all people, shower sympathy on me for putting up with Kaka's sarcastic tongue?

DASRAO: I don't deny what you say, Hematai. But I, too, was helpless, you know. Three grown-up daughters, waiting in a queue to be married off. My father bedridden with paralysis. No land. No source of income except my job. I really had no objection to Satish as a tenant, otherwise I wouldn't have taken an advance from him . . . but . . .

HEMA: But . . . ? Go on.

DASRAO: If I'd rented rooms to Satish, then the other tenants would have immediately vacated their rooms. They warned me about that!

HEMA: You would have got other tenants.

DASRAO: Got other tenants? That's where you are wrong, Hematai! You don't know the ways of this world!

HEMA: This answer certainly doesn't become you, Guruji. You're a freedom fighter!

DASRAO: Even a freedom fighter has a stomach to fill. Come to think of it, it was easy to fight the Nizam. Facing these small problems in life is far more difficult.

HEMA: And yet you'll hang the certificate of a freedom fighter on your wall. Never mind! Whatever happens, happens for the best. Since then, Satish has firmly resolved to form a housing society. Along with other problems, he's trying to solve the problem of housing too. The loan will be sanctioned next month.

DASRAO: I have always had great respect for Satish.

HEMA: (*Trying to gauge him.*) Did you have any specific work with him?

DASRAO: Yes . . . no . . . I mean . . . nothing special, you know . . .

HEMA: There he is!

SATISH: (*Enters.*) Namaskar, Guruji! (HEMA *takes his books and puts them on the table.*) Why don't you sit down? When did you come?

DASRAO: Just now. Some twenty minutes ago. It seems as if you were out of town. Were you?

SATISH: (*Taking off his shoes and socks.*) Ah, yes. There's a camp going on at Kasarakhed. NSS camp. (*Puts his shoes in their place.*) But you didn't send Sonal to the camp. (*Relaxing.*) She had really set her heart on it.

DASRAO: I, too, wanted to send her, you know. But these days her mother just doesn't allow her to go out anywhere.

SATISH: Are you sure it's her mother who doesn't allow her? Guruji, Sonal is old enough, now! She's in second year B.A.

DASRAO: That's why her mother is so concerned, you know!

SATISH: Then you should convince her.

DASRAO: It's no use.

SATISH: Why?

DASRAO: Nature, you know.

SATISH: Nature. (*Remembers something.*) Something interesting happened in the camp today.

DASRAO: What happened?

SATISH: There was this project for simple toilets, you know. A group of four or five boys was working at a moneylender's place. In spite of their protests, the moneylender arranged for tea for them. The tea came, eventually. The moneylender distributed the cups among the boys. When, however, they looked at one tea cup, they were furious and immediately walked out of his house without drinking his tea. They told their teacher that they would never go to the moneylender's place again.

DASRAO: Why?

SATISH: The teacher in charge of the NSS made enquiries and discovered that one of the cups was distinctly different! It was set aside specially for Dalits.

DASRAO: Say what you like, but the villages haven't changed much.

SATISH: Of course, we are aware of that. And we also brief our students about that. (*Pauses.*) That cup was given to one ugly, dark boy from that group. You know who that boy was? Arvind Deshmukh. (SATISH *starts laughing,* GURUJI *stiffens.*) Really, what funny ideas people have! If it's an ugly dark boy, he must be a Dalit! Deshmukh was furious, Guruji. He was virtually seething with rage. My god! I just said to him, Deshmukh, don't be so angry. What you can do is to destroy all such cups and glasses in your own house, those set aside specially for Dalits. It's good to feel angry, Guruji, but not sufficient. That anger has to be given the right direction. (*Looks at* GURUJI.) Why, you seem to have become very serious all of a sudden!

DASRAO: Arvind Deshmukh? He's in third year B.Com., isn't he?

SATISH: Yes. You know him?

DASRAO: Yes. He's the son of Nanasaheb Deshmukh, from Jawale.

SATISH: Oh yes?

DASRAO: They've asked for Sonal.

SATISH: For Sonal?

DASRAO: They're very rich. Besides, they don't want any dowry.

SATISH: Guruji, your Sonal's too young. Aren't you concerned about that?

DASRAO: I am more concerned about my responsibilities.

SATISH: Have you given your consent?

DASRAO: Does everything in life take place with one's consent?

SATISH: Yes. If one wants it to.

DASRAO: That's possible only for some individuals.

SATISH: No. It's possible for all individuals. Provided they are prepared to suffer a bit.

DASRAO: I really have great respect for you, sir. But when I am in cornered circumstances, rationality just deserts me. And the ways of the world aren't so straight as to allow reason to guide one. Oh well, experience will teach you too. You'll learn gradually.

SATISH: Experience! Your special weapon to render us young people speechless.

DASRAO: Why go far away? Here's an example at hand. I never wanted to obtain a false certificate for Shewanta. But Kaka was bent upon it and, finally, I had to agree.

SATISH: You shouldn't have.

DASRAO: What would you have done in my place?

SATISH: I would never have given a false certificate. Instead, I'd have made her take classes for weak students.

DASRAO: But she would have lost one year in that.

SATISH: But you've lost the importance of that certificate itself, Guruji! She could have done her B.Ed. next year as well.

DASRAO: But her convenience was more important for me, as it was for Kaka!

SATISH: So convenience is more important for you! Then what's the difference between you and that moneylender? He found the convenience of tradition more important, and you found the convenience of Shewanta more important! Now please don't be angry, Guruji. Such convenient thinking does yield some benefits, it's true. But aren't they only temporary? No. You'll never realize what a great price you have to pay at each step for such conveniences. Well, never mind. I forgot to ask you why you'd come.

DASRAO: Um . . . nothing special really, but you know . . .

SATISH: Please go on.

DASRAO: You know, those houses built by the government. For the flood affected people. Arjun, they say, is going to acquire those houses by force.

SATISH: Who told you that?

DASRAO: He has submitted an application to the *tehsildar.*

SATISH: But I don't see any force in that.

DASRAO: Did he say anything to you?

SATISH: No. Actually, I haven't seen him for a couple of weeks.

DASRAO: Ask him when you see him then.

SATISH: What? Whether he has made such an application?

DASRAO: Oh, it's true he has submitted such an application. But since the *tehsildar* hasn't given any answer, he's going to break the locks and acquire the houses by force. That's what they are saying.

SATISH: I don't think Arjun will do any such thing.

DASRAO: Nor do I. But Pawar Sahib said . . . Pawar Sahib, the president of our institution! He's the contractor, you know, of that colony. He has not yet submitted the completion report. But if some such thing happens before that, the real flood victims will be left out in the cold and an altogether different conflict will erupt in our town.

SATISH: I'll ask Arjun when he comes.

DASRAO: Don't just ask him, sir, enquire into it. After all, Pawar Sahib is president of our institution. He knows of our friendship. That's why he specially sent me to you. Well, so long, then.

SATISH: So long. How much you worry about your job, Guruji!

DASRAO: N . . . No, not really.

SATISH: Come on! Even I work in Pawar Sahib's college. See you then.

(DASRAO *goes.* SATISH *somewhat uneasy.*)

SATISH: Hema . . .

HEMA: *Ji.*

SATISH: *Ji?* So Kaka has finally persuaded you to adopt his ways too!

HEMA: What could I do? I can argue with you and resist, but . . .

SATISH: It's impossible to argue with Kaka, isn't it? I know Hema, the trick is never to argue with him. Once you make concessions to some of his whims, he'll behave like a lamb. Please Hema, I know it's such a bother to you!

HEMA: You think I'm complaining?

SATISH: Then who's complaining? Me? (*Both laugh.* HEMA *goes in.*) Hema, has Arjun been here? (ARJUN *enters.*)

ARJUN: *Jai Bhim,* sir.

SATISH: Oh Arjun? Come on in! Aayushyaman Arjunrao Jadhav, please come in. You're going to live a hundred years.

ARJUN: Hundred years! I don't mind, sir. I don't mind at all, living on for a hundred years. Even a hundred years would be too short a time to cleanse this society of all the filth it has accumulated over thousands of years. Well, let it pass, sir. This is an endless topic. Kaka said you wanted to see me.

SATISH: Yes. We haven't met for two weeks. I didn't see you even at the college. I just couldn't understand what you were so involved in. So I did tell Kaka . . .

ARJUN: No, I wasn't involved in many things, sir. Only the question of houses for the flood affected people. The rainy season is so close, knocking at the door almost . . .

SATISH: So? What have you decided to do?

ARJUN: What else, sir? It's been a month since the colony for the flood victims was built. But there are still no signs of the completion and distribution of the houses. So we . . .

SATISH: What did you do then?

ARJUN: We settled the affair today, in our own way. We forcibly broke the locks open and gave the houses to the flood victims.

SATISH: What?

ARJUN: People are rushing there. All the flood victims in Bhim Nagar are occupying those houses.

SATISH: And Kaka? Where is he?

ARJUN: I've asked him to wait there, to supervise the whole operation.

SATISH: Arjun, you really broke the locks open and acquired those houses?

ARJUN: Yes, sir. Right to the T.

SATISH: Broke the locks open?

ARJUN: Yes.

SATISH: But the houses are for the flood victims.

ARJUN: Then those occupying the houses are none other than the flood victims.

SATISH: All?

ARJUN: Well, maybe one or two aren't. So what?

SATISH: Are you sure you have done nothing wrong, Arjun?

ARJUN: Absolutely, sir. You know that Pawar, the contractor? It's been almost a month since the houses were complete, sir. But he wasn't ready to hand them over to the B.C.'s, sir. You know why? He wants to push his own relatives into those houses in the guise of flood victims. His list wasn't getting finalized. That's why he kept on postponing it.

SATISH: How do you know? What's the evidence?

ARJUN: You can't give evidence for everything.

SATISH: But one has to at least make sure.

ARJUN: How? And when? You would be convinced, probably, only after he'd settled all his relatives into those houses. But then the people in Bhim Nagar would be left in the lurch, without any houses.

SATISH: Arjun, your action is illegal.

ARJUN: I know that.

SATISH: Arjun, this is called *goondaism*.

ARJUN: Sir!

SATISH: And *goondaism* isn't social service.

ARJUN: Only needy people have occupied those houses. You call that *goondaism*? You call me a *goonda*?

SATISH: Arjun, think with a cool head. How many people are you pushing into a sea of trouble along with yourself? Our housing society has been registered now. We'll get a loan next month.

ARJUN: Why take that? Ask them to give those houses to us instead.

SATISH: Do you have no thought for tomorrow?

ARJUN: Tomorrow will take care of itself! Who's seen the future?

SATISH: (*In a hard tone.*) Arjun, think carefully. Think of the future. You are courageous, intelligent. But you can't afford to treat the law so casually. Nobody can.

ARJUN: Let whatever happens, happen, sir.

SATISH: But think at least of the real flood victims. They will be furious and say you've been true to your caste.

ARJUN: Who says so? Guruji? Dasrao Guruji says that? Who are the real flood victims? If we aren't, then is Dasrao Guruji one? Even his name appears in the list of flood victims.

SATISH: Dasrao Guruji's name? In the list of flood victims?

ARJUN: And these are the people who brand me a casteist! People in Bhim Nagar have been living in hutments that leak. The rains are just round the corner. I made arrangements for them. I don't have monopoly rights to think on behalf of everybody! I won't think for the others. I'll think only of my caste. That's all.

HEMA: Arjun, has somebody insulted you?

ARJUN: Yes.

SATISH: Who?

ARJUN: My caste. The caste I wasn't born into by choice. I don't want an education. Is there any dearth of those who are educated and unemployed in this country? Anyway, what will I get from this kind of education? Who's going to wipe off the stamp of caste from my name? You, too, are educated. Plus yours is an intercaste marriage. Did Dasrao Joshi rent you his house? And now he poses as a reformer.

HEMA: Did Dasrao Guruji say anything to you, Arjun?

ARJUN: I can only give a *guru* like him a kick in the pants!

SATISH: Arjun!

ARJUN: I am saying that deliberately. I want to trample on those who pretend to be reformers. I want to expose those who capitalize on our caste. I want to tear the masks off their faces. I have chosen my path, sir, consciously. With my reason intact. I know what the ultimate consequence will be. Handcuffs, prison. What else! I'm prepared for that! (*The* POLICE INSPECTOR *enters.*) Goodbye, sir. Come, Inspector. Come in. You have nothing whatsoever to do with order. Protect the law. The law may be an ass, stupid, merciless. But what's that to you? Here, come on, arrest me.

INSPECTOR: (*To* SATISH.) I'm sorry, sir.

(*Lights fade slowly as the* INSPECTOR *puts handcuffs on* ARJUN'*s wrists.*)

SCENE TWO

The same place. It's eleven in the morning. Two months after the events of scene 1. When the curtain goes up, KAKA *is seen sitting on the couch, with a fat volume in his hand, reading it as if it were the scriptures.* SONAL, *a young girl of eighteen, enters while he's busy reading. She turns to watch him closely, hesitates for some time, then unable to suppress her curiosity any longer, calls out—*

SONAL: Kaka—

KAKA: *Ji.* Who's that? Ah, Sonal! Come, come.

SONAL: Isn't Madam at home?

KAKA: No. Probably gone out shopping. Why?

SONAL: Nothing. (KAKA *is once again absorbed in reading.*) What are you reading, Kaka?

KAKA: *Buddha and His Dhamma.* It's a book written by Babasaheb.

SONAL: *Dhamma?*

KAKA: Yes. *Dhamma.* Not *dharma. Dharma* is yours. Ours is *dhamma.* We've begun a *parayana* in Milind Nagar.

SONAL: Milind Nagar?

KAKA: That new place where our Arjunya has settled the flood victims, don't you know?

SONAL: Is it called Milind Nagar?

KAKA: Yes. We've named it so. We're planning to install the statue of Bhagawan Gautam there soon, say in a month's time. These days we're holding a *parayana* there each night.

SONAL: *Parayana?*

KAKA: What? Don't you know *parayana?* And you come from a good Brahmin family. Don't you know what it means?

SONAL: Of course, I know what a *parayana* means. But a *parayana* of this book . . .

KAKA: Why? Is a *parayana* supposed to be only for typically Hindu books? Like *Harivijaya,* or *Pandav Pratap?* Is there any such rule? The Hindus may do the *parayana* of their books. But the Buddhists do *parayana* for this book only. (SONAL *starts to go to the kitchen.*) I know, you won't accept this. Never! Ha! You don't even have elementary manners. How can you understand our *dhamma?*

SONAL: (*His last sentence stops her abruptly.*) Did I make some mistake, Kaka?

KAKA: Yes, you did. Come here. (*She does.*) You go to a college, don't you? Which standard?

SONAL: I am in second year B.A. (*Pauses.*) Um . . . you can say in the fourteenth standard.

KAKA: Fourteenth standard, she says, but doesn't even know that she's to say "*Jai Bhim*" on meeting an elderly person! Come on, say it, can't you? (HEMA *is at the door.*) No? Why? Does the tongue refuse to say it? Of course, you're Dasrao Joshi's daughter! How can you say "*Jai Bhim?*"

SONAL: *Namaskar,* Kaka.

KAKA: That's it! What else can you say except "*Namaskar.*" Okay. That isn't bad in a way! Otherwise saying "*Jai Bhim,*" you might catch hold of a Jai Bhimwala!

HEMA: Good! So the day seems to have begun for you! Don't you ever bother to consider whom you are talking to? Whether it's one of the family or an outsider?

KAKA: Oh hell! I thought you weren't around!

HEMA: So you think you can go on talking like that if I'm not around!

KAKA: Sunbai, is Sonal an outsider? We accepted you as our own, so naturally Sonal is also one of the family.

HEMA: "Our own" he says! And never bothers to respect my feelings. Sonal sit down. I'll be back in a minute.

KAKA: You know Sunbai . . . no, you won't understand the point of this! You know there was this *satyagraha* at Parvati . . . (HEMA *goes into the kitchen without paying any attention to him.* KAKA *continues, looking at* SONAL.) And we were such strapping young men then, you know. I still carry the lash marks on my back.

SONAL: Wow! You participated in a *satyagraha?*

KAKA: What's so surprising about that?

SONAL: Well, I just asked.

KAKA: Your father, Dasrao! He, too, was jailed, wasn't he? Why? Because he'd participated in a *satyagraha.* Right?

SONAL: Right!

KAKA: What with that government certificate he's got which says that he's a freedom fighter, he thinks he has earned some knighthood! I, too, was jailed! Do you know Rajbhoj Sahib? Such a great man! When they *lathi*-charged us, I virtually fell on him like this, and saved him from the blows. Took them all on my back.

SONAL: Did you have to go to a hospital then?

KAKA: Bah! This body had thrived on *murdad!* Who would go to a hospital?

SONAL: *Murdad?* What's that, Kaka?

KAKA: Meat. Of dead cattle!

SONAL: Yuk!

KAKA: Not now! We used to eat it then! In our childhood. But Babasaheb said, don't eat such beastly things. Give it up! We immediately gave it up! Haven't eaten it ever since!

SONAL: Kaka, I don't think there are any *satyagraha*s now. I don't remember seeing any.

KAKA: How can you? Nobody does it now. Now you have *gherao*s, *morcha*s. Our Satish—your Sir, you know—he, too, was in some movement. Now, what was it called . . . ?

SONAL: Vikranda?

KAKA: That's right! Why, you seem to know about it!

SONAL: Well, Sir tells us about it sometimes.

KAKA: Vikranda! When we participated in a *satyagraha*, it was *lathi*s for us. But when he participated in a *gherao* . . .

SONAL: Yes, Kaka?

KAKA: (*Looking at her meaningfully.*) Ask your Madam!—*Gherao* someone and get a girl! *Gherao* someone and get the girl! Bravo! Three cheers for a *gherao*!

SONAL: (*Blushes.*) Kaka!

KAKA: (*Laughs. Pauses. Then gives her a penetrating look.*) Aren't you, too, in some *gherao*? Maybe you are. Who knows! You visit this house so often! So you probably are!

SONAL: (*Blushing.*) Kaka!

KAKA: If you ask me, girls should never be educated. The moment they come of age, they should be married off. With a "bridle" around their neck, they should be packed off with their husbands!*

SONAL: Come on Kaka! You call yourself an Ambedkarite. How can you say girls shouldn't be educated?

KAKA: I mean, shouldn't be educated before marriage! After marriage, let them learn to their heart's content! Sonal, I've told Dasrao Guruji this year he must pack you off!

SONAL: (*Changing the subject.*) Kaka, that day when Arjun was arrested, did you go to the police station?

KAKA: Why my wench? Why this sudden sprint from the marriage *pandal* to the police station?

SONAL: Tell me, Kaka, please! Did you?

KAKA: Of course, I did! Who else would? Our Sattyawan started blabber-

---

*A reference to the *mangalsutra*, a necklace that is fastened (or, in common parlance, "tied") around a Hindu woman's neck during her wedding ceremony.

ing about what is lawful and what isn't . . . He wouldn't go. So I got up and went. From there I went straight to Milind Nagar. Come on, let's go, I said. Not a soul was ready even to stir! They dreaded the police, you know! Then I appealed to the women and children in the name of Babasaheb! What then! The women came out and started marching to the police station! Along with their children! Their men, of course, followed them. The police station was bursting with people! The *thane-dar* was utterly bewildered. Virtually tied himself up into knots. When I gave him an application for bail, he started demanding property documents. There was I, standing like a mountain and asking for bail papers, and he demanded property documents from me! Are those documents greater than human beings? Then what! We started a verbal fight! Fortunately, our Sattyawan entered the scene at that point! Don't know by what miracle, but enter he did! He took the *thanedar* to task right away! In English, you know! Then what! The *thanedar* had to release Arjun immediately. I felt so happy! For educating him! (*Remembers something.*) Bless me! What time is it?

SONAL: Eleven.

KAKA: Got to rush. There's a *morcha* today. The guardian minister is coming on a visit. Have to give him that memorandum. Arjunya must be waiting for me. Sunbai! (HEMA *comes.*) I'm off to Bhim Nagar. (*Leaves.*)

SONAL: He's quite jolly, isn't he?

HEMA: Mountains look lovely only from a distance!

SONAL: Does he ever get angry at you, ma'am?

HEMA: No. He doesn't. But he often taunts me.

SONAL: Taunts you?

HEMA: Forget it! You won't understand it.

SONAL: He appears to be quite a veteran!

HEMA: He was an activist in the movement, you know. Satish, your Sir, lost both his parents when he was quite young. It was Kaka who brought him up. Satish thinks the world of him.

SONAL: But where did you meet him?

HEMA: Who, Satish?

SONAL: You call him by his name, ma'am?

HEMA: Why not? I met him at a Vikranda camp.

SONAL: You knew who he was before marriage?

HEMA: What do you mean who he was? Oh, his caste, you mean! Of course I knew.

SONAL: And yet . . .

HEMA: I loved him, you know. Why should I have asked him about his caste?

SONAL: Then how did you find out? You asked him?

HEMA: Oh no. He told me himself. After he proposed.

SONAL: My, weren't you afraid?

HEMA: Afraid of what?

SONAL: That your parents might get angry?

HEMA: My father is a judge, you know. Ours is a family of reformers. My father fought in the freedom struggle right from the beginning. But yes, my mother was a bit unhappy about it to begin with. But all that is over. She's forgotten her displeasure now. Both of them paid us a visit quite recently.

SONAL: Kaka opposed your marriage, ma'am?

HEMA: Opposed? He even refused to see us for one and a half years!

SONAL: Kaka opposed it! But he says he was in Babasaheb's movement!

HEMA: So what if he was in Babasaheb's movement! Does anyone here like to break off caste ties so easily? (*Sensing something.*) But why are you asking me all this?

SONAL: Just like that, for no particular reason! Ma'am, what does Arjun's father do?

HEMA: He has lost his father. Now he has only his mother. The poor thing is a wage laborer.

SONAL: Ma'am, doesn't Arjun come here these days?

HEMA: Of course he does.

SONAL: I haven't seen him in the college for quite a few days. Actually, since that affair about the flood victims.

HEMA: You came here expecting to see him, then? And you haven't been to the college today, either. (*Looks at her steadily.*) Sonal . . .

SONAL: (*Pauses. Then, in order to relieve her own tension, bursts out.*) I like Arjun, ma'am!

HEMA: (*Speechless for a second. Then controls herself and says.*) Sonal, all this must stop at once.

SONAL: Is Arjun bad, ma'am?

HEMA: No, Arjun isn't bad. It's your age that's bad. Once this age of dreams flies away, you'll be left with nothing but the barren sands of harsh reality.

SONAL: Aren't you happy, ma'am?

HEMA: Who says so?

SONAL: Then why did you say . . .

HEMA: No. I didn't say that out of personal frustration. I just told you about the reality that experience has taught me to see. Of course I'm happy. But one has to suffer a lot before one is granted that happiness.

SONAL: What does one have to do exactly?

HEMA: Well, one has to take one's own decisions. With full responsibility.

SONAL: That's all? Then I, too, am taking a decision to get married with full responsibility.

HEMA: But listen, my dear, this is such a small town. What will your parents say? Have you given it a thought?

SONAL: Had you, ma'am?

HEMA: It was different with me. My father was in the freedom movement.

SONAL: But so was my father! My father is a freedom fighter, too.

HEMA: But not a reformer!

SONAL: My father doesn't believe in this caste business! I'm sure he doesn't.

HEMA: And what makes you so sure?

SONAL: Oh, I was his student in school, you know. Besides, I observe things at home too. Arjun visits us often and my father always treats him with such affection.

HEMA: Affection! Like what a disabled person gets in a crowded compartment! It's like that.

SONAL: The other day I did a funny thing, you know, ma'am. When I say the other day, I mean, two months back, of course. I wrote Arjun a letter.

HEMA: What?

SONAL: Oh, it wasn't meant for Arjun. It was for father to read. I put it in one of my books and kept the book on my father's table. You know why? Because I was scared to tell my father directly.

HEMA: Did he read that letter?

SONAL: He must have. I'm quite certain.

HEMA: What makes you so sure?

SONAL: Because the next day the letter wasn't there in the book.

HEMA: What did your father say?

SONAL: Not a word, ma'am! He must have approved.

HEMA: Does Arjun know anything of this?

SONAL: That's what I want to talk to him about. But I haven't seen him for the last two months. Since that episode about the colony for the flood victims.

HEMA: But does he at least know that you love him?

SONAL: Why shouldn't he? All his friends tease me, taking his name in a voice loud enough for me to hear. Shouldn't he know then?

HEMA: Sonal, all this is a figment of your imagination. This has got to stop. Because I tell you so.

SONAL: Ma'am, you? You of all the persons are saying this! I came to you with such hopes . . . and . . .

ARJUN: (*Entering.*) Kaka . . . (*Seeing him,* SONAL *hides behind* HEMA. ARJUN *looks at her with disgust, then completely ignores her.*) Where's Kaka, ma'am?

HEMA: He just went out saying he wanted to see you. What's tomorrow's *morcha* for?

ARJUN: What else? About Milind Nagar! What can be the demands of the slum-dwellers? They want a house. (*Deliberately looking at* SONAL.) The freedom fighters are ruling the country. What do they care whether Dalits get houses or not!

HEMA: Now why that sarcastic tone? And why don't you attend college these days.

ARJUN: Me? College? After all, we're *goondas*, ruffians, you know! All that we're capable of is teasing girls from respectable families. We aren't the ones who deserve an education. Besides, all respectable girls must be sighing with relief now that I don't go to college. (SONAL *is at first confused at this barrage. Then hurt. Starts to go away, downcast.*) Stop Sonal. Why did you come here?

HEMA: Arjun! (SONAL *raises her head only once to look directly into* ARJUN'S *eyes. Then stands still with her head bowed.*)

ARJUN: What else do you propose to do now? Eh? Have you been poisoning Ma'am's mind against me? You want Ma'am to blast me too? You want to deprive me even of this home? Come on, speak up. Why did you come here?

HEMA: Arjun, what's wrong with you?

ARJUN: But Sir isn't like your father, you know. Or did you think Madam was? They won't even scold me till they've heard my side of the story.

HEMA: Did Dasrao Guruji say something to you, Arjun?

ARJUN: Say something? He insulted me. She complained to her father about me. Said I had written her letters. And that I chased her around. Not just me alone. My entire group of friends is supposed to have teased her. Who the hell is she? What does she think she is? Queen of England or Miss World? Speak up, now. When your father was hurling insult after insult at me, you didn't even come out. Open your moth at least now.

HEMA: You are under some misapprehension, Arjun!

ARJUN: I was. But not now! Ask her, ma'am, ask her please. Have I ever said even four sentences in a row to her? Just because I live in a slum, am I shameless? Because I am an orphan, am I a ruffian? Because I am poor, am I a hooligan? I don't give a damn for such respectable people. I kick them in their teeth. I spit on their wealth. (SONAL *finds it unbearable and goes out.* HEMA *is disturbed too.*)

HEMA: Arjun, calm down! Arjun!

ARJUN: Do you know what else her father said? I used to respect him so much because he had taught me. But how was I to know that a man who was such a fine teacher had a perverted heart? He said, can all Mahars be Ambedkars just because they receive an education? Receive as much education as you want, he said, but you'll never lose your habits! You'll never be civilized! I would've endured it had it been just that. But then he added, "You've grown so insolent only because that Godghate pampers you. God knows where he's brought that female from—and goes around boasting that she's a Brahmin! Godghate may say what he likes, but why should we believe it? That Mahar only wants to show off and fool us into believing that he is great." He said, "Keep your wisdom to yourself, wise guy! I'll pluck your eyes out if you so much as even look at Sonal!" (*Pauses.*) What the hell do they take the government *tamrapata* for? A license to lash people? And how simple he looks! What honeyed words glibly roll off his tongue! But what poison lies in his heart! And he has an addled, rancid brain in his head! Bloody Brahmin! This bloody Brahmin caste! You can never suspect the deceit in their heart!

HEMA: Wait, Arjun! Answer one question. (*Stressing each word.*) Do you like Sonal? (*Pauses.*) Do you love her? (ARJUN *looks into* HEMA's *eyes and bows his head.*) Why don't you speak up? I want an answer. (ARJUN *starts to go.*) Arjun, I'm waiting for your answer!

ARJUN: No. I don't like anyone now. I had forgotten myself. But thank God, I've woken up in time. No. Now I won't be deceived. And I know you'll only take her side.

HEMA: Arjun, did you say all this in front of Dasrao?

ARJUN: No.

HEMA: Did you notice that Sonal left crying? No. Did you bother to notice that I was standing right in front of you when you spoke? No. Why? Why don't you look beyond yourself a bit? You were insulted. I agree. But why should you insult everybody who crosses your path? Who gave you that right? What's the difference between you and Dasrao Guruji then? You think he lashes out at anybody just because he's got the freedom fighter's certificate. But do you think you've got a right to insult others just because you're born a Dalit?

(SATISH *has come in and is standing at the door.*)

ARJUN: Yes. I am a Dalit. I am. Did you realize that only today? I am glad that I heard that word from your mouth! Yes. I am a Dalit. I shall live as a Dalit. And live for Dalits. I won't be a hypocrite. Good-bye.

(HEMA *calls out "Arjun," then goes into the kitchen.* ARJUN *turns to go and sees* SATISH.)

SATISH: Where are you going?

ARJUN: We're planning to *gherao* the guardian minister tomorrow. There's a meeting in connection with that.

SATISH: I see. Sit down for a while.

ARJUN: I am getting late, sir.

SATISH: I am aware of that. But I, too, want to talk about the *gherao*.

(KAKA *enters.*)

KAKA: (*To* ARJUN.) Now what are you yapping about here? People have been waiting for a long time. Come on, let's go.

SATISH: Wait, Kaka. Will you be there in tomorrow's *morcha*?

KAKA: Yes.

SATISH: Then please sit down. (ARJUN *and* KAKA *sit down.*)

ARJUN: But it's getting late, sir!

SATISH: I won't stop you, don't worry. Who's participating in the *gherao* today?

ARJUN: What do you mean, who? It's our *gherao*, ours.

SATISH: There is going to be another *morcha* of the flood victims tomorrow. You know that? With a demand for those houses.

ARJUN: Really? Who told you that, sir?

SATISH: Students have given a call for a college *bundh* tomorrow to support the flood victims. They're taking the *morcha* to the collector's office. What about you?

ARJUN: We'll be going to the Rest House.

SATISH: All *savarnas* have united on this issue.

KAKA: All *savarnas* always unite in crisis. And I thought he was telling us something new!

SATISH: Now don't add fuel to the fire, Kaka. The town is tense. They've got an extra police force.

KAKA: Trying to put fear in me, eh? What will the police do? Open fire? On so many people? On women and children?

SATISH: A *morcha* isn't meant just to build up pressure alone, Kaka!

ARJUN: Who's building up the pressure, sir? We? By taking out a *morcha* in the most peaceful manner possible? The one to build up pressure is that Pawar of yours. The president of your college committee. He's the contractor of that colony. He has two *lakh rupees* at stake. Besides his relatives haven't got houses.

SATISH: Right. But he's doing it with the help of the law. And he's using the flood victims. They are an excuse. He has the sympathy of the whole town. Besides, he sees to it that he himself remains nowhere in the picture!

ARJUN: I, too, have organized the homeless. And there are plenty of flood victims amongst them, too. And why should I hide behind anyone? My conscience is clear. I shall make my demand out there in the open. Because my demand is a demand for justice.

SATISH: And what about the flood victims who aren't Dalits.

ARJUN: Sure! They, too, should be given houses.

SATISH: But there aren't any more houses left.

ARJUN: Then build new houses for them.

SATISH: Arjun, you aren't prepared to respect the law. You don't bother about earning people's sympathy. You aren't prepared to consider other castes even as a strategy. Where are you leading them all? Where? Arjun, the fight for justice can't be fought with crowds alone. That is sheer mobocracy. It always claims the poor man as the victim. Forget about the others. At least we have to fight more carefully.

KAKA: Oh Sattyawan, Our Lord of Truth! Why are you telling me all this? Don't give me that bullshit! What will happen? Jail, at the most. All right. I have been jailed before! Dadasaheb Gaikwad had organized that *satyagraha*. And on what a grand scale! Even Gandhi had never been able to organize such a mammoth rally. You know what it was for? For the grazing lands to be given to the rural poor. Thousands of poor people went to jail. Endured *lathi* charges. Their children suffered utter starvation. And did the poor get that land finally? No. None of them got any. But today this Arjunya has indeed achieved a miracle! People have got houses in just one day. Now let them jail us. Who cares? Come on! He may be your student, but he's working far more effectively than you. Pat him on the back, instead of boxing his ears! What's the use of your education otherwise?

SATISH: Kaka, you've always thought of me as an armchair intellectual. It's true, I'm no activist like you. But I want you to answer a few questions. There were ten thousand activists in the Mahad *satyagraha*, right? Each one had a *lathi* in his hand, a fire in his soul, and the strength of an elephant! And how big was the group of the stone throwing, orthodox Brahmins? Only a handful. Had they really wanted to, the activists could have burnt down the whole of Mahad. Those few reactionaries would have been grist for their mill. Babasaheb had just to say the word, and they would have done it in a second. But it never happened. Babasaheb didn't utter even a single curse in retaliation. Why? The activists quietly faced the showers of stones and pellets to protect their leader. But no one lifted even a finger in retaliation. Why did that happen? It was a temporary set-back for him, Kaka. But he did sense one thing acutely. It was a historical moment. A moment when the Dalits realized their collective power. He refused the help offered to him by the non-Brahmins. Not because he didn't want their support. In fact, he did want the majority to support his cause. He refused to accept the support of the non-Brahmin party because their condition was—

"Exclude the Brahmins." Taking the support of the law and appealing to the conscience of the people when law was found to be weak—that's how Babasaheb lived! He never used his political acumen to grab the seat of power. Rather, he exercised it to make the movement stronger, more dynamic. We are the followers of that Seer, Arjun. We must never forget that. We can't afford to think only of temporary gains. Remember, Babasaheb warned, "It doesn't matter if you can't advance this chariot, but never, never reverse it!"

ARJUN: What do you suggest I do, sir?

SATISH: I think, at the moment, we should call off the *morcha*. And we should take in some *savarnas* too, if we can.

ARJUN: Neither of these is possible now, sir. They are all ready for the *morcha* there—at this very moment!

SATISH: Come on, let's go there. Let's change the date of the *morcha!*

ARJUN: But if they've come to know of this counter *morcha* now, they will be raging. And then it would be sheer cowardice to take the *morcha* back.

SATISH: Cowardice? Whose? Yours or theirs?

ARJUN: All right. Suppose we cancel this *morcha*. Will it solve the problem? On the contrary, people taking out the counter *morcha* will feel that we consider their demand just.

SATISH: Are you aware of the implications if both the *morchas* are taken out at the same time?

ARJUN: There'll be *lathi* charges, firing, a few will be injured, and someone may become a martyr, too.

SATISH: Those will be the immediate results. What about the long-term implications? Have you considered that? It doesn't matter if Kaka doesn't consider this. But you? You can't afford to avoid thinking about that. That will be dangerous.

ARJUN: Don't you dare taunt me by talking about danger!

SATISH: Oh it is undoubtedly dangerous for you! But more importantly, it would be dangerous for the Dalit movement. All the needy Dalits will have to do without the sympathy of the others.

ARJUN: All right. (*Gets up.*) Kaka. What have you decided?

KAKA: What's there to decide? Come on. (*Starts to leave.*) This is how the white-collared people always behave, Arjunya. Trust them to help out at the critical moment! They'll immediately back out!

(HEMA *is at the door, listening to all this.* KAKA *goes out, followed by* ARJUN. SATISH *looks in their direction. Then, dejected, sits in a chair.* HEMA *comes near him. Her fingers ruffle his hair, consolingly.*)

HEMA: Eating your heart out?

SATISH: Huh? No. Depressed. A bit!

HEMA: It's the same thing happening everywhere. How can you possibly control it all alone! After all, you aren't a politician!

SATISH: That's exactly why I'm depressed! Those politicians who could control the circumstances are extinct now. Today, the one who can ride the wave becomes the leader! And the people! They just follow him who dazzles them most with alluring baits! What do you think? The Dalits who are supporting him today will continue to support him tomorrow, too? They've got houses, thanks to him, without any sweat. Now if somebody comes with a bigger bait tomorrow, they will dump him like dirt! Where will Arjun be then? He'll either be frustrated, or become a puppet in the hands of some big boss in politics! The Dalit movement will go to the dogs! Will be shattered into fragments! Shattered by the weapon of alluring baits! (*Lost in himself.*)

HEMA: You've done your duty. You have explained everything to him. Now it's up to him! Finally, everyone has to decide for himself!

SATISH: (*Waking with a start.*) That's true! Finally, everyone has to decide for himself.

Act Two
SCENE ONE

The same place. Second day. The morcha *of the Dalits is passing.* HEMA *at the window, looking at the* morcha. SATISH *enters. He is back from the college, distracted. Puts his books on the table and sits down in a chair. Still lost. After the* morcha *is out of sight,* HEMA *turns and sees* SATISH.)

HEMA: Oh! When did you come?

SATISH: Just now.

HEMA: Did anything special happen in the college today?

SATISH: Special? Unh uh . . . nothing really special as such! But the *savarna* students, supporting the flood victims, wanted to observe a *bundh* in the college . . . You know who their leader was?

HEMA: Who?

SATISH: Arvind Deshmukh!

HEMA: The future son-in-law of Dasrao Guruji?

SATISH: Wrong! The one insulted by the moneylender in the NSS camp! You know, the one who was taken for a Dalit and given the broken cup of tea, set aside for the Dalits! That same one!

HEMA: How come he's become so active?

SATISH: After that incident, I'd thought he would do some introspection. But his ego seems to be terribly hurt! He's desperately trying to pull something off which will declare to the whole world that he's got *savarna* blood in his veins! (*Pauses.*) Hema, do you remember Vijay Kundkar? From two years back? The poet?

HEMA: Of course, I do. What lovely poems he used to write!

SATISH: What committed poems! He was an orphan. Used to attend every Dalit literary convention! His own relatives, his caste people—none had ever helped him. And so scornfully he did talk about them! But I gave him a helping hand, took a little interest in his life. And how he respected me for that! He respects me even today. Now he's a teacher. But do you know what he does these days? I read all his published poems. Do you know, he invariably writes his name as Vijay Kundkar, followed by "Patil" in brackets. (*Sighs.*) You know why? Because he's a Maratha. Now he doesn't find his status as a poet sufficient. He craves the status given by birth! I met him today. I asked him why. You know, Hema, he just smiled in reply. Hema, I think we're proving to be worthless in this battle of life.

HEMA: Come on, now! Come in with me. Let me make you some tea!

SATISH: No. Let me sit here for some time. Could you bring the tea here?

HEMA: You've become so nervous!

SATISH: Not really!

HEMA: I'll be back with the tea in a minute.

(*Goes in.* SATISH *relaxes a bit. Skims through the newspaper on the table.* DASRAO JOSHI *enters.*)

DASRAO: May I come in, sir?

SATISH: Come on in, Dasrao Guruji! So you, too, seem to have got a holiday today!

DASRAO: (*Sitting.*) Of course! All the teachers have gone to participate in the *morcha*. So I thought, why sit alone in the school! Let's go to Professor Satish for a chat. You know what—I met Shewanta on my way!

SATISH: Shewanta? Why, isn't she at the *morcha*?

DASRAO: At the *morcha*? Who'll allow her there?

SATISH: Why not? They're taking out the *morcha* with women and children as well.

DASRAO: That may be so. But she's a defaulter!

SATISH: Defaulter? How come? I don't get you.

DASRAO: I didn't either, at first! But then she told me.

SATISH: What?

DASRAO: Each family in Milind Nagar has to pay housing tax. Twenty-five *rupees* a month! But she hasn't paid a single *paisa* in the last two months.

SATISH: Who collects this housing tax?

DASRAO: Who else? Arjun. Arjun collects it!

SATISH: Arjun collects housing tax?

DASRAO: What's so surprising about that? After all, it was he who got them the houses, so he must collect taxes from them too. Now Shewanta's poor. Maybe she doesn't have money to pay him. Still, how long can Arjun allow her to stay in the house?

SATISH: You mean Arjun drove her out of the house?

DASRAO: Maybe he couldn't help it, you know! But all her belongings lay scattered on the road. The house was locked. There was no one to keep an eye on them. So the poor thing was hanging around in utter desperation. She couldn't even get away, you see. She said she wanted to talk to Kaka.

SATISH: This is simply horrible! Arjun's behaving atrociously. (*He's disturbed.* HEMA *comes in with tea for all three. To* HEMA.) Hema, does Arjun collect housing tax from people in Milind Nagar? Did Kaka say anything to you about it?

DASRAO: Sir, Kaka probably doesn't even know about this. I hurried to inform you because you have a different image, sir. We consider you half Brahmin, sir! By that, of course, I mean rational!

SATISH: Are only the Brahmins qualified to be rational, Guruji? (*Gives him tea.*) Have tea, Guruji. Don't worry. It's been prepared by Hema. (*Takes his tea and sits down in a chair.*) Kaka's quite right. People'll never forget caste. (HEMA *sits down somewhere in the hall, looking for an opportunity to enter the conversation.*)

DASRAO: People are so funny, sir! Irrespective of your intentions, despite your behavior, they'll always say certain things. Now Kaka has joined the *morcha*, right? You know what people say? Professor Godghate must have instigated him. So what if he hasn't gone himself, that's because he has a job to protect. Besides, Pawar Sahib is the president of the college committee.

SATISH: So people think I am a coward!

DASRAO: No, no. Not a coward. But what can you do if Kaka doesn't listen to you.

SATISH: Why should he? He's an old hand of the RPI. I was never in any political party myself. I resigned from Vikranda the day it became a political party. Kaka is entitled to have his own opinion—

DASRAO: Of course, of course. But then people don't know all these details, do they?

HEMA: You certainly seem to know them, though! Then why don't you tell them your own opinion?

DASRAO: Who, me? Oh no, Hematai. I'm no scholar like you.

SATISH: You don't have to be a scholar to understand this, Guruji. You can understand it even by reading a newspaper. I can give you a number of examples of blood brothers working in different political parties. How many examples do you need of fathers and sons who stay in the same house and still support different political ideologies?

DASRAO: Oh yes. There are. There are.

SATISH: But here you'll apply different yardsticks! It may be Panthers, Mass Movement, Republican Party of India that you are talking about. But you will find that they have one factor which is common to all of them. Dalit. Dalit! Right?

HEMA: Why do you lose your temper at him? Guruji, have you ever heard the name, Vishnupant Ranade?

DASRAO: I . . . I think I have. He's the . . .

HEMA: The sessions judge of our district!

DASRAO: Of course! He's just been transferred here.

HEMA: He's my father.

DASRAO: Oh really? Great.

HEMA: I'll surely invite you when he comes to visit me. To introduce you to him.

DASRAO: That'll be very nice!

HEMA: You were asking Arjun about my father, I heard!

DASRAO: Me?

HEMA: How would Arjun know, Guruji? You could've just asked me, instead!

DASRAO: But I never asked Arjun! Who told you that? Arjun?

HEMA: No. Sonal did. After you read her letter to Arjun.

(DASRAO *is totally bewildered*.)

SATISH: What's this, Hema?

HEMA: You'll know by and by. Why, Dasrao himself will tell you!

DASRAO: I knew Sonal would blabber something like that here.

HEMA: Isn't it true?

DASRAO: But when did she come here?

HEMA: So now you'll go and take her to task! Why don't you tell her frankly, instead, that you're arranging her marriage?

DASRAO: Look here, Hematai . . .

HEMA: Who did you take us for? Managers of an Intercaste Marriage Bureau?

DASRAO: No. No . . . Hematai . . .

HEMA: I know everything you said to Arjun.

DASRAO: (*Getting up*.) There was no other way left for me, Hematai. Just think what a small town this is! What will people say?

HEMA: Please don't lie any more. You aren't as straight as you look. It was Sonal who had written that letter for you to read, but it was Arjun you blasted. Why? Why? Now come on. Did you have a single letter written by him?

DASRAO: But . . . he kept quiet when I scolded him . . . so . . .

HEMA: He loves Sonal.

SATISH: Hema?

HEMA: It's true. So Guruji wanted to know whether they'd maintained any correspondence. And at the same time, he was careful enough to keep Sonal in the dark about what he was doing. He wanted to preserve his image as a progressive father in her eyes. At any cost. You know how to protect your selfish interests don't you? Your status . . . ! Oh how very well, indeed!

DASRAO: I'll take your leave now, sir. Hematai seems to be in an angry mood. That Arjun must have come and told her what I did say along with what I absolutely didn't. Well, see you. (*Starts to go.*)

HEMA: And don't you forget that Sonal is a major!

DASRAO: I'm sure, Hematai, the occasion will hardly arise. (*Leaves.*)

SATISH: Hema, how angry you were! I didn't even dare to intervene! What has happened?

HEMA: Nothing.

SATISH: Won't you tell even me?

HEMA: (*With tears in her eyes.*) Guruji called Arjun and not only did he revile his caste but . . . but . . .

SATISH: Go on Hema!

HEMA: He said, "God knows from where this Godghate has brought that female! Boasts she's a Brahmin! But who knows what she really is!" That's what he said about me, that man! And he comes here so often! Speaks such honeyed words! But what a filthy mind! And he's a teacher, even a freedom fighter!

SATISH: Take it easy, Hema! It's difficult to make out people who have a honeyed tongue. It's only when their interests are hurt that the filth in their hearts comes out like this.

HEMA: (*Still angry.*) Kaka has his own brand of eccentricity. He feels I've come into this house solely to ruin the girls from his caste.

SATISH: Kaka's a very old fashioned person, Hema. Please try to understand him. But mind you, he'll never say anything behind your back.

HEMA: (*Still lost in herself.*) Sonal thinks I must support her. Why? Simple! I've married out of caste! Then there's Arjun! A boy who's almost one of the family. But the way he lashed out at me in a fit of anger! If you call someone a Mahar, that's an insult! And what if you call someone a Brahmin? Is that supposed to be an honor? I rejected my caste when I married you. It's a deliberate insult to me to be called a Brahmin! A downright affront! Everybody claws at me with their savage caste nails.

Deliberately or without being aware of it. Whatever their intentions, every blow inflicts a new wound on me. But who cares? Who feels it's wrong? (*Silent.*) I accepted this reality with my eyes open. And I must, alone, build the inner strength to endure all this. But at the moment I feel weak. A little support is all I want, Satish, please! Let me lean on your shoulder.

(ARJUN *comes in, running.*)

ARJUN: Sir, Sir, isn't Kaka home yet? (*Startled, stands rooted.*)

(HEMA *turns and goes inside.* SATISH *regains control over himself.*)

SATISH: Arjun? Anything wrong? How was the *morcha*? Okay?

ARJUN: No sir, the *morcha* was totally ruined. They threw the belongings of everyone in Milind Nagar out on the streets and set them on fire. They're making a bonfire of each Dalit home. And—

SATISH: But the police? What are the police doing?

ARJUN: Police? The bastards opened fire on us! That bloody minister never arrived. With his tail between his legs, he ran away to safety. The situation has gotten totally out of control.

SATISH: And what about you? When the situation went out of control, what did you do? Ran away, didn't you? You are responsible for this disaster. I warned you not to take out the *morcha* today. But you didn't listen. You provoked the Dalits. And now when the *basti* is burning, you condemn the police? Who invited this catastrophe on the heads of the poor illiterate people in the first place?

ARJUN: (*Furious.*) It's easy to hold forth in the safety of four walls. But reason and rationality don't provide a roof over your head when you have lived in leaking huts for ages. The houses are built specially for us. How can we tolerate it if people like Dasrao Joshi brazenly occupy them before our very eyes? Can *you*? That man had even refused to rent you his rooms. Bloody bastard! They've been claiming every damn thing around as their own. But even *our* things? Do they also belong to them? Then what do we have which belongs to us here, sir? What can we call our own? We've just one thing left as our own, sir, and that's suffering! Oppression and injustice are crushing us to extinction and you still want *us* to think? Oh no. That's not on, sir; that's just not on. This is no ordinary struggle and no ordinary movement. It is an all-out war. Even greater than the two world wars. And anything is fair in war. The path which leads to victory is the right path.

SATISH: All right. No one will dispute that Dasrao Joshi has no right to live in that house. But Shewanta? What about Shewanta? She is both a Dalit and a flood victim. Then why wasn't she in the *morcha*?

ARJUN: Who told you that? Did she come here?

SATISH: So, Shewanta was not in the *morcha*.

ARJUN: Sir, let me tell you—

SATISH: No, let me tell you. Shewanta was not there in the *morcha* because she hadn't paid her housing tax. Right? So Arjunrao Jadhav, the self-proclaimed savior of the Dalits, threw her out of her house along with her belongings. And forbade her from joining in the *morcha*. For just fifty *rupees*. Because she couldn't pay fifty *rupees*, Shewanta became homeless. Was thrown out onto the streets. You took a sane and rational decision to allow her to be crushed to extinction, under oppression and injustice, just because she didn't have fifty *rupees*. Arjun, what has turned your head? Today you are God for the Dalits in Milind Nagar. Their hero. And you collect money from them! Even the *goonda*s on the footpaths are better than you. They, at least, do it as a profession to stay alive. Why, Arjun? Why were you collecting the money?

ARJUN: I had to give bribes, sir, in order to maintain the status quo of the colony. Where could I have got such an amount from, sir? I had to make several trips to Bombay. Where was I going to get money for them? The others understood and gave money without complaining, didn't they? Were they stupid fools? Besides it wasn't as if Shewanta didn't have the money. But she didn't want to pay. She insisted that I declare the accounts of the collection.

SATISH: What was wrong with that?

ARJUN: Was I supposed to declare to all and sundry how much I had paid as bribes and to whom? I just wanted to shake her a bit. But she started demanding accounts right there, in front of everyone, on the very day of the *morcha*. What if the *morcha* had suffered?

SATISH: Look here, Arjun. Think coolly. Apart from Shewanta, didn't everyone else pay without complaining? If they knew why they were paying, why were you reluctant to disclose the accounts in front of them? Is Kaka aware of this? Where is Kaka? Kaka?

(*Gets up to go out.* KAKA *enters. A wound on his forehead. With him,* SUBHAN, *a party worker. He has come to know about Shewanta.* ARJUN *goes to support him, but* KAKA *vehemently pushes his hand away and looks at* ARJUN *scornfully. The look reveals all—even to* ARJUN.)

KAKA: Stay away. Don't you touch me.

ARJUN: Kaka . . .

SATISH: What happened? What has happened, Kaka?

KAKA: Ask Arjun. Ask him. There was firing in Milind Nagar. Poor Shewanta was killed, Satish!

SATISH: What? Shewanta killed! But . . .

KAKA: He! It was he who drove her out of her house for fifty *rupees*! For just fifty *rupees*! Yes. That's what he did. A poor widow who had even got herself an education, because she wanted to stand on her own feet. But—

ARJUN: Kaka . . .

SATISH: Calm down, Kaka. Please. There, there.

(*Supports him.* ARJUN *looks guilty, stands in a corner.* KAKA *sinks to the ground, sits with his head between his hands, absolutely drained. Darkness.*)

SCENE TWO

The same place. Eleven in the morning. Fifteen days have passed since the events of the last scene. When the curtain goes up, the stage is empty. Notes of some auspicious instrument like the shehnai *float in.* KAKA *enters hastily. There is a band-aid on his forehead. He carries a packet of candles, a packet of flowers, and a big cardboard box with a statue of Buddha in it. He brings out the statue from the box and puts it on the table. Lights a candle. Starts to worship and pray. Sings "Trisarana."* HEMA *comes from outside. Sees him engrossed in worship.*

HEMA: Beautiful! It's just beautiful!

KAKA: Isn't it? I ordered it specially from Bombay. Satish himself gave me the address, you know. Cost five hundred *rupees*, it did. (*Offers flowers.*) Had got it specially for that Vihara in Milind Nagar! (*Sighs.*) But what's the use, now? (*Looks at her pathetically.*)

HEMA: (*With affection.*) Kaka . . . (*A pause.*)

KAKA: I haven't lost my heart, Sunbai! Our Satish is forming that housing society, isn't he? This statue of the Buddha can be set up there. (*Pauses.*) You, too, can offer flowers. This is our God, you know. Not yours. Your God believes in inequality; discriminates between people. But our God won't ever reject your prayers. (HEMA *smiles. Doesn't move.*) What has happened? (*Realizes his mistake.*) Come on. Tell me (*Laughs.*) Sunbai, say what you like, but old habits die hard, you know! This habit will be with me till the end. All right. Don't pray if you don't want to. I won't insist. (*But in the meantime,* HEMA *has already picked up the garland of flowers.*) No. Don't. That garland is for Babasaheb's photograph. Take some flowers instead. You can't offer a garland to the Buddha!

HEMA: Why not, Kaka?

KAKA: Because that's the custom!

HEMA: Yes. But why?

KAKA: How should I know? I'll ask the Bhante and tell you. (HEMA *laughs.*) What are you laughing at?

HEMA: Nothing. Just like that.

KAKA: (*Offering the garland to Babasaheb's photograph.*) I know why you laughed, Sunbai.

HEMA: Tell me.

KAKA: Your God, Maruti, is always offered a garland of *rui* flowers. Why? Because that's the custom! Similarly, this is also a custom.

HEMA: All right. All right. Let's have lunch.

(HEMA *goes in to the kitchen.* KAKA *is looking at the Buddha.* DASRAO JOSHI *stands at the door.*)

DASRAO: Kaka . . .

KAKA: *Ji.* Who's it? Oh, Dasrao Guruji . . . *Jai Bhim.*

DASRAO: *Namaskar.*

KAKA: Come in, Guruji, please sit down.

DASRAO: No. Not now. No time. Actually, I was on my way to Milind Nagar. There's some program there, you know. So I thought I could go along with you. That's why I came.

KAKA: Milind Nagar? What's left of Milind Nagar now?

DASRAO: Haven't you been there recently? All the damage has been repaired. They've even painted the houses.

KAKA: Who has?

DASRAO: Why, the government, who else?

KAKA: And who had burned them in the first place?

DASRAO: Now who can tell us *that* Kaka? There are some twenty-five accused. The case is going on in the sessions court.

KAKA: Who are the accused ones? Aren't they the relatives of the guardian minister?

DASRAO: Huh? Oh yes. I suppose you could say that.

KAKA: Then why call it Milind Nagar? Milind Nagar was burnt down. Call it the government colony.

DASRAO: They say the government's going to give each family some utensils, clothes, and five hundred *rupees* as aid.

KAKA: Let them avail themselves of it!

DASRAO: From the hands of the guardian minister.

KAKA: He'll certainly come now. Why couldn't he come earlier? At least this disaster would have been averted.

DASRAO: Where's Arjun?

KAKA: I don't know.

DASRAO: It was Arjun, they say, who greased the palm of everyone at the top there.

KAKA: Maybe.

DASRAO: You don't know.

KAKA: Ask him to climb a little higher than that if he can, and bring back Shewanta's life! Now that she's dead and gone . . .

HEMA: (*Calling from within.*) Kaka . . .

KAKA: *Ji.*

HEMA: (*Enters.*) Oh, Dasrao Guruji! When did you come?

DASRAO: Just now.

HEMA: You probably have some work?

DASRAO: I was going to this program, you know. In Milind Nagar. But Kaka doesn't seem inclined. Otherwise he would have been good company for me.

HEMA: Of course! You're going to deliver a speech there, aren't you?

DASRAO: I am. I am invited often as the old hand in the town. Oh well, Hematai, the court is coming here next week, they say, for spot inspection.

HEMA: Perhaps.

DASRAO: Er . . . The court—that is, Ranade Saheb himself—is coming, they say. You had said, remember, that you would introduce me to him? You have only to send word, I'll come.

HEMA: If he's coming on some official work, Daddy won't come here. He'll go straight from the Rest House.

DASRAO: Oh will he?

HEMA: You can go to the Rest House, if you like!

DASRAO: All right.

HEMA: Is Arvind Deshmukh one of the accused?

DASRAO: No. (*Immediately catching her drift.*) Oh, no, no. It wasn't for anything like that Hematai, that I wanted to see him. I just wanted to meet him informally. Goodbye. (*Goes.*)

HEMA: Let's go in, Kaka.

KAKA: Okay. Let's go in.

HEMA: Such a shrewd man. And a close one, too. Won't reveal anything!

KAKA: After all, he's a Brahmin!

(HEMA *looks at him with mock anger. Both laugh and go in.* SATISH *enters. He seems disturbed. Notices the statue of the Buddha on the table. Stands watching it for some time. Then takes off his shoes and socks. Throws them into the corner and sits down.*)

SATISH: Hema . . .

HEMA: (*Enters.*) You? Back so early today?

SATISH: So the statue has arrived! Where's Kaka?

HEMA: Inside. Having his meal. But don't you have college today? Why are you back so early?

SATISH: I just came back. No particular reason.

HEMA: Aren't you well? Have you taken casual leave?

SATISH: The students have boycotted classes. Things have been heating up for the last four days. Today they came to a head and exploded.

HEMA: What has been going on for the last four days?

SATISH: Chicken-hearted buggers! They're so scared of the students! . . .

HEMA: Who?

SATISH: Who else? My colleagues. For the last four days the students have been demanding Arjun's expulsion from the college.

HEMA: Arjun's expulsion? What for?

SATISH: Because he's been charge-sheeted under 302 and 307. The police have held him responsible for Shewanta's death. The students say they are afraid of him. They say a murderer must not be allowed in the college. The principal's singing the same tune. And such namby-pamby policies he has. Actually, he should have firmly told the students right on the first day that no one's guilty until the law proves him so. The law also considers the accused person innocent till he's sentenced. Instead of that, he kept on driveling in front of the students! "Arjun doesn't come to the college, anyway . . . Why stretch things too far unnecessarily . . . etc."! Rubbish. Naturally such spineless drivel roused the students even more.

HEMA: Is Pawar Sahib instigating the students?

SATISH: It isn't like that, Hema. Why should Pawar Sahib instigate the students? It's the principal who's exploiting this opportunity to please him. What else!

HEMA: You believe Pawar to be neutral in Arjun's affair?

SATISH: He can't afford to get involved in it at this time. As it is, there's tension in the town! Besides, his last payment for the flood victims colony is still pending. So he must be wishing to hear the last of this affair as early as possible. He won't get his money till then!

HEMA: But how did the students reach that stage?

SATISH: It was like this. Yesterday the principal called a meeting of the discipline committee. The teachers sensed which way the principal was inclined, and played up to him. They kept on repeating the same words. "When does Arjun come to the college these days, anyway?" So everyone assumed that Arjun was guilty; but because he didn't come to the college, there was no need to worry. I vehemently criticized this assumption. I plainly told them, Arjun can't be legally expelled from the college till his guilt is proved. That gave them a jolt! Then someone guardedly said, "He's been consistently absent, so he can be expelled on that ground!" Offering again a new escape route! I said, "Okay. If that's the stand, expel all those who've remained absent throughout the whole year." Then someone came up with yet another trick, "We should suspend him till the court gives its verdict." The best middle way. Any skin-saving device is a middle way. Kill both birds with one stone. Satisfy the students and create the illusion of having punished Arjun! I opposed that too. I was the only one to oppose his suspension. Finally I told them, if you suspend Arjun, I'll resign from the discipline committee. That was the end of the meeting!

HEMA: Do you sincerely believe that Arjun is innocent?

SATISH: Come on! Shewanta was burned in Milind Nagar. He was in the crowd at the Rest House at that time. The distance between the two places is one and a half kilometers. How's that possible, tell me? Arjun has got a fiery temper all right, but he certainly isn't such a brute! Of course, what I feel is unimportant. The verdict the court gives is important.

HEMA: What happened today?

(*There is a great commotion outside. Slogans are shouted: "Down with Satish Godghate." "Satish Godghate Murdabad, Expel Arjun Jadhav from the college." etc.*)

SATISH: These are pressure tactics, pure and simple! Hema, you go in. I'll take care of this. (HEMA *goes in.* KAKA *comes out, wiping his hands on his dhoti.*)

KAKA: What's happening? What's the commotion outside?

(*Again slogans are heard.*)

SATISH: Don't go out, Kaka. Come inside.

KAKA: Down with you? Who's that? You there, come here.

HEMA: Kaka, don't go please.

KAKA: But what's happening? Who are they?

SATISH: (*Goes near the door.*) Only one of you should come forward and say what you want. I don't mind if you want to shout slogans. But if you want to talk, I'll allow only one person.

FIRST STUDENT: We want to ask you some questions.

SECOND: And we'll ask them only from here.

THIRD: Go on, you two.

SATISH: Come in. (TWO STUDENTS *come in.* "Don't take too long" *somebody shouts from outside.*)

SATISH: Now don't shout any more slogans. You want me to talk to you, don't you? (*All become quiet.*) Come in and sit down.

FIRST: We haven't come to sit down.

SATISH: You've come to talk, haven't you? You might as well sit down and talk.

SECOND: (*Without sitting down.*) What happened to the resolution regarding Arjun?

FIRST: You opposed his dismissal?

SATISH: Not just me alone. We all opposed it.

SECOND: You are lying.

SATISH: His dismissal wouldn't have been legal. So we all opposed it. You appear to be only half-informed.

FIRST: Who is lying? You or the principal?

SATISH: Did the principal himself give you this information? I opposed his suspension.

SECOND: So you did oppose it.

SATISH: His suspension.

SECOND: Same thing! Why did you oppose it? Why did you turn down everybody's request?

SATISH: Request? You call this a request? You closed the college by force today. Threatened not to enter classes until Arjun was dismissed. You call that a request?

SECOND: What else could we do? We tried speaking to you. Then gave a written application. Yet your discipline committee did nothing. What could we do then? And if that wasn't a request, what was it?

THIRD: (*From outside.*) Come out, you two, we're getting late. Let's go to Pawar Sahib. We'll see how he isn't dismissed!

SATISH: So! You're going to Pawar Sahib?

FIRST: Of course! But we came to ask you a question before going there. How can we sit in the class with a murderer? And look at you! You make such a great show of educating us in culture and values!

SATISH: Arjun has yet to be proven guilty.

SECOND: Now what else is left to be proved? Our fathers were handcuffed because of him.

SATISH: The handcuffs were for setting the houses on fire, weren't they? They've been accused of it. The police have charged them with it. Now will that make you drive your fathers out of your houses?

THIRD: (*Standing near the door.*) What the hell are you discussing with him? Come on. We just wanted to get at the truth. We've got it now.

SATISH: So what if I opposed it? The principal has a right to take the final decision, doesn't he? Ask him to take it then. Ask him to suspend Arjun!

THIRD: Oh yes, so you can wax eloquent about the oppression of the Dalits! Come on. Let's go. How can he possibly say anything against Arjun? Let's get out of here.

SATISH: (*Furious.*) Have you lost your heads?

THIRD: We asked you to expel Arjun, a murderer. And you advise us to drive our own fathers out of our homes? And on top of it, you ask us if we've lost our heads? I'm off.

(*The* THIRD STUDENT *comes near the door and shouts, "Satish Godghate." The other students respond, "Murdabad!" "Down with casteists!" The remaining two students leave. Slogans get weaker as the students go away.* SATISH, *tremendously hurt, stands rooted to the spot.* KAKA *pats him on the back.*)

KAKA: Come on. Take it easy.

SATISH: I don't know what to do anymore, Kaka.

KAKA: Look Satish, after all, I'm an ignorant chap. I don't understand all this. But I do know one thing. Finally, birds of the same caste flock together.

SATISH: Kaka, you really don't understand anything. The fathers of all these boys have been charge-sheeted by the police. They are the accused. But they are the flood victims as well. Firstly, they didn't get the houses that were built for them. On top of that, they were handcuffed!

KAKA: You think they didn't set the houses on fire?

SATISH: Oh, that they did. But they were misled. They are *savarnas* all right, but they, too, are poor. It's the poor who are fighting the poor. Moreover, they are taking the law into their own hands.

KAKA: But why do you think of all the poor? Granted, of course, that they are all poor. But that certainly didn't prevent them from burning the houses down. Arjunya broke the law. All right. They should have burnt down the police station. But no. What they burned down was the *basti* of the Dalits. What they burnt down was the living Shewanta. Why? Because we are Dalits. Never will they forget that.

SATISH: What simple answers you have for everything, Kaka! It's good, isn't it, in a way? Very convenient! No problem, however big, can shatter your inner convictions. An activist must be like that. He must have ready-made answers! He can then wash his hands of the entire responsibility of the thing for himself!

KAKA: You son of an ass! You are calling me an ass! Isn't that what you called me in your Brahmin language? Satish, we are ignorant people. Why should we think? We leave that to people like Babasaheb. To educated people like you.

ARJUN: (Entering.) Jai Bhim, Kaka.

KAKA: (Looking straight into his eyes.) Here comes yet another educated guy.

ARJUN: What?

KAKA: Nothing, I was just talking about the wisdom of educated people, and you entered.

ARJUN: The people are waiting for you there, Kaka. (Notices the statue.) Wow! So it has arrived! Wonderful! (Offers flowers to it.) Aren't you coming, Kaka? There's a big program today. Everyone's going to get utensils, clothes, and five hundred rupees.

KAKA: From the hands of the guardian minister? Why, once upon a time, you used to curse him!

ARJUN: Curse, I will. Even in the future! If that's the language they understand, then that's the language I use.

SATISH: Arjun, you're making yet another mistake! You curse them and yet accept their help, that's exactly what they want. If your curses fetch you a good Dalit following and yet make it easy for you to follow the ministers, then why should they prevent you?

ARJUN: Are they spending out of their own pockets? It's government money. Our money. It's our own money they're paying us. Not obliging us.

KAKA: Then why do you offer them garlands? So that they can set your houses on fire and be the ones to put the fire out? Ah, what magnificent justice! Don't you boast in front of me.

ARJUN: What did I do wrong? How could they live after having suffered in the fire? People didn't even allow them to enter the town.

KAKA: Well done! Well done, indeed! Now go and become their henchman.

SATISH: Kaka, please take it easy. Why don't you go in and rest? What did the doctor tell you? He advised you not to talk too much, didn't he?

KAKA: Who's talking? I've opened my mouth for the first time in two weeks. And that too because this Arjunya came.

ARJUN: Kaka, shall I take the statue of the Buddha?

KAKA: Hold it. Don't you dare touch that statue. Take back your money and your contribution! No, I shall not allow you to take that statue there.

ARJUN: But now people know that it has arrived, Kaka. They all want it very much.

KAKA: Don't they have any sense of shame? They want the government's money and they also want this statue. And you, too, are asking for it shamelessly.

ARJUN: Hunger makes people helpless, Kaka.

KAKA: (*Furious.*) Hunger! As if you alone are hungry! Even cats and dogs have hunger. Even prostitutes sell their bodies because of it. Even a pig has it! You ass! Didn't we have it? Babasaheb said, don't drag dead cattle. We gave it up. What did we eat once? Meat of dead cattle, didn't we? But we gave it up. The whole town boycotted us. We could get no work. No wages. No one even allowed us to stand at their door. Meat they refused us. Their leftovers they refused us. As if that wasn't enough, they attacked us with sticks. But we didn't give in. We didn't collect contributions from anyone. We hid in the hills. Amongst the rocks. With our children, we wandered in exile, without any food. Survived on *tarotha* leaves. On crabs caught in dirty ponds. On grains we sifted out from dirty soil. At times, on ears of corn that we stole. And if we got nothing, then plain water quenched the pangs of hunger that gnawed our insides. And you talk to me about hunger! You didn't collect contributions just to bribe the officers. You put them to your personal use, too. You embezzled that money. Otherwise you wouldn't have driven Shewanta out of her house. Had you needed more money, you would have asked me. But you didn't want me to know. That's why you collected the money in a hush-hush manner! To hell with you!

SATISH: Calm down, Kaka, please, calm down.

KAKA: What will happen at the most? I'll die. That's much better!

SATISH: Please don't say things like that, Kaka. Arjun, you'd better leave now.

ARJUN: But Kaka's hurling heinous accusations at me, sir!

SATISH: Okay. But this is not the time to set the score straight.

KAKA: Satish, my heart had expanded like the sky when I saw Arjunya's daring. I felt as strong as an elephant! I said, at last there's one amongst us who's man enough! People like you had proved to be a pure waste. Your education has ruined you. But here was a ray of hope at last! But alas . . . Satish, when Dadasaheb chased power, this heart was stupefied. Then Bhandare went the same way. Rupawate followed suit. Gavai, Khobragade didn't exactly go the same way, but come elections, there they all took the same path. It was just like a clay fort, dissolving on the spot, under torrential rains. There was nothing but mud everywhere. My spirits sank. These boys showed a new courage, and I felt alive again! But even they are going the same way now. Go, go, all of you. Go the same way. But this Kaka is the genuine heir of Babasaheb. Go accept those garlands! Bow down before them if you want to. But I won't. Never! Who is that, offering me five hundred *rupees*? The minister? Oh, the guardian minister? Whose guardian? Go away, you scum! Go get your knighthood from them! This old man will break but will not bend. Don't you dare touch this statue! Even your shadow, your murderer's shadow, will defile it. You murdered Shewanta! Took the life of that poor widow! Get out, get out of here, get lost!

(KAKA *gesticulates wildly, loses his balance, trips, and falls down.* SATISH *tries to support and hold him.* HEMA *quickly gets water.* KAKA *stretches his legs on the divan, lifts his right hand up to Satish's head, dies.* SATISH *lets out a heartbroken wail.* ARJUN *stands transfixed. All freeze. The notes of "Trisarana," full of pathos, float from the background. Darkness.*)

SCENE THREE

The same place. Six months have passed since Kaka's death. When lights come on, Kaka's photograph can be seen on the wall. Below is the Buddha statue on a high stool. A calendar on the wall with a picture of a child. On the couch lie half-knitted baby socks. HEMA *enters. Picks up a garland from the packet on the stand. Arranges it neatly on Kaka's photograph. Offers flowers to the statue. Lights a candle and bows with folded hands. Then she walks to the outer door. Lingers there for some time. Sitar music, full of pathos, floats in from the background. Listless,* HEMA *sits down on the couch and starts knitting.* SATISH *comes in.* HEMA *is sitting with her back to him. He approaches her stealthily and places his hand on her shoulder. She is startled.*

SATISH: Scared?

HEMA: (*Holding his hands on her shoulder.*) Why are you so late?

SATISH: Well, I got a bit late somehow. Angry with me?

HEMA: No. But this house becomes oppressively lonely when you aren't around, you know.

SATISH: Come on, Hema. You aren't alone now. You've got a four-month-old companion with you! (HEMA *blushes.*) Wow! It's ages since you blushed so beautifully.

HEMA: (*Scolding him.*) Professor Satish Godghate, you seem to be in a very romantic mood today.

SATISH: What romantic mood! Call it a family mood.

HEMA: So that's why you're back so . . . early! I am fasting today.

SATISH: Fasting?

HEMA: It's *poornima*, full moon day, today.

SATISH: What's this new fad?

HEMA: Nothing new in it. It's six months now. I have told you about it only today. I've been fasting on every *poornima* day since Kaka left us.

SATISH: How come you never told me that?

HEMA: What was there to tell? I felt like doing it, so I did it. That's all.

SATISH: What for?

HEMA: Nothing really.

(SATISH *notices the garland on Kaka's photograph.*)

SATISH: A garland of fresh flowers on Kaka's photograph! And what's this? You seem to have worshiped the Buddha as well! Hema, can I ask you something?

HEMA: Of course.

SATISH: You won't be angry, will you?

HEMA: Of course I won't!

SATISH: Did you really feel like worshiping the statue?

HEMA: I offered the Buddha statue flowers the day it arrived, but that was because I couldn't offend Kaka. But if I hadn't offered flowers today, who was there to feel offended anyway?

SATISH: You mean you really offered flowers today with full faith?

HEMA: I feel nice after worshiping. Now if you think that's being faithful, I won't object.

SATISH: You are a Vikrandian. You never prayed or worshiped.

HEMA: So what? Now that I feel like doing it, I do it. What do you think? That I am becoming a reactionary?

SATISH: So you do this to divert your mind from the oppressive loneliness you feel these days?

HEMA: I don't know. I mean, I can't explain the reason.

SATISH: (*Serious.*) Are you doing this in order to please me? Because you know I loved Kaka?

HEMA: (*Angry.*) You can replace the statue with a Ganesha idol, if you like.

SATISH: Hema, do bring a Ganesha if you like. I won't mind.

HEMA: Oh! What did you think? That I actually wanted to worship Ganesha, but worshiped the Buddha instead because I thought you would feel bad? Imagining all the while that I was worshiping Ganesha? Oh no. That's not what I meant at all. I just wanted to tell you that I wasn't being a hypocrite when I worshiped the Buddha. These days, quite honestly, I sincerely feel like praying. I'm almost on the verge of tears. When I pray, I really feel light! Free of all tensions!

SATISH: I am sorry, Hema.

HEMA: Come on, what's happened to you today?

SATISH: Do pregnant women really feel a craving? And what about reincarnation?

HEMA: Reincarnation?

SATISH: Is Kaka taking another birth? Is that why you get that craving?

HEMA: How much you do think, Satish! You know why, because you insist on a logical explanation for all the complexities of life. Leave it. Come, let's go in.

SATISH: No. I'm not depressed, Hema. I just feel curious. Kaka must have got some inner strength by doing such things. Now you, too, have started praying. Do you get that inner strength too? That's all I wanted to ask you. (*Lost again in his own thoughts.*)

HEMA: What's this about inner strength that you keep harping on these days? Has something happened in the college today? And you were in such a romantic mood just a while back! (*Pause.*) Satish, I asked you something.

SATISH: Eh? What?

SONAL: (*Entering.*) May I come in, ma'am?

SATISH: Ah, Sonal? Come in. It's been ages since you last visited us. Do come in.

SONAL: *Namaskar,* sir.

SATISH: *Namaskar.* Why don't you sit down? (SONAL *sits down.*) How's your father?

SONAL: Okay.

SATISH: Even he hasn't been here for a very long time.

SONAL: Yes.

SATISH: How are your studies going? Okay?

SONAL: Okay.

SATISH: Just two more weeks left for the exams! Don't neglect your studies just because this is only the second year.

SONAL: No.

HEMA: What's wrong Sonal? You aren't your bubbly self today. (SONAL *quiet.*) Just dropped in to see us? I didn't mince words at all when I scolded Arjun! He misunderstood . . .

SONAL: Ma'am! (*Tries to control her tears, then stands up resolutely.*) I want your blessings, ma'am. I want you to give me strength. (*Bows down and touches* HEMA's *feet.*) Sir, I want your blessings, too.

HEMA: What's this? You're speaking as if you're leaving for your husband's place.

SONAL: I am. They've fixed my marriage with Arvind Deshmukh. The engagement is taking place today.

HEMA: Sonal!

SONAL: With my consent, ma'am. No one has forced me.

HEMA: Arjun's innocent. He's not a murderer. The court has acquitted him. He's innocent.

SONAL: That was madness, ma'am. There are two more sisters to be married off. Allow me to go now. (*Starts to leave.*)

HEMA: Wait, Sonal. Tell me the truth. Is this decision really yours?

SONAL: Yes, ma'am. I'll go now.

(SONAL *leaves. Seems to be near tears.* HEMA *collapses on the couch.*)

HEMA: O God! What's happening?

SATISH: This was to be expected, Hema.

HEMA: No. It isn't like that, Satish. It was purely a misunderstanding between them. But that scorched the delicate shoots of love in their hearts. Both of them loved each other. But both of them refused to budge from their positions. They should at least have talked to each other frankly. What they needed was our support.

SATISH: No. We can't do anything, Hema, we really can't. We can neither stop this marriage nor can we clear up the misunderstanding between them. It's too late now. And, in a way, what's happened has happened for the best, Hema. It was really good that she wasn't too involved with Arjun. It would've been difficult for her to cope with Arjun's rebellious nature. Basically, she's hardly the type to put up with his hectic life. Has Arjun been here?

HEMA: No. Maybe he doesn't know about this yet.

SATISH: Even if he comes to know about it, he will accept it. I know him only too well. People just notice his quick temper, but . . . Okay. Let's go in. Come on.

(HEMA *gets up, puts her hand on his shoulder for support. They slowly go up to the door leading inside.* DASRAO *enters running.*)

DASRAO: Godghate, sir, Godghate, sir, please save my Sonal, save her please.

SATISH: (*Supporting him.*) What's happened, Guruji? What's happened to Sonal?

DASRAO: Riots have broken out. And Arjun has kidnapped her. His friends have carried her off.

HEMA: Impossible. Guruji, you're lying.

DASRAO: No, no, Hematai. I swear that's the truth. Eyewitnesses told me so.

SATISH: Guruji, please, tell us exactly what happened.

DASRAO: Today the court gave its verdict. The sessions court.

SATISH: I know that. Go on.

DASRAO: All the accused were declared not guilty and released.

SATISH: Go on.

HEMA: You knew this, Satish? You didn't tell me!

SATISH: Just a minute, Hema. What happened then?

DASRAO: They took the evening bus to the town. They burst into the town shouting slogans.

SATISH: Then?

DASRAO: I don't know what happened then, but suddenly fighting started in the city square. Sonal's mother told me that Sonal had come to you here. So I started towards your house. On my way, I saw riots breaking out in the city square. For the sake of my daughter, I started to run towards your house. But some people stopped me and told me that Sonal had been kidnapped. Sir, today she's getting engaged. Sir, her whole life will be ruined, sir. Only you can talk to Arjun. Only you.

HEMA: Why are you naming only Arjun, Guruji?

DASRAO: Because the people named only him.

SATISH: But what people? What were their names?

DASRAO: How could I know all that, sir? When I was running to get here, I heard some people shouting.

(*Voices from the crowd. Police whistles. The sound of the siren stops.* POLICE INSPECTOR NAYAK *enters. Looks at all three. Gives the house a searching look.*)

INSPECTOR: Did Arjun Jadhav come here?

SATISH: No.

INSPECTOR: He may come then. He set the police van on fire. And he's hiding somewhere. (*Looks at* DASRAO.) What brings you here, Guruji, at this time?

DASRAO: (*In two minds. Whether to tell him or not. Looks at* SATISH *and the* INSPECTOR *alternately.*) Nothing significant, really. Dropped in casually for a chat.

SATISH: Guruji often pays me a visit.

INSPECTOR: All right. But don't go out immediately, okay? (*Goes to the door. Looks out.*) No. He isn't here. You go to Milind Nagar and search for him there. I'll go to the city square. (*Turns.*) Mr. Godghate, I'll come again after some time. (*Goes. Sound of the police car speeding away.*)

SATISH: Guruji, why did you lie to the police inspector?

DASRAO: I was scared, sir. Only you can find Arjun, please. My reputation will be ruined. Save me from public disgrace, sir. It's her engagement today.

HEMA: Guruji, even in such a critical moment, all that you can think about is your reputation!

SATISH: Let's go.

HEMA: Where are you going?

SATISH: To look for Arjun.

HEMA: You're rushing out in the midst of a riot?

SATISH: Sonal's life is at stake.

HEMA: Wait a minute. Don't rush.

(ARJUN *enters running. Starts going towards the kitchen. Sees* HEMA *near the kitchen door.*)

ARJUN: Please help me, ma'am. The police are on my trail.

DASRAO: Ask him, ask him.

SATISH: Arjun!

ARJUN: You? You are here, Guruji? Sir, the police are following me. Please.

SATISH: You kidnapped Sonal?

ARJUN: Who says so, Guruji? Is that why he's here?

SATISH: Is it true?

ARJUN: I'll explain that later, sir. A policeman noticed me running through the square.

SATISH: No. I won't support you. When you erred for the first time, it was I who got you out on bail. So that you could reform yourself and mend your ways.

ARJUN: Ma'am, at least you tell him, please.

SATISH: You have committed a crime. And you are afraid of the police. Why?

ARJUN: I haven't committed any crime. I haven't. (*Sound of the police car.*) Sir, please. I'll explain everything later.

SATISH: I'll hand you over to the police myself.

ARJUN: Sir, I wish Kaka were alive today. He wouldn't have forsaken me.

HEMA: Arjun, go in. (*He goes.*)

SATISH: Hema, what are you doing?

HEMA: Give him some time, at least. He isn't some savage beast.

INSPECTOR: (*Suddenly appearing.*) Has Arjun come here? I saw him running through the city square in this direction.

HEMA: No. He hasn't come here.

INSPECTOR: (*Looks into her eyes.*) Professor Godghate, Arjun didn't come here?

SATISH: No. He didn't.

INSPECTOR: Sir, I can search this house.

SATISH: Go right ahead.

INSPECTOR: No. I believe you. You won't hamper law and order. See you, then. (*Starts going.*) The situation is under control. Guruji, I can take you home if you want.

DASRAO: Eh, what? No. Thanks very much, I'll go later.

INSPECTOR: Okay. As you wish. But it would be a major crime to hide Arjun. Don't forget that. Hand him over to us if he comes.

(POLICE INSPECTOR NAYAK *goes out. Sound of the car driving away.* ARJUN *comes out.*)

ARJUN: Thank you, ma'am. Actually, I must thank Kaka. It was only when I uttered his name that I got help. I have committed no crime whatsoever.

HEMA: Then why were you hiding?

ARJUN: To avoid arrest. I must get bail before the police arrest me.

HEMA: Arjun, tell us exactly what happened.

ARJUN: Those who'd burned down our houses escaped scot-free today. In the absence of strong evidence. It was your father who gave that verdict. And sir, what faith you have in the law!

SATISH: So that's why you started the arson?

ARJUN: Yes. (*Pauses.*) The accused were released. Proved innocent. As if that had given them a license to insult us. The moment they entered the town, they started a volley of abuse. Where were the police then? We were unprepared. They caught one of my friends in the city square. He was alone. Unaccompanied. They thrashed the life out of him. When we heard this, we rushed to the place. We found two policemen at the pan stall, rubbing tobacco in their palms. The so-called guardians of law! You always advise us not to take the law into our own hands. But who really violates the law? We? What were the guardians of the law doing at that time? There are limits even to the endurance of the poor. They stretch it to the limit. On top of that, whenever there is any stone throwing, looting, arson, it's the poor who are threatened by the law. What sort of justice is that? Some people burned Shewanta. And the same people charged me with murder. They were the ones who trapped me. Okay. I know what has to be done now, sir. There's a technique for escaping safely. I know it now. I've found my own way, sir. Attack is the best defense. The movement has no other alternative but struggle.

HEMA: Wait, Arjun. You haven't said a word about Sonal.

ARJUN: Oh! So that's why Dasrao Guruji's here. Tell me, what letters had I written to Sonal? And when did my friends tease her? You are no teacher. Nor are you a freedom fighter. Coward! That's what you are. And what did you say about Madam? Now say it in front of her.

DASRAO: Arjun, I admit to all my mistakes, but return my Sonal to me.

ARJUN: What? You came here just to defame me once again!

DASRAO: Where is Sonal, Arjun?

HEMA: Where is Sonal?

ARJUN: All of you believe that I've kidnapped her? Ma'am, Sonal is safe in her house.

DASRAO: What?

ARJUN: I recognized her even in that crowd. Those bastards would have made another Shewanta out of her. I got her home with the help of some of my friends.

DASRAO: I am deeply obliged, Arjun. I'll never forget this. Never. Never. (*Goes.*)

ARJUN: I loved her, ma'am. I didn't say it so explicitly then. But today I say it. She, too, loved me. I knew it. But I didn't dare to ask her. She's getting engaged today. She talked a lot to me even as we hurried through the streets. She talked sincerely, from the depth of her soul. It was so exhilarating . . . getting her home safely! Every fiber of my being was vibrant! But it's a good thing she's got engaged. I wouldn't have said yes even if she'd proposed. Sonal was like a beautiful tempest. But ma'am, she'd have taken me away from my movement. And I don't want to leave the movement. Goodbye.

SATISH: Wait Arjun. What you call a movement is nothing but an explosion. A devastating explosion.

ARJUN: Explosion? A devastating explosion? Then what do you call all that is happening now? Those who burned and looted our colony have escaped scott free. Isn't that devastating enough? I'll leave now, sir. I'll come to you when I don't have anything important to do. To "discuss" things. It will be a nice entertainment for me, and you will get the satisfaction of having done a lot, too. You always told us, didn't you, that you have to pay the price! If you want to be in the movement you have to pay the price! What does it mean—paying the price? To protect your job, reputation, and face a little mudslinging? That too for merely holding a discussion. That's what paying a price means to you. That's how you interpret your favorite principle. How very convenient!

(ARJUN *storms off.* SATISH *slumps down as if someone has slapped him.* HEMA *comes near him and puts her hand on his back.*)

SATISH: He's right, Hema. I know one has to pay the price. I am even willing to pay it. But does it mean destroying everything? Who's to pay the price for this utter destruction? How? No, Hema. There's something wrong somewhere. What's wrong? Where? Kaka educated me so that I could think. And me? I do nothing else but think. Nothing but impotent thinking! I have become irrelevant in this system. I can do nothing. I can neither be an extremist nor can I live like vermin. Hema, I am losing faith in humanity, in people.

HEMA: Humanity never dies. You want to work, don't you? Arjun could've taken revenge on Sonal had he wished to. But he didn't do that. He got her home safely.

SATISH: Right! You're right, Hema. Absolutely right! We must protect that tiny shoot. Not by remaining outside, on the banks, but by being with him, right where he is. Come, let's go. I'll bail him out. Let's go.

(SATISH *gets up.* HEMA *supports him. They start out. Both freeze. The curtain falls slowly.*)

Glossary

ACHHA: "Okay," "yes," or "so." Often used as an expression of general understanding, sometimes of agreement.

ADHVARYU: The priest who chants the *Yajur Veda* during the *yajña*. He is also responsible for building the altar, preparing the sacrificial vessels, lighting the fire, and butchering the animal(s) to be sacrificed and offered to the deity (in this case Indra).

AJWAIN: A spice that is used as a digestive.

ALTA: Red dye used to decorate the feet. Believed to have a protective medicinal value.

AMBEDKAR: Bhimrao Ramji Ambedkar (1891–1956), "lawyer, statesman, author, reformer, educator, law minister in India's first cabinet, and chairman of the drafting committee of the Indian constitution; known affectionately as Babasaheb in his capacity as the revered spokesman for India's Untouchables . . . Ambedkar graduated from Elphinstone College . . . secured a Ph.D. from Columbia University in New York and a D.Sc. from the University of London, as well as passing the bar from Gray's Inn." He was the second member of the Mahar caste to receive a college degree. "Ambedkar worked to reform, invigorate, and unify Untouchables through his newspapers and widespread Depressed Classes Conferences. He also worked for political rights and economic opportunity as a member of the Bombay Legislative Assembly . . . Ambedkar's educational and religious concerns have had a far-reaching effect. The People's Education Society, established in 1945, and other Ambedkar-inspired groups now run complexes of colleges in Bombay, Aurangabad, Mahad, and Nagpur. The stress on education has produced an important . . . literary movement in Marathi" (*Encyclopedia of Asian History,* Charles Scribner's Sons, 1988, p. 52). (*See* Dalit.)

AMBEDKARITE: A follower of Dr. Babasaheb Ambedkar. (*See* Ambedkar.)

AMMA: Mother.

ARRE: An exclamation, roughly equivalent to "Hey!"

ARRE BAAP RE: An exclamation roughly equivalent to "Oh my god!"

ATTA: Wheat flour.

ATTAR: Perfumed oil.

AVJO: An expression in Gujarati used while parting company. It literally means "do come again" but is also used by the person departing, probably to mean "please do visit my home." It is a formulaic expression, because in almost all Indian cultures it is considered extremely rude to say "I am leaving" or "I have to go now" without adding "come again" or "I will come again."

BABASAHEB: *See* Ambedkar.

BABU: Father. It is used in many situations as a more general, and respectful, term for a male.

BADIS: Spicy lentil-paste balls which are dried and stored, then fried and added to vegetable curries.

BAHU: Daughter-in-law, or wife.

BAPPA: Father. An affectionate term. It can also be used when addressing a male child.

BARTHEENI: "I will come again" in Kannada. Similar to *avjo* in Gujarati.

BASTI: Colony.

BEDA: Literally "don't want" in Kannada.

BETA: Son.

BHAGAVAD GITA: (*The Song of the Blessed One.*) The *Bhagavad Gita* is one of the most widely known Hindu religious texts, found in the sixth book of the *Mahabharata*. It is a dialogue between the god Krishna and the warrior Arjuna on the Kurukshetra battlefield as Arjuna is about to fight members of his own family on the other side. It outlines a "doctrine of duty and order (*dharma*) . . . in terms of reciprocal cosmic and human activity (*karma*)" (*Encyclopedia of Asian History,* Charles Scribner's Sons, 1988, p. 153).

BHAGWAN GAUTAM: God Gautam Buddha.

BHAI: Brother.

BHAIYA: "Brother" in Hindi. In *Rudali*, it is used as a form of casual address, or tagged onto the end of an exclamation. In *Tara,* it is also used loosely as a term for "milkman," because it is a familiar way of addressing men in the state of Uttar Pradesh, and in Bombay most milk deliveries are made by men from Uttar Pradesh.

BHANGIS: Members of an Untouchable caste.

BHANTE: A leader of Bikkhu Sangha. A Bikkhu is a Buddhist priest, or one who teaches the Buddhist way of life. Sangha is a religious order of monks and nuns.

BHARATIYA BODH SABHA: An organization established by Dr. Ambedkar to propagate Buddhism. *Sabha* literally means "assembly" and refers to an organization of like-minded people. *Maha* simply means "great," so Bharatiya Bodh Mahasabha is roughly the same thing.

BHAUJI: Brother-in-law or sister-in-law.

BHINDI: Okra.

BIDIS: Because cigarettes are a Western import, they indicate a more citified lifestyle. A *bidi* is a poor man's smoke. It is tobacco rolled in a leaf. It is very cheap and is sold everywhere.

BIKKHU SANGHA: *See* Bhante.

BODH GAYA: A Buddhist holy city in the state of Bihar. Gaya is the name of the town; Bodh means knowledge of Buddha. The Buddha was enlightened while sitting under a bodhi tree at Bodh Gaya, so it is the most important pilgrimage site for Buddhists everywhere.

BODH VIHARA: A small Buddhist temple. A place for prayer.

BRAHMAN: "Sacred power. The term is derived from the root *brh* (to grow, to become great). Originally the *Vedas* [were] regarded as *Brahman* in verbal form, and the performance of sacrificial ritual (*yajña*) was the means of access to this power" (*Historical Dictionary of Hinduism,* Scarecrow Press, 1997, p. 47).

BRAHMA RAKSHASA: A demonic spirit. According to the *Manusmriti,* a Brahmin who has associated with outcastes, seduced another man's wife, or stolen the property of another Brahmin will, when he dies, become a *brahma rakshasa*. (*See* Rakshasa.)

BRAHMIN: "The highest of the four traditional *varnas*, or broad delineations of caste, in Hinduism. The term originally meant 'one possessed of *brahman*,' . . . and it referred to specially trained priests . . . By the end of the Rig Vedic period (c. sixth century B.C.E.), the term was used for all members of the priestly group, whether family priests, kings' advisors, or teachers of the *Vedas* (or of other branches of learning) . . . Writing by Brahmins about Brahmins has been an integral part of Indian social history from ancient times and has often been intended to justify and maintain the high social status and privileges of the Brahmin caste" (*Encyclopedia of Asian History*, Charles Scribner's Sons, 1988, pp. 173–74). (*See* Brahman; Caste; Sacred Thread.)

BRINJAL: Eggplant.

BUNDH: Strike.

CASTE: "Portuguese seafarers traveling to India in the late fifteenth century first used the term *casta* ('genera, breed, race, lineage') to describe the society they found there. Caste is still used to designate the system of social stratification in South Asia. Commonly defined as corporate groups formed through descent and marriage, most castes are endogamous and associated with hereditary 'traditional' occupations." No one knows what the origin of the caste system is, but there is one Vedic reference to caste, which "tells of the sacrificial division of Purusha, the primeval man, into the four *varnas* [or caste categories]: from his mouth came the Brahmins . . . ; from his arms the *Kshatriyas*, or warrior rulers; from his thighs the *Vaishyas*, or landowners and merchants; and from his feet the *Shudras*, or artisans and servants. The so-called fifth *varna*, the Untouchables, those at the bottom of the hierarchy, was not mentioned, nor were the many thousands of named endogamous groups (*jatis*) evident in later times. A given *jati* (Hindi for 'descent group, breed, lineage') sometimes cannot even be assigned to one of the four *varnas*, so far has empirical reality diverged from the classical model" (*Encyclopedia of Asian History*, Charles Scribner's Sons, 1988, p. 229). Many people still identify themselves as members of a particular caste. India's constitution, adopted in 1950, outlaws discrimination on the basis of caste. (*See* Brahmin; Shudra; Dalit; Untouchable.)

CHACHA: Father's brother.

CHACHI: Father's brother's wife.

CHAKKI: A stone mill operated by hand.

CHAMPAK TREE: The frangipani. Also called the "temple tree."

CHANNA: Chickpeas.

CHARPOY: A string cot.

CHIVDA: Parched rice.

DAAIN: A witch, often believed to devour children.

DADIA: Affectionate version of *dadi*, father's mother. *Doda* means father's father.

DAHI: Curds, like yogurt.

DAL: Lentils.

DALDA: Hydrogenated vegetable oil.

DALIT: Dalit means "ground down" or "oppressed" in Marathi and is the term used by politicized ex-Untouchables to describe themselves with respect to the oppression they have endured. "Their insistence on the use of Dalit has been recognized officially, and the state governments of Maharashtra, Madhya Pradesh, and Uttar Pradesh have issued orders that Dalit be the term used, rather than Harijan, Scheduled Caste, or Untouchable" (Eleanor Zelliot, *An Anthology of Dalit Literature,* Gyan Publishing House, 1992, pp. 1–2). (*See* Ambedkar; Caste; Untouchable.)

DAROGAJI: A *daroga* is a village police officer or head of a police station. *Ji* is a suffix indicating respect.

DEVI: God.

DHAMMA: A term used by Ambedkar, specifically with reference to *dharma,* in order to emphasize the difference between Buddhist and Hindu teachings.

DHARMA: Duty, law, righteousness, virtue, law, honor. According to the *Mahabharata, dharma* protects *dharnat* (everything); it maintains what has been created and is, by extension, the principle that can maintain the universe. "A concept of multiple connotations, *dharma* includes cosmological, ethical, social, and legal principles that provide the basis for the notion of an ordered universe. In the social context, it stands for the imperative of righteousness in the definition of the good life. More specifically, *dharma* refers to the rules of social intercourse laid down traditionally for every category of actor (or moral agent) in terms of social status (*varna*), the stage of life (*ashrama*), and the qualities of inborn nature (*guna*). Put simply, for every person there is a mode of conduct that is most appropriate: it is his or her *svadharma,* which may be translated as 'vocation'" (From T. N. Madan, "Religion in India," *Daedalus,* Fall 1989, pp. 117–18).

DHAT: An exclamation of annoyance, roughly equivalent to "get lost!" or "stop it!"

DHOTI: A cloth tied around the lower half of the body. Worn only by men.

DIWALI: *Diwali* celebrates the return of Rama to Ayodhaya after fourteen years of exile (as told in the *Ramayana*). Because he returned on a moonless night, *diyas* were used to light his way home, and Diwali is often referred to as the "festival of lights."

DIYA: Small clay lamp filled with oil or clarified butter. Associated with festive and religious occasions.

DOMS: Members of a low caste who tend cremation grounds.

DOODHWALLA: *Doodh* is Hindi for "milk." A *doodhwalla* is someone who sells milk, or a milkman.

DUSHADS: Members of an Untouchable caste.

GADDA: Hindi for "mattress" or "futon." Having a futon on the floor is a typical North Indian informal seating arrangement.

GALI: A word of Hindi origin meaning "alley" or "narrow street."

GANJUS: Members of a low caste.

GERHARD HANSEN: The first scientist to identify the bacterium that causes leprosy.

GHAGRA: Traditional full-length gathered skirt worn by women in rural Bihar.

GHATI: A derogatory term for Maharashtrians; it literally means people from the ghats. The American equivalent would be *hillbilly.*

GHEE: Clarified butter.

GHERAOS: Political demonstrations.

GODOWN: A warehouse or storehouse.

GOONDAISM: A *goonda* is a hooligan.

GOPI MANHARI: A reference to Krishna as the beloved of the *gopis.* The *gopis* are female cowherds who followed, and played with, Krishna when he was young. (*See* Govinda.)

GOVINDA: Another name for Krishna. Krishna figures so often in *The Wooden Cart* because he has the ability to love, and be loved, by all. He embodies all-encompassing love, even for those who have been rejected by everyone else.

GUJARATI: Refers to the language spoken in the state of Gujarat and to the people who live in, or who are from, Gujarat.

GUR: Jaggery, or molasses.

GURU: "Literally meaning heavy, or great, or respected, . . . often used for one's spiritual preceptor or teacher" (*Historical Dictionary of Hinduism*, Scarecrow Press, 1997, p. 92).

HAI HAI: An exclamation of distress, sorrow, grief, or disapproval, depending on the context.

HAI MAIYYA: An exclamation literally meaning "Oh Mother!"

HAI RAM: A common exclamation, usually an expression of shock, distress, or grief. Similar to "Oh god!" (*See* Ram.)

HAKIM: A practitioner of traditional Islamic medicine.

HALWA-PURI: A sweet dish made out of carrots, lentils, or semolina; similar to Middle Eastern *halwa*. *Puri* is a round, deep-fried bread. Eaten together, this is a typical festive or religious meal served at birthdays, *pujas*, etc.

HANUMAN'S DESCENDANTS / RAM'S DISCIPLES: Hanuman is a monkey (often worshiped as a deity in his own right) who figures in the *Ramayana* as Rama's loyal follower and companion. In the final battle between Rama and the demon Ravana, "Hanuman was sent to Mount Kailasa for healing herbs but, unable to distinguish which were the ones he needed, he brought the entire mountain back with him. For his devotion and the service he rendered, Rama granted Hanuman longevity and eternal youth" (*Historical Dictionary of Hinduism*, Scarecrow Press, 1997, p. 93). Hanuman's descendants then, are monkeys, who are also referred to as Ram's disciples. (*See* Rama; *Ramayana*.)

HARI: Another name for Krishna. (*See* Govinda.)

HARIVIJAYA: A long religious poem composed by a popular eighteenth-century writer, Shridhar. *Harivijaya* (which literally means "victory of God") is about the life of Krishna. (*See* Parayana; *Pandav Pratap*.)

HEG IDDIRA: "How are you" in Kannada.

HUZOOR: A term of respect, like *sir*, usually used for a master or someone of higher seniority.

HUZOORAIN: Female version of *huzoor*.

INDRA: God of the firmament, a personification of the atmosphere and the lord of the rains. "Indra was clearly the most popular deity among the poets of the *Rig Veda* . . . almost a quarter of all the hymns are addressed to him. He is the dominant deity of the middle region, the region between Earth and Heaven . . . A few [of the hymns] make him the son of Tvastri, the Great Father and Creator of all creatures . . . His chief characteristic, accorded unstinted praise, is his powers, both on the human plane as the god of battle . . . and mythologically as the thunder god who conquers the demons of drought and darkness, thus liberating the waters or winning the light. The most basic myth connected with Indra concerns his battle with the serpent Vritra, who is obstructing the waters and the sky" (From J. L. Brockington, *The Sacred Thread: A Short History of Hinduism*, Oxford University Press, 1992, pp. 10–11). (*See* Vritra.)

JAI BHIM: A greeting used by the followers of Dr. Ambedkar instead of *namaskar* or *namaste*, which is used primarily by Hindus. *Jai* means "welcome," and Bhim is a shortened form of Dr. Ambedkar's first name, so followers of Ambedkar use this greeting proudly, as an identity marker.

JAI BHIMWALA: A staunch follower of Dr. Ambedkar.

JAI MAHADEV: Literally, "glory to the Great God." *Mahadev* is specifically an appellation for Shiva. In Hindu practice one often refers to deities by their many names or manifestations.

JAIPUR: A city in Rajasthan.

JI: A term of respect attached to the end of someone's name. (For example, Mahatma Gandhi is referred to as Gandhiji.)

KAALI KAMLI: He or she of the black blanket. (This is an affectionate reference to the girlhood friendship between Sanichari and Bikhni. Bikhni always dressed in a dirty *ghagra* [skirt] made out of a black blanket, which is how she got her nickname.)

KAILASHNATH: A form of Shiva. (*See* Jai Mahadev; Loknath.)

KANCHIPURAM IDLIS: An *idli* is made from fermented dough that is steamed in special *idli* makers; it comes out looking like a small, round cake or dumpling.

KANNADA: The language spoken in the state of Karnataka.

KANNADIGAS: People who speak Kannada (which is spoken primarily in the state of Karnataka).

KATHAKALI: *Kathakali* is possibly the best-known of India's classical dance-drama forms. *Kathakali* literally means "story play." It dramatizes stories from the *Ramayana* and *Mahabharata* in plays that can last all night (although these days select scenes from a *kathakali* play will be performed for three or four hours in the evening). *Kathakali* is referred to as "the art of the nonworldly" because it depicts not everyday human life but clashes between good and evil as represented by gods, demons, and heroes. It uses no set and very few props. There are, however, elaborate costumes and makeup and an elaborate system of hand gestures known as *mudras*. (*See* Mudra.)

KEM CHCHO? MAJHJHA MA?: "How are you? Fine?"

KHOI: A type of puffed rice.

KOEL: A cuckoo.

KRISHNA MURARI: A joyful way of referring to Krishna. (*See* Govinda.)

KRITYA: "A female deity to whom sacrifices are offered for destructive and magical purposes." (V. S. Apte, *The Practical Sanskrit-English Dictionary,* Prasad Prakashan, 1979.)

KRIYA CEREMONY: Post-death religious rites.

KUTTIYATTAM: *See* Introduction.

LADDU: A sweet or dessert in the shape of a ball.

LAKH: One hundred thousand.

LATHI-CHARGED: A *lathi* is a wooden stick carried by a policeman. "*Lathi*-charged" means that a group of policemen charged into a group, hitting people with their *lathis*. Supposedly a form of riot control, it can also be a form of police brutality; many people get injured in *lathi* charges, some severely.

LOKNATH: The god of lepers. Loknath is a form of Shiva. It is also a temple in Puri which is supposed to have special powers for those affected by leprosy. This comes from the belief that Shiva can drink poison and that he can therefore swallow (and thereby cure people of) leprosy.

MAAI: A variant on Ma, meaning "Mother." It is also used as an exclamation.

MAHABHARATA: *The Great War of the Bharatas,* one of India's most famous epic poems. "The story can be summarized as follows. The ruling family of north-central India, the Bharata clan, split into two groups in a dispute over succession to the throne: the Pandavas (five brothers, sons of Pandu who had ruled earlier) and their cousins the Kauravas (100 brothers, sons of Dhritarashtra, who was ruling currently). The Pandavas had as their friend and ally Krishna, a prince from a nearby area who was also an *avatar* (God incarnate in human form), on earth to restore *dharma.* At a Vedic ritual called *Rajasuya* (Royal Consecration), which would have declared the eldest Pandava Yudhishthira the emperor ruling over many kings, the Kauravas cheated at a dice match that was to have celebrated the conclusion of the rite, and the Pandavas were exiled with their [one] wife, Draupadi. After twelve years of exile in the wilderness, followed by a thirteenth year spent in disguise as they reentered society, the Pandava brothers returned to the kingdom to claim their share but were rebuffed by their cousins. Both sides assembled their allies and met to fight a battle for sovereignty. After eighteen days of fierce fighting, the Pandavas won back the decimated kingdom and ruled righteously for many years. The poem's characters are depicted as the gods and demons in human form, so that a character who represents a god is depicted in ways that remind the audience of that deity. The characters and situations they are involved in are regarded by many Hindus as providing guidelines on how they should live their lives, even today. The *Mahabharata* also includes many passages that explicitly teach religious and philosophical doctrines, the most significant of which is the *Bhagavad Gita*" (*Historical Dictionary of Hinduism,* Scarecrow Press, 1997, pp. 127–28).

MAHADEV: Literally, "Great God." (*See* Jai Mahadev.)

MAHAJAN: A moneylender. (*See* Malik-mahajan.)

MAHAR: "The Mahars, a large Marathi-speaking caste now eighty percent Buddhist and disclaiming caste, had a traditional role of 'inferior village servant,' as the British called them . . . Along with the other Untouchable castes in the area, Mangs and Chambhars, the well and temple were closed to them, and their living quarters were removed from the village proper. Before the nineteenth century the only recorded voice of the Mahar was that of Chokhamela, a fourteenth-century poet-saint." (Eleanor Zelliot, *An Anthology of Dalit Literature,* Gyan Publishing House, 1992, pp. 2–3.) (*See* Ambedkar; Dalit.)

MAHARAJ: Literally, "Great King."

MAHARASHTRIANS: People who live in or come from the state of Maharashtra.

MALIK: Literally, "master." (*See* Malik-mahajan.)

MALIK-MAHAJAN: Both the landowning employer and the moneylender. In rural Bihar the landowner also functions as the moneylender so that he can keep the people who work for him under his thumb.

MANUSMRITI: *The Laws of Manu,* "a collection of laws based on custom and precedent and the teaching of the *Vedas.*" It asserts that the ultimate goal of mankind is to achieve not individual immortality but union with *brahman.* "Divine revelation and empirical knowledge are drawn upon to define the Law of Conduct and to apply it . . . to all classes of the community" (*A Dictionary of Hinduism,* Routledge, 1977, p. 182). It should be noted that the *Manusmriti* has been used by Brahmins to delineate duties according to caste and gender—delineations which have often served their own interests.

MARATHI: The language spoken in the state of Maharashtra.

MAVANDA: A special religious dinner, arranged when a person returns from a pilgrimage. This is a Hindu custom.

MELA: A fair.

MOKSHA: "The *purusharthas* are the four ethical goals of human existence: *dharma, artha, kama,* and *moksha.* Very roughly, *dharma* relates to the spiritual sphere, *artha* to the realm of political and economic power, and *kama* to that of sexual or aesthetic gratification. In these cases, what a person understands as his or her *purushartha* could vary according to his or her background, stage of and station in life, sex, etc., as well as the nature of the crisis he or she is facing. The fourth goal, *moksha,* is release from the cycle of births and deaths and hence final liberation from human bondage. This is the supreme goal, the achievement of which relates the human being to the Absolute. The concept therefore belongs to a realm beyond where the first three are relevant. Thus the harmony of the first three may be seen as a means to realizing the fourth" (from Karnad's notes to the Oxford University Press edition of *The Fire and the Rain,* pp. 71–72).

MORCHAS: Agitation.

MUDRA: A hand gesture. There are three kinds of gestures used in performance: those used to depict nouns and verbs (such as hair, tiger, to see); those which demonstrate emotion (such as for love, anger, fear); and those which symbolize concepts (such as the three worlds). A *mudra* is a way of visualizing, or embodying, language and thought. (*See* Kathakali.)

NAGAR: Neighborhood.

NAMASKAR: Like *namaste,* a greeting, similar to "hello."

PAISA: One hundredth of a *rupee,* the unit of currency in India. *Paise* is the plural form.

PANCHAYAT: The village council that decides local civic matters.

PANDA: Priest of a Hindu temple.

PANDAL: A canopy.

PANDAV PRATAP: A long religious poem composed by Shridhar, a popular eighteenth-century writer. *Pandav Pratap* tells the story of the Pandava brothers (from the *Mahabharata.*) (*See* Parayana; and *Harivijaya.*)

PANDIT: A learned person.

PANTHERS (DALIT PANTHERS): "An organization founded in 1972 by writers to protest both atrocities against Untouchables in the villages and the ineffectiveness of the Republican Party [which was founded by Ambedkar to represent the interests of the Dalits at the national level]. The Dalit Panthers, named after the Black Panthers in the United States, is still in existence, although its effective militant stance has been reduced by splits in leadership and by its inability to curb village violence. The founders of the Panthers, Namdeo Dhasal and Raja Dhale, were poets, committed both to literature and to literature as a weapon against social [in]justice" (Eleanor Zelliot, *An Anthology of Dalit Literature,* Gyan Publishing House, 1992, pp. 9–10).

PARAYANA: A Hindu ritual of reading the epics during the rainy season. In some villages, Buddhists follow the same ritual, but they read Ambedkar's book *Buddha and His Dhamma* instead of the *Ramayana.*

PINDA: A ritual offering made by offspring for the peace of a departed parent's soul. (Same as *pinda dan; dan* means "offering.")

PIPAL TREE: A variety of tree sacred to both Hindus and Buddhists. People find refuge under its branches. It is never cut.

POORNIMA: Full moon night.

PUJA: Literally, "sacred offerings."

RAKSHASA: A demon. *Rakshasas* often wander around at night, and, although they are usually described as having fiery eyes and abnormally long tongued, they can transform into and appear as dogs, vultures, husbands, and lovers.

RAM: Ram is the Hindi-language version of the name Rama. "The name, in its Hindi-language form . . . is often regarded in northern India as a name for the Absolute, or God, and recited repeatedly as a *mantra*" (*Historical Dictionary of Hinduism,* Scarecrow Press, 1997, p. 179). (*See* Rama; *Ramayana.*)

RAMA: Hero of the *Ramayana.* "He is depicted as a human hero and as an *avatar* or incarnation of Vishnu . . . Rama is traditionally understood as an exemplar of Brahminical values and maintenance of *dharma*" (*Historical Dictionary of Hinduism,* Scarecrow Press, 1997, p. 179). The years in which he ruled Ayodhya are thought of as "golden years." (See Ram; *Ramayana.*)

RAMAYANA: *The Adventures of Rama,* one of India's most famous epic poems. "The story centers on the hero Rama, a prince of Ayodhya, who married Sita and was about to become king when he was forced into exile in the forest by intrigue in the palace. His wife and younger brother Lakshmana accompanied him into the forest. Sita was abducted by the demon King Ravana, taken to his home of Lanka, and held captive there while Ravana tried to persuade her to marry him. Rama assembled an army of allies made up of residents of the forest, including the monkey Hanuman. They attacked Ravana's army and succeeded in killing Ravana and liberating Sita, reuniting her with Rama. To the question whether she had been faithful to Rama in captivity, she called on the gods to bear witness to her truthfulness, which they did. Rama and Sita returned to Ayodhya, where they ruled for many years and had two sons" (*Historical Dictionary of Hinduism,* Scarecrow Press, 1997, p. 183).

RAM BHAGWAN: *Bhagwan* means "god," so Ram Bhagwan literally means "the god Ram." (*See* Ram; Rama.)

RAM NAM SATYA HAI: Literally, "Rama is truth," a chant that accompanies the corpse to the cremation ground.

RE: A multipurpose exclamation, tagged on for emphasis. It can mean whatever the emotional context implies. In "Budhua re" it emphasizes the dead person's name.

RICKSHAWALAS: A *rickshaw* is a vehicle for getting around town, like a taxi. There are three varieties: a two-wheeler pulled by a person; a three-wheeler which looks like a cart attached to a bicycle and which is operated as a bicycle; and a motorized three-wheeler, like a motorcycle with enclosed seating in the back. A *rickshawala* is the person who pulls the two-wheeler or cycles the three-wheeler. Operators of motorized three-wheelers are usually referred to as "rickshaw drivers."

ROTI: Homemade bread.

RUDALI: The *rudali* is a funeral ritual unique to Bihar and other eastern Indian states, among the Rajput landowning community. When a family member dies, female mourners wail, praise the dead person, and accompany the funeral procession to the cremation ground. If sufficient numbers of women within the family are not available, it is customary to hire mourners, known as *rudalis.*

RUI FLOWERS: The *Ramayana* (*The Adventures of Rama*) tells the story of Rama, who is worshiped as the seventh incarnation of Vishnu and as a god. His loyal follower Hanuman is also worshiped as a god, and in every village in Maharashtra there is a temple to Hanuman. Each Saturday the villagers garland Hanuman (also known as Maruti) with *rui* flowers.

RUPEE: The unit of currency in India.

SAAB: Shortened form of *sahib,* a term of respect.

SACRED THREAD: "Persons of the three upper castes (Brahmin, *kshatriya, vaishya*) traditionally received the sacred thread in their youth in a ceremony of initiation supervised by their *guru.* Such a ceremony is one of the twelve rites of passage incumbent on the three upper castes. Properly initiated persons are called 'twice-born' because they have received a new identity through the ritual" (*Historical Dictionary of Hinduism,* Scarecrow Press, 1997, p. 192). (*See* Brahmin; Caste; Shudra.)

SANGHA: A religious order of monks and nuns.

SANICHARI: One born on a Saturday, or Sanichar.

SARI: Garment worn by women in India. The *sari* is a piece of material (usually sixteen meters long) which is gathered and draped around the body.

SARKAR: Literally, "government" but also used to mean "sir" or "master."

SARVAN KUMAR: A legendary figure of the perfect son.

SATI: The practice in which a widow joins her dead husband on the funeral pyre and is burned alive as he is cremated; both the act and the victim are referred to as *sati.* The word *sati* comes from the Sanskrit *sat,* meaning truth; *sati* originally referred to a virtuous woman, a woman who was "true to her ideals." But because *pativrata*—or loyalty to one's husband in the form of taking on his experiences as one's own—has become an ideal for women, *sati* came to be seen by some as the ultimate act of loyalty and fidelity. It is therefore occasionally demanded of the widow by her husband's family, because it confers a higher status on them. (From Sakuntala Narasimhan, *Sati, A Study of Widow Burning in India,* Penguin, 1990, pp. 11–12.)

SATTU: Flour, usually made from ground chickpeas. A cheap but nourishing food eaten by the poor.

SATYAGRAHA: Literally meaning "truth action," *satyagraha* is a demonstration for truth, or "a legitimate, moral and truthful form of political action by the people against the injustices of the state, an active mass resistance to unjust rule." (Partha Chatterjee, *Nationalist Thought and the Colonial World,* University of Minnesota Press, 1993, p. 103.)

SAVARNAS: Upper-caste Hindus.

SERS: A measure of weight equivalent to one kilogram or of volume equivalent to one liter.

SEWADAL: Rastra Seva Dal, a nonpolitical organization of youths actively engaged in social reform. The organization sells calendars to raise money.

SHEHNAI: A reed instrument akin to the oboe.

SHIVJI: The god Shiva (with *ji* added as a term of respect). An amulet or charm blessed by Shiva would be a powerful protection.

SHIVLING: A Shiva lingam. Shiva is known as the great destroyer. As Rudra or Mahakala, he destroys so that things can be reborn or recreated. As Shiva, or Shankara, the auspicious, he embodies reproductive power and is represented by the lingam, an abstract representation of a penis. Some people think there may be a connection between the formlessness of the lingam and the formlessness that afflicts the limbs of people with leprosy.

SHLOKA: Metrical verse, composed in stanzas.

SHUDRA: "Serf; servant. *Shudra* is the name of the social class ranked fourth and lowest in the caste system. *Shudras* were and are regarded as non-Aryan in heritage, in contrast to the three higher-ranked caste groups," which are theoretically of Aryan heritage. "While these three groups receive an initiation that is regarded as a second birth, which causes them to be regarded as the twice-born classes and entitles them to wear the Sacred Thread and perform Vedic rites, *shudras* receive no such initiation and are not to wear the Sacred Thread, nor to hear the *Veda* recited nor witness a Vedic sacrifice" (*Historical Dictionary of Hinduism,* Scarecrow Press, 1997, p. 219). (*See* Caste; Sacred Thread.)

SINDOOR: A red powder that women wear in the part of their hair as a sign of marriage.

SITAR: A stringed instrument.

SOMRI: One born on Somvar, or Monday.

SUNBAI: Daughter-in-law. In Maharashtra, elder family members do not call their daughters-in-law by name but refer to them respectfully as Sunbai.

TAMRAPATA: In ancient times, the commands of the king were inscribed on stone or metal. *Tamrapata* is a name for a king's orders inscribed on a copper sheet. In this case it refers to a right or privilege assured by the government.

TAROTHA: A kind of green grass which grows in the rainy season.

TEAPOY: A small wooden stool.

TEHSILDAR: A county commissioner.

THAKUR: Master, idol.

THAKURAIN: Wife of a *thakur.*

THALI: A steel plate.

THANEDAR: Police inspector.

THATHA: "Father" in Sanskrit. Used in colloquial Tamil and sometimes in Kannada to mean "grandfather" in general or the patriarch of the house (who could be the great-grandfather).

TILAK CEREMONY: An auspicious occasion celebrating a young man's coming of age.

TRISARANA: A prayer to be recited at the beginning of a holy act:

> *Budhan Sharanan Gachamiyn*
> *Dhammam Sharanan Gachamiyn*
> *Sanghanan Sharanan Gachamiyn*

Translation by Eleanor Zelliot:

> I go for refuge to the Buddha
> I go for refuge to the *Dhamma*
> I go for refuge to the *Sangha*

UNTOUCHABLE: "Its origins are obscure, its development difficult to trace, but it is clear that the basis of untouchability and the presence of Untouchable castes in India is the concept of purity and pollution. While all humans are considered impure after a death in the family, and women during menstruation and childbirth, more than four hundred castes came over time to be viewed as irrevocably impure from birth.

"Manu's harsh restrictions [in the *Manusmriti*] on *chandalas* [the prototype of the Untouchable] the 'basest of men,' and the idea of groups having lower status than the *shudra* in the fourfold *varna* classification are repeated and developed in later legal texts, along with the occasional use of the term *asprishya* ('untouchable') for certain low castes." In the early nineteenth century, many people (including Gandhi and Ambedkar) worked to bring about caste reform. "Untouchability and its practice were 'abolished' in the constitution of independent India . . . and such practice made punishable by law." Members of the scheduled castes (based upon a list or schedule of Untouchable castes made in 1935 which includes "specific castes in specific areas that were customarily denied religious rights of entry into temples and civil rights of entry into public places and the use of wells") now receive "political, educational, and governmental job privileges as compensation for previous" discrimination. (From the *Encyclopedia of Asian History,* Charles Scribner's Sons, 1988, pp. 169–71.)

UPASAKAS: Followers of the Buddhist faith.

VAIDJI: A *vaid* is a practitioner of Ayurveda, an indigenous system of medicine; *ji* is a term of respect.

VIKRANDA: Datta Bhagat says there is no organization by the name of Vikranda, that it is an imaginary organization. The sound of the word, however, is reminiscent of Yukrand, the name of an organization that does exist. From 1970 to 1990, young people in Maharashtra were heavily influenced by the Yukrand.

VISHWARUPA: *See* Vritra.

VRITRA: Demon of drought whom Indra always fights. Indra always wins the battle, thus releasing the rains.

"The slaying of the demon Vritra by Indra is one of the archetypal myths of India . . . In the *Rig Veda,* Vritra, 'the shoulderless one' (a serpent) swallows rivers and hides the waters inside him. Indra, by killing him, releases the waters and 'like lowing cows, the rivers flow out.' The importance of this deed to the Vedic culture is borne out by the epithet 'Vritrahan' or the slayer of Vritra, by which Indra is repeatedly hailed." (From Karnad's notes to the Oxford University Press edition of *The Fire and the Rain,* p. 68. He quotes from Wendy O'Flaherty, *Hindu Myths,* Penguin, 1975, pp. 74–86.)

"The exact nature of [the] liberation of the waters has given rise to much speculation. In the nineteenth century it was interpreted as bringing down rain . . . But the Vritra myth is now generally accepted as a creation myth with Vritra symbolizing chaos" (from J. L. Brockington, *The Sacred Thread: A Short History of Hinduism,* Oxford University Press, 1992, p. 11).

"By the time we come to the version [of this story as it is] recorded in the *Mahabharata,* Indra has lost his central position in the Hindu pantheon. The sectarian gods, Vishnu and Shiva, now hold sway. In the later version of the myth, Indra is anxious that Vishwarupa (also called Trishiras, the three-headed one), son of Tvastri, may dislodge him from his throne. He therefore destroys Vishwarupa treacherously. Tvastri then gives birth to another son, Vritra, by a female demon, and tells him: 'Kill Indra.' Indra, unable to overcome the new enemy, again has to resort to ignominious trickery to survive. Having killed Vritra, he suffers from the guilt of Brahminicide.

"The myth can be seen as expressing a deep anxiety that informs the whole of Indian mythology: the fear of brother destroying brother." (From Karnad's notes to the Oxford University Press edition of *The Fire and the Rain,* p. 68). (*See* Indra.)

WANDH TARAH: An untranslatable expression. It literally means "one type" in Kannada. The American equivalent might be *oddball.* It is not as strong a term as *freak.*

WANDU TARAH: A corruption of *wandh tarah.*

YAJÑA: A ritual sacrifice. According to Vedic thought, the world was governed by an objective order, inherent in the nature of things, which was guarded by the gods. The *yajña* can be seen as a sacrifice to the gods, a ritual by which the universe is recreated and order restored. (From J. L. Brockington, *The Sacred Thread: A Short History of Hinduism,* Oxford University Press, 1992, p. 34.)

Divinity in the Vedic period was associated with *rita,* which originally meant "cosmic order," and which the gods were supposed to maintain. *Rita* later "came to mean 'right,' so the gods were conceived as preserving the world not merely from physical disorder but also from moral chaos." *Rita* also means sacrificial correctness, so "ritualistic *punctilio* thus comes to be placed on the same level as natural law and moral rectitude." (From M. Hiriyanna, *The Essentials of Indian Philosophy,* George Allen & Unwin, 1949, pp. 12, 16, 17, quoted by Karnad in the notes to the Oxford University Press edition of *The Fire and the Rain.*)

As the *yajña* developed over time, it became more and more elaborate; as it became more complicated to perform, a special class of priests developed who were believed to be the only people capable of officiating. The spirit behind the *yajña* changed over time as well: "what prompted the performance of sacrifices was no longer the thought of prevailing upon the gods to bestow some favor or to ward off some danger; it was rather to compel or coerce them to do what the sacrificer wanted to be done." (From M. Hiriyanna, *The Essentials of Indian Philosophy,* George Allen & Unwin, 1949, pp. 12, 16, 17, quoted by Karnad in the notes to the Oxford University Press edition of *The Fire and the Rain.*)

ZAMINDAR: Landowner.

Notes on Contributors

DATTA BHAGAT (*Routes and Escape Routes*) has published four collections of one-act plays in Marathi and three full-length plays (*Kheliya, Ashmak,* and *Wata-Palwata* or *Routes and Escape Routes*). Many of his plays are available in Hindi translation. He has also published two collections of critical essays, one titled *Dalit Sahitya Disha Ani Dishantar.* Bhagat is a member of the Sahitya Akademi, a former chairman of the Board of Studies in Marathi, Chancellor Nominee of S.R.T. University, and a Reader in the Marathi Department at the Dr. Babasaheb Ambedkar Marathwada University in Aurangabad. His research interests focus on the reflection of social movements and reform activities in literature.

MAHESH DATTANI (*Tara*) was born in Bangalore in 1958 and studied at Baldwin's High School and St. Joseph's College of Arts and Science, Bangalore. His theater group, Play-pen, was formed in 1984, and he has directed several plays for them, ranging from classic Greek to contemporary works. In 1986 he wrote his first full-length play, *Where There's A Will,* and since 1995 he has been working full-time in the theater. In 1998 he set up his own theater studio, dedicated to training and showcasing new talents in acting, directing, and stage writing, the first in the country to focus specifically on new work. In 1998 Dattani won the Sahitya Akademi Award for *Final Solutions and Other Plays,* published by East West Books, Madras. He is the first playwright writing in English to win this award. Dattani also teaches theater courses in the summer session at Portland State University, Oregon, conducts workshops regularly at his studio and elsewhere, and writes plays for BBC Radio 4. He lives in Bangalore.

USHA GANGULI (*Rudali*) began her career as a Bharatanatyam dancer but took to acting in 1970. Although she played leading roles in many productions in Calcutta, she was disappointed by the Hindi theater. This prompted her to form her own company, Rangakarmee, in 1976. Rangakarmee has presented a number of plays, including *Mahabhoj, Lok-katha, Holi, Vama, Court Martial, Khoj, Beti Aayee,* and *Himmat Mai,* an adaptation of Brecht's *Mother Courage.* Ganguli won the state government's Best Actress Award in 1982 for her performance in *Guria Ghar,* the Best Production Award in 1987 for *Mahabhoj* and later for *Court Martial* and *Rudali,* and the Shiromoni Puraskaar for *Holi.* For her immense contribution to theater, she was awarded the Dayavati Modi Shree Shakti Samman in 1998 and the Safdar Hashmi Award. Ganguli lives in Calcutta and is a lecturer in Hindi language and literature at the Bhawanipur Education Society College.

GIRISH KARNAD (*The Fire and the Rain*) is a Kannada playwright and filmmaker. He was educated at the Karnatak University, Dharwad, and at Oxford, where he was a Rhodes Scholar. After working with the Oxford University Press for seven years, he resigned to concentrate on writing and filmmaking. He has served as the director of the Film and Television Institute of India and as the chairman of the Sangeet Natak Akademi, India's national academy of the performing arts. In 1987–88, he was at the University of Chicago as Visiting Professor and Fulbright Scholar-in-Residence. His play *Hayavadana* (1971) won both the Sangeet Natak Akademi Award and the Kamaladevi Chattopadhyaya Award. *Nagamandala* premiered in the United States at the Guthrie Theater, Minneapolis, as part of its thirtieth anniversary celebration in 1993, and has since been staged the world over. *The Fire and the Rain* was commissioned by the Guthrie Theater. In 1999 he received the Bharatiya Jnanpith Award, India's highest literary award. His first film *Samskara,* for which he wrote the script and played the lead role, was initially banned by censors and, when released, went on to win the President's Gold Medal. Subsequent films, directed by him mainly in Kannada but also in Hindi, have won several national awards and have been part of international film festivals. He also acts and has appeared in the films of Shyam Benegal as well as the television serials of Satyajit Ray and Mrinal Sen. He was awarded the Padma Shri in 1974 and the Padma Bushan in 1992 by the president of India. The Karnataka University conferred a D.Litt. on him in 1994. He lives in Bangalore with his wife and two children.

ANJUM KATYAL (translator of *Rudali*) is the editor of *Seagull Theatre Quarterly,* an all-Indian journal of contemporary theater and performance; and Seagull Books, a Calcutta-based publisher specializing in arts publishing, particularly the visual and performing arts. In the course of her work she has studied, interviewed, researched, documented, and written extensively on contemporary theater around the country. She lives and works in Calcutta.

ERIN B. MEE (editor) has made numerous trips to India in the past ten years (once as a Fulbright Scholar); there she has directed an adaptation of Goethe's *Faust* with Sopanam, one of India's leading theater companies, and a production of *Aramba Chekkan.* She directed *The Imperialists* at the Joseph Papp Public Theater and was Resident Director at the Guthrie Theater for two years, where she directed *Troilus and Cressida* and several Pinter plays. Her most recent piece was an adaptation/deconstruction of *Mrs. Warren's Profession* at Mabou Mines, where she was a Resident Artist. With her own company, The ARK Ensemble, she has directed the American premieres of Girish Karnad's *Divided Together* and K. N. Panikkar's *Ottayan.* Her articles have appeared in *Performing Arts Journal, American Theatre,* and *Seagull Theatre Quarterly.*

MAYA PANDIT (translator of *Routes and Escape Routes*) teaches English at Shivaji University, Kolhapur. She has translated G. P. Deshpande's Marathi play *Chanakya Vishnugupta* into English, and Dario Fo's *Accidental Death of an Anarchist* into Marathi. She has written extensively on the theater.

KAVALAM NARAYANA PANIKKAR (*Aramba Chekkan*) is a playwright and director and the founding director of Sopanam. His plays include *Sakshi* (1964), *Avanavankadamba*

(1975), *Ottayan* (1978), *Karimkutty* (1983), *Koyma* (1986), *Arani* (1989). *Theyya Theyyam* (1980), *Faust* (1993), and *Poranadi* (1995). He has directed his own plays as well as the plays of Bhasa (*Madhyama Vyayogam, Urubhangam,* and *Karnabharam*) and Kalidasa (*Shakuntalam* and *Vikramorvasiyam*). His awards include the prestigious Kalidas Samman Award for Theatre (1996), the National Award from the Sangeet Natak Akademi for Theatre Direction (1983), the Kerala State Sahitya Akademi Award for the best Malayalam Playwright (1974), the Critic Circle of India Award for Theatre Direction (1982 and 1984), and a Ford Foundation Fellowship. His productions have been presented in Greece, Japan, Austria, the United States, the Soviet Union, and Korea.

MOHIT SATYANAND (translator of *The Wooden Cart*) was born in Delhi in 1956. He performed with renowned Indian theater director Barry John from 1970 to 1989 in amateur productions of *The Snow Queen, Amadeus, Cactus Flower, Find Me, On the Razzle,* and other plays. While pursuing a corporate career, he led a weekly workshop for the actors of John's repertory for one season. In 1987, he gave up the corporate world for documentary film production, specializing in films for and about voluntary work in rural India. He produced and wrote scripts for more than forty films in the succeeding eight years, and he supervised the translation of at least twenty-five of those from English into Hindi.

TRIPURARI SHARMA (*The Wooden Cart*) has conducted numerous theater workshops around India to develop scripts around social issues and local problems with women's groups, college students, factory workers, and others. She has developed and directed many productions for her own theater company, Alarippu, as well as directing such plays as *Galileo* (B. H. U. Varanasi) and *Six Characters in Search of an Author* (I. I. T. Kanpur). For the National School of Drama (NSD) in Delhi she has directed *Adhe Adhure* and her own *Kaath Ki Gaadi* (*The Wooden Cart*). She was the Indian representative at the first conference of female playwrights, held in the United States in 1988; coordinated a year-long project on women and theater for the Women's Conference in Beijing; and is co-director of the TV serial *Shakti,* on women's issues. She is a recipient of the Sankriti and Natya Sangh awards and is an associate professor of acting at the NSD.

Library of Congress Cataloging-in-Publication Data

DramaContemporary India / edited by Erin B. Mee.
    p. cm. — (PAJ books)
    "Plays by Girish Karnad, Kavalam Narayana Panikkar, Usha Ganguli, Tripurari Sharma, Mahesh Dattani, Datta Bhagat."
    Includes bibliographical references.
    ISBN 0-8018-6621-9 — ISBN 0-8018-6622-7 (pbk.)
    1. Indic drama—20th century—Translations into English.   I. Title: Drama contemporary. II. Mee, Erin B. III. Series.

PK5437 .D73 2001
808.82'00954'09045—dc21   00-053470